Lying about the Wolf
Essays in Culture and Education

Addressing some of the major issues plaguing education, particularly the scandal of illiteracy and growing mediocrity in academic performance, David Solway argues that the current state of affairs in education is the result not simply of poor training in elementary school or the disappearance of grammatical study from the overall curriculum but of a larger cultural problem.

Solway explains that the current generation of students, raised in a non-historical and iconic environment, do not live in time as an emergent, continuous medium in which the complexities of experience are parsed and organized. Their psychological world is largely devoid of syntax – of causal, differential, and temporal relations between events. The result is precisely what we see about us: a cultural world characterized by a vast subpopulation of young (and not so young) people for whom the past is an unsubstantiated rumour and the future an unacknowledged responsibility. Solway claims that contemporary educators have become cultural speculators who disregard a basic truth about how the mind develops: that it needs to be grounded in reality and time. But in education, as in almost every other cultural institution, the sense of reality and the dynamic of time have "virtually" disappeared, leading to the deep disconnectedness we experience on every level of "human grammar," from the organization of the community to the organization of the sentence.

Lying about the Wolf is not only an analysis of current pedagogical issues but also, and perhaps primarily, a cultural analysis for which the subject of education is really a pretext. Solway argues that we cannot hope to solve the educational problem unless we are prepared to deal with the larger cultural predicament.

DAVID SOLWAY is a poet and professor of English literature, John Abbott College. His previous nonfiction books are *Education Lost* and *The Anatomy of Arcadia*.

Lying about the Wolf

Essays in Culture and Education

David Solway

McGill-Queen's University Press
Montreal & Kingston • London • Buffalo

© McGill-Queen's University Press 1997
ISBN 0-7735-1535-6 (cloth)
ISBN 0-7735-1536-4 (paper)

Legal deposit first quarter 1997
Bibliothèque nationale du Québec

Printed in Canada on acid-free paper

McGill-Queen's University Press acknowledges the support received for its publishing
program from the Canada Council's Block
Grants program.

Canadian Cataloguing in Publication Data

Solway, David, 1941–
Lying about the wolf: essays in culture and
education.
Includes bibliographical references.
ISBN 0-7735-1535-6 (bound)
ISBN 0-7735-1536-4 (pbk.)
1. Educational anthropology.   I. Title.
LB1025.3.S64 1997   370.19'2   C96-900920-8

For Professors Wayne Shute and Clark Webb,
for Monsignor Dan Dever,
and for Frank Smith,
who each in his own way helped me to look the wolf in the eye.

Contents

Acknowledgments

The line of thought that stitches together the essays in this collection owes whatever modulus it has to the work of a small number of contemporary writers who circulate throughout these pages and whom I wish to acknowledge at the outset. Peter Sloterdijk's *Critique of Cynical Reason* has provided me with a kind of angular, southpaw perspective on cultural issues which I find particularly congenial, as has Andrei Codrescu's brilliant *The Disappearance of the Outside* which, though remaindered, remains with me. (Its disappearance is symptomatic of its central theme.) John Ralston Saul's analysis in *Voltaire's Bastards* of the rational prepossession of the modern era is essential reading for anyone interested in isolating the causes behind the socioeconomic malaise in all areas of public life, including education. I should also mention Arthur Kroker's and Michael Weinstein's *Data Trash* which sets forth with a certain technoclastic zeal a sharp critique of virtual culture under the heading of Crash theory: its application to educational concerns is especially pertinent. I greatly admire as well Andrew Nikiforuk's *School's Out* and *If Learning Is So Natural, Why Am I Going to School?* for their aggressive candour and rough-hewn good sense. Mikhail Bakhtin in *The Dialogic Imagination*, Roman Jakobson's essays on language, and Gregory Ulmer in *Teletheory* furnish invaluable insight into the nature of dialogue, the narrative contract, the multidimensional class, and the question of grammatical displacement that form the basis for any genuine understanding of the literacy crisis that has so far defeated our best efforts toward solution. Like anyone writing on educational themes today, I would be found in default if I failed to acknowledge Lev Vygotsky's *Thought and Language* and *Mind in Society* for guidance through the wilderness of learning theory. I regard Agnes Heller as a philosophical mentor and credit her *A Philosophy of History in Fragments* for helping me to contextualize current educational issues in the larger framework of the contemporary *zeitgeist*. Though Jacques Ellul's irascible and unmodish *The Humiliation of the Word* reads disturbingly like the Fifth Gospel, it deserves wide and serious attention: its denunciations remain both analytically and prophetically acute even if one does not share its Christian premises. Clifford Stoll's *Silicon Snake Oil* is a potent remedy for anyone who has been spammed by such popular books as George Gilder's *Telecosm* and Lewis J. Perelman's *School's Out* with their fatidic enthusiasm for the unmonitored distractions of hyperlearning. Stoll's book, a muniment of reasonableness, effectively debunks the current crop of hi-tech education speculators. Jane Healy's *Endangered Minds*, which develops the thesis that habits of mind become structures of the brain, puts a neuropsychological spin on the contemporary educational debacle. This is a brave and brilliant book and should be read by anyone trying to come to grips with the incompetency-based learning that goes on in our schools. I have been strongly influenced by the "neoconservative" writings, far more radical than reactionary, of Wendell Berry, Christopher Lasch, and Michael Oakeshott, whose work constitutes on the whole a quiet enclave of good sense in a clamorous world of pseudo-revolutionary upheavals. They urge us to recall the nearly despoiled gift of good land, a remote culture beyond narcissism, and the fading conversation of mankind. While revising my text I began reading Camille Paglia's *Sex, Art, and American Culture*, and found, with both delight and dismay, that not a few of my own commendations and condemnations had been anticipated by that ardent and redoubtable writer, particularly in the chapter "Junk Bonds and Corporate Raiders: Academe in the Hour of the Wolf." I put this down to serendipity. Although balking at her cowcatcher scoop and toss of the semiotic French, I cannot but applaud her defence of the western intellectual tradition which has come under attack from so many incendiary quarters today. *A History of Education in Antiquity* by H.I. Marrou, an indispensable source text, anchors the library shelf which would be incomplete if I did not mention as well the work of Hilda Neatby, Northrop Frye, and Neil Postman, revered teachers all. Thanks go out to my philosophical adversary Professor Fred Wilson of the University of Toronto for motivating or rather provoking two of the essays in this volume. With such enemies, who need friends?

I am indebted to Frank Smith, François Victor Tochon, and J.T. Dillon, whose encouragement was always sustaining and who in various guises, whether as correspondents, drinking companions, or critical analysts, have contributed to the shaping and trimming of these pages. I have also benefited from the kindness of my intellectual mentors, Jacques Barzun and Umberto Eco, who suffered importunacies with customary grace.

On a more personal note, I wish to acknowledge the considerable help given me by my son, Ilye, in typing, processing, and preparing these pages. It must have seemed to him over the years a truly Sisyphean labour. I am grateful to my wife, Karin, who risked divorce with her rigorous criticism. And I am obliged as well to Professor Louis-Marie Ouellette of the Université de Sherbrooke who, in the course of many conversations on the subject of educational style, suggested a more tolerant and pacific mode of discourse than I am comfortable with; nevertheless, I do appreciate his civility.

My thanks to Helene Robert and Doug Armstrong in the reference library at John Abbott College, and to Eric Ormsby, director of libraries at McGill University, and his administrative assistant, Bruna Ceccolini, for their patience, humour, accessibility, and skill at bibliographic detection.

I should also like to mention, with genuine respect, my colleagues in the English Department at John Abbott College, in particular Larry Weller on whose wisdom and sympathy I could always rely, Peter Henbury who managed more than one impossible task, and our founding chairman, Murray Napier, whose passionate concern with educational issues set the tone for our parietal life. On the whole it has been a privilege to be associated with a department of such calibre and versatility.

Thanks are due to my editors at McGill-Queen's University Press, Phil Cercone, Joan McGilvray, and Maureen Garvie, for their professional acumen and unfailing congeniality.

Finally, my gratitude to the Canada Council for its timely and generous intervention.

Note on the Text

The reader will find a modicum of cross-references throughout owing to the occasional manner in which most of the essays started out on their eventual careers. Some began as talks or lectures and others as formal articles but all have been shaped up as semi-independent instalments in the development of a general theme. Most of the *ritornelli* have been revised out of the text, but a few have been allowed to remain on the assumption that points of importance need not suffer from tactical repetition.

"Dead Teachers Society" is a revised and extended rendition of a lecture delivered at the Conference on Educational Leadership held at Brigham Young University in the summer of 1991. An abridged version appeared in *Matrix* (no. 44, Montreal, 1994).

"Balnibarbian Architecture" was initially presented in 1995 as a short contribution to the John Abbott College quarterly *Bulletin* on the subject of the Quebec *réform pédagogique*. It expanded to its present shape in an attempt to deal with the reform prepossession itself and the larger question of contemporary attitudes to education.

"The Anecdotal Function" is a revised version of an essay that appeared in the symposium section of *Interchange* (vol. 22, no. 4, Toronto, 1991). It was originally intended as a defence of my previous book, *Education Lost*, in response to an editorial request, but developed its own momentum and gradually assumed its present form as a discourse on narrativity.

"What About Food?" is a response to Professor Fred Wilson's impeachment of "The Anecdotal Function," entitled "Solway on Losing Education," which appeared in the *Interchange* symposium mentioned above. But it is more than a polemical rejoinder, taking issue with the current agenda that seeks to therapeuticize education.

"The Bipolar Paradigm" was originally drafted in 1992 as a proposal to the Quebec Ministry of Education for repositioning the classroom model then, and currently, in place but took on a life of its own and settled after some time into its proper niche here.

"Charlie Don't Surf" started out, somewhat extemporaneously, as the keynote address delivered to the Maurice J. Sullivan Builders of Hope Conference held in Honolulu, April 1994; it now contains enough material for several more keynote addresses.

Diverse portions of "Teaching Down or Learning Up" emerged from behind the podium at the Calgary City Teachers' Convention in February 1993 and at Brigham Young University in July of the same year during my stint there as visiting professor, rounding into shape in early 1996. A modified version of this chapter was accepted in April 1996 by the University of Sherbrooke as an Educational Research thesis.

The remaining two essays, "Grammatical Fictions" and "Script and Nondescript," were independent ventures, beginning at the writing table in 1993 and gradually completed over the next two years.

Note on Notes

The reader will remark, perhaps ruefully, that each chapter generates an extensive battery of notes. I urge that the endnote section be regarded as a kind of chapterette which may be read uninterruptedly if the reader so desires. Sometimes these notes merely give the referential address, sometimes they constitute a local expansion of the subject under discussion, sometimes they will operate as a sort of textual counterpoint or meandering paratext, as Rousseau famously suggested in the "Notice Concerning the Notes" which he appended to his *Discourse on Inequality*. Footnotes and endnotes constitute a fascinating subject in themselves.[1] They may even be considered as reversing the usual relation of precedence and generating the book to which they are nominally attached (which may very well be the case here), operating as its content-addressable memory, a connectionist network in which items are linked across readerly time and textual space and upon which the central argument draws in its construction of a theoretical position. But the text itself should be negotiated with as little interference as possible despite the cloud of dancing, numerical gnats that often distracts the eye. These are simply part of the bibliographic climate.

Lying about the Wolf

No story comes off if I do not know whether I speak about the wolf or the lamb. Certainly, in a dream, the wolf and the lamb can be the same figures subsequently, also simultaneously.

Agnes Heller

Tomorrow assumes the dual character of inconsequence and probable catastrophe; somewhere in between, a small hope of getting through lingers.

Peter Sloterdijk

Introduction

What do you mean? You still believe in the Big Bad Wolf? First of all, are you sure that somebody really stole your skateboard? If so, let us try to find out who really could have done it.

Umberto Eco

Comehome to roo, wee chickchilds doo, when the wild worewolf's abroad.

James Joyce

Much of the analysis and perhaps most of the conclusions associated with research in education seem to me increasingly otiose and redundant. Researchers such as T.M. Amabile have discovered, for example, that extrinsic motivation tends to undermine intrinsic motivation and to produce inferior results. David Perkins, surveying the current situation, solemnly avers that "an abundance of research shows that youngsters generally do not understand very well what they are learning." Brian Mullen conducts an elaborate methodological study to discover at the end that the frequency of first-person-singular pronouns correlates inversely with group size, from which he deduces that smaller groups tend to promote a higher degree of self-attention; in other words, small groups favour more intimate relationships than large ones! Years of research by a high-profile team of education scholars have culminated at last in a consensus definition of reading: "Reading is the process of constructing meaning from written texts."[1] The number of such examples in the current research literature approaches infinity. Yet who ever doubted for a nano-second that intrinsic or self motivation is more effective than the external variety or that young students in contemporary American and Canadian schools are performing very poorly indeed or that one can be more effective as a teacher among a group of five students than 500 or that reading, *mirabile dictu*, has to do with making sense of written texts? Have we become so insecure or so fashionably postmodern and decentred that we can no longer trust, credit, or even *possess* our own most evident perceptions? Do we need to commission expensive projects that deplete our dwindling financial resources in order to confirm or discover what half an hour's experience and a thimbleful of common sense would bring home to us with cometary impact? Do we need to spend years exploring Lupusland, run endless simulations, correlate data, and write painstakingly analytical books to establish that, yes, wolves *do* bite – in fact, they megabyte – especially when they are hungry?[2]

Like many of my colleagues who have purchased their experience by their penny of observation and not in the leisure provided by research grants and frequent sabbaticals, I have seen the wolf face to face in the wilderness of school and classroom, not in the safe and artificial environment of a theoretical fable. And I can reliably report that the wolf, in ironic defiance of even the most well-intentioned theories, doctrines, and recommendations, has indeed stolen our skateboard, and is in fact flourishing as never before, its belly full not of stones but of tender, flocculent sheep, of pink little pigs (including the most puritan of porkers), innocuous ducks, ailing grandmothers, bonneted girls, young Prokofiev adventurers, and especially ferocious hunters armed with the latest weapons intended to parry or subdue the lycanthropic appetite of our most dedicated adversary, Reality.

For the wolf cannot be deceived or evaded. It must be acknowledged, respected, feared, modestly and intelligently come to terms with. What it swallows does not reappear courtesy of a fairy-tale Caesarian. If it is ignored, the farm is inexorably depopulated. Brick houses do not keep it out, and chimneys are child's play. Thirty years of intermittent psychotherapy does not cure Sergei Pankejev, Freud's celebrated Wolf-man, whose infirmity persists linguistically. The wolf is clever and insatiable, and only those survive, and only for a time, who remain alert and adopt appropriate measures. In education especially, one must take Isengrim seriously if one is ever to out-Reynard him. One cannot indulge the luxuries of forgetfulness and indolence, of trust in systems or the promise of new "strategies" of avoidance or domestication.[3] We have nothing to oppose to the wolf but vigilance, hard work, and cultivated intelligence – and perhaps the wisdom to recognize that we must not expect victory in this unequal contest but only, if we are very lucky and very diligent, the well-earned reward of authentic joy, the realization of identity, the benefit of fortitude, and a certain amount of time in which to enjoy them. These are the gifts whose conditions of possibility we can hand down to our children through the medium of home and school. But let us make no mistake about our current situation, for it is precisely in the home and the school that the wolf now finds its richest crop of victims.[4]

Education cannot act as if Isaiah 11: 6 offered a plausible alternative to the world in which we are constrained to live, without producing considerable devastation in the sequel, including the destruction of the child intended to lead. I have written this book to testify, in what is truly a desperate hour, that we can no longer afford to continue lying about the wolf.

· 1 ·

Grammatical Fictions

If I do speak of a fiction, then it is of a grammatical fiction.
  Ludwig Wittgenstein, *Philosophical Investigations*

But reflectiveness and articulateness about the self take time to grow.
Short term developments slow its growth.
  Walter J. Ong, *Orality and Literacy*

Anyone remotely concerned with the fate of education today is uncomfortably aware of a state of crisis perilously close to Red Alert. The arena of debate and contention has witnessed a noisy proliferation of theories proposing one or another radical or accelerated solution of the crisis. Everything from the dismantling of the educational establishment to the privatizing of the public-school sector to the resurgence of the movement of what we might call grammatical technology (a universal panacea) has been advanced as an answer to the crucial question that confronts us.

I am here and for the moment concerned mainly with Gramtech. It is no secret that at least half the students graduating from high school do not possess the scholastic equipment needed to succeed in college and university. The solution envisaged by certain grammar technicians, so far as English departments go, is to reduce or de-emphasize the higher-level "academic" courses and open a larger number of "effective writing," "language skills," and "composition" courses to supplement and/or replace them. As a recent article in the student newspaper of my college asserts, quoting generously from departmental sources, "Too often, Core English courses concentrate on what the teacher wants to say, and not enough on what the students need to hear." What is now required, it appears, is a re-intensified focus on "teaching basic communication skills," a practical introduction to the study of vocabulary, grammar, and the "technical aspects of English" via an increasing number of what are somewhat pompously called "foundational courses." Naturally, many teachers will resist the revolutionary implications of these proposals and bundle up even more incorrigibly against the freshening winds of change. "People who have taught the same material for twenty years aren't going to be enthusiastic about change," one departmental spokesman presciently remarks.

That students need to be helped to strengthen and augment their "minimal communication skills" is a proposition no one can reasonably deny. The issue is, rather, how to go about doing this. I am convinced that the insensate ramification of writing-skills courses, whether "foundational" or complementary, is at best only marginally profitable. No less an authority on the subject than Richard Ohmann concedes that composition courses are "notoriously ineffective."[1] The intractable nature of the problem has been addressed by many other educational scholars. Jacques Barzun writes: "People who are half articulate cannot properly listen or read; hence lacking *early and continuing* attention to language, the 'problem of communication' is bound to be chronic." More recently, E.D. Hirsch has argued, with considerable vigour, plausibility, and evidential force, that literacy "is far more than a skill and ... requires large amounts of specific information." That is, the level of literacy to which we wish to raise our students depends, unfortunately for us, "on the relevant *background information* that the person possesses."[2] Students who arrive at college or university lacking in substantive information, deficient in the "schematic associations" shared by the culture in general, innocent of the protocols of reasoned thought and lucid speech, having *read* very little[3] and reflected even less, not having enjoyed what Theodore Roszak calls the "Homeric interlude" or Umberto Eco describes as "inferential walks in the cultural encyclopedia," cannot be expected to emerge from a composition course (or even two or three) with more than a fractional command of grammatical structure. Their writing may improve parenthetically but, with a few redeeming exceptions, by no means significantly.[4]

It is a catastrophic error to conceive of literacy as a purely formal skill that can be effectively taught or inculcated in a utilitarian communication-skills course. "The skills model of education," Hirsch writes, "is illusory because it overlooks the fact that reading and thinking skills alike depend upon a wide range of specific, quickly available information." As Hirsch observes, even so resolutely technological a thinker as Herbert A. Simon, the Nobel laureate in artificial intelligence research, doubts whether there is such a thing as a general or transferable cognitive skill. Our mistake lies in part in conceiving of grammatical facility as a purely *mechanical* or *technical* skill rather than as a *cognitive* achievement undetachably integrated into the larger, sustaining processes of reading and thinking, *even at rudimentary levels.*

At present, fifty years and more after the advent of descriptive and structural linguistics, and at least a full generation since the speculations of the semiotic thinkers became common intellectual property, the recommendations of the grammar technicians seem sadly futile, weary for all their brisk-ness, unconsciously belated, exhibiting, as James Finn Garner would put it, a condition of advanced rudimentariness. For, as Edward Sapir writes, summing up a lifetime's study of the correlations between language and culture, "It is quite an illusion to imagine ... that language is merely an *incidental* means of solving specific problems of communication or reflec-tion."[5] And Benjamin Lee Whorf concludes that "the background linguistic system (the grammar) of each language is not merely a reproducing in-strument for voicing ideas but rather is itself the shaper of ideas."[6] Though the Sapir-Whorf hypothesis has come under attack from various quarters in the last academic generation and has undergone significant modification, this line of thought still carries conviction in the complex realms of cultural and symbolic systems. It is the ways in which experience is punctuated and categorized, or the forms in which knowledge is organized, assimilated, and recombined, that determine (and are themselves determined by) the ways in which we assemble the schematic coherencies of language. Form and formulation always ride in tandem.

We see these relations between linguistic structure and *sensed*[7] reality at work almost automatically on the simplest levels of ordinary English syntax as a mimetic reproduction of the temporal order of experience. "Next Thursday and Friday are holidays." We seldom hear anyone saying, "next Friday and Thursday." Even the *reversal* of the order of events in the system of predication, as in countdown, can be understood as a function of the syntax of felt experience. Apart from activating the numinous property of zero, reverse countdown simulates the *spring* effect: compression generating propulsion. The rocket is propelled upward through the coil and snap of released energy: $\rightarrow 3$-2-1-0-1-2-$3 \rightarrow$ (infinity) is how we syntactically *experience* the event.

Analogously, but at levels of pretty well insoluble complexity, the ways in which the disparate items of our experience – perceptual, mental, and affective – are cognitively integrated and related to the external context must be treated from the standpoint of education as *reciprocally implicated with the grammatical and syntactic shaping of that experience*. The relation, as is now well understood by the various semiotic disciplines (linguistics, structuralism, psycholinguistics),[8] is not one that holds between a pre-existent mental substance and an *incidental* or extraneous structuring me-dium, so that in the absence, impairment, or incompleteness of the former, the latter can nevertheless be competently inculcated or applied. Grammar, in the largest sense of the term, representing the scansion of the world in which we live (culturally inflected as that may be), is the reflex of the ordered and intelligible self which it is the promise of education to sponsor and reinforce. The relation is one of mutual causality and reciprocal ef-fectiveness. If our sense of the world is, let us say, rather too discontinuous,

sketchy, or attenuated, and lacking, as Hirsch contends, in material content
as well, it should be obvious that the eleventh-hour teaching of the rules
of orthography, punctuation, phrasing, sentence-structure, and paragraphing
will not gain much in the way of grapple and drag, since, as Jonathan
Culler has noted, the real problems of writing and reading are "the problems
of articulating a world."[9] And this is precisely why the results of grammatical
instruction in a partial void will often seem disconcertingly bathetic. For
the issue we face requires us to engage with "deep elaboratives" rather than
"shallow derivatives," but as instructors we have developed a farcical resemblance to a corps of misguided draegermen at the site of a disaster,
who, instead of descending into the mine shaft to attempt a rescue, appease
their consciences by monitoring the traffic.

As I am not attempting a systematic mapping of such intricate noetic
regions (both space and competence forbid), let me give a modest example
of what I am getting at. One of my better students submits a term paper
on a poem called "The Dolphin"[10] in which that emblematic creature is
represented as swimming past a group of boys hunting for oysters on a
reef. The event approximates a *parousia*, "the flat tail-flukes / like the wings
of a solitary angel, sailing / easily through the boys' wild yells." My student
writes: "The dolphin comes from nowhere and swims in the poem past the
boys." This is a simple assertion and perfectly "grammatical" in itself (repeated later as: "The dolphin swims in the poem so that the reader wonders
where it is going"), yet it represents an inappropriate mixing of different
orders or levels of event, a minor category-mistake that the reader registers
as faintly humorous. We are not at present concerned with the analytic
interpretation *of the poem*, which is another matter entirely, but with the
way in which the student "reads" and amalgamates two different experiences:
the experience of decoding the poem and the experience of reconstructing
the situation as it occurs "in the world." Dolphins, I point out, do not
usually swim in poems, unless one is thinking metaphorically (which the
writer assured me she was not); they happen to swim in the sea. My student
was perfectly aware of the fact. What she was not aware of was a series
of correlative facts: (1) that the statement as it swims past us on the page
does not represent the order of "reality"; (2) that its semantic content, as
written, offers another version of "reality"; (3) that metaphorical redemption
would have been eminently possible (or transferred epithet, as in Coleridge's
mock-studious eye, fixed "on my swimming book," in "Frost at Midnight");
(4) that the reader of the paper, who *shares the world* with its writer and
whose presence as addressee needs to be imagined or taken into consideration, will almost inevitably register this grammatical statement as un-
grammatical in another way, as distinctly inconsistent with the *rational* and
mutually endorsed structure of experience.[11] (I once knew an elderly man
who had retired into poetry, and who claimed that he habitually saw dolphins

swimming in the sky. His confession was grammatical in both senses.)[12] In other words, with respect to (4), what this *aporia* involves is a failure of the imagination – that sense of being in the world with others whose responses to one's testimony must be at least to some extent anticipated – and not a failure of grammatical expertise.

I do not wish to labour the point, and my student's supra-grammatical solecism is by no means capital. Its exemplary value resides in the symptomatic *absence of awareness* which it betokens as well as in the illustration it affords of the gap, the (occasional or frequent) lack of fit, the possible disjunction between grammatical ordonnance *as such* and the cognitive parsing of the world of shared experience, or of what we might call the economy of semantic hierarchies. As Neil Postman suggests, while giving English teachers the strap for their "consistent obtuseness," semantics should form one of the major subjects on a revised curriculum. If English teachers "do not teach anything about the relationship of language to reality ... I cannot imagine how they expect reading and writing to improve."[13] The problem is that solecisms or discrepancies of the sort I am describing here are epidemic, and, what is central to my deposition, generally run much deeper, somewhere far below the Plimsoll line of everyday communication, at levels that the instruments of grammatical technology *per se* are incapable of sounding.

And it is precisely these sub-Plimsollian levels that constitute the gravity and magnitude of the quandary we are in. What I have somewhat loosely (and, perhaps, unavoidably) called the "sense of reality" is intimately bound up with what I will now call, equally loosely (and unavoidably) the "sense of time." The depths that a belated grammatical intervention cannot plumb have to do with the dark and to some extent unfathomable element of prenoetic temporality in which the sensibility generates a vectorial relation to the world, a kind of "psychic momentum by which we are driven and impelled toward the rational ordering of experience."[14] This interior dimension of time is carried, expressed, and *realized* in language as it simultaneously, so to speak, dyes and saturates the linguistic structures that are themselves *realized* in time. Language and time are indissolubly related, not merely in the crude sense that it requires time to produce an utterance or write a sentence but in the sense that the coherent evolution of a linguistic sequence, whether at the level of the sentence or of the larger narrative transformations we call stories or texts, depends upon the interior, prenoetic, vectorial impulse of linear temporality itself. Time-lines and sentences coalesce in our experience of *lineation*, enabling us not only to project, reconstruct, or participate in but ultimately to *know* a world that is both rational and temporally unified. This is by no means a mere filleting point but the very core and substance of our predicament. As Heidegger says somewhere, we do not simply live in time; we "live time."

It follows from this that if the faculty of memory is impaired in either or both of its two parallel modes, personal and historical, that is, *if the sense of constituent temporality is disordered*, then the grammaticization of experience will be correspondingly halting, erratic, and discontinuous. The individual suffering from what I have elsewhere called "time-sedation" or the "chronosectomy" will have no choice but to *rediscover time*, to grow back the prenoetic organ that generates and reinforces the temporal scansion of experience on the level of personal continuity as well as that of historical connectedness, if that experience is ever to become coherent, substantial, non-entropic, and genuinely literate. The causes responsible for this condition of interior temporal deformation are manifold and not entirely isolable (see *Education Lost*, chapter 5, for an attempted diagnosis of the predicament, in particular the discussion of the disorienting effect of the technological imperative that envisages the abolition of time by collapsing the distance between beginnings and ends, input and output, in its striving for pure, luminal velocity). But what I am mainly concerned with now is the failure of grammatical technology. On the one hand, education will have to counteract the forces that lead to the stultifying of the deep sense of linear temporality, of which the technological paradigm with its stress on instantaneity, on the abolition of intervening time, is pre-eminent (aided and abetted by the diffusions of the videotronic syndrome, the replacement of the word by the image, the page by the screen). On the other hand, education, if it is to be worthy of the name, will have to double back and rediscover for itself – reactionary as this may sound today – the value of the humanistic disciplines, the power of intelligibility inherent in history, literature, and philosophy, if the substratum of the personality is to acquire content *and* direction: if it is to become potentially grammatical.

It might be useful in this connection to reflect upon the analysis of the phenomenon of aphasia undertaken by Roman Jakobson, not as a psychologist preoccupied with discovering a cure but as a linguist interested in the way language works.[15] For Jakobson, elaborating on the insights of Ferdinand de Saussure, language operates along two constitutive axes.[16] The vertical or paradigmatic ladder, subsumed under the heading of metaphor (the axis of selection), is the virtual dimension or code, a repository or storehouse from which the components of our phrases and sentences are chosen. This axis represents the synchronic mode of language, invisibly present (and hence virtual) even after the selection has been made, a coexistent inventory of all the parts of speech which both supports and encompasses the structure of phrasal sequences. It implies *substitution* of lexical items and is the process whereby metaphor is generated. The horizontal or syntagmatic plane, subsumed under the heading of metonymy (the axis of combination), manifests in the syntactical ordering of the component parts of sentences, the linear contiguity of verbal elements. This represents the diachronic mode of language, the sentence extending itself *in* time and *as* time, rationalized, ordered, and unit-linked, that is, the phrasal sequence itself. It is the process whereby lexical items are combined horizontally across the sentence, with a concomitant emphasis on syntactic and grammatical functions.

Extrapolating from these two planes of linguistic signification, Jakobson distinguishes two basic forms of aphasia which he denominates "selection deficiency" or "*similarity disorder*" and "contexture deficiency" or "*contiguity disorder*," related respectively to metaphor and metonymy. In similarity disorder the ability to construct associative relationships – the raw stuff of metaphor – is impaired, with only the syntagmatic or combinative aspects of language seeming to remain in place. In contiguity disorder the "syntactical rules organizing words into higher units are lost." Speech is then largely confined to the *substitution* of words by "similarities ... of a metaphoric nature," since abstract or connective functions tend to disappear or grow increasingly tenuous.

Now it is my contention that a considerable proportion of student writing, which in many respects functions as a *correlate of speech*, betrays the symptoms of what Jakobson has defined as contiguity disorder – not that such student writing is to be regarded as pure aphasic production but that it *resembles* the forms of discontinuity associated with secondary aphasic dysfunction. We should not confuse this latter with vocabulary deficiency or paradigmatic weakening which may give the impression of *similarity disorder*, for the lexicon can always be restored or augmented – this is in part what Hirsch means by the acquisition of "cultural literacy." Rather, the disturbance in the written specimens we are trying to repair tends to occur along the axis of combination which should ideally connect the various "lexical substitutions" into an intelligible syntactic chain, but which instead appears as radically dislocated, causing the sentence to degenerate into what David Lodge calls "a mere word heap ... giving rise to the so-called 'telegraphic style.'"[17] In the intermittent light of these syntagmatic incongruities blinking along the combinatorial axis of much student writing, the concerted effort to remedy such defects manifestly requires an analysis of the underlying causes of quasi-contiguity disorder and not the compulsive piling up of remedial projects or the single-minded instruction of grammatical usage (or the introduction of computer-oriented learning programs like Seymour Papert's LOGO). The central question is: *why does student writing by and large display the features of the second type of aphasic disturbance*?

I do not pretend to have a ready, convenient, marketable answer to the problem, but I am convinced that the phenomenon of temporal distortion or obstruction is causally related to the question of contiguity disorder. Similarity disorder or selection deficiency is not the primary issue. Student writing clearly displays the operations of metaphorical substitution, even if meta-

phorical *vitality* or exuberance is often conspicuously lacking. If the right
word cannot be found, the wrong word, with which the right word is in
some way associated, can be confidently expected to deputize for it. And
this should not surprise us, since as Saussure and Jakobson have established,
the paradigmatic axis is virtual, present and co-existent *at every moment*,
subtending the horizontal extensiveness of the linear phrase as a set of latent,
constant, vertical possibilities.[18] There is a sense in which the axis of selection can be understood as non-temporal (that is, it functions in the mode
of *simultaneity*, lexical forces converging on the instant), and therefore the
speaker or writer in whom the dimension of constituent temporality is underdeveloped will still be able to perform synchronically or paradigmatically,
that is, metaphorically or associatively. Students will often write like latter-
day Viconian poets.

The dilemma we are confronting is, on the contrary, largely *metonymic*
in origin, an aspect of the temporal or diachronic process extending itself
syntagmatically along the axis of combination. The weakening of the deep
sense of time is in this view one of the principal sources or reasons for
the widespread diffusion of a grammatical dysfunctionality (sometimes
called "functional illiteracy") which looks a lot like aphasic contiguity disorder or contexture deficiency, even if it is not to be vigorously identified
with it. In the Saussure/Jakobson theory, discourse connects topics and
items (themes and words) because they are either similar or contiguous:
meaning propagates via selection and/or combination. In the present educational context, the attempt to produce or make sense of a text, whether
that text be a simple sentence or a longer, narrative or theoretical, discourse,
demands the strengthening of the sense of relationship and temporality, a
re-invigorating of the principle of metonymic contiguity. But this cannot
be accomplished overnight. *It takes time.*

The Catholic philosopher Paul Virilio makes a similar point in the course
of an anti-technological argument about the modern hunger for pure velocity. The technological agenda, he claims, is dedicated to the disappearance
of the self (which makes distinctions between the various orders of spatio-
temporal experience) by seducing it to identify not with a place or a time
or a cultural locus but with the neutralizing transparency of extreme speed,
the "ideal vector" or prosthesis of acceleration that relieves us of the demands
and anxieties of concrete existence and produces a "taste for ubiquitous
absence." The individual becomes increasingly "picnoleptic," that is, begins
to suffer frequent time lapses, gaps in the felt continuum of conscious life
as time is progressively eclipsed (or rather whited out) in the pure luminosity,
the blur and blend, of insensate, world-telescoping speed. This results
in the erosion or attenuation of those faculties most intimately associated
with the sense of continuous time of which, I would assume, the self-
coherence generated by language would be paramount. Virilio's conclu-

sion seems inescapable. The "victim of movement," he writes, has "become *aphasic.*"[19]

The aptness of this line of thinking for education today cannot be doubted. To adapt Edward T. Hall's terminology once again (see note 14), education may be understood as a slow, polychronic, *high-context* message that requires many years or even a lifetime to unfold. The more information about a system that is already shared through a process of *gradual mutuality*, the higher the context, demanding fewer specific instructions and less spelling out of rules. Low-context systems, on the other hand, require a plethora of explicit detail, leaving little room for suppleness or innovation. Though the study of *specific* subjects may be *initially* low-context, education in the larger sense is necessarily high-context, leading to a high degree of cognitive reciprocity. In other words, when understanding has been slowly and painstakingly acquired, one reaches a point at which communication can in certain circumstances be extraordinarily fast. The paradox is only apparent. High-velocity communication, of course, may be either thin and impoverished (little content) or rich and thick (polyvalent content). Rich, high-velocity communication, however, depends upon what we may term a *low-velocity medium* which provides for the gradual accumulation of implicit, core-component knowledge, making fast, relatively effortless, complex communication possible. "High context messages," Hall writes, "take longer to learn to read accurately but are much faster once learned."[20]

In a context defined by the absence or attenuation of shared knowledge built up piecemeal over time, communication is often laborious, repetitive, and obstructive, clogged with tedious minutiae, as most of the information is vested in the coded, explicit, transmitted part of the message. Everything needs to be explained and what may at times resemble speed is merely a function of illusory or non-vectorial motion, of the rapidity of *repetition* that often begins to approximate stasis, like swiftly rotating spokes or whirling propeller blades. In any event, within a high-context system, fast communication and a slow, evolving, complex, lifelong message are by no means incompatible processes.

Thus, another way of formulating the problem afflicting both teacher and student at this time is to say that the student, on the whole under-instructed and poorly prepared, requires that the educational milieu function as a high-velocity, low-context environment. This generates the need for immediate, repetitive, basic informational input to repair the deficiencies in his or her prior equipment, with the inevitable deferment of the low-velocity, high-context process associated with the desiderata of genuine education. As a result the harassed teacher is in the unenviable position of having to transmit or inculcate *isolated competencies*, injecting high-pressure streams of information that should have been gradually absorbed many years before, which has the inadvertent and prejudicial effect of swamping the educational context almost beyond reclamation. This means that education regarded as a *message-system in itself*, as something we endorse, anticipate, experience, and *read* in its slow, metonymic unfolding, so that education is always partly about itself as it is about us, suffers an inescapable subversion and disintegration. Such is the case precisely because *the educational process is itself educational* and in fact constitutes the major, permeating subject in the Calendar we are all so industriously flagging and codifying to very little effect, undercutting our own laudable intentions. There is no workable, instantaneous way out of our predicament, but given the choices that confront us, we are probably better served making a pedagogical virtue out of a temporal necessity and proceeding toward the *reinscription of time* as the basis of the curriculum rather than giving up on *Bildung* altogether or postponing it indefinitely.

Moreover, the baptism in time is essential not only with respect to viable utterance or sentence-production but with respect to the *interpretation* of texts as well. That the hermeneutic faculty remains woefully undeveloped in the majority of contemporary students is merely the obverse of the contiguity dysfunction apparent in their written work. One cannot be a stranger to time, inimical to the slow, almost proprioceptive medium in which perception, thought, and language cohere, and expect to preside insightfully over the semantic exfoliation of a text. One needs to take one's time, to exercise the composite power of memory, anticipation, and patience (Chaucer's "conquering virtue"), if one is to learn to write and read intelligibly, to produce not only grammatical sentences but *grammatical interpretations* of what one is given to read. At the same time, the material must be reasonably demanding, with a reasonably high modulus, not the sort of porridge that often passes for course content these days, if the student is going to have anything to work with and to some extent *against* – anything solid and consistent to attach grammatical instruction to. But as every teacher knows these days, if the majority is not entertained or distracted, if it is not provided with immediately accessible material, and if it is subjected to lengthy or circuitous tangents of explication, local perturbations are almost certain to ensue.

One popular but all too quodlibetical "solution" to the dilemma is to try to avoid it entirely by simply *displacing* it onto another level, adopting a kind of managerial or systems-analysis perspective and treating the class as a problem in interpersonal relationships. Thus teachers are too often prone to retitle their courses in order to attract a larger enrolment, rearranging the material to conform to the perceived requirements of *relevance*, and playing with the grading protocols so that normative evaluation (already thinned down to formative evaluation) eventually becomes dormative evaluation, ensuring that no one is awakened to the enormity of the question that remains conveniently unaddressed. What seems to resemble progressive, enlightened, and rehabilitated pedagogy turns out on closer inspection to be nothing less than a massive cop-out, a species of instant, undeferred gratification *masking as a solution* which assuages the teacher's sense of malaise as it satisfies the student's insistence on *timeliness* – an imperative that has nothing at all to do with time.

For the only authentic solution to the problem entails the gradual recuperation of time, regardless of how much time this takes, through a renewed emphasis on the value, as well as the values, of the humanistic and historical disciplines and the subtle discriminations of literary study, that is, on the value of *education*.[21]

Furthermore, turning from the macroscopic perspective of the curriculum to focus on what we might call the grammatical event itself, it would appear that the rediscovery of time or the restoration of the sense of the past as it moves through the verbal transformer at the heart of the sentence toward the amplifications of anticipated meaning *reproduces the historical dynamic in miniature*.[22] The metonymic chain of historical circumstance finds its processional image reflected and multiplied in the tiny mirror of the sentence, repeated over and over again along the syntagmatic axis of linear intelligibility. As George Steiner puts it, "what is meaningful in history is gathered into the dynamic, elucidative custody of the rational sentence."[23] This is why the grammatical episode cannot be understood in isolation from the larger temporal continuum which it both re-enacts and articulates on the level of molecular event, a little diachronic monad. Every sentence possesses a history and generates a history even as it mimes the historical process in its specular or cameo role as an instance of temporality, an aspect of the larger timescape. Otherwise what we mistakenly call a sentence is really an opaque or static *fragment* of discourse, a verbal shard that fits no sustaining, encompassing, or continuous pattern of coherent intent.

We have entered, to rephrase Plato's definition of time in the *Timaeus*, into the repetitive stasis of eternity. It seems reasonable to assume that continuous memory and normative syntax go together in the mode of reciprocal determination, reflecting ordered sequences of experienced time. Where time is sensed or apprehended as haphazard, disordered, and accidental, the binding force of memory is weakened at the same time (so to speak) that analytic syntax is disrupted. Syntax as it disintegrates merely reflects the metonymic discontinuity of experience delivered in momentary images whose logic defies temporal scansion. That is, these images or pictorial instantaneities may be *reproduced* – in idea maps, collages, or syntactical *analogues* – but they cannot be adequately described or explained at higher levels of abstraction requiring not reproductive succession but progressive, conceptual integration. This latter is a function of the complex relations of development and organization dependent on the deep, vectorial sense – the *current*, as it were – of the temporal medium of existence. Language, in Chomsky's sense as the set of all possible sentences, must be liberated from its encapsulation in the present moment of discourse in which it can only resemble gesture or expletive, trapped in the dimension of the paradigmatic, a kind of ana-phoric poetry without content or force. For a language that bears no traces of its past is a language without a future.

I suspect we are all covertly aware of this, only we are like heavy sleepers who, faintly hearing the cat howling at the window, try to dream their way around it. But at some point we are going to have to wake up and let the cat in, the basic psychological truth that Hopkins noted in his journal: "From much, much more; from little, not much; and from nothing, noth-ing."[24] We can be grateful for the good students whom we are privileged to teach and who are equally privileged to be in a position to pursue and manage their education. But for what is probably a majority, the emphasis we are increasingly constrained to place upon empirical techniques and dis-embodied skills at the expense of material instruction and genuine content is at best nugatory and at worst counter-productive. Our job is to bring the nothing up to the little and the little to the much; as for the much more, we can leave that in good conscience to the student.

If it is true, as suggested above, that the writing down depends upon the reading up, then the causal decoupling of these reciprocal functions both assumed and promoted by contemporary forms of grammatolatry will have only a tangential effect on the problems our students continue to face. Offering them an *education*, not just a compendium of heuristic and op-erational tactics of doubtful remediation value, and doing this as early as possible in their formal schooling, remains the only way of providing them with the egg tooth they require to saw their way out of the shell of their immaturity – which is the *real* and unnamed predicament that confronts us all. Anything else is only tinkering.

If we could turn the clock back or deploy some sort of pedagogical tractor beam to recover what too many public-school students missed along the way, remedial courses might have something to work upon. But failing the irruption of miracle, we remain trapped, teacher and student alike, in the paradox of trying continually to catch up with ourselves, like Charlie Cha-plin with his trayful of glasses hurrying to prevent himself from falling. I think we have no choice but to face the fact that at present there is no ready way out of the dilemma. but should it ever come to the decision, playing catch-up *teaching* is certainly preferable to acting as grammatical Handy Andys.

And this is the crux of the matter. Without a prior and continuing ex-posure to books and conversation, without *some* knowledge of the fables, legends, myths, and stories on which our civilization has cut its teeth,[25] without at least a passing and superficial acquaintance with history, the arts and the sciences, and the exigencies of language as both a memorial and expressive medium (that is, with *articulation*), the student who sits baffled, resentful, and dysfunctional in our classes will seldom experience a communication-skills course as anything but the quickest of fixes leading to no durable and genuinely remedial conclusion. This is why, to repeat Ohmann's lamentation, such courses are "notoriously ineffective," why they do not really help us in our Lernaean morass.

A good example of this quick-fix approach may be found in the teaching of essay composition, which sublimates the struggle of writing coherently into the routine and dogmatic enchantment of a "system" whose real purpose is to eclipse or accelerate the years of study and practice most students have not experienced. The "system" works approximately as follows. Students are informed that there is only one way to organize an essay. The opening paragraph must begin with a "thesis statement" and conclude with a "funnel sentence." This in turn leads into a variable number of subsequent paragraphs, the fewer the better, which "develop the theme." Each of these paragraphs should contain a sentence that signals or consummates its particular contents. The essay then crowds toward a penultimate paragraph that assembles the major points that have been scored along the way and then shoehorns into a concluding or summary paragraph reaffirming the original "statement of intention," which has now presumably been proven or justified. And there we have it. A rigid template or blueprint, blindly adhered to, has succeeded in domesticating a seething ferment of rudimentary or volatile notions – or what is perhaps more to the point, in bringing structure and content out of an approximate vacuum. Order has been imposed on chaos. Clarity and force have somehow, in the best mystical tradition, emerged from a state of inchoate unpreparedness, lexical inadequacy, and intellectual famine, thanks to the magical properties of a talismanic formula or a staple recipe of rhetorical simples.

It is easy to see what is wrong with this methodological delusion. It presupposes, first of all, that there is only one right way of doing things and that so long as we conform to a specific format discovered or invented by an accredited "expert," a given task can be readily accomplished. That such an attitude to education in general and composition in particular is basically impoverishing, that it limits, distorts, and shrinks one's verbal response to the level of a mere conditioned reflex, and produces, when it comes to writing, nothing worth reading, seems to have escaped the pedagogical conscience altogether. Next, it assumes that form can mysteriously double for content, that an abstract or apriori set of procedures can make up for lack of substance, frivolity of intention, and deep cognitive disarray, in short, that a mere *technique*, a formal or disembodied "skill," can generate *matter* (not to mention ardour, conviction, lucidity, and epistemic cohesion). And to cap it all, as we might have expected, in the real negotiations that necessarily ensue in putting this approach into practice, the teacher almost always ends up more or less rewriting the student's draft submissions and grading a final product that can only charitably be attributed to the student's ostensibly growing competence.

It seems to me that we have failed to address the central question, which may be formulated as follows. How can we really expect to organize non-producerly or *cenographic* texts in which syntactical and rhetorical structures necessarily find little to methodize in the first place? If the student writer who approaches the job of structuring an essay comes equipped with neither 1) a lattice of coherent ideas or scaffolding of background information, nor with 2) *the implicit sense gained over time of the logical relations that obtain between ideas* and which grammar and syntax materially reflect, then all the task-wizards we bring to bear upon the process remain in the long run virtually useless. (Or to put it in computer lingo, you cannot simply notch a low-density disk and turn it presto into a high-density disk. The result is always unreliable).

Thus our current theory of composition, like our theory of education in the larger sense, reveals itself as 1) monistic and inflexible; 2) contaminated by the secondary smoke of a textbook authority; 3) prone to substituting adjectival form for substantive content; 4) a short-term attempt to close the "wound," the metonymic lesion, that only time can heal; and 5) inherently disingenuous in order to camouflage its patent bankruptcy. These related symptoms of our pedagogical condition, as I have argued throughout, attest to both a collapse of common sense and a failure of intellectual nerve in many of those who are presumed to know.

And the result, after fifteen or so years of dedicated futility, is that no genuine progress in resolving the literacy crisis has yet occurred or is likely to. Teachers continue to rely on a mechanical series of prescriptions and regimens that remain as ineffective as the professional terminologies that accompany them are empty of real content. And students go on handing in essays that are as grammatically insoluble as they are intellectually embarrassing, devoid of nuance, insight, verbal appositeness, logical consistency, and the sustaining or underlying *apprehension of reality* that serves as a prerequisite for textual coherence. What is the point of the now preferred five-paragraph format leading inexorably from thesis to summary via a sequence of infundibular transitions if the student applies this template in order to establish the conclusion – to cite from an essay I recently graded on the effects of the conversion of arable land to pasture in sixteenth-century England – that "The enclosure of Arab lands, the land that used to be owned by Arabs who used to cultivate agriculture and cattle was a bad thing"?

Consider the following typical sentence from a student analysis of an assigned poem. "So in this sense his poem is not an elegy but an Eulogy because an elegy is so a lamentation and mourning of someone's death and it concludes with words of joy of or an affirmation of life and an Eulogy does and it doesn't too really and an elegy does." The syntax is faulty not only because the student is unfamiliar with the rules of phrasal sequencing but because the thought process we can discern at work here relies upon the simple concatenation of phrasal units rather than upon a logical relation of causal precedence and semantic coordination. Stripped of infelicities, the sentence should read: "So in this sense his poem is not an elegy because an elegy, while a lamentation, also concludes with an affirmation of life." What is lacking in much of our students' writing (apart from background knowledge – what Gérard Genette has called the "architext") is the deep schematization of logical and temporal relations implied by little words like "while" and "also" in the previous sentence. The absence or misuse of such "little words" (what the medieval nominalists called "syncategorematic terms") that reflect or embody the metonymic links between ideas, in particular the relations of synchronicity, contiguity, concessive function, subordination, conditionality, precedence, and causation, suggests that the problem has a lot more to do with a profound weakness in the cognitive or logico-temporal *structuring of experience* than with the lack of organizational skills in the structuring of a sentence, paragraph, or essay.

It is important, once again, to realize that there is no immediate solution to the crisis. It will take at the very least years of effort, of lucid, unsentimental, non-technical thinking, to resolve our predicament. But there just may be the slenderest chance of an eventual solution, if we are willing to proceed with dogged patience[26] and install a program of concrete, demanding, rigorous education that requires our students not only to learn to write coherently (the term "communication skills" is facile and misleading) but to master the prerequisites of intelligent reading and clear thinking, and moreover – an absolute necessity in the current situation – *to develop a sense of emotional and intellectual responsibility for their own education.* "Is it possible," asks Hilda Neatby, "that the playing down of individual responsibility for individual achievement ... may be one cause for the necessity of so much remedial work?"[27]

But the job that awaits us is staggering, close to Augean proportions, which none of the now all-too-familiar pedagogical hexafoos will help us to accomplish. Too much in the way of prior knowledge, informed thinking, and the *attitude of conviction* has been lost in too many of our students to the devastations of a deficient family life (see concluding appendix) and an impoverished formal training in the schools, as well as to the onslaught of what Neil Postman has called the First Curriculum, the image-saturated analogic medium of television and film.[28]

At the same time I am not suggesting that we give up wholesale on composition courses but rather that we learn to see them as ad hoc outriders of limited usefulness, and that we scale down our hybristic and eupeptic ambitions of programmatic retrieval. I *am* suggesting that we approach our task with a certain saving diffidence, in fear and trembling, with stern compassion and unaccustomed clarity. One cannot teach *literacy* with any hope of success without teaching *literateness*, and teaching it neat, not diluted or fizzy. One cannot teach writing without teaching reading. One cannot attach a set of adjectival "skills" to a carrier deprived of cultural and intellectual substance – even if that substance may strike us at times as being far from substantial. If we refuse "to listen for intimations of deprival," in George Grant's poignant phrase, and to direct ourselves to furnishing the emptiness, both temporal and substantial, we come to resemble the teachers and students in the cooking schools of the defunct Soviet Union suffering from chronic food shortage: *education proceeds by simulation*, as everybody is driven necessarily to pretend that the foodstuffs on which to practise are readily available, but the pots and pans are empty. And as teachers, we cannot treat the ineptitude unless we do something first about the emptiness.

"I have been a good teacher," says Dunstan Ramsay in Robertson Davies's *Fifth Business*, "because I have never thought much about teaching; I just worked through the curriculum and insisted on high standards." In our current situation, prone to incessant canon-deformation, acrimonious debate, competing righteousnesses, and the growing influence of the edutainment-and-indolescence factor, such an affirmation may appear a trifle naïve, yet its deflationary modesty has much to recommend it. Today we have little choice, given the educational disaster that threatens (if it is not already upon us), but to think long and hard about teaching – provided we resist the temptation to opt for fashionable solutions predicated on a displaced technicity.[29] We are inundated with unprepared students, and we have to tell them precisely what their newspaper article referred to at the start of this chapter says they "need to hear." But what they "need to hear" is not what they subliminally *expect to hear*,[30] which latter is the veridical translation of the implications embedded in the cited phrase.

What most of these students certainly need to hear, and what some of their teachers probably need to know, is that the quick technological fix only exacerbates the disaster; that communication-skills courses cropping up in the educational wilderness are merely one more mirage, traducing us, as Joyce puts it in *Finnegans Wake*, "into jinglish janglage for the nusances of dolphins born"; that endless bricolage yields no long-term results; and in short, that there is no Waldo to be found in the grammatical logograph we are so busily contriving. The operations of the Gramtech "school of thought" will succeed chiefly in producing a new student writer not much different from his or her predecessor, and one bearing a disconcerting resemblance, after the finderscope has been adjusted, to the Quebecois novelist

Rejean Ducharme's *écrivantome*, the writer-ghost who remains in need of the ghost-writer to get the writing done.[31]

APPENDIX

One of the reasons the issue we are addressing remains so resistant to solution is located in the communication patterns associated with the home in an increasingly under-educated, market- and media-dominated society. As a prodigious number of studies have shown, and as personal experience tends to reconfirm, young people are less and less exposed to the educational benefits of serious and prolonged conversation in the midst of family life. Middle-class parents are often too busy or too distracted to cater to the intellectual needs of their children ("lower-class" or immigrant parents, except in those ethnic sub-societies imbued with a tradition of learning and the virtues of discipline, are inattentive for other well-documented reasons). The discussion of interesting subjects at the supper table, the vigilant perusal of schoolwork and the assignment of reading material, the introduction of absorbing guests into the family circle (Hirsch stresses the importance of the "literate stranger" in the development of a child's education) and the sponsoring of "cultural" activities (theatres, symphonies, museums, book fairs, monitored travel) all take a back seat to the trivial-pursuit syndrome, programmatic neglect, and especially to ubiquitous television (so that much of what passes for family conversation consists in the exchange of random comments with respect to the events occurring on the screen).

The polls and questionnaires I habitually conduct and distribute among my chiefly middle-class students have yielded results calculated to produce a state of terminal depression in the teacher, who cannot be made responsible for the apriori stupefaction with which he or she must daily contend. Only a small percentage of students remember being read to *da capo* by their parents or introduced to the myths and stories that most teachers have until recently assumed they were familiar with. As Bruno Bettelheim writes, "Nothing is more important than the impact of parents ... second in importance is our cultural heritage ... When children are young, it is literature that carries such information best," especially the fairy tale. This is nothing less than a desideratum: "reading and being read to are essential means of education."[32] An even smaller minority have profited from parental attention to their homework and to their intellectual life in general (one of my students, the son of a high-school principal, was, to put it bluntly, illiterate), and almost none can report having engaged in the discussion of *ideas* within the family in any consistent way. (In the same vein, a recent polling venture of mine turned up only *one* out of a group of 142 students who could identify even a few of a number of crucial events, dates, and persons in Canadian history: e.g., What was Lord Durham's Report? the

Canada Act? the Jesuit Relations? Who was Lord Elgin? Louis Riel? What
happened in 1812–14? Some of my victims thought that Mackenzie King
was an early Canadian monarch. It turned out that the one knowledgeable
student, his uncle a well-known Canadian writer, enjoyed a literate family
life.)

It is safe to say that until the preschool home environment, the ecology
of family life, is radically and significantly changed to provide the early
instruction and the para-educational upbringing the child needs not only
to establish a grounding but to cross the *pons asinorum* towards an education, the teacher's most dedicated efforts are bound to be only cosmetic
and provisionally successful at best. One should consult the findings of
the Plowden Committee (1967) in England which determined that home
factors accounted for three times as many of the variations in scholastic
achievement by age eleven as did school factors. Benjamin Bloom discovered
that something in the order of two-thirds of individual differences in intellectual performance by the age of eighteen were predictable by the age
of six.[33] As the Swedish educator Torsten Husen comments, the important
factors "include the amount of time parents devote to their children, encouraging them to learn, training them to acquire learning skills, and imparting a useful vocabulary." His summing up is chilling indeed: "The school
exerts a moderate influence compared with the home."[34] And as Lionel
Trilling writes, "Traditionally the family has been a narrative institution:
it was the past and it had a tale to tell of how things began, including
the child himself."[35] What Hirsch, Roszak, Postman, and a host of other
socio-educational researchers have found in the last few years merely serves
to ratify what we have known for a very long time. As David Guterson
writes in an article in the November 1990 issue of *Harper's*, "We should
recognize that schools will never solve the bedrock problems of education
because the problems are problems of *families*, of cultural pressures that
the schools reflect and thus cannot really remedy."

Consider, for example, the terse summation provided by Pierre Bourdieu
and Jean-Claude Passeron who develop the notion of the "habitus," defined
as "a durable and culturally determined set of schemata." The habitus "acquired within the family forms the basis of the reception and assimilation
of the classroom message."[36] Until the problem of the formation of the
underlying habitus is addressed, educational theory, curriculum design, and
the practical reforms that may ensue will have only a limited effect on scholastic performance. This pedagogical judgment was brought home to me
with renewed force at a recent departmental meeting in which we were addressed by eight of our premier students, voluntary members of the peer-
tutoring program in the ad hoc Writing Centre. Apart from their regular
workload, these students gave freely of their time and expertise to assist
their less-advantaged peers to improve in "writing competence" and to de-

velop "the habit of literacy."[37] When I asked the tutors to account for their evident superiority as students, it turned out that seven of the eight had benefited from a rich and productive home life, having been taught by their parents to read at an early age and introduced to the central texts of the cultural incunabulum prior to entering school: fairy tales, myths, Bible stories, tales from Shakespeare. The eighth student did not credit his parents with the kind of strict and loving attention that had enabled his fellow tutors to prosper but owed a debt of gratitude to an energetic high-school teacher who taught him *Macbeth* with such enthusiasm that, in his own words, "My life changed from that point on." Once again the conclusion seemed inescapable: good teaching may from time to time exercise a redemptive function on receptive students, but *nothing* can replace education in the home, the influence of the dedicated and enlightened parent, in producing eager, literate, and grammatically capable students. It is not only moral character that is formed in the cradle of the family but language facility and the basis for intellectual coherence as well. The autodidact or opsimath one very occasionally meets is the exception that proves the rule (in both senses of "proves," i.e., tests and confirms). This general line of thought has been further reinforced, perhaps unintentionally, by the work of Richard Herrnstein and Charles Murray who argue persuasively that childhood IQ is strongly correlated with achievement status in later life and that IQ is heritable, but also – a thesis which they unfortunately do not develop in greater detail – that "the *heritability of a trait may change when the conditions producing variation change.*" In other words, there exists a strong family basis for both higher IQ and rising heritability (or, conversely, for stasis or decline).[38]

It is therefore clear that as long as conditions of apriori neglect continue to exist, or, what is more likely the case, continue to deteriorate, the teacher's mandate will remain (for the most part, unconfessedly) implausible. In the absence of that foundation of *basic grammatical reflection*, a composite bedrock of constituent temporality in which the requisite "background information" is fused and melded, no durable superstructure can be erected. Thus the culminating irony must be confronted: *the teacher's remedial efforts become more necessary in exact proportion as they grow less feasible.* Yet, so long as he or she sticks with the job, it may as well be performed with insight, ardour, and stubbornness, provided that the collective delusion that currently besets the profession concerning the effectiveness of belated grammatical technology at the expense of *authentic renovation* can be punctured.

A CBC television news documentary of 29 April 1992 predicts that by the end of the century, if the situation in the schools is not rectified, we can expect something like a million dysfunctional high-school graduates incapable of the most elementary operations of literacy and numeracy. The report ignores the influence of the home environment and gives added clout to the case the grammar technicians are myopically constructing. I am afraid that if such reports, which are bound to proliferate, are not *interpreted* and contextualized, their effect will only compound the dilemma we are facing.

Thus an article in the *Montreal Gazette* of 2 May 1992, pounding the same bombinating chord, quotes from a host of educators who advocate the boringly predictable "back to basics" approach. If "back to basics" means re-introducing grammar into the elementary school curriculum, abolishing the infamous worksheet which wastes the student's time while it saves the teacher's, stemming the videocy tide, and restricting the computer to its support role as a "learning tool" (or treating it as an academic subject) rather than abetting its marauding incursions into the system as a ratiocinative paradigm as well as a usurper of the teacher's legitimate functions (computers are not "interactive," despite the propaganda hype), then I would have no quarrel with the hard-line recommendations. If, on the other hand, back to basics is piously regarded as a universal panacea prescribed in the absence of genuine course content, a revised syllabus and the *indispensable advancement* of performance capacities (so that what students regularly study in their matriculation year could be moved up in the curriculum to their high-school entrance year), then the new emphasis on "fundamentals" will be nothing more than another in an indefinite series of pedagogical illusions. Our students would still remain several years behind their European counterparts. And even if the back-to-basics program were successful, the leisurely and frivolous attitude to learning, coupled with the re-infantilization of the sensibility promoted by current pedagogical practice, would yield the farcical spectacle of a new generation of grammatically competent nincompoops.

In any case, the so-called back-to-basics movement must be regarded with hepatic suspicion. As John Ralston Saul writes, back to basics is "a narrow and absolute solution to what is a general problem," which in Saul's analysis has to do primarily with "the disastrous divorce of the humanities from the systems which control our societies." He suspects that "the call for a return to basics in the classroom probably has more to do with the attempt to quiet growing public fury over ballooning illiteracy than with a serious desire to understand the problem."[39] Is it not instructive how all these reforms and movements in education, all these fresh starts, inevitably come to stale conclusions? What we require more than ever today is not another breakthrough in curriculum design or formal methodology, not another *régime pédagogique* imposed by costive and isolated ministries suffering from the usual gaseous platitudes, but a *revolution in attitude* to the fetishes, delusions, and infatuations that infect educational thinking in our increasingly technocratic environment.

Thus as a "progressive" counterpull to the back-to-basics reaction we find something euphemistically called the "new pedagogy" – also known as "open pedagogy," media-sensitive teaching, or AG (Applied Grammatology).[40] This is understood as an educational discourse for the video age. Its intellectual procedures, according to Gregory Ulmer, are appropriate for students "whose experience of language is largely shaped by continuous exposure to cinema and television." These procedures foreground the non-discursive and imagistic dimensions of thought and communication as a means not so much for the transmission of ideas as for the evocation of appropriate epistemic attitudes and for the participation of the student in the space of teaching as a primary contributor. According to this way of thinking, increasingly popular among avant-garde educators, in order to reach the media-soaked contemporary student, teachers must adapt to the prevailing *weltanschauung* of mass communication by depriviliging the traditional mode of academic discourse and concentrating instead on the *mise-en-scene* of classroom technics in which students behave more like a TV quiz-show audience than an assembly of learners. This requires a new cognitive style: the reliance on electronic hardware like video terminals and movie projectors, the selective replacement of the academic term paper by the "creative" collage or in-class "performance," and the presentation and discussion of class material through the development of pictorial "strategies" rather than via the diachronic, expository methods associated with a now-superseded print culture and the long sift of rational inquiry. We are thus presiding over the demise of the "writerly student" (Ulmer, extrapolating from Roland Barthes) and fostering instead an open pedagogy which is "not simply one style among others but is the one necessary for the cognitive use of film/video in education."

But this is a terrible mistake. The motive itself behind the new media-oriented pedagogy, invoking the potential of television as a model or template for "deep processing of thought," is both understandable and even laudable: the desire to find ways of teaching a distressingly non-teachable student population by drawing on the electronic paradigm currently in place rather than on the humanistic encyclopedia of knowledge and methodology in order to create a responsive environment. But the problem here is that it simply doesn't work, regardless of how advanced and enlightened the new procedure may appear. To begin with, the thinkers whose ideas are usually invoked to provide the intellectual backing for this "revolutionary" proposal – for example, the grammatology of Jacques Derrida or the *lalangue* of Jacques Lacan – are largely unintelligible to the videotronic generation fidgeting in our classrooms. The irony is that the filmic and pluralistic discourse of grammatological pedagogy can be "processed" only by the beneficiaries of a rigorous, linear, print-oriented education. The texts in which Derrida

argues for a poststructuralist pedagogy, reducing the role of verbal discourse
in favour of an emphasis on staging and spectacle, exemplary and figurative
material; or in which Lacan promotes the "audience" or reader to the position of the analyst stethoscoping for semiotic pulsations in the cryptophoric
discourse of the analysand-teacher; or in which Ulmer himself proposes
"mounting a pedagogical discourse that takes into account the functioning
of the double inscription" – all these "texts" are so gnarled, obscure, esoteric,
and largely unreadable that they require a heroic breed of lectors trained
in the strenuous subtleties of traditional academic philosophy if they are
to enjoy any chance of being interpreted and applied.

This revolutionary cadre of mediologists, for all its pedagogical fervour
and presumption of enlightenment, is really enacting nothing less than the
latest instalment of Benda's *trahison des clercs*, involving a wholesale ca-
pitulation to its audience, a pedagogical sellout to the analogic media justified by prodigies of intellectual casuistry. A generation of students nurtured
on television and video should not be appealed or catered to by being provided with more of the same under the auspices of a progressive education.
These students cannot be taught to *think* by being drenched in the viscosities
of a grammatological pedagogy which is only a distillation of the processes
that account in great measure for their mental stagnation. Going to school
only becomes playing hooky by another name. The very teachers most in
favour of this Golden Fleece, mediatric pedagogy – Bernard Pautrat, Leslie
Fiedler, Gregory Ulmer, to name only a few – are precisely those who cut
their cognitive teeth on the long tradition of humanistic pedagogy, and who
have mastered the *texts* of Plato, Aristotle, Dante, Shakespeare, Montaigne,
Descartes, Kant, Hegel, Nietzsche, Dostoevsky, Proust, Joyce, Mann, and
Wittgenstein. And further, it is only owing to the traditional protocols of
humanistic study that our incendiary caucus of pedagogues finds itself in
the position of intellectual transcendence enabling it to analyse and reflect
upon the electronic paradigm and to propose *reasoned arguments* in *written
documents* in its behalf – exactly what the majority of students *cannot*
do as they sink ever deeper into a condition of intellectual paralysis and
lexical anorexia, abetted by their ostensible patrons.[41]

The problem, of course, is that television operates (to use C.S. Peirce's
terms) as an *iconic* rather than a *symbolic* medium. It provides an instance
of first-level decodability that does not invite the viewer to subject its protocols, functions, and techniques to second-level analysis unless the viewer
has already profited by continuous exposure to the procedures of a symbolic,
differential, rigorously coded, non-iconic, linguistic, and transformative educational structure. To put it differently, we cannot expect to *see* what seeing
involves unless we have first learned to write and converse.

Thus television, video, and film, when we succumb to the temptations
of indiscriminate and unfiltered enjoyment they proffer, are directly respon-

sible for the diffusions of attention and thought that make education a near-unworkable proposition today. As Paul Fussell writes: "Although now and then it tries to cover its shame and put on airs, television is a grossly proletarian medium, efficient at merchandising ... but death to books, ideas, the sense of history, and the complexities, subtleties, and ironies of civilized discourse."[42] Moreover, the ubiquitous television, switched on almost all the time, is especially disastrous not only because it prevents conversation, as Fussell argues, but also because it inhibits silence, which is another form of conversation or discourse. Language is precisely the medium that permits not only communication but the gift and possibility of *genuine*, literate silence (not dumbness) which in turn fosters meditation and self-knowledge. As A.R. Luria believed, we all need a rich and elaborate language to be silent in. But the great casualties of the electronic media are precisely language and its deeper, resonating silence (and therefore that indispensable language of inaudible reflection) that make us educable, enabling us to establish reasonably integrated and stable identities.[43]

Thus when I consider the recommendations of our contemporary mediologists to reshape and cinetextualize our educational practice, I am put in mind of Matthew Hodgart's curious and proleptic novel, *A Voyage to the Country of the Houyhnhnms*, in which Gulliver, upon his ill-advised return to the island of the horses, discovers that the noble Houyhnhnms have destabilized their intellectual economy and, in the interests of a harmonious and viable future, have opened their gates to the horde of self-indulgent and unlettered Yahoos. The progressive educator, the worthy Chestnut, explains the new pedagogy to a bemused Gulliver: "We have of late made Changes in the Upbringing of our Youth. Some few Teachers still insist on the daily Training of the Canter on the Downs, and the Plunge into the Cold River, and the Study of the ancient Odes; but many of us have come to feel that this is too circumscribed a Way of imparting Knowledge and Skill ... I would banish all the old Tales and Epics of our Ancestors from the Curriculum ... Above all we must *permit* them to develop all their Capacities without Let or Hindrance; and in this the Yahoos do set us a good Example." The upshot, of course, is that the horses are duly stampeded and forced to abandon their island, swimming for their lives as they are swamped by the cresting wave of the future.[44]

EXHIBITS

In a course I have been teaching for several years under the general heading "Survey of Literature," but that might be more accurately rendered as "Theories of Interpretation," I will usually by mid-semester introduce my students to the first ten or so lines of *Finnegans Wake*. I need not be reminded that this is a notoriously difficult and inaccessible text, capable of driving post-graduate students to the brink of madness and suicide. But one-third of a prefatory page, set in the narrative context of Joyce's life and literary purposes, unfolding over a period of three hours and conducted in the manner of a parlour game or crossword puzzle (or Joyce's "crossmess parzle"), generally leads to much boisterous fun, a certain amount of second guessing, and some interesting discussion. The point I am trying to get across to my class is that such a text, which might appear as labyrinthine and eccentric, a parody or limiting case, is centrally implicated in the way all literary texts operate, foregrounding the properties of literary language in itself: its volatility, materiality, intertextual echoes and incorporations, and ultimate freedom from strict, determinate, intentional sources and referents. As Derek Attridge argues, in *Finnegans Wake* the novel "ceases to be the writing of a story to become the story of a writing,"[45] which is demonstrably the way most postmodern fiction operates (though we can go back a couple of centuries to *Tristram Shandy* for the *modus operandi*).[46]

In any event, after a three-hour session devoted to a small number of carefully selected lines, in themselves no more complicated, really, than many of Wyatt's or Shakespeare's sonnets, students no longer appear repelled or intimidated. If they remain perplexed, this is not because they cannot understand the passage in question but because they cannot understand why anybody in his right mind would waste seventeen years compiling a parzled folio of this nature and then have the temerity to demand "an ideal audience suffering from an ideal insomnia." They are, of course, perfectly entitled to this verdict, which I myself am occasionally tempted to share. But when they come to write or comment on the text in response to a prepared question already thoroughly ventilated in class discussion, the results are somewhat disconcerting, though no less edifying for all that.

I give two exemplars, the first of which (exhibit 1) I consider an average production from a batch I have recently corrected (there were twenty or so comparable performances, another half dozen totally undecipherable *non licets*, and five or six lucid answers). From a Jakobsonian perspective, the student was able to manage the job of lexical substitution with commendable facility – the piece could be rewritten without altering its form to allow for the production of *local* meanings – but the arrangement of lexical items along the horizontal axis of combination would continue to defeat the attempt at intelligible scansion. The problem with this passage is precisely the tenuousness of abstract, implicit, or connective functions (of which standard grammar is the *material correlate*) on which Jakobson has focused, so that the reader is left to struggle with a Lodgean "word heap" – an excellent example of the "telegraphic style." The words themselves are by no means cryptonyms. The air of secrecy that pervades or surrounds the text and so many others like it derives chiefly from the absence of what we may call syntactic interiority: words as correlates of thoughts that are

Q. Why may *Finnegans Wake* be regarded not as an exception to but as a representative of the practice of literature?

A. Because it has the intra/intertextuality of the essence to understand in literature – it provides a most definite fact to estimate the difference between the author's notions or intentions and the reader's understanding and influence. It is not regarded as an exception to because it doesn't have the right influence to show the means of practice of literature. It doesn't have that certain development where it provides the appropriate exception of an understanding text.[47]

Exhibit 1

not only poorly formed and curiously empty but also, insofar as they evince any semantic weight at all, are logically *disarticulated*, as if the axis of combination behaved more like a Procrustean bed than an assembly line – a morphological chopper rather than a syntactic belt.[48]

The critical point here is that grammar should not be regarded, as it almost always is, as an autonomous, self-sustaining, adjustable structure in itself, like a kind of independent lexical palatinate within the "empire of signs." One should approach it, on the contrary, as the "phonetic" manifestation of a complex system of latent, "phonemic" relations by which the mind is ordered and structured. The syntactic rules organizing words into higher semantic units function as a glossing device or second-order signifying system, what I have denoted above as a "material correlate," corresponding to a "deep structure" of interior regulating principles. As Paul Feyerabend suggests, grammar in this deeper sense contains "a cosmology" that influences thought, behaviour, and perception.[49]

The implications of this notion are perhaps no longer as revolutionary as they must have appeared, for example, to Hume's contemporaries when the great philosopher tackled the subject of personal identity, concluding that questions of self-identity "are to be regarded rather as *grammatical* than as philosophical difficulties. Identity depends on the *relations* of ideas; and these relations produce identity."[50] In the light of semiotic reflection in which we currently perceive these questions, the issue is understood as one of *isomorphic miming* between a deep grammatical structure which organizes (or as some thinkers would claim, *constitutes*) the self (and its "sense of the world") and a surface grammatical system which differentiates, arranges, and classifies the various parts of speech making up sentences.[51] The relation between latency and manifestation is of course a reciprocal

Exhibit 2

one, which explains why isolated grammar courses are not *completely* use-less; but the tacit structures that enable us to process experience enjoy a sort of ontological priority, which accounts for the general ineffectiveness of the Gramtech approach.[52] (Note the adequacy of spelling and punctuation in the first exhibit. What effect could a grammar course possibly have on this student's writing?)

The second item (exhibit 2) is a visually coherent, analogic transcript of the student's reaction to author, text, and teacher, which adroitly sidesteps the pitfalls of metonymic linearity. The fact that the writing in the cartoon bubbles is clear and well formed is due in part to its brevity and in part to the comic-strip template on which it is predicated. This student experienced greater difficulty organizing his thoughts and perceptions in his "official" written projects.[53]

· 2 ·

Dead Teachers Society

A baggy figure, equally pathetic
When sedentary and when peripatetic.
Robert Frost, "The Bear"

And once (when? That too is forgotten):
felt the barb
where my pulse dared the counter-beat.
Paul Celan, "All Souls"

Films dealing with the unlikely subjects of pedagogy and poetry have been enjoying a certain vogue of late, their tendency to clog partially neutralized by generous infusions of those twin aperients, alcoholism and humour. A good example of the pedagogical category would be *Educating Rita*, in which Michael Caine, playing an updated version of Professor Higgins, boozes his way through burnout, professional cynicism, and middle-age crisis with a little help from Blake and a timely romantic infatuation. In the course of his staggering progress, the essential democracy of education is re-affirmed as the patrician teacher is gradually revitalized by his proletarian student before embarking upon a redemptive exile in Australia, the prison continent that ironically reinforces the theme of self-liberation and *la vita nuova*. The most successful recent instance in the poetic category would probably be *Reuben Reuben* in which Tom Conti, playing a lovable and harmless reincarnation of Dylan Thomas, boozes his way down the New England seaboard ("cutting a sexual swath," remarks one of the characters) generating hilarious one-liners[1] to compensate for a prolonged bout of creative sterility. In the course of his typically canzicrans progress, the poetic stereotype is duly confirmed: poets are congenital losers, erotic insatiables, chronic alcoholics, abusers of the word, and though capable of genuine insights into the human condition and at least marginally endearing, will inevitably go to the dogs in an access of rhetorical volubility. Meanwhile the social clichés governing the ways in which we perceive teachers and poets, the former inferior to their students and the latter a species of suicidal entertainers, are playfully ratified.

These two increasingly popular subjects converge and fuse in the immensely successful *Dead Poets Society*, a film that not only did well at the box office and received numerous awards but has now embarked upon a second life as an audiovisual aid in our schools and colleges.[2] One reason for its réclame is, of course, the inimitable Robin Williams, whose curiously laconic and understated performance as the dedicated, funny, and *sympatico* Mr Keating, poetry teacher in a prestigious private school, gives his character a certain dimension, a sort of "reality" that helps to ensure his survival in our memory. Everyone has had at least one teacher who may not reproduce but at least approximates to Mr Keating's personal blend of pedagogical devotion, love of his discipline, and that wryly comical manner of approach and delivery that serves to humanize his subject, make it less formidable or repellant, and connect it with daily life as it is experienced by his audience. Another reason, no less important, has to do with the adroit treatment of cultural stereotypes and clichés, the valourizing of conventional wisdoms guaranteeing that the educational (and cultural) system ostensibly under attack will continue to operate even more smoothly and efficiently than before. In other words, the film is an exercise in the dialectics of sentimentality whose function is to preserve that which it nominally criticizes or rejects by assuring that the alternative it sympathetically proposes may be safely co-opted and assimilated by the larger structure submitted to abrasive scrutiny. (The manner in which it does this, of course, is implicit in the making and distribution of the film itself – financed, marketed, absorbed, and underwritten by the same society it critiques.) The film theoretically opposes good teaching to bad teaching,[3] a sensitive pedagogy that affirms the human spirit and establishes an intimate relation between the world of books and the world of practical affairs on the one hand, and on the other a merely efficient pedagogy: sclerotic, dry, systematic, unresponsive, concerned exclusively with verifiable success and outward respectability. But what generally goes unnoticed, even in the classroom where the film is rapidly becoming an unimpeachable text, is that *Dead Poets Society* succeeds primarily in opposing *two forms of bad teaching* – one less austere and indigestible than the other, be it said – but nevertheless two systems of pedagogy, the collectivist and the personalist, which are equally contra-indicated and equally destructive of genuine learning.

For what the film has effectively done is to set up a pair of rigged alternatives. No one who watches this movie doubts for a moment that the educational system under attack, *institutionalized* in the form of the conventional teaching of poetry, is scandalously incompetent. The infamous introduction to the class anthology, by Dr J. Evans Pritchard PH D (later signalized as "excellent" by the martinet headmaster) recommends as a test of relative merit a kind of trigonometric manipulation whereby a sonnet of Shakespeare can be measured against and rated superior to one by Byron.

The crassest instrumentalism triumphs in the teaching of literature, a point that excites disbelief and indignation in the heart of even the most sceptical viewer. It is immediately clear that we have come upon a telling and pervasive symbol, the *modus operandi* of the introduction suggesting an attitude to the educational transaction that considers it as essentially a quantifying procedure, every unit of instruction bearing, as it were, a price tag, a list of ingredients, and a specific weight establishing its status as a marketable commodity. Whatever is being learned exists in the last analysis to serve the requirements of trade and not of integration, of mensuration not absorption, to privilege exchange-value at the expense of use-value,[4] to ensure success and reputation first in the school and afterward in the larger sociocultural economy in which the graduate must not only survive but excel. All that reeks of the unorthodox and the unconventional must be rigorously controlled, securely sanitized, or ruthlessly expunged. A poem is something that may be temporarily memorized for examination purposes, rated on a scale of competitive excellence, and finally committed to the oblivion that so feeble and effeminate a product of the cultural enterprise patently deserves. The arts as a form of cultural output are necessarily suspect. A young boy who wishes to devote his life to the theatre is driven to suicide by an anal-retentive father who lines up his slippers tidily by his bedside and dreams of the sacrifice, the *investment*, that his son's education represents. No room for the wayward, the unpredictable, the disruptive resources of the spirit in this prototypical family of which the school is merely the analytic and corporate form. Meanwhile the masters go about their duties unobjectionably teaching their subjects without much in the way of personal involvement, flushing into the American mainstream generations of students whose only record of passage is the anonymous group photo (its function as mirror none but Mr Keating recognizes), and upholding the honour of the school, its priorities, once again, success and reputability, microcosm of the cultural multinational it serves and replenishes.

And the viewers, scandalized to the roots of their being, recognizing the trauma and debacle of their own educational experience, naturally object. This is plainly not what education was ever intended to be! Few are the students, current or erstwhile, who do not acknowledge that familiar and poignant tugging of the spirit away from the empirical and the instrumental, the devastating pragmatism of their upbringing, the subtle yet always detectable lie in the propagation of the humanities, the essential insincerity of their teachers. They recall the deeply felt wish for "self-expression," the desire to indulge their creative impulses, the compelling need to be thought unique, sensitive, "special," even where these desiderata are cloaked by an assumed indifference – and then turn with regret or indignation upon the institution that thwarted such desires either by direct repression or by a kind of meretricious pandering that glorifies the spirit for two periods a week only to diffuse its claims at end of term by receipting it with a grade. The anger would appear to be justified until those graduates, now adults with children of their own, improbably observe that the assumptions by which they live and the hopes and demands they impose upon their own offspring tend to underwrite the very institution against which, as they watch the film, they passionately rebel. The same holds true, *mutatis mutandis*, for younger viewers who identify uncritically with the doomed Mr Keating or with those more innocent and improvisatory students who respond to his brand of charismatic pedagogy. No one, of course, identifies with the confirmed pragmatist, the crafty and viverine Cameron, who subsumes and represents a far greater proportion of the student "clientele" than most of us are willing to accept.[5]

Disapproving of everything the school stands for, its rigidity and hypocrisy, its narrow-minded self-righteousness, its tidy, coprolitic packaging of both subjects and students into profit commodities, its preoccupation with appearances, its callow rhetoric of success, the viewer greets the *parousia* of the roguish Mr Keating with relief and jubilation. His initial gesture of having his students rip the offending Dr Pritchard's introduction out of their anthologies is a sign of better things to come, a long-awaited liberation from the fakeries and stultifications of conventional education. And we are not to be disappointed. For in John Keating we have a necessary corrective to all this oppressive Pecksniffery, a true practitioner of the pedagogy of enthusiasm (the Keat(s) embedded in his name, fortified by the obligatory John, promising authenticity and poetic exuberance as we observe him Keat-ing his way along into the Great Tradition). We listen with pleasure as he recites extemporaneously and with obvious sincerity and delight from the poets he is assigned to teach, indicating that he has *incorporated* his material. We relish his (in)appropriate and limber clowning as he hops on his desk and tips the bell with a terpsichorean toe, and makes his students adopt the same attitude to alter their perceptual habits. We applaud his supple adaptiveness, his timely quotations, his constant and warm accessibility, his caring for what and whom he teaches – wishing only that we had been fortunate enough to have studied under that wise and benevolent gaze, that agile stewardship, in the prolonged embarrassment we remember as our high-school careers. And we commend those students who revive Mr Keating's Dead Poets Society and hold clandestine meetings in a cave after nightfall to recite verse, exchange jokes and ideas, and inject a certain verve, a certain adolescent exorbitance, a quality of living immediacy into their literary education as the dead poets come to life again via the incitement of their lines and their residence in the souls of the young.

But as we are swept along in this irresistible tide of feeling, participating vicariously in the resurrection of precisely that which our education has betrayed, and revelling in the unexpected advent of that rarest of beings, the genuine teacher, we tend conveniently to forget certain disquieting elements which the film has not chosen to foreground and of which its director, the highly talented Peter Weir, was probably unaware. To begin with, that notorious introduction to which we so rightly take exception: How many of us have ever made the acquaintance of a Dr J. Evans Pritchard PH D in our high-school poetry classes? Granted, many of the introductions to which we have been exposed, just as many of the instructors who hovered over the anthologies in the intervals between teaching history and gym, carried out their duties in the most amateurish and perfunctory way imaginable, chopping up the material like a Grade Three blackboard pie. Still, I have never encountered a teacher or an introduction that proposed anything like a mathematical assault upon the contents of a poetry anthology, graphing out scalar values or vectorial quantities for the purpose of competitive ratings. The recent standard anthologies, such as the *Heath Introduction to Poetry* (preface by Joseph de Roche), the Random House *Western Wind* (foreword by John Frederick Nims), Holt, Rhinehart, Winston's *To Read Poetry* (introduction by Donald Hall), and Prentice Hall's *An Invitation to Poetry* (introduction by Jay Parini), to name only a few, all go about their business with professional aplomb and expertise and even with considerable tact and sensitivity. And I would hazard the guess that some of the worst teachers I can recall would have felt somewhat nonplussed and hamstrung before the redoubtable Dr Pritchard and, although perhaps not going so far as ordering an *auto da fé*, would have prudently circumvented those barbarous pages. The function of the scene in the film is to predispose us immediately in favour of Mr Keating while condemning the sterile and unimaginative use of the textbook and the policies that certify it. In virtue of this single episode, Mr Keating's character as rebel and iconoclast, implacable enemy of institutionalized humbug, is solidly established. What is forgotten is the manifest *unreality* of the introduction (as the pleonastic "Dr ... PH D" should make clear).

Another factor that tends to get glossed over is the little matter of Mr Keating's repertoire. It generally escapes the viewer's attention that the instructor's citational fluency is confined almost entirely to the illustrious past, and in particular to the Romantic and Victorian periods. (The film's title is, perhaps, unintentionally apt.) The *poetic language* he deploys and his students are prone to copy is one that has safely weathered the test Mr Keating never sets or invigilates but habitually assumes, namely, the test of time. Most of the material *has already passed* and can be found stamped with the seal of approval in an Oscar Williams treasury, endorsed, as it were, by the Better Business Bureau: a touch of Elizabethanism, a goodly measure of Walt Whitman, some unexceptionable and spirit-rousing Tennyson (whose Ulyssean closure is obviously intended to apply to Mr Keating himself).[6] In effect, Mr Keating is a poetic arch-conservative, a sort of booklicker, harbouring all the right cultural sentiments, who would not be out of place in the pages of *Reader's Digest*. The fact that he takes his poetry seriously, which might have cast him in the role of cultural renegade, is immediately qualified by the fact that it is the kind of poetry calculated to outrage no one either in terms of content or technique. It is a poetry that has already been culturally processed, Krafted, blanched, creamed out, milled of all disturbing rugosities. Mr Keating, for all his surface flamboyance, is really *defensor fidei*.[7]

But Mr Keating, let it be admitted, does make one memorable sortie into the twentieth century, quoting at a pertinent moment that old chestnut of Frost's, "The Road Not Taken." No harm is done to his credibility by this uncharacteristic gesture, for there is much in early-to-middle Frost that still smacks of archaism (an occasional 'tis, ere, 'twixt and lo); the poem is dated 1916, and the sentiment it apparently promotes – don't be afraid to go your own way, dare to be unconventional – has been resonantly drummed into American and Canadian high-school students for three-quarters of a century with great *éclat* and no observable effect.[8] It cannot come as a surprise that Mr Keating, ever prone to moralizing, should elect to cheer and encourage his students by quoting the poem's famous conclusion:

Two roads diverged in a wood, and I–
I took the one less traveled by,
And that has made all the difference.

A cursory analysis of the piece would seem to reinforce the pioneering thrust of its message. After all, it begins:

Two roads diverged in a yellow wood,
And sorry I could not travel both
And be one traveler ...

and continues, after the speaker has dithered for a bit,

Then took the other, as just as fair,
And having perhaps the better claim,
Because it was grassy and wanted wear ...

It all totals up nicely, and most teachers, after pausing to draw attention to the poem's beauty and power, sum up its accomplishment by dwelling lovingly on its *fortissimo* closing lines (which resemble the fragment from Tennyson's "Ulysses" quoted by the young Neil Perry: "To strive, to seek, to find, and not to yield") and exhorting their students to imitate the master,

oblivious to both the contradiction implicit in their advice and the contradiction lurking in the very heart of the poem itself.

If Mr Keating were half the teacher his students as well as the film's
viewers credit him with being, he would have lingered to observe that the
poem's presumed thesis collapses on itself directly at its centre (lines 9–12
inclusive of a 20-line poem), where Frost writes:

> Though as for that the passing there
> Had worn them really about the same,
>
> And both that morning equally lay
> In leaves no step had trodden black.

Or in other words, there is no question of the speaker having taken the
road "less traveled by," since in fact, given the central attestation, there
is no such road to be found in the poem at all. As far as the passing there
goes, the two paths are absolutely identical, and even more to the point,
they are identical *negatively*, as the title clearly indicates ("The Road *Not*
Taken": Why should the "not" be so conspicuous if the poem is about the
other path, the one not not taken?) As the protagonist contemplates which
of the two roads he should choose, it is evident to the attentive reader that
neither has been travelled on, that both are "grassy" and covered in leaves
"no step has trodden black," that both are, in a sense, "not taken." Given
these tangible conditions, the conclusion makes no sense if it is read at
face value. The poem presents us with a blatant contradiction.

And any competent teacher would recognize it is precisely the contradiction in the middle of the poem that must be confronted and resolved.
Of course, one is free to assume that if Homer can nod, Frost might be
expected occasionally to doze, but the slightest acquaintance with Frost's
biography and with his work in general would suggest otherwise. The man
who drove his family half insane, who wrote about witches, who developed
in the small compass of a sonnet ("Design") an entire gnostic theology (already implicit in the early "The Demiurge's Laugh"), who beneath a Bun-
yanesque exterior concealed a brooding, mischievous, and perhaps demonic
personality, and who was at the same time a superb technician and crafts-
man[9] (one who would surely have endorsed Robert Duncan's remark, "I
work with the mistake") – this man would not have stumbled so egregiously
and clumsily in the midst of what is arguably his most celebrated poem.
A responsible instructor, an *authentic* Mr Keating, would certainly have
resisted the temptation of surrendering to the conventional bromides of interpretation and *really have chosen the road "less traveled by" into the heart
of the poem.* He would perhaps have observed that the poem has something
to do with the complex nature of choice which always carries a certain

doubleness with it, and that, from the point of view of someone in the position of having to make an important decision in life, neither way that opens before him has as yet been travelled – *by him*. That both ways represent *terra incognita*, that they are, so to speak, *privately* untravelled.[10] But in terms of their *public* use, one may indeed be "less traveled by" than the other. There are more farmers than poets in the world, more doctors in the suburbs of London than alligator hunters in the sewers of New York (Pynchon's Benny Profane is the only one of the latter I am familiar with) – but from the perspective of an individual who has been neither and yet is required to make a choice, both alternatives as life-long vocations are equally unexplored. If the public and private dimensions of choice are taken into consideration, the contradiction evaporates – although the irony remains.[11] The reader can still affirm his integrity, his courage, his unconventionality, can still choose the less travelled path in the wood of life (as did Dante at the beginning of his great quest midway through "life's journey," in the middle of the "dark forest," although, at first, "the right path appeared not anywhere.") But there remains a number of beguilements the teacher should perhaps resist: the temptation to preside inattentively over a complex and demanding subject, the lure of purveying recommendations inhibited by the poem's content (be unconventional – all of you), and the refusal to take the untrodden path of close reading into the wood of the poem itself.

And these are all seductions which the vivacious Mr Keating permits himself to practise with a clear pedagogical conscience, and which render him, although an inspiring presence, a rather mediocre teacher. By contrast with the general run of his colleagues and a reactionary administration, he radiates presence and commitment. But the melancholy fact remains that his scholarship is inadequate, his taste in poetry tame and conservative in the extreme, and his habits of interpretation and analysis undeveloped. All this makes him no threat to the institution he ostensibly opposes but unconsciously serves, and his forced dismissal is merely the external sign or concomitant of his fundamental innocuousness. If the young Neil Perry had not committed suicide, an event that imparts a "tragic" complexion to the cinematic unfolding of the plot and ensures the protagonist's downfall, Mr Keating would have remained loyally at his post, have been duly regarded as something of an eccentric with a tendency to "unsound methods," and while receiving the occasional reprimand, have continued to function as the necessary outsider, the one whose contestation is absorbed and transmuted by the system, which closes around it and finds itself thus strengthened and conserved.[12] For Mr Keating's otherness is precisely of the kind that is assimilable and provides the system it combats with the opportunity to rejuvenate itself through the inclusion of the "foreign," the revitalizing element. It is, in short, an otherness that survives in the heart of the same, taking up towards that which the cultural economy regards as a marginal pursuit the attitude of precedent and conventional validity, of *stare decisis*, which that same cultural economy regards as mandatory. It is just sufficiently exotic – like Panasonic, just a *little* ahead of our time – to create the impression of novelty and threat, yet, for all that, remaining comfortably within the boundaries of the predictable, the safe, the accommodating, the ritualized, affirming the patterns of social expectation and relying on what we might call the *predisposition toward the canonical*. The writing and study of poetry is plainly a border phenomenon in "American" culture, existing precariously on the fringe of serious pursuits. But the attitude generally brought to bear upon it by the "best" teachers cannot be readily distinguished from that adopted by the most thoroughgoing poetasters. The methodology of appreciation as well as the range of examples corresponds more or less exactly to the basic assumptions by which the society at large regulates its practice. The new and the strange is rendered acceptable by an unexceptionable context, founded in precedent, that has been elaborately prepared for it. But genuine originality consists precisely in *reformulating the context* or establishing one that is culturally unexpected, that is to say, in what Thomas Kuhn calls a "paradigm shift," a notion familiar to all good (i.e., revolutionary) teachers.[13]

Given a somewhat different and less theatrical twist of circumstance, one perhaps more in "conformity" with our own educational experience, the school would find itself in the same position vis à vis Mr Keating as the spinster in the old joke who, sampling a heady and unfamiliar wine, comments: "I relish its impertinence." The point is, the wine may be strange, but it is neither vinegar nor antifreeze. There is always room in the system for an impertinence that adds a certain *frisson*, a flicker of spiciness, but nonetheless abides by the ideological protocols by which that system is controlled and unified. The less travelled path, as we know, is studded with rest stations and patrolled by traffic helicopters. Nobody gets lost on it. A member of an important cultural institution, Mr Keating, it would appear, is not the fifth column but the fourth pillar.[14]

And hence the bathos of the film's conclusion, a departing Mr Keating leaving a host of diminutive Keatings behind him, standing on their desks in a transient gesture of solidarity. But when the credits have rolled off the screen, as we are well aware, they will seat themselves again to ponder Dr Pritchard's introduction before turning the semester into a cautionary anecdote tinged with the sentimental overtones of a deceptive authenticity.[15]

· 3 ·

Balnibarbian Architecture

There was a most ingenious architect who had contrived a new method for building houses, by beginning at the roof and working downwards to the foundation.

Jonathan Swift, *Gulliver's Travels*, Bk. III, Gulliver in Balnibarbi

While the substructure of a society is rotting away, the superstructure continues to prosper, living off the decay below. But when the substructure is finally gone, it is only a matter of time before the glorious surface crashes down under its own weight.

John Ralston Saul, *Voltaire's Bastards*

FIDDLING ON THE ROOF

As we are all uncomfortably aware these days, we find ourselves increasingly embroiled in discussion and controversy over a swarm of academic questions calculated to lead to polarization instead of answers. These issues, which populate the now-familiar educational realm of the Quasiplausi (quasi-plausibilities that rarely work), range across the entire pedagogical spectrum from institutional reforms generated by arachnoid ministries at one end to small, local prescriptives regarding teacher evaluation at the other. In between, when we have time, we worry about contract settlements that are neither contractual nor settled, student retention that has nothing to do with students retaining what they learn and everything with keeping them in our classrooms regardless of merit, and abstruse curricular directives that fudge the distinction between requirement and recommendation, leaving us as often as not in a state of unproductive confusion rather than, at the very least, creative anarchy.

What *seems* to unite us at the manifest level through all this turmoil is a putative generosity of spirit, an ostensible concern with the welfare of our students and the health of the educational institution. But I suspect that what really binds us beneath all the rhetoric and pedagogical bustle is something quite different, namely, a latent desire to avoid genuine issues and to neutralize the unsettling recognition that something has gone terribly wrong with a system that co-opts our best intentions, so that even opposition will often become a secret form of participation.[1] The result is, in the words of the underground grammarian Richard Mitchell, that education has now become "the consolidation of the mundane through the accumulation of the trivial."[2]

For example, at the lower end of the scale, the recent fuss over teacher evaluation, a non-starter if there ever was one. Common sense tells us that if a teacher finds class assessments of his or her performance useful, then by all means let these be adopted, despite the ensuing hermeneutic problem of assessing the assessments. If, on the other hand, such evaluations are regarded as a form of catering to a "clientele" barely capable of consistent scholarly performance, or alternately, as a form of political correctness in an increasingly repressive environment, then let the teacher bravely rely on his or her own intuition and judgment. Given the large number of un-reflected variables involved in the matter, it seems reasonable to assume that teacher evaluation should be both discretionary and cautious.[3]

In any case, genuine *teaching* has little to do with such orthopedic dis-tractions, which can only clutter the central issue of learning in the current milieu while enabling teachers and administrators to maintain the fiction of pedagogical purpose and moral uprightness. And the central issue has been clearly articulated for us by the influential educator, Quaker theologian Parker Palmer, who writes: "Truth is evoked from the teacher by the obe-dience of those who listen and learn – and when that quality is lacking in students, the teacher's words are taken away." The desire to learn is what we should expect and encourage in our students, but this requires "a spirituality of 'sources' in education rather than one of 'ends'," an ability to welcome ambiguity and *real* diversity rather than the inclination "to dic-tate the desirable outcomes of education" – whether in the form of the tacit presuppositions behind questionnaires, the rigidities of competency-based pedagogy, or the demands of crude authority. How could what Palmer calls the "desert teacher" require anything less from his students than labour and respect, modesty and a willingness to learn, if he is not to return their tendency to premature judgment or mere indifference with, as he suggests, pedagogical silence?[4] But, as things stand, we have grown so bemused with outcome that we have forgotten all about input. Naturally, Palmer's message is precisely what many of us do not want to hear; it is simply too true to be good.

Or on the upper end of the scale, we find ourselves confronted with a *fait accompli* imposed by a nonconsultative ministry that has taken it upon itself to substitute one disaster for another, as if structural reorganization were ever an antidote for substantive disorganization. The new system of numbers and weightings and ponderations, hours spent in the classroom, designated outcomes (which is more like designating the drinker than the driver), procedural calisthenics, exit tests, and so on, while affecting our lives and vocations in profoundly adverse ways (including the discernible spread of a certain institutional sullenness), constitutes little more than an expensive, cosmetic evasion of what is little less than a vast cultural deformity – a perfect case of what Michel Foucault dismisses as reformers wishing "to change the institution without touching the ideological system." Structures change; the structure remains the same. This passion for wanton and unbridled reform, this endless recycling of dead theories and false hopes, is a symptom of what we might call, paraphrasing Arthur Kroker, Crash pedagogy: "One result of Crash is that there can be no new contents, just rearrangements of the old ones."[5] This is why such alterations amount to exercises in futility, since the real purpose of "reform" is not to launch us into the redemptive world of millennial expansions but, quite frankly, to preserve the status quo under another name. The lamentable fact is that the reform mentality, so much a part of the technolatric disposition of our time, has grown more robust as it has become less effective. Educational reforms are mainly a way of doing less with more and thus operate as a parody of the efficiency construct that determines the growing absurdity of our professional behaviour. Put another way, educational reform is generally a mixture of cutback economics (that almost never works) and institutional takeover (that almost always does). The essential point, of course, is that prescriptive reforms cannot be vertically imposed if they are to be truly effective. As Paulo Freire warns, educational programs must be planned "from the bottom up, rather than from the top down,"[6] if they are not to collapse into Balnibarbian paradox, generating less teaching and more administration as a top-heavy ceiling subsides with all its decorative excrescences into an inadequate foundation.

As for the current curriculum reform in Quebec, it will, I suspect, eventually result in nothing more than an increase in workload accompanied by a reduction in the number of teachers, this latter happily offset by the creation of several hundred new bureaucratic appointments to administer the manipulated shortfall. The best that can be said about this procedure is that it at least demonstrates the virtue of consistency in a province that employs, at minimum count, 5,000 education paper-shufflers to administer a population of 90,000 teachers. Lise Payette, a former cabinet minister, points out that Denmark, which has 180,000 teachers, is served by a cadre of 50 education administrators. (Compare also the superior quality of Danish education with the catenary sag of the local product. Further, the dropout rate in Denmark is 2 per cent; in Quebec it is closer to 40 per cent.) An educational system counting twice the number of teachers serving a slightly smaller student population and administered by 1 per cent the number of bureaucratic personnel – and doing a significantly better job into the bargain – boggles what remains of the Quebecois mind.[7]

Aside from a small number of, let's say, prebendary advantages that may arise from the more sensible aspects of the reform (those involving second-language learning, for example), the entire operation will eventually take its place as one more shambles in the barren landscape of contemporary education crammed with Potemkin villages. The approach is all wrong from the start: top-down, aprioristic, anti-conciliar planning, predicated on an objectives model of learning which, with its stress on prespecified competency and criterion projection, is already intrinsically obsolete.[8] To begin with, reform – if it is to be meaningful – *must proceed under a local description*, taking into account the claims and diversities of the domestic moment in respectful consultation with those *who do the work*. Secondly, those responsible for planning must strive to exorcise the ghostly metaphors and presuppositions about education that will certainly haunt their thinking on the subject, that is, *they must proceed under a conviction of a preconception*. One of the ways to accomplish this end (aside from radical or autonomous reflection, always in short supply) is to consult, not flowcharts and spreadsheets and organagrams but the work of the most reputable thinkers in the field. Only thus can Mission Control gain some modest assurance that it is not in danger of inflicting on society massive educational damage from which it may never fully recover. Reform must start with *teachers* in the class and *thinkers* in the field (preferably non-cognitivists), with those who nourish a capacity for difference and who are often forced to be original, and not with Laputan specialists in remote and splendid confraternity practising the higher karaoke of intellectual reprise.[9]

There is not much one can do about it now except, as always, to try to minimize the inevitable consequences of the debacle by staying as alert and lucid as we can, despite the temptation to scepticism or despair.[10] Teaching has always, among other things, been a form of damage control, but in the present environment of perpetual emergency it has come to resemble something even more implausible, a curious kind of catastrophe management. Curious because, often with the best of intentions – a laudable desire to train and encourage their students – teachers find themselves playing down, *normalizing*, the extent and nature of the calamity we call education. The tendency toward soft grading is epidemic, as if in sympathy with the students' dilemma rather than their condition. The unfounded belief that "technique will generate content,"[11] especially in writing courses, aligns the teacher with the hierophants and mystagogues of the technological paradigm who base their reform programs on exactly that principle. The rigid conformity to schedule, procedure, and blueprint that is growing more and more pronounced, presumably as an expression of concern and involvement but really, I suspect, as an affectation of legitimacy, works against the improvisatory and serendipitous, which is the soul of all good teaching. Sometimes the teacher manifests as Draconian legislator, sometimes as boisterous companion. But in the absence of demanding content, strict marking, and scrupulous research (none of which precludes common sociability), and without a hospitality for the unpredictable, it all comes down to the same thing: unwitting complicity with the administrative master. The teacher is now reduced to the subordinate task of implementing a complex set of directives and regulations imposed by fiat instead of responding with an informed conscience to the exigencies of the real situation. The job now consists not of enacting a cultural imperative but of determining what constitutes an entry-level course or how to construct and invigilate an exit test. No longer *teachers*, we are in danger of becoming little more than a parcel of human screen-savers, or just waiter-friendly servitors traying in courses that freeze well and are readily catered for, like lobster tails and carrot cake.[12]

What we see in operation, in other words, is a species of the centralist or monistic ideology, which envisions an aggregate of individuals released from communal or associational ties and subject to the unilinear authority of a controlling organization. This program almost never works. In education, as in society, the only feasible and productive approach to communal existence is pluralistic, de Toqueville's celebrated "art of association," beginning with the concrete and immediate relations that obtain between the smaller, interstitial communities that comprise the larger grouping and privileging the local centres of authority and allegiance which, as Robert Nisbet argues, "are vital not only to the human personality but to any genuine sense of the larger community."[13] This is not an argument for deregulation – broad parameters and enforceable standards of consistency remain obligatory – but for decentralization (what Proudhon aptly called "defatalization") which allows for initial contributions to proposals for change and considerable latitude in their domestication on the part of the constituent communities – in this case chiefly teachers as groups of concerned professionals and their departments as collective decision-making bodies.

The correlation between my various instances, then, from the frenetic busywork of teacher evaluation to the ponderous restructurings of education ministries, may be seen to entail what many thinkers and writers from Martin Heidegger to John Ralston Saul have considered as the pervasive idolatry of our time: the infatuation with rational structure and disembodied technique that works to the advantage of the administrative apparatus while diminishing real creative enterprise and local initiative to the status of a nostalgic reminiscence. Call it "enframing" if you're reading the former or "solutioneering" if you're reading the latter. The larger process is the same: the gradual assumption of the instrument to the level of the reality it presumably measures or regulates, and the consequent investment and consolidation of power in the bureaucratic caste controlling the instrument.[14] In this instance, I fail to see why "collaborative learning" theory, as developed by, for example, Kenneth Bruffee, among others, should be applied only to student performance and not, *mutatis mutandis*, to the decision-

making process enacted by administrators. Bruffee argues for the validity
of participation and conversation, peer tutoring and classroom group work,
in the improvement of learning. If collaborative learning, then why not
collaborative administration and reform involving both teachers and students as well?[15] But it is the High Priori road, as Pope termed it in *The
Dunciad*, we continue to travel down.

In education the results would be distressingly evident were not so many
of us, or all of us too much of the time, so blinkered and seduced by
the same self-serving ideology, insensibly participating in what William Gib-
son in *Neuromancer* calls "consensual hallucination." For we do not need
more structure and new techniques – of which the barrage of pedagogical
protocols and methodologies, departmental reshufflings, canon deformation,
numerical projections, curricular excesses, and complicated rational scaffolding are mere symptoms – imposed from above by self-declared experts,
often incompetent, in the interests of procedural tidiness, abstract logic,
and technical progress. These are delusions dear to the technocratic "soul"
and form no part of the Kendo.[16] We need authentic substance reflected
in demanding course work, high expectations on the part of both teachers
and students, the education of the culture itself in the requisites of genuine
literacy, a cultivated respect for the past, and an emphasis on continuous
memory. On the practical front, we need to elevate standards, reduce the
size of our classes, double the number of teachers, and drastically curtail
the insensate proliferation of administrators uncloaking around us like Rom-
ulan warbirds. Anything less is merely counter-productive, a deception prospering in direct proportion to our collaboration with the rational mandarins
of our day – a collaboration, be it noted, that tends to pass itself off as
a *moral passion* for beneficial reconstruction while its principal effect and
partial purpose is to ratchet up our self-esteem at the cost of genuine reconstruction.[17] Meanwhile the enormous weight of the unessential, the proliferation of rules and details and codes and programs and theories and
reforms and cognitive scenarios for refunctioning the class – mere Quasiplausi stuff – leads us toward inevitable catastrophe in the literal sense
of the word: down-turning, collapse, decadence.

And this is the nub of the issue. Attractive-sounding notions that have
recently hit the academic marketplace like Roy Pea's "distributed intelligence" and David Perkins's "distribution of cognitive functions" in the classroom to refine and upgrade the learning situation merely reformulate those
practices that all teachers worth their salt have regularly employed – practices
that may also be easily abused. It is not the distribution of cognitive functions that counts towards a renewed learning environment but the redis-
tribution of financial resources towards the downsizing of administration
and the re-allocation of the multi-million dollar quotient into smaller classes,
higher salaries for teachers, and sabbatical time *for all teachers*, at whatever

level in the hierarchy they find themselves, to pursue their own ongoing education. Psychotropic as this may sound, *nothing else will ultimately work*, not Paideia, not the Smart School, not educational reform, no matter how engaged, compassionate, or innovative (qualities, by the way, which are in sharp decline) we may happen to be. I do not wish to imply that new theoretical models and inventive practices are necessarily factitious or chimerical. *Pedagogical* reflection and experiment remain a *sine qua non*. Obviously, we have to continue thinking as teachers about the problems and approaches of teaching if we are going to make any sort of difference. But I am suggesting that no degree of structural rethinking and no quantity of official reforming is going to have any significant long-term effect in the absence of *cultural* reflection and a massive fiscal restructuring which privileges *real teaching* – that is, which gives the teacher the time, prestige, and remuneration that rightfully accrues to the profession and consequently favours *real learning* by giving the student seminar-type classes, more individual attention, and the benefit of the teacher's growing competence, reflectiveness, pride, and enthusiasm. Otherwise, those nominally praiseworthy efforts toward reform of one kind or another amount to no more than expensive fooling around.

Nor is there any need to boost the overall education budget; it might even be decreased. The problem resides in its grossly inefficient administering and allocation, based on a systemic misconception of the value of centralized and authoritarian structures of organization. As I have argued here and elsewhere, 90 per cent or more of the *administrative* budget could be beneficially diverted to where it legitimately belongs: schools, classes, and teachers. (According to Jeff Polenz, writing in the *Montreal Gazette* of 17 April 1996, the administrative budget in Quebec for the fiscal year 1996–97, accounting mainly for a plethora of "public and para-public agencies and commissions," will be a staggering $1,114,000,000.) Thus, *a secondary function usurping a primary purpose* – precisely the modern form of Iscariotism – is one of the major factors that has made education so wicked pricey, a haven and a pretext for bureaucratic and political careers at the expense of those whom the structure was originally intended to serve. We see the demolition going on all around us beneath the misleading sign of increased efficiency: teachers' wages, already anorexic, relentlessly eroded; support staff compelled to accept buyout packages which are really sellout packages; class sizes inflating exponentially (when I met my first class this semester under the auspices of the new reform ostensibly designed to *reduce* the student-teacher ratio, there were fifty-two students, a full deck, filling every chair, shuffling in corners and crammed on window sills); the classrooms themselves resembling Third-World army barracks complete with deteriorating furniture and malfunctioning air conditioners producing only acoustic mayhem; and departments of forty served by one harassed secretary.

At the same time the typical director-general, a lineal descendant of Gilbert and Sullivan's Sir Joseph Porter, earning twice the salary of the average teacher while performing half the labour – and not very much of that, be it said, of any real or abiding educational value – "pursues his mandate" cradled by two secretaries in an admiralty office equipped with plush carpeting, a private bathroom, and all the conceivable amenities. And, judging by precedent, there is always the additional incentive of a possible double-dipping future to lighten the onerousness of the job. The allegorical implications of this vignette, of this scandal of multiples, are unmistakable and profoundly disturbing.

It should be brutally clear to all of us that the vast sums invested in maintaining a top-heavy and saprophytic educational establishment that jealously protects its powers and privileges is out of all proportion with the real, productive work it does. The issue is not only that bureaucracy is wasteful: *this* bureaucracy is the very incarnation of waste. And it continues to flourish not only because it bends its efforts towards its own "progressive" entrenchment but also because it ironically pre-empts and conscripts *local* administrations and a significant number of teachers as well into its procedural ambience. Unless this establishment is eventually demonstered, what we used to call education will continue to be found only in small Escalantean patches and enclaves scattered randomly across the mediascape, in the better private schools and in the roseate hues of nostalgic reminiscence.

And the beat goes on. The busier we are, the more advanced our touchtone pedagogy grows, the greater our preoccupation with committees, liaison building, council meetings, query sessions, and intermittent pedagogical workshops, all accompanied by incessant need for clarification that continues to recede as we approach – the less real work and substantive change we manage to achieve. We are coming increasingly to resemble Wittgenstein's bicyclist who has "to keep pedalling, to keep moving, in order not to fall down," racing ahead not to reach a destination but to preserve a precarious balance, a dubious parody of intention. Meanwhile we have all become specialists in an auxiliary discourse tailored to the requirements of formulaic evasion which has nothing to do with the passion for education or the desire to remain in the vanguard of our disciplines. We still believe we are teaching our students, and perhaps we do have our moments from time to time. "Good teachers know," writes Andrew Nikiforuk, "that effective classroom teaching cannot be reduced to technocratic problem solving, statistical research or happy students."[18] But mainly we are just responding to the pressure of norms and specifications articulated by authoritarian legislators who are versed primarily in the manipulation of political, economic, and pedagogical abstractions couched in the pretend language of technological expertise. And the joke is that some, perhaps too many, of us assume we are actually accomplishing something, mobilizing the latest solution to a stubborn and deteriorating crisis, when all we are really doing is applying arsy-versy ideas to pretty straightforward, if complex, predicaments.

We have, in effect, now descended to the level of pedagogical farce. A recent "innovation" proposed at my college enjoins that we supplement our teaching of reading and writing by teaching "speaking and listening" as well. But how we are to instruct our students in the art – or is it technology – of actual *listening*, and how we are to assess for it, must transcend the ineffable. The next logical step will be to mandate protocols for the teaching of undeniable prerequisites like sitting and breathing and to devise sophisticated tests for assessing the degree to which these projected competencies have been mastered.

The modern tendency is to do things backwards or upsidedown, to rely on the priority of polls, statistical analyses, conical projections, the segmentation of the natural and the accessory into artificial components, and on abstract logic in general – what we might call the *systemic fallacy* – rather than beginning with what Clifford Geertz has called "thick description," working up from the ethnographic instance[19] in close consultation with those who are centrally implicated in or affected by proposed innovations, and in a manner that takes their *humanity* into account. This functional distortion is really a case or subset of a much larger deprivation, having to do with the modern inability to tolerate ambiguity and to recognize that in the most important areas of our experience we have little choice but to live in riddle and obscurity. Reality is not optional. It is merely fanciful to rely on the good offices of a "Virtual World Generator" as if life were only a somewhat messier analogue of the F-16 Super Cockpit. We cannot just turn the world off and replace it with a convenient and thoroughly pre-scripted simulacrum guaranteed to produce anticipated effects. Certain forms of relationship and desire, of affective existence – love, filiation, spiritual growth, friendship, self-reflection – cannot be controlled or prespecified or subject to a transcendental audit without distorting their essential nature.

This is equally true of education. The relationship between teacher and student, if it is to be *productive*, necessarily resists the importation of techniques with the primary function of abolishing doubt and insecurity, whether these methods take the form of preconsidered norms and projections, continuous assessment, specified outcomes and competencies, or of little class plebiscites designed to help the teacher provide for the greatest number of *satisfied* students. Perplexity is part of the package. Naturally the teacher will bring certain concrete aims and aspirations to bear in his or her classroom agenda – for example, to provide for the greatest number of *educated* students consistent with the severe limitations and handicaps under which the work proceeds – but such purposes remain saturated with ambiguity and risk. All roads lead to the fall of Rome; the trick is to prolong the

journey, to celebrate the detour. Thus, the teacher *takes chances*, swings
off on promising tangents that may suddenly arise, aborts a lesson plan
in the interest of unpredictable rewards that may turn out to be losses,
introduces unplanned material if the situation warrants,[20] hesitates to regard
a course outline as a legal contract (since the angel of enlightenment avoids
prefiguration), is willing to make judgment calls that can backfire and lead
to – heaven forfend! – unpopularity, and will occasionally interrogate the
unspoken premises behind his or her congenial theory of pedagogy for the
sake of critical detoxification, despite the temporary drop in confidence and
effectiveness such moves compel. This is the gamble all good teaching entails, one which by nature cannot be monitored, enumerated, tested, or
pre-assigned. But such an attitude is also the sign of the good student as
it is, *mutatis mutandis*, of the competent administrator. Given such considerations, how are we to proceed?

We have to start humble, with the understanding that we can never be
sure of making things better, we can only do the best we can, and in education this means, above all, not putting Descartes before the horse.[21]
We must begin where we happen to find ourselves, in the concrete moment,
building from foundations, aware of obstinate deficits of intellect, will, and
appetite that won't go away no matter what advanced methodology or no-
mothetic arrogance we like to brandish. We must accept in all diffidence
what may be a law of life, namely, that long-term solutions (or even any
solutions) to *essential* human predicaments do not fall within our sphere
of competence and that it is both hybristic and dangerously Procrustean
to impose abstract or premeditated structures on forms of *lived* experience
which are always partially unpredictable, fluctuating, and risk-oriented.
There is no single right way to bring up a child. There is no prescribed
manner for falling in love. There is no universal protocol for worshipping
or rejecting the divine. There are no rules for creating a work of art. There
is no recipe for individual freedom or enlightenment.[22] All such experience
is coupled to imperfection and error, the possibility of which functions *as
a condition* of attainment. The same condition applies to education all across
the board, on the level of reform as well as on the level of class polls
and the psephological excesses these produce. And in between the parentheses of reform and evaluation falls the rich amalgam of teaching itself,
alloyed with doubt, riddled with astonishment, boredom, and delight, and
refusing the depravity of rigid structuration to alleviate the inherent defect
of the real.

For it should be clear by now that all the systematic and prestructured
remedies and the prodigies of technique we habitually rely upon are no
longer working since, as John Ralston Saul cogently remarks,[23] these have
to do primarily with "structure and method" and not with substance and
scholarly rigour. Method, of course, is intended to produce *results*, but this
is by no means the same thing as producing *quality*. Results can always be

cooked or calibrated, exactly as class averages are routinely jockeyed, to fit a prescribed requirement so that so-called results will often end up reflecting not a change in substantive abilities but the manipulation of techniques of measurement in the service of administrative objectives and quotas. For all the lip-service we abundantly pay to the ideal of ensuring the happiness and success of our students, we are really doing little more than turning them into contented integers, mere *numerons* who figure more prominently on retention lists, performance graphs, and bell curves than in any calculation of genuine learning and proficiency. No alteration in method or technique can generate a good student any more than a hi-tech milking machine can increase the yield of a poor milker. Only diet and care, over a long period of time, can do that. The same is true of academic competence. Without discipline, good studying habits, considerable reading, and early exposure to the intellectual heritage, a C student will remain alphabetically immobilized, despite what the results of any new methodology may seem to promise.[24]

The main responsibility lies with the parent, but afterward it is only the teacher – not the administrator, the professional planner, the ministerial specialist, or the pure theorist – who can supply the nourishment and exercise the student needs to grow and to excel. Nor can the theorist continue to ply his intravenous machinations in the vain and costly attempt to control the teacher's stabilizing functions. We have got the relationship between the theorist and administrator on one side – Burke's "sophisters, economists and calculators" – and the teacher on the other hopelessly reversed. It is not so much supervision that we need as super-vision. Unfortunately, in the current milieu, the administrator washes the damask while the teacher rinses out the colostomy bags.[25] Worse, we are in danger of actually endorsing the reversal, legitimizing our susceptibility to rational but unreasonable ideas parasitic upon our genuine functions.

But education, writes Saul, "is above all the result of teaching. And teaching requires teachers, the more the better." And, I'm tempted to add, the more of us there are, the better we would be. Provided, of course, we understand that the slavish devotion to rational structure is not a moral but an eschatological force that flourishes virally on the body of genuine content and vocational merit,[26] and that real teaching is inevitably crushed between the Clashing Rocks of the technological mindset and the bureaucratic mindsit. But such a recognition also entails a saving paradox, as unexpected as it is desirable. For only with the restoration of substance and the retrieval of discipline, unlikely as this may be, may theory itself be recovered and structure and method rise upon commitment, in full awareness of their native fallibility, so that we need no longer find ourselves in the position of the Shakespearean protagonist,

Seeking that beauteous roof to ruinate
Which to repair should be thy chief desire.

OMSITOG MEETS GRAMMATIK 5

I attach three "exhibits" as illustrations of the technomorphic mindset at work. The first, in two parts, is a set of directives, in the form of a description of a new Arts and Letters program, which will give the reader an idea of how the current *réforme pédagogique* is conceived by the Quebec Ministry of Education and the cryptolect in which it is expressed. The second is a character-education model emanating from the Utah Board of Education. The third consists of portions of an article by Professor Alan Weiss that appeared in the *Language across the Curriculum Bulletin*, John Abbott College, Montreal, Spring 1993, which provide the occasion for an extended critique of current pedagogical attitudes. (This is not presented separately but selectively in text.) I append as well a fourth "document" prepared by one of my students as a commentary on the previous item.

Exhibit One

The Quebec document, as the reader will note, is an uneasy hybrid of Tyler Objectivism and the Adlerian column-mongering of the Paideia Proposal. It attempts to impose on the teacher an exact set of pre-stipulated objectives and structures spread across the field of literacy-acquisition, as if the elements of genuine pedagogy were *logically* separable and distinct. It is also rife with errors of judgment and unverified assumptions about the nature of teaching and learning. I will cite just a few here.

To begin with, the program is entirely *static*: it makes no allowance or provision for accident, surprise, the sudden irruption of insight or inspiration, unspecified exigencies, conceptual freedom, alternative scenarios, in short, for the *possibility of emerging possibilities* that cannot be premeditated and that forms the deep core of effective classroom performance. Instead, students are envisioned as inert material, like pastry dough, while teachers, armed with a battery of pedagogical cookie cutters, stamp the desired shape into the mass of undifferentiated substance before them. This predisposition favours procedural replication at the expense of flexible response and discourages independent and improvisatory thinking. It works against the rich and severe freedom of the teacher's defining activity, the revels of disciplined improvidence. Under so crude and narrow a dispensation as imposed by the reformist travesty of educational procedure, how may a class be expected to *evolve* over the space of a semester? For the teacher is not there merely to transfer "dead" information, conform to timetable, or inculcate pre-specified competencies but to awaken in the student a *desire* to learn and to come to noble terms with a given course of study. The teacher does not only teach a subject but, over and around the material, by virtue of comportment and example, a certain attitude to the demands of learning itself. In addition to the subject, the teacher teaches curiosity, passion, joy, the love of knowledge, the craving for intellectual experience, and the pleasures of attainment through the conquest of difficulty. And this means that a class is always *in process*, open to new possibilities of insight and assimilation and to new combinations of ideas that cannot in the nature of things be legislated, controlled, or stipulated in advance. The genuine class, in any discipline and at every level, *develops* as it goes along since it carries within its structure of expectancy a built-in but undictatable friendliness toward the spontaneous and the unprecedented – precisely that which reformist pedantry, in its fear of the elements of risk, challenge, and even failure associated with all authentic questing, is designed to stifle and expunge. I am not suggesting that the syllabus is dispensable but that it is contingent; in other words, it should be sufficiently flexible to accommodate what cannot be foreseen, those occasions of genuine discovery or recognition or insight that can flourish only in an atmosphere of invitation and surprise. Every good teacher, however scholarly, will have a touch of the gypsy within, an inclination to embark on unplanned but promising journeys into *terra incognita*. Thus the class must be permitted to *unfold*, the teacher to digress, and the student to encounter the unanticipated, to limpet off the time to appraise and appreciate what is not in the lesson plan and which may be of far greater value than any pre-specified competency, if learning is not to degenerate into repetition, dullness, and the scandal of minimal accomplishment or rigid production. As Edmund Burke wrote: "Nothing in progression can rest on its original plan. We may as well think of rocking a grown man in the cradle of an infant."

Secondly, the definition of both "elements of competency" and "performance criteria," apart from the mutual implication that renders their logical dissociation from one another completely *artificial*, rests upon a very shaky platform of banality and presumption that renders their articulation almost entirely *unnecessary* as well. What teacher ever doubted that correctly developed sentences or accurate recognition of the main ideas in a particular discourse were "desirable outcomes" of classwork? At the same time, why should "appropriate use of program-related communication strategies" or even the identification of "forms of discourse" constitute an educational standard or objective? How do program-related communication strategies attach students to the history of their civilization or discipline or improve their ability to think lucidly, consistently, and independently? What purpose is served by identifying forms of discourse? *What* forms of discourse? And how, for that matter, is student writing to improve if, as many language thinkers now suspect, specialized knowledge of the rules and conventions of writing is not picked up by (w)rote through deliberate formal analysis but from extensive reading and the assimilation of models of good prose? In short, the basic tendency of such programs is to equate abstract distinctions and merely notional constructs with substantive reality and genuine performance, which is nothing but the practice of administrative hybris,

Matrix of Skills Specific to the Arts and Letters Program

General Objectives	Skills	Languages	Letters	Visual Arts	Performing Arts	Media Languages	Units	Status	Culture	Creation	1. Knowing	2. Understanding	3. Applying	4. Analyzing	5. Integrating	6. Assessing
1. To enable students to locate themselves in the world of contemporary culture and in the history of the arts and letters.	1 a) To adapt to postsecondary studies in the arts and letters.	O	O	O	O	O	2	Core program*	O		O	O	O			
	1 b) To identify major movements in the field of arts and letters.	O	O	O	O	O	4	Core program	O		O	O	O			
2. To introduce students to various types of language and means of expression.	2 a) To recognize the characteristic features of languages and means of expression used in the field of arts and letters.	O	O	O	O	O	2	Core program	O		O	O	O			
	2 b) To illustrate the mechanisms of communication used in the field of arts and letters.	O	O	O	O	O	2	Core program	O		O	O	O			
3. To develop students' ability to communicate in a language other than that of the educational institution.	3. To communicate in a language other than that of the educational institution.	O					2	Profiles**	O		O	O	O			
4. To enable students to apply basic concepts in the field of arts and letters.	4 a) To use methods of analysis in one of the languages of arts and letters.	O	O	O	O	O	2	Profiles	O		O	O	O			
	4 b) To use techniques of creation or performance in one of the languages of arts and letters.	O	O	O	O	O	2	Profiles		O	O	O	O			

5. To develop students' capacity for thought, analysis and criticism in the field of arts and letters.	5 a) To analyse a work in the field of arts and letters.	O O O O O	2	Profiles	O O O O O O
	5 b) To criticize a work in the field of arts and letters.	O O O O O	2	Profiles	O O O O O O
6. To enable students to experience the process of creation in the field of arts and letters, displaying intuition, originality and expressivity, while respecting appropriate requirements.	6. To produce, distribute and evaluate an original creation in the field of arts and letters.	O O O O	4	Profiles	O O O O O O O
7. To develop students' capacity for integration, as well as their ability to transfer the various skills they have acquired and to make connections between them.	7. To bring together, in an original project, all of the skills acquired.	O O O O	2	Core program	O O O O O O O

*Each core course deals with all of the various fields of knowledge.

**Courses vary according to discipline.

Exhibit I

BLOCK B

ENGLISH FOR SPECIFIC PROGRAMS

OBJECTIVE	STANDARD	LEARNING ACTIVITIES
STATEMENT OF THE COMPETENCY To communicate in the forms of discourse appropriate to a given field of studies.	**ACHIEVEMENT CONTEXT*** Individual production of a 1000-word discourse. From a selection of discourse related to the field of studies. With the aid of reference material.	Discipline(s): 603 Prerequisite: None Ponderation: 2 - 2 - 2 Units: 2
ELEMENTS OF COMPETENCY 1. To identify the forms of discourse appropriate to a given area of studies.	**PERFORMANCE CRITERIA** – Accurate recognition of specialized vocabulary and conventions. – Accurate recognition of the characteristics of the forms of discourse.	
2. To recognize the organization of facts and arguments of a given discourse.	– Clear and accurate recognition of the main ideas and structure. – Appropriate distinction between fact and argument.	
3. To use communication strategies related to a given field of studies.	– Accurate choice of tone and diction. – Correctly developed sentences. – Clearly and coherently developed paragraphs. – Appropriate use of program-related communication strategies. – Thorough revision of form and content.	

*ACHIEVEMENT CONTEXT: Student work specified is not intended as either a maximum number of words written by a student in a course or as what a student would produce in examination conditions. The work specified is what a student could produce while meeting the performance criteria described when this work is produced at the end of the course and in conditions which do not involve an artificial time constraint.

Exhibit I

the routine sublimities of the systemic. And the writing programs in particular, whether technical or discipline-related, are especially misguided, based as they are on the false assumption that writing can be taught as an isolable practice, "standing apart from any application that is real to the student. Language is wrongly treated as a separate entity, unrelated to other manifestations of social behaviour."[27]

Thirdly, the *language* of the document typifies it as little more than a professional scam, an effort to dress in what the poet Ricardo Paul-Llosa calls "casino-appropriate clothes." (The vestamentary metaphor also gives rise to the possibility of considering these self-declared reformers as pedagogical revisionists, what the French call *experts en sinistres* or dry-cleaners who specialize in restoring smoke-damaged fabrics.) This language sounds properly starched, brisk, mercerized, authentic, official, *unquestionable*, despite the fact that it is largely devoid of substance and has almost nothing in its pockets. It is simply the latest development in *educatese* or reformspeak, which Jacques Barzun called "this ghoulish Desperanto," a language given over to "reifying and obnubilating," that is, to "making objects out of the intangible and using words to becloud the real" – hence the sly appositeness of "obnubilating."[28] What is a "communication strategy," for example? A way of slipping messages past enemy vigilance or of persuading people to drink Pepsi? And where, pray tell, does that elusive Wolpertinger live, the "matrix of skills" that bunnies its way across the pages of nearly every document associated with education ministries? Why "matrix"? Is the propagation of "skills" a function or property somehow connected with the miraculous profusions of the womb or with the *vas mirabile* of the alchemist where the *filius philosophorum* gestates? And what, when we get right down to it, is a "skill"? Skills, after all, refer to motor coordination and muscle tone, which improve with exercise and drill. But literacy, as Frank Smith cogently argues, is not "a matter of honing skills ... The basis of learning is understanding ... Reading enhances familiarity with texts, an expansion of understanding that is the opposite of practising a skill," in the same way as learning to spell derives from reading, not only from memorizing scores of correspondence rules. Students should practise reading and writing "not as a drill but as an avocation."[29] What makes learning possible is *what we know*, accumulated knowledge embedded in a context of meaningful application and use and (to modify an earlier metaphor) leavened with the enthusiasm, knowledge, and spontaneity of the teacher.

But the classy, rented, pleonastic jargon of education documents merely disguises the underlying truth of language acquisition, or rather of the student's acquisition by language, which has nothing to do with developing a "capacity for integration" *in vitro* or with that bizarre form of prestidigitation known as "transference of skills" (it is not "skills" that are transferred but attitudes and habits) – and everything to do with reading copiously, engaging in informed and even passionate discussion, and learning that coherent writing, patient reading, and lucid speaking *genuinely matter.* That is, such attainments apply intimately to the conduct of daily life, are meant to be put to constant use, and are vital to the building of a rich and authoritative sensibility. But to acquire the skill (sic) "to produce, distribute and evaluate an original creation in the field of arts and letters," duly monitored in units, axes, and sundry taxonomic levels like analysis, integration, and assessment, leads inescapably to bathos, logophobia, and confusion. (Moreover, I should mention that in twenty-five years of teaching I have come across a modicum of good and even promising student work, but I have yet to meet an "original creation in the field of arts and letters.") This is the use of language tailored to the needs of evasion and fabular production in the interests not of its putative beneficiaries but of a professional community of adepts and initiates – the kind of language that Foucault has called the "exclusionary archive."[30]

Exhibit Two

The Utah document graciously spares us the labour of argument by being so evidently self-condemning. One need only remark that moral or spiritual development is almost always stultified by formal and technical inculcation and flourishes mainly in informal contexts. One learns best about moral issues and imperatives, or develops character, by observing and participating in *other activities,* by indirection and example, by doing things in a context of need and responsibility under the guidance of loving tutors, especially parents. All teachers can do here is teach by example, not precept, that is, show compassion, sincerity, and responsibility in thorough preparation of class material, in scrupulous grading, and in *practical* concern with the student's long-term welfare. The basic misunderstanding that vitiates this document and the mindset it betokens involves the now normative displacement of the essentially *human* – which depends on the primacy of will and choice actuated by a sense of freedom, that is, on moral agency – by a *theoretical construct* subject to the manipulations of technique and artificial programming. (The comment at the bottom of the page, which exposes the absurdity of the entire scheme and schedule, comes courtesy of the pen of the education writer J.T. Dillon. One thinks as well of Emerson's remark with respect to wisdom, poetry, or virtue in his essay "Experience," that "we never got it on any dated calendar day.")

Thus the general ineffectiveness associated with most *schemes* of moral instruction, from the now infamous Lord's Prayer syndrome (scarcely a single member of my (admittedly small) graduating high-school class was able to jog through the ritual Paternoster from beginning to end without stumbling, despite having recited it, eyes closed and hands clasped, every morning for eleven years) to the current MRE non-elective in which congeries of prov-

CHARACTER EDUCATION

STANDARD
8000-0700

Students will learn, demonstrate and practice personal integrity in all situations at school, home and in the community.

OBJECTIVES		Date Taught	Date Mastered	P/G Notes	I
8000-0701	Define personal integrity and find examples in own life.				
8000-0702	Understand judging appropriate and inappropriate behavior by learning to follow and accept consequences for breaking rules and laws at school, home and in the community				
8000-0703	Define honesty as being true to self and others and recognize that it is necessary to gain trust, loyalty, and respect of others at school, home, sports activities and in the work place.				
8000-0704	Understand sincerity as being fair, truthful, and genuine in word and actions.				
8000-0705	Demonstrate a humane attitude for all living things by showing compassion and empathy.				
8000-0706	Practice personal integrity in all aspects of life and understand there is a consequence for every decision and action.	7/31	8/1		

*It was about
11:00 AM — or
maybe 11:15.*

Exhibit 2

erbs, abstract imperatives, bits of disembodied history, edifying fables, tests, and simulations generate even higher levels of boredom and incredulity than was originally the case. Ethical character grows by the absorption of paradigms presented or embodied in the conduct of activities dedicated to ostensibly different ends, most effectively in the context of family life. The articulation of principles *in vacuo* is worse than useless, and in the classroom smacks of hypocrisy, deception, and sentimentality – defects of character to which young people are inordinately sensitive.

One demonstrates the virtue of hard work by working hard. One teaches the Golden Rule by doing nobly unto others, including one's children and students. One reveals and endorses the value of truth by not lying – *even about the dubious value of truth itself* in certain social situations, or the vulnerability of honesty and rectitude to the depredations of cunning and mendacity. (Honesty does not always pay, at least, not immediately. In fact, most of the time, honesty costs.) Parents and teachers must be candid with their charges when it comes to educating them about the nature of the real world or the real world of nature. The refinement of the moral sensibility, the passion for truth, the desedimenting of the feelings, the desire for intellectual achievement must be openly confessed as problematic, inconsistent, tenuous, enigmatic, ambiguous, subject both to self-delusion and objective distortion. At the same time one must bear testimony in speech and conduct to the central importance of these values and to the paradox of human life that can flourish *inwardly* only in candour and difficulty, a wick of troubled light in an environing darkness.[31]

This is why ethics cannot be a part of education in a formal, abstract, or technical sense, unless one is educating either for contempt or servitude. Put in the language of sociology, "prosocial behaviour in children is increased by adults who ... engage in prosocial behaviours (although not by adults who demand prosocial behaviours; do-as-I-say-not-as-I-do does not work)."[32] But we have become so dazed and stupefied by the presumed advantages of the rational prosthesis that we have willingly undersold our essential humanity for a mess of diagrams, procedures, schedules, and menus. This is merely cyborg pedagogy, wiring moral precepts and segmented behaviours like artificial circuits or spare parts into the living tissue of experience (or, in a more ancestral idiom, paying tithes of mint, anise and cumin at the expense of the weightier matters of the law).

Exhibit Three

"As a result of the John Abbott LAC Workshop with John Bean, I now require my students to prepare an 'idea map' and a 'tree diagram' before writing their rough drafts."

So begins Alan Weiss's article in the Language Across the Curriculum bulletin on the subject of improving student writing, furnishing us with an excellent exposition of the trendy and loser-friendly pedagogy we are all being urged to adopt. "An idea map is a focused brainstorm. A tree diagram gives students a visual picture of how they will actually organize their paper." In this way, apparently, students "can write more quickly and with greater concentration and creativity." Thus, we set our students on hunts for buried intellectual treasure, assuming they will now be able to chart their way through a wilderness that is far more refractory and insoluble than such contrivances suggest. The belief underlying this assumption is that a mere technique, a methodological doodle, will suffice to generate insight and order. But surely there are as many ways of inciting ideas or regulating their sequence as there are individuals who entertain ideas and desire to organize them. We should certainly encourage students to find whatever preliminary approach to writing suits them best, whether this may be, like Schiller, sniffing an apple kept in the desk drawer for its stimulating effect, or taking long walks or cold showers, or defacing the walls of one's room with inspirational graffiti, or – drawing idea maps and tree diagrams like cartographers with a taste for dendrology. But we should also be aware that these devices amount to nothing more than calisthenic warm-ups for the real task at hand, which is to think hard and struggle for clarity, toil assiduously through the research, tax the memory unmercifully, and work up as many drafts as eventual lucidity demands. A tree diagram (like that aging chestnut, concept-mapping)[33] is not a substitute for hard work, and the initial satisfaction it produces will often deceive the student with the fiction of realized purpose or substantive accomplishment. Maps and charts, so dear to the technomorphic soul, are only empirical tricks or idiosyncratic spasms or, at best, heuristic gadgets that accompany effort, but they do not coincide with effort. Once again the irrelevant or the merely propaedeutic is elevated to the level of real, substantial achievement in an act that reflects our contemporary infirmity of mind, *the canonization of the accessory.*

We see the effects of this epidemic tendency everywhere in the cultural wasteland we inhabit in the information technologies where data take precedence over knowledge, facilitating the communication of the trivial and ancillary as we mobilize progressively sophisticated means for increasingly primitive ends; in literature where the postmodern syndrome focuses on the status of the observer while dismissing the objective constituents of experience as illusory or fictive; in the economic sphere where financial assets are favoured over physical investments, generating an access of mergermania and corporate "restructuring" in which capital is put to work expediting transfers, divestitures, acquisitions, and leveraged buyouts rather than expanding business or increasing production of real goods; and, of course, as I am contending here, in education where the pedagogical apparatus replaces pedagogical substance and structural reform doubles for genuine performance. The situation in which we find ourselves is one in which what the Zen masters dismiss as "roof chatter" has driven out and silenced, to our inestimable loss, what Michael Oakeshott has so aptly called "the conversation of mankind."

Thus, David Perkins in *Smart Schools*, plumping for various ways of distributing cognitive functions in the classroom, encourages the practice of brainstorming, taxonomizing, tabulating, concept-mapping, and the like and would certainly entertain no objection to ramifying tree diagrams. Nothing wrong with this in moderation (i.e., selective pruning never hurts). But when he takes the next step and suggests that *much of our thinking is actually done by the cognitive environment*, that "what really counts is not where the knowledge is – inside or outside the skull – but what might be called 'access characteristics' of relevant knowledge," and that "what is in the notebook, whether the person-solo remembers it or not, is part of what the person-plus has learned," he treads on dangerous cognitive ground. If knowledge need not be deposited in the self but may be distributed throughout the epistemic system, why then, to take a simple example, should one bother memorizing a poem when one can always look it up? If we are concerned not with the intellectual possession or emotional integration of a given content but rather with its "access characteristics," we can obviously spare ourselves enormous and presumably unremunerative labour by simply consulting an anthology or the crib on the inside of our shirt cuffs, should the need arise. (Cheating devices would form an integral part of the person-plus network.) Yet it is evident from even minimal experience that the absorption of a passage, for example, from Shakespeare or Gray – its incorporation in the self – alters the quality of our living, realigns our perception of the world in unexpected and rewarding ways, emerges as a part of the conversational flow to enrich or complexify our dialogue with one another, and helps us to deepen and summarize the little odyssey of our days, whether poised in the sessions of sweet, silent thought or adrift in the madding crowd's ignoble strife.

Education has at least as much to do with the smart skull as with the smart school or, to put it differently, it crucially addresses the problem of the experiential ordering of the *non-distributable self*. This by no means rules out collaboration with other people or with the diverse media and instruments that further knowledge-acquisition and optative performance. But one must ask a potentially embarrassing question: what if most of the cognitive "residue" ends up in the notebook, the concept map, or the hard disk and correspondingly little in the memory of the learner? This transforms the learner into an accessory portion of the larger cognitive system and education becomes merely a technique for booting up the software self. But insofar as cognition enters into and *structures the personality*, and therefore cannot reasonably be construed as a utilitarian adjunct ensuring external performance or as a kind of auxiliary knowledge-system plugged into a composite abstraction, then what counts is precisely where the knowledge is and what it does there. The person-plus can be a helpful construct, but we must never forget that it is the person-solo who loves, labours, experiences insight and joy, suffers and dies. In this sense it is only the person-solo who is *real*, that is, *constitutively non-accessory*, and whose centre in memory, ardour, and reflection should be honoured and reinforced.

The perverse notion of the nomadic or dispersable self is growing increasingly popular in cognitive circles these days. This is due in part to a lamentable confusion of knowledge with expertise. As Lewis J. Perelman confidently asserts, "expertise [is] ever more embedded in networks and smart tools, rather than personal 'masters'," as education preferentially comes to rely on collaborative relationships, telecommunications networks, and groupware facilities (*School's Out*; cf. n. 28). What Perelman says is true – but true mainly of the instrumental and empirical domains which lend themselves naturally to teamwork and netscaping. In an increasingly utilitarian world dominated by economic anxieties and the pressing need to acquire new and profitable skills before they are rendered obsolete, the core-identity of the individual based on contemplation, conscience, inner leisure, productive solitude, and the patient acquisition of cultural and historical knowledge tends to atrophy with disuse or vanish entirely with contempt or neglect. The self as classically understood – and it is doubtful whether it can be meaningfully conceived in any other way – has become archaic, the detritus of the archive surviving only in the mists of humanistic pathos and elegiac recollection. In effect, the "well-rounded" educated person envisioned by the nearly defunct liberal curriculum has yielded to the geek and the hacker, the long-distance thinker to the nimble telecommuter, the prophet to the futurologist, and the old ideal of the autonomous individual to the new ideal of the corporate specialist.

It may be apt at this point to recall the Heideggerian concept of "being toward death" (in other words, of being toward authentic life) or Jaspers's notion of "boundary experience," which suggests that reality sits in the self, problematic as it may be, and not in the surround or in the theoretical superstructure. The current infatuation with *constructed systems* incorporating the individual as a functional element in a non-sensible totality and promising improved results in the process is merely another symptom of the rational hegemony of our time. This also explains why reforms are so readily imposed from Balnibarbian altitudes, *de haut en bas*, even though (in the rhetoric of Macbeth) "palaces and pyramids do slope / Their heads to their foundations." Top-downing reflects the invasive function of a systemic ideology, the belief that changes in rational organization and abstract structure are the most efficient way to guarantee progress or development on the ground. The real person, whose core of perishable subjectivity provides the source and touchstone of meaningful experience, is simply factored out of the ontological equation. Perkins's person-plus, if not sceptically monitored, has a distressing habit of morphing into the person-minus, like Carroll's Snark that can turn on the instant into a deadly Boojum.[34]

Our predicament *as teachers* is not hard to detect. We have become an underclass of epistemological rejects. Certainly we are no longer *masters* of field, discipline, and appropriate method but are more like keyboard cowboys and socket jockeys hooking into cyberspace, a dreamworld of phantom schematics and instant solutions, in the service of a corporate technocracy[35] made up of bureaucrats, technicians, and salaried cognitivists. We have come progressively to rely on the quick fix, the seduction of artifice, the installation of virtual protocols in the place of genuine commitment, the *frisson* of consummation in lieu of painstaking labour fuelled by self-criticism and dissatisfaction – all the while prone to the congratulatory rhetoric which the facility of CADifying, brain-storming, and data-accessing, as opposed to the stubborn resistance of actual writing, tends to reinforce.

Thus, the purr-word "creativity" makes its mandatory appearance in the
Weiss article, as if so rare and indeed sublime an attribute can be warehoused
in a typical class, whereas, for Jacques Barzun, who is certainly entitled
to use this epithet with impunity, creativity "is a sacred word, forbidden
except to describe extraordinary achievements."[36] Weiss then provides a scoring guide (in unwitting tandem with the Reform document) that assigns
points for "original thought," a readily available commodity, it would appear,
but as H.I. Marrou approvingly observes in his encyclopedic history of
education, "the schoolboy of antiquity was not obliged to be original: all
that was required of him was that he should learn to write."[37] Today such
modesty of address or requirement flourishes in inverse proportion to a
benign alacrity of praise and the instant inflation of goals, grades, and
gratifications, all somehow supported by abstract and subsidiary procedures.

The environment we have "created" for ourselves may be characterized
as one that is hospitable to the hypertrophy of announced intentions at
the expense of actual achievement. In this case, for example, Weiss "models"
(in part by growing another stand of tree diagrams) how students are to
fulfil a slate of objectives and expectations in their writing assignment, of
which the following, according to the text, are the most important:

- that the students develop their polemical arguments through their role
  plays and not as an abstract statement
- that their paper includes at least one fully developed analogy
- that they state one or several arguments of the opposition and refute
  them

Weiss's approach does not differ except in rhetorical force and intellectual
persuasiveness from, for example, David Hitchcock's recommendation of
the OMSITOG method, which at least enjoys the mystique of an acronymic
imprimatur: begin with an Overview of the item to be critiqued (or by
extension, written), establish Meaning, order the Structure, verify Inferences,
assess Truth claims, consult Other items for possible incorporation or evidence, and finally Grade the material.[38] But OMSITOG is just another Wolpertinger, a piece of glitzy nonsense that possesses only virtual existence
but *sounds* dandy and is tailored to give teacher and student the impression
of having accomplished something solid, complex, and, best of all,
progressive. It is as if plain hard work, conscientious reading, and serious
thinking had become obsolete, mere childish habits associated with our benighted pre-technotronic ancestors whom we have providentially outgrown
and resolutely shrink from repatriating. (As Jacques Lacan remarks in one
of his Seminars, "knowledge is worth exactly as much as it costs.")[39]

Thus the mixed tone of rueful apology and gratitude with which Weiss,
having been rescued by a colleague at the eleventh hour from the Slough
of Unsound Method, claims, "I now follow sound pedagogical practices

that I should have been doing all along." These practices also include introducing his students to a cyberlinguistic messiah called Grammatik 5 which will enable them to "become more self-reliant" and furnish them with "repeated reinforcement" while eliminating student resentment of the taskmaster.[40] "Now I require that students use this program before submitting their final drafts," he writes. We are not to read this pedagogical requirement as an autocratic or abitrary demand on the part of the teacher, since it is clearly intended for the benefit of the students who, "if they start using Grammatik 5 regularly ... will reduce the number of grammatical and mechanical errors they make, their grades on writing assignments will rise, and their general attitudes toward writing will improve. Hence one can hope with Grammatik 5 that students will experience noticeably and continuously developing improvement long after they have left the course." Curiously, many of my own students seem to have grown less self-reliant by habituating themselves to grammar programs and spell checks; in fact, they have become alarmingly dependent on their computers and processors, less capable of writing *on location and demand*, and are increasingly prone to the lure of phonetic spelling, probably because the relation between orthography and semantics largely escapes them. And the fact that Grammatik 5 is obviously incapable of correcting the trendy-poor spelling of its own designation does not auger well for its putative effectiveness. (Weiss concludes his article with the rider: "P.S. This essay has been analyzed by Grammatik 5." Given the solecisms scattered throughout, which I have left to the detection of the reader, the postscript was probably unnecessary.)

The three exhibits I have assembled here should serve to alert us to the "structural" heresy of our ostensible enlightenment. They are fundamentally ways of avoiding real issues, depriving us of our substance, and deluding us into the conviction that we are making genuine progress in the seven-league boots of technical expertise while keeping us securely bound in the Quasiplausi.[41] The truth is, this unreflected faith in the "technological paradigm" portends little but disaster and will only consummate the parody of learning we have been perpetuating for far too long. What we have decided to call "instructional technology," predicated on the unfounded belief in the effectiveness of programmed sequencing, rational structures of assimilation, competency-based learning protocols, and informational instantaneity, is nothing but the latest instalment in the educational farce to which we insist on contributing. Less gets done with ever more chatter and hype. We measure our ascent by following a VGA colour chart or diagram while remaining oblivious to the ongoing, grey, precipitous decline of standards, levels of accomplishment, and future potentials. The map is not the territory, said Korzybski, but we have substituted the former for the latter in an orgy of simulations, exactly like the cartographers in Borges's *A Universal History of Infamy* who "evolved a Map of the Empire that was of the same Scale

as the Empire and that coincided with it point for point."[42] The inevitable
result in the course of time as the Map eventually disintegrates is that "in
the whole Nation, no other relic is left of the Discipline of Geography."
Nor, we might add, is there much left of the Nation either.

Exhibit Four

I owe the following account to Karl Hemeon, one of the more proficient
students in my Utopian Satire class, an appropriate place in which to discuss
deliriums like Grammatik 5. Karl met the latter face-to-interface and survived the encounter, owing it would seem to a certain saving resilience,
a robust sense of humour, and precipitate flight.

REFLECTIONS ON GRAMMATIK 5
KARL HEMEON

A student's lot is not always dull. This class in particular promised a unique
experience as our professor, trembling with excitement, proclaimed, "It can
teach! It can teach!" Anxiously, he gathered his students, led them to the
computer lab, and introduced them to their new brains, Grammatik 5.

I must admit that as I sat, facing the computer screen, I not only felt
degraded, but extremely sceptical of its ability to improve my writing. Writing, I always believed, required much thought and creativity to be effective.
Could a computer that could neither think nor create possibly teach me
to write better? I looked towards the other students in the class. The answer
became strikingly clear, no.

The guy to my right was annoyed that even his computer was "politically
correct" as it was advising him to replace "fisherman" with the less gender
specific term "fisher." Why do this? I asked myself. Why change the voice
of the author, which may very well assume that most fishers are men, to
a more socially acceptable one. The computer does not know better. The
computer, which has no personality of its own, tries to impose one – that
of its programmers. Anyone who has met a computer programmer knows
that his personality (and most probably his writing) is about as interesting
as his floppy disk.

The guy to my left was frustrated in trying to understand the computer's
jargon. With auxiliary verb "be," a subject pronoun is needed in the object
position instead of the object pronoun "Us." Suggested replacement: We.
Another flaw I found with Grammatik 5 was that it could not teach. It
could only process. A good teacher is *someone* you can ask questions. They
don't just command you to "press F10," they explain "why." You can learn
from a teacher by playing off his personality, by asking questions and being
intuitive. The only thing you can play off a computer is Space Invaders.

On my own screen, I was startled to see that Grammatik 5 revealed a secret that not even my parents were aware of. It seems that my last name, Hemeon, is a spelling error. According to Grammatik 5, my name should be Karl Hereon! Yes, while this example is exaggerated, it does illustrate a point: computers have no common sense. The concept that a computer – which has no common sense – can improve one's writing becomes horrifically more ridiculous. It would then be possible for a student to write a completely incoherent, senseless paper and still get 100 per cent from Grammatik 5.

Our final Grammatik 5 papers reflected the flaws in computer teaching. They had no personality, made no sense, and resembled manufactured, processed papers. Long sentences did not exist because the computer deemed them incomprehensible. Completely abiding by Grammatik 5 resulted in a Dick, Jane, Spot story. See Karl Hereon run. Run Karl run.

The computer brain may be able to correct a spelling error here and there, and it may be able to rearrange a misplaced comma, but it cannot improve one's writing. Our professor fails to realize that his computer cannot possibly teach written English when it can only read binary. When he finds out, my dear mad teacher will crumble to his knees, clutch his hair, and cry, "I've created monsters!"

Is it possible that Karl's session with the latest in instructional technology is merely anomalous? Most of the students whom I have queried, when asked to reflect honestly on their experience and to resist the hype to which they have been exposed in manual and classroom, report similar unsatisfactory encounters with these intrusive and rigid devices. Yet we are assured by no less an authority than Lewis J. Perelman in *School's Out* that the "fundamental technology of programmed instruction – focused on continuous feedback, self-pacing, timely reinforcement for success, and mastery of subject matter – has been applied successfully in military and corporate training." I would have thought that this would be precisely why it should not be applied in the schools. "Continuous feedback" is trivial and disruptive; "self-pacing" is really controlled by the programming agenda in the software as well as inherently problematic in that it rules out serendipitous leaps – the soul of the learning process; "timely reinforcement" is hokey and unconvincing since it is a mechanical, not a human response (real encouragement is always personal); and "mastery of subject matter" requires a slow and meditative absorption period and very likely human intervention as well in all but menial or instrumental tasks. But I am afraid that, with the escalating propaganda for and relentless diffusion of this "fundamental technology," for every Karl Hemeon who has seen through the illusion of efficacy and progress, there will be a growing number of Karl Hereons whose education will have been even further compromised or wholly sabotaged before we pause to take inventory.

• 4 •

The Anecdotal Function

Different parts of the Ocean contained different sorts of stories ... the Ocean of the Streams of Story was in fact the biggest library in the universe.

Salman Rushdie, *Haroun and the Sea of Stories*

Inferential walks are supported by the repertory of similar events recorded by the intertextual encyclopedia.

Umberto Eco, *The Role of the Reader*

I once had a landlord who would adroitly evade any requests his tenants might make for repairs or renovations by activating an anecdotal talent of consummate and unstanchable fluency. For the first couple of years of his dispensation, I dreaded telephoning this master of avoidance to complain about a broken skylight, a leaning balcony or a defective furnace. The results of my petitions were tediously predictable: nothing was ever done and the flat fell into a progressive slummy decrepitude. But after a time, recognizing the inevitable, I stopped worrying about the state of my lodgings and found myself perversely enjoying Mr Bergman's narrative ingenuity and copiousness. I would occasionally invent some minor problem or other just for the privilege of hearing this proto–Shah of Blah release his accumulated sea of stories. His refusal to act was always prefaced by the standard formula, "Mr Solway, let me tell you a story," whereupon he proceeded to make good his promise, the only one he ever honoured.

As more time passed I began to understand that these anecdotal inundations were nothing less than Mr Bergman's characteristic *way of acting*, his technique for ordering the chaos of experience into manageable, stabilizing, and endlessly inventive diegetic structures, their purpose not only to avoid expenditure but to construct a narrative of the self, to establish and consolidate an identity. Before I finally moved into my own dwelling, our converse had grown into a symbiotic affiliation that far outstripped the original landlord-tenant relationship and had in fact blossomed into a kind of loving competition of story and argument. The day of my departure was a sad one for both of us, but I left, enriched and instructed, to occupy my own house and make my own repairs and renovations. Language, as Heidegger said, is indeed the House of Being. Narrative, he might have added, is Being itself, inflected in the language of Dasein.

In his recent book *Teletheory*,[1] conceived as a challenge to the hegemony of academic discourse in the age of television, Gregory Ulmer proposes the viability of a counter-analytic genre which he calls, somewhat infelicitously, "mystory." This is a mode of thinking and writing that vigorously opposes and arguably supersedes the reigning technology of alphabetic literacy based on the so-called scopophilia of print: linear reflection in the analytico-referential register.[2] Rejecting the protocols of standard methodological discourse, the teletheoretical project allows for private, popular, and disciplinary forms of address to be mapped unto one another, drawing from all the codes and resources of the cultural incunabulum: the video script, the joke (one of Andre Jolles's "simple forms"), the macaronic pun, the private reminiscence, the Derridean gram, the Joycean collage, and even, by the way of co-optation, the "alphabetic melancholy" of the specialist. The result is a multi-track text called mystory, defined as "a hybrid in which the oral-anecdotal and the literate-theoretical articulate a *third meaning* (italics mine).

The mystoriographical mode, it must be admitted, is not as new or revolutionary as its neologistic formulation might suggest, since the genre is already populated (though not overpopulated, it is true) by resident exemplars which Ulmer does not fail to cite, especially Barthes's *A Lover's Discourse*, Francis Ponge's *The Making of the Pre*, John Cage's *Mushroom Book*,[3] and N. Scott Momeday's memorable *The Way to Rainy Mountain*. One might also add such provocative works as Jacques Derrida's *The Post Card*, Luciano De Crescenzo's *The History of Greek Philosophy*, Ivan Illich's *H²O and the Waters of Forgetfulness*, Witold Rybcynski's *The Most Beautiful House in the World*, and Luciano Canfora's postmodernist reconstruction of the library of Alexandria, *The Vanished Library*. (While one is at it, one could just as well include Petronius's *Satyricon*, Aulus Gellius's *Attic Nights* and Dante's *La Vita Nuova*, inter alia.) Momeday's book in particular with its deft, almost metacarpal, play of registers – the mythological, the historical, and the autobiographical – provides us with an unlikely yet productive opportunity for retheorizing academic discourse by permitting us to focus on the pleated overlaps of the anecdotal function, that is, the evocation of an experience for the sake of the constitution of an argument. Such refocusing is doubly necessary in educational discourse which is notoriously artificial, dull, alphanumeric, mackled, hydroponic, lutarian, given to excessive textolatry, and equally prone to riding the Buick. To put it another way, there is nothing more disheartening than the practice of black-box pedagogy, whether it is carried on by the teacher in the classroom or by the educationalist in treatise or journal. One begins to long for a little redemptive jocktalk instead of chalk talk, for the sound of beer bottles banging in a bicycle basket outside the classroom window or a reference to ornamental Transylvanian soup-strainers in an article on research paradigms.[4] Even in the realm of pedagogical practice – teaching or writing – one must make room for what Roland Barthes called "third meanings," those stray elements that the irreducible plurality of the signifier scatters indiscriminately and providentially about, items "left over" as a kind of "luxury, an expenditure without exchange" in the process of representation. Such aliquant traces rescue us from the pretentious sobriety of academic discourse and provide us with the elements of narrative or of the "truly filmic," thus permitting us to stave off the temptation to ideological closure which is the besetting vice of academic *declamatio*.[5] But the effort to lay down the pudding-stone of experience to serve as a foundation of a "text" – whether "document" or "performance" – will almost always be met with charges of levity, distortion, and irresponsibility.

Thus I was by no means surprised when I read a recent review by Prof. Fred Wilson of my *Education Lost*, in which the anecdotal layer that underlies and supports the book's theoretical articulations was rather severely impugned.[6] Not only was the veracity of the narrative structure called into question but the equally important theoretical edifice it evidently served was dismissed from consideration. The reader of the review would never have known that the book was attempting to develop a serious polemic on the state of education in the western world or to pursue an analysis of time-deletion (the "chronosectomy") partly responsible for the disintegration of grammatical literacy in the contemporary student. I do not, I hope, take undue offence at a poor review (well, perhaps I do, a little), but I am troubled by the lack of insight into, or the missing effort to understand exactly what is at stake in the deployment of the anecdotal mode in the midst of what is at least in part a theoretical discourse.

An essential element of the book's thesis has to do with the uncertain status of memory in a technological age that *institutionalizes* the memorial function, displaces it, and deposits it for safekeeping in a complex electronic apparatus effectively severed from its original source in the mind and imagination of the individual (as if Thamus's fear in Plato's *Phaedrus* had been updated and realized). This process is intimately related to a technological project that, in the interests of an ultimate efficiency, proposes the *abolition of time*, the rejection of the prolonged and slowly assimilated vector of lived experience (as well as of reflective thought) that both substantiates and refines the educated sensibility.[7] The victim of this species of hirudinal subversion is memory in both its historical and personal dimensions, a catastrophe that accounts at least partially for the precipitous decline of literacy in our time or for the reduction of what I call in *Education Lost* "the literate scansion of the universe." Given this analysis, progressively elaborated in the body of the text, it should become clear that the anecdotal function serves an essentially strategical purpose and, moreover, operates on two parallel levels at once.

The text strives (whether successfully or not is another question, the only *legitimate* question) to counter the inexorable drift or, rather, plunge into Uchronia by staging its own constituent temporality, implicitly enacting its central prescription by interrogating its own unconscious and reviving the faculty of memory, thus allowing for the return of the repressed, the forgotten, the ignored, the dismissed, the repudiated, even at times the instructively mundane. The anecdote as a "simple form" or narrative device functions as both an example and a unit, an expression of as well as an expression – on the one hand a demonstration and on the other a condensation of personal memory itself. Thus chapter 4, dealing with the new barbarians of programmatic atemporality, opens with the phrase "I remember," which gradually becomes the leitmotif or verbal refrain insistently resonating through to the end of my deposition. For the same reason the chapter begins with a series of reminiscences meant to lead the reader into the middle of an argument that treats of the terrible nostalgia of the void, of forgetfulness and silence, and at the same time generates an implicit plea for literate paramnesis.

But in order for the anecdote to be effective as a performative technique in its desire to enact, to play out, to reproduce a theoretical claim on the level of material demonstration, it must also *generalize* and expand its personal or immediate features into the historical dimension, relying on but also exemplifying the long memory of the race. Consequently, citation and reference, the vast reticulated network of allusion, demonstration, inference, and "proof" that binds the pages of what Umberto Eco calls the "cultural encyclopedia," must take over from personal recollection and provide the groundwork of the argument. As Ulmer writes, with a glance no doubt in Eco's direction, "The encyclopedia is mine to think with ... as much a part of my memory as the stories told me by my grandmother, with an absolute conflation of artificial and living memory." In order to rediscover time, to *rediscover oneself* in time, one must not only activate memory but enter memory, or to put it paradoxically, one must *remember memory*, become part of the great flow of cultural and historical anecdote brought as far as possible to conscious recognition, so that quotation assumes the function of recollection. Creating a past that conditions one's present in the mode of the Lacanian future anterior, one will have become what one essentially is, reassembling the "morcellated" self along the lines of its potential unity and completeness as a cultural entity. The apparatus of reference and citation, parenthesis and footnote, name and idea, works as reminiscence by other means, as the macroscopic anecdote which, globalized and extended in time, complements personal memory and redeems it from both insuffiency and narcissism.

Thus anecdote, when it is successful, necessarily defeats itself, for anecdote is etymologically linked to silence and repression. The *anekdotos* remains the literally unpublished, the *an ek/dotos* or "not given out," with its lexical emphasis on privacy and intransitivity demanding its own cancellation, a warning and an exhortation. It is precisely the subversion of "anecdote" that accounts for this narrative effectiveness, the breaking of the spirit out of the tomb of the literal, for its essential function is to challenge the entrapment of the self in the closed circle of its silent, oneiric revery. The congenial or primal self is experienced as separate and unassailable, hoarded in secret like Gollum's glittering Precious, unuttered, unpublished, jealously protected, the message whispered in the circuit of election, and most effectively immured in one or another form of theoretical discourse. But the story that is dreamed in the privacy of the sanctum or entombed in the sepulchre of theory must be *told*, spoken aloud, published (made public), constructed, edited, and even written, reaching out into narrativity so that at its ideal limit the self as signifier moves toward its conceptual alliance with the larger historical signified, becoming eventually coherent and representative, unified in the sign, significant.

Education Lost was also planned to reflect a certain optative classroom practice in which the teacher presumably attempts to mobilize the full range of anecdotal method in its double acceptation as selective biography and historical scholarship. The relative proportions that hold between the personal archive and the cultural encyclopedia will obviously vary from teacher to teacher. In many cases this relation may become skewed or lopsided. Encyclopedic hypertrophy is nearly always oppressive and clumsy and leads neither to transmission nor evocation but to educational blockage, to the sedative or the costive. Anecdotal glibness in the private register leads on the other hand to mere dissipation as colloquial illustration volatizes the subject to be mastered, the teacher turning into a pure raconteur minus the campfire and the guitar. One teacher I knew used the classroom as a kind of gymnasium in which he exercised a truly prodigious memory for historical facts and dates, leaving everyone amazed and unredeemed; another taught us more about his son's dyslexia and his passion for computers than about the sinuous intricacies of the *Four Quartets*. These two teachers and their congenial practices represent the ideological limits of anecdotal fluency. Competent teachers move somewhere in between on the sliding scale of performative technique, drawing in more or less equal measures from both the slide collection and the *Britannica* as they seek to enliven, contextualize, and humanize the subject for which they are responsible. But in so doing, in wedding the doxa of "history" to the episteme of their dis-

cipline, they perform in a conscious and imaginative manner precisely \
Ann Berthoff defines as the double function of language, the memorial \
the communicative. They wield the naming or *hypostatic* power that enab..s
them to remember and reflect at the same time that they mobilize the
discursive function which, owing to its "tendency to syntax," brings the
memorial (the historical/anecdotal) into a dialogical relation with their interlocutors.[8] Naming the past leads to telling in the present, which, narratively inflected and synthesized, provokes additional naming, shared glos-
saries of experience and thought. By activating memory in its two-fold aspect
and by engaging the interlocutor, the anecdotal function, hypostatic as well
as discursive, empowers the individual to organize the welter of experience,
to heddle and weave the threads of perception and knowledge, insight, and
recollection, into something coherent and meaningful – a discernible figure
in the carpet. In this way one achieves intelligibility.

The structural homology between textual and classroom practice, though
often unremarked, assumes a *constitutive* significance: that is, the former
should determine the *modus operandi* of the latter. This requires that the
classroom scenario be viewed from the perspective of the teacher rather
than from that of the student. Here the teacher regards his or her performance *sub specie fabulae*, understanding that the *act* of teaching will
always to some extent reflect a narrative procedure and, indeed, gradually
subsume the teacher as protagonist into the narrative diegesis. Narrative,
says Fredric Jameson, "is the fundamental instance of the human mind,"
or as Tzvetan Todorov claims, "Narrative equals life; absence of narrative
is death."[9] Gregory Ulmer develops the idea in his proposal for a versatile
mystoriography that elaborates a "euretic" or inventive rather than a hermeneutic discourse: "human identity is a function of a life story ... The
story operates less by referentiality than by coherence." The teacher in the
classroom, regardless of the particular discipline that organizes his schema
and delivery, is in the process of constituting and establishing – one might
almost say, accumulating – an identity whose signature is repeatedly practised and indelibly paraphed in a kind of narrative momentum, which is
to say, anecdotally. The constant editing of personal reminiscence for purposes of illustration goes hand in hand with an epical and transumptive
relation to the great historical muniment of which the teacher is the carrier
and representative. He finds himself situated in that trembling and undecidable middle ground between recollection and paramnesis, between the
personal chronicle and the cultural transcript, as he strives to shape the
first to conform in some obscure yet *telling* manner to the testimonial imperative of the latter. In so doing, with strict attention leavened by narrative
joy and interest, he progressively becomes, in virtue of his retrospective
future, that which he implicitly sees himself as being or as always having

been. We are witnessing the progressive manifestation of an intrinsic self
– one of the fringe benefits of teaching, which in certain cases may become
its "central instance" and, ultimately, its *raison d'être*.

This is a practice well known to writers of fiction and poetry who understand their craft as, *mutatis mutandis,* a means of creating a unified
and productive self or at least the genetic and necessary illusion of one.
À la recherche du temps perdu, for example, relying on involuntary and
affective memory, concludes with the *emergence* of the protagonist, a capable
and educated Marcel who is now in a position to write the book that he
has remembered and we have just read.[10] In Lacanian terms, he has emerged
from the realm of the Imaginary reasonably intact and entered the domain
of the Symbolic, of the law of the Father, of language, discipline, and coherence. He has been both textualized and empowered. The same holds
true of the narrative voice that animates and recounts the meandering, in-
tersecting tales of Leopold Bloom and Stephen Dedalus whose shared experience produces an author capable of writing *Ulysses*. "One can only
become a philosopher," said Friedrich Schlegel, enunciating a romantic dictum with ubiquitous applicability. The philosopher, the poet ("I am my Collected Works," said Yeats), the novelist, the teacher, the *person* is in a sense
professionally engaged in constructing a cohesive and retrospective identity,
though with varying degrees of success (or rather failure), since the process
is at best merely asymptotic and too often scanted. The medium used in
the construction is what I should like to call anecdotal literacy: the assembling of a series of syntactical narrative units culled from both the log-
book and the almanac, personal time and historical time, into the grammatical image of a lucid, amalgamated self. The *pedagogical* value of this
narrative project derives from its representative and exemplary nature: the
teacher signifies the kind of person, one who has realized an achieved self,
whom the student would presumably, in his or her own way, like to become.[11]
(But how often does this happen?)

In the same way I set out to write a book, originally named *The Mystery
of Teaching* (with "mystery" echoing the Greek "mysterion," a secret rite)
but retitled *Education Lost*, with the purpose in part to put together a
fabula in which a narrative ego might eventually take shape, an "I" qual-
itatively *other* than the sloppy, empirical, distressingly accidental teacher-
person slumped over the writing table. In other words, the book itself was
intended as my education, so that under the Miltonic nomination of disaster,
with wandering steps and slow, with luck, grace, and discipline, I might
one day find myself leaving the Edenic (or Lacanian) Imaginary in the
direction of a viable hypostasis, an Education Regained. The quasi-fictional
nature of this semi-coherent identity would be redeemed by internal consistency and staying-power.[12] The "I" in *Education Lost* (the first word
in the actual text) which rants, prophesies, laments, analyses, explains, con-

demns, begs, threatens, and above all *remembers* is not the "I" who conceived of the project of escape from between the Scylla of domesticity and
Charybdis of profession. It is the Ithacan "I," the one that sets out on
the journey while, in the aporetic mode of the future anterior, having already
arrived at its destination – the Augustinian "already and not yet." I knew
what I had to do in order to become what I knew I was – and wasn't.
The entire project was animated by a certain textual *faith* (the last word
in the text proper) in the outcome. And the medium in which I tried to
negotiate both voyage and arrival was precisely that of anecdotal literacy
in its twin register of diary and scroll, forming an intentional palimpsest
of recorded event.

So to reply to the charge of narrative distortion, I might suggest there
is a sense in which it does not matter whether the *personal* anecdote, at
any rate, is "true" or not, provided it is credible, informative, and educational. (As Italo Svevo says, a story begins to be true the moment it
cannot be told in any other way.)[13] I confess that as a teacher I have occasionally "made up" stories in class for expository reasons. On the other
hand, though such assurance is doubtlessly idle, I certainly felt no need
to invent anything in my text apart from a believable and functional identity
as a writer, teacher, and person. The private anecdotes with which the text
is prolifically strewn are all "true" in the sense that I remember them as
having occurred, both in terms of actual event and emotional impact, in
exactly the way in which they are recorded. Clearly, memory is unreliable.
It fails, deforms, and embellishes involuntarily, yet one cannot be held consciously responsible for such manipulations of the "real" if one's intentions
– problematic as the concept of intention may be – are honest and genuinely
felt to be transparent. One cannot do more in this vale of deontological
opacity. But the anecdotal function per se, selective and controlled, implicitly
as well as explicitly, governs the classroom procedure of the teacher and
the textual operations of the writer as it does – subject to the inevitable
lapses and distractions – the ongoing psychography of everyday life.[14]

At a lecture I gave recently to a Montreal Leisure Society audience, which
consisted exclusively of elderly people, I was asked why the favourite reading
of "senior citizens" was demonstrably biographical. Apart from the obvious
fact that such material is less taxing than most serious literary genres, it
seemed to me that the answer had something to do with the category of
narrative itself (in this case, experienced vicariously in the reading of bi-
ographies). If life is structured as narrative, which provides our daily experience with its existential vigour, weight, and value, then nothing is so
critical as running out of stories to tell or suffering the drainage of narrative
content associated with old age and retirement. Telling the story of the
self, as Peter Brooks claims, "remains our indispensable thread in the laby-

rinth of temporality."[15] This is probably the reason vigorous people upon retirement often collapse or grow quickly debilitated and may also explain why elderly people tend to repeat themselves or to recount the history of their illnesses or the trivial events that all too frequently constitute their daily life. It is not just a question of physical weakness or mental deterioration as such. The problem is that the anecdotal function has run out of grist. Even younger people who for one reason or another lose the capacity to regard their lives as narrative structures tend to become aimless, lost, marginal, or "unsuccessful." The first casualty of anecdotal tabescence is the sense of order, direction, and purpose that informs existence in both its empirical and theoretical aspects. And following inevitably into desuetude are the qualities of enthusiasm, joy, and interest – without which the educational transaction, or any other personal enterprise, becomes merely parodic.

This process may go some way toward explaining the evident uneasiness or boredom many students feel in the class of a teacher who is anecdotally illiterate. The impression conveyed is that of sclerosis, "dryness," superannuation, and probably accounts for the pejorative connotation of the word "academic," which ironically derives, according to one theory, from the name of the farmer, Akademos, from whom Plato rented the grove in which he founded his Academy. All that fresh air and peripatetic freedom (Plato was peripatetic before Aristotle, both in an ambulatory and diegetic sense) leading eventually to the paralysis associated with the word, the discipline, and the pedagogical scriptures!

One is put in mind of Richard Rorty's *Irony, Contingency and Solidarity*,[16] which privileges "imagination" over "inquiry" in its proposal for a "liberal utopia" predicated on a saving, non-totalizing ironism. "That recognition would be part of a general turn against theory and toward narrative," writes this proponent of the new pragmatism, who sees fiction as a more cogent epistemological instrument than analysis. (But as if to illustrate just how difficult this proposition is, his study proceeds – as does Ulmer's – on the whole theoretically rather than narratively. One is encouraged to note that Paul Feyerabend, making a more or less similar point in his celebrated *Against Method*,[17] manages at least to bring the book to an absorbing anecdotal conclusion and caps his cadenza by warning, "argument without illustration leads away from human elements which affect the most abstract problems.") The tendency toward selective narrativity is something all "educators" should be encouraged to promote in both their teaching and their writing. Some people are manifestly better at telling stories than others, but the issue here involves developing a feel for the narrative *structure* in which one's practice is contained as well as mediated. In this connection, one might consider Richard Ohmann's inquiry into the status of teaching as theoretical practice, with particular reference to the humanities and English literature. Ohmann asks whether theory should enter into academic discourse and answers in the affirmative. Yet such theoretical discourse is seldom dispensed in raw, unmediated chunks; rather it is whipped into a narrative remoulade and appropriately flavoured with commentary and revelation. This is done by "incorporating the theoretical terms in a relaxed, conversational style ... it is important to fix my discourse in that key ... I want to project in the lecturing my own appropriation of these ideas, their integration into my whole outlook [and] I want to contest the routine segmentation of academic discourse into special languages."[18] To move my culinary metaphor to the back-burner, I think what Ohmann is pointing to here is the bibliomorphic nature of the classroom scenario, its governing paradigm that of the text, primarily the novel. In every class there are (or should be) swatches of metalinguistic description or explanation jostling for space with elements of dialogue and passages of confessional disclosure. Both teacher and student *enter* into the text while they are at the same time *reading* it, as it were, and in the case of the teacher, in large measure *writing* it as well. The overall form of the class, even as it absorbs its theoretical dimension, is that of the narrative fiction in early draft mode, with its controlled distribution of planned improvisations, its allowance for unexpected irruptions, and its confident sense of anecdotal momentum. (Clearly, in the teaching of science courses the ratio between the constituent features of the macroscopic narrative would need to be readjusted. Nevertheless, as long as there are teachers and students to be found in classrooms, the narrative paradigm – and therefore the anecdotal function – continues to apply.)

Thus it is not simply a question of having a large repertory of stories at one's disposal or of some sort of spry mimetic gift – though these are helpful – but of being able to recognize the *constructed* nature of the event in which one is participating – an event that resembles a macroscopic narrative including in its subsidiary components everything from rumination, questioning,[19] and dialogue to anecdote in itself. This in turn involves regarding the classroom scenario *as a text* which is, to put it paradoxically, *written orally* (or conversely, to approach one's text as a classroom event that is recounted graphically). In either case the redemptive Mr Bergman who lives at the other end of the line in the remote banlieue of the psyche must be dialled and consulted. The lodging may not be repaired, but the time spent in it will be fruitful, interesting, and, in the best sense of the term, educational.[20]

• 5 •
What About Food?

Some, indeed, will fail; but even if none failed, the outcomes would always be variable, since individuals have different potentials to start with. A society based on sentiments that discount difference in potential and excellence emasculates healthy competition, initiative and achievement, and risks promoting collective mediocrity and private resentment. It also saps itself of the incentives that unite individual pursuit of happiness with the collective good of the community.

Peter Emberley, *Zero Tolerance*

I have known an hospital, where all the household-officers grew rich; while the poor for whose sake it was built, were almost starving for want of food.

Jonathan Swift, "A Short View of The State of Ireland"

I do not believe that anyone familiar with my writing would ever accuse me of being a professional scholar. Neither am I a professional education writer or theorist – an avowal some of my pedagogical critics would be only too happy to endorse.[1] I certainly do not see my work in such a depleted, oxymoronic light, and if I had to characterize my congenial practice, I would call it polemical, rhetorical, and committed. I try to avoid monotony and lexical drabness, the menial sin of academic discourse. I would also hope the work is motivated by a spirit of honesty, though I am acutely conscious of the *structurally* problematic nature of such a claim. Nevertheless, so far as I am aware, the essential *nisus* of my writing, whether analytical or hyperbolical, is at least governed by the effort towards an always difficult and elusive candour. Effort alone is insufficient, let it be said, but I am prepared to stand by the results. At any rate, I have always – until now – tried to stay away from *personal* controversy, to resist the temptation to insinuendo, and to avoid the sly, vicious, or merely quodlibetical exchanges too often associated with scholastic debate.

I cannot, of course, guarantee the overall success of this writing ethic, only the attempt to put it into practice. Clarity begins at home; who knows where it may end? But I have always felt that ideas should be argued on their merits, that the articulation of doubts should be framed in a basic idiom of scrupulous inquiry (which does not preclude a certain verbal rubrication when that is a function of the *joy* of expression), and that as a writer one may permit oneself certain proprietary excesses provided these are aerated by the spirit of self-deflationary irony, however tenuous that might be. And one should always be aware of one's resident fallibility regardless of one's presumed assurance, moral rectitude, or "political correctness." Not an easy bill to fill, but still an asymptotic possibility.

It is for this reason (or these reasons) that I feel impelled to challenge Fred Wilson's most recent swivet, his "second review" of *Education Lost* and his reply to my essay "The Anecdotal Function." I hope it is understood that I am not responding merely to negative, critical, or uncharitable assessment of the book. When one decides to publish, one accepts the attendant risks and learns to live with them, developing precision callouses. But I am troubled and at moments a little appalled by the invidiousness of the piece, its tone of discourtesy shading into what one might almost suspect as a form of calumny, its violation of the implicit Robert's Rules of disinterested argument. A marked inclination to replace an objection with a flamefest belongs, it seems to me, on the Net and not in a presumably analytical inquiry or critique. The evangelical and stentorian spirit that seems to animate Prof. Wilson's deposition is evident in a multitude of ways from outright misrepresentation to more subtle and disingenuous tactics of presentation to an ultimate trivializing of both the terms and the substance of the dispute. Perhaps I am myself reacting too astringently to what is after all just another article – like my own – in another educational journal in a world that pays scant attention to such productions. Still, and for whatever it may be worth, it strikes me as important to reply to the illegitimate use of argument in what purports to be a scholarly *declamatio*.

Let me cite a few concrete examples of the sort of "inductive" solecisms and tactical MacGuffins I decry in Prof. Wilson's paper, which damage rather than strengthen his case. For it is entirely possible that my position in *Education Lost* needs to be modified, adjusted, or re-thought, and I am not averse to recognizing the force of a good counter-argument if it is made with rigour, probity, and rhetorical vitality. (See, for example, Wesley Cragg's rather styptic article in the same issue of *Interchange*, which, while by no means lupercalian, is at least measured.) A bit of humour mixed into the censure might help, too. But when a kind of obtuseness is allied with a tendency toward the partisan handling of evidence – or is it the agelastic grooming of pet peeves – a counter-challenge is perhaps in order.[2]

(1) It is clear that Prof. Wilson is not overly fond of Heidegger, with his "tedious and convoluted prose," by whom I have presumably been infected. Neither am I. This does not prevent me from plunging into the tenebrous inferno of *Being and Time* to see what I can learn, what fragments of genuine wisdom I may cabbalistically redeem and bring back to the upper world, even if these shards of light are blithely dismissed as "bits of continental philosophy and occasional Germanisms." For Heidegger, whether we like him or not, happens to be one of the great philosophers and truly

original thinkers of our era despite his torpid and saturnine style, his passion for errant etymologies and bizarre neologisms, and, even worse, the moral dubiety of his association with Nazi ideology. Even a Jewish thinker like George Steiner, while unsparingly anatomizing all that is objectionable in Heidegger, ruefully acknowledges his greatness and importance as a philosopher. I, too, am a Jew and find myself wholly sympathetic to Steiner's moral agonizing, to Gunter Grass's scathing parody in *Dog Years* of Heidegger's phlegmatic language, and to the rigorous prosecution of Victor Farias.[3] But as Steiner recognizes, one cannot simply dismiss the profound and seminal or at the very least influential thought of Heidegger on stylistic grounds (or for that matter, on the basis of unsupported assertions such as Prof. Wilson's "And the British empiricist psychologists had many more interesting things to say about [memory] ... than Heidegger." What interesting things? which empiricists?) without opening oneself to the charge of frivolity or philosophical irresponsibility.

But I can understand Prof. Wilson's chagrin and his consequent animadversion. Heidegger is not everybody's seidel of Bavarian dark, and there are times when I drink with deep reluctance. Hence my no-doubt misguided effort at salting the philosophical foam with a few grains of ostensive humour.[4] The point of the sentence that concludes the preamble to "The Anecdotal Function," to which Prof. Wilson takes such rancorous exception ("Language, as Heidegger said, is indeed the House of Being. Narrative, he might have added, is Being itself, inflected in the language of Dasein") depends on its being placed in context. I had just been analogically speaking of my relationship with a former landlord, of the fact that he had refused to keep my lodgings in repair, and that I had eventually moved into my own dwelling. The allusion to Heidegger's notion of language as the House of Being[5] and his description of man as being *unbehaust*, homeless, unhoused (an Odyssean condition), was simply my way of practising a kind of post-anecdotal *aufhebung*, of sublimating my introductory story with what I hoped was a certain saving facetiousness into the Heideggerian register. I assumed nobody would take the reference with total seriousness. After all, the hero of my account was not the philosopher Heidegger but the landlord Bergman. Prof. Wilson apparently was neither to be *aufgehoben* nor nostofied. (I could, of course, just as easily have chosen another analogue, for example, Oliver Wendell Holmes's chambered nautilus, moving into larger and more complex life "as the frail tenant shaped his growing shell." Or had I been so inclined, and perhaps writing for a different audience, I might have referred instead to Beethoven's famous Sonata Op. 81a, known as *Les Adieux*, and have extemporized on its three movements: *Das Lebewhol* (the Farewell), *Die Abwesenheit* (the Absence), and *Das Wiedersehen* (the Return).)

But my declared subject in the essay being anecdote and narrative, the fictional structures in which we live, reflect, learn, teach, and practise constant *bricolage*,[6] the Heidegger metaphor of the house struck me as curiously apposite, almost serendipitous, even amusing. Unless I am gravely mistaken, it takes a pretty solemn heavy-handedness or a deliberate effort at (non-Bloomian) misreading to miss the point with such haustorial fury. As Peter Sloterdijk remarks, "In laughter, all theory is anticipated."[7] All I was trying to do here was to blend a little Merlot of pantagruelizing commentary with the Cabernet Sauvignon of my argument to impart a morbifuge risibility to the analytic vintage.

(2) It may seem a minor quibble but Prof. Wilson's tendency to append the handy enclitic, "sic," in square brackets to the third-person masculine pronoun in quotations from my book suggests a somewhat ludicrous politicizing of the argument with the intention of making me appear archaic, phallogocentric, reactionary. Thus he can discard my "elitism"[8] as "a vision of the teaching profession in which most of the students are white, male, and middle-class" (and, at least preferentially, the teachers as well), accuse me of epidemic crimes like "sexism and ethnocentrism," and contend that I will dismiss certain students in my classes "as proletariat or something worse, like women." Perhaps I should quit the teaching profession pronto and take to rape, wife-beating, and white mercenary activity before retirement forces me to regret a lifetime of lost opportunities? Cool it, Wilson, I should like to say, my kids still love me and, *mirabile dictu*, most of my students do not appear entirely unappreciative of my classroom efforts.

It is true, I must confess, I use the pronoun "he" impenitently and I hope appropriately throughout my writing. There are times when I settle for the meristic "he or she" (sometimes even "she or he") but insistent repetition leads to stylistic clutter, which I would like to avoid even more than accusations of gender insensitivity. I append a parenthetical rider on page 4 of *Education Lost* in the phrase "The man (or woman, as it should go without saying)," in the hope that the reader will not object to the subsequent use of the generic pronoun with a traditional warrant I think it is tendentious and grimly ostentatious to condemn. I have come across certain writers who will regularly use "she" in place of "he," a forced artificiality even more vulnerable to the charge of sexism. Other writers are content with the ubiquitous slash, giving us a stylistically grotesque composite that makes for a somewhat bumpy sentential ride. Yet others vary the "he" and "she" with a sort of musical abandon so that the reader feels she/he is participating in a kind of square dance, do-se-do-ing through a medley of pronominal evolutions rather than negotiating a passage of lucid or epideictic prose. Sometimes a strict, implicit system governs the distribution of pronouns in a politically over-correct manner, as when Richard Rorty, loading the pronominal dice, covertly derogates the liberal metaphysician as "he" whereas the protagoniste of his drama, the liberal ironist, is preferentially "she." The counter-practice is thus instantly refuted and condemned as a form of linguistic infibulation, obsolete and cruel.[9]

For my part I can do no better than to take as my authority and precedent the brilliant Ursula Le Guin who, in discussing the pronominal difficulty experienced in her novel about androgynes, *The Left Hand of Darkness*, writes: "In the third person singular the English generic pronoun is the same as the masculine pronoun ... And it's a trap, with no way out, because the exclusion of the feminine (she) and the neuter (it) from the generic/ masculine (he) makes the use of either of them more specific, *more unjust*, as it were, than the use of "he".[10]

As for my "elitism," I know full well that the word is interpreted pejoratively these days, but as I try to indicate in appendix 2 of *Education Lost*, elitism and democracy are not antithetical notions. "It is generally questionable," writes Agnes Heller in a similar vein, "whether 'elitism' is so alien from the spirit of democracy." In her interesting discussion of Kant's *Anthropology from a Pragmatic Point of View*, in particular the passages treating the nature of the symposium, she distinguishes between the negative elitism of wealth, power, and celebrity that is a typical and unfortunate feature of mass democracy, and the positive elitism that maintains what Kant calls the discipline of the will, based on ethical, cultural, and intellectual virtues. The point is not whether elites should or should not be abolished; they flourish inevitably in every society, and perhaps most virulently in democratic society where egalitarian rhetoric frequently serves as a form of camouflage for inequality, privilege, and fraud. The point is, rather, to struggle to replace negative elites by their positive counterparts, "because democracy cannot survive without ... intellectual-cultural elites. Without them, democratic reality is a dead body politic ... It was, after all, the elite gathering at the Symposion of Plato and not the crowd cheering in the Roman circuses ... that kept the idea of democracy alive for more than two thousand years."[11]

All this should be massively obvious. We habitually assume that best effort and best intention are necessary qualities of the achieved personality, but we do not automatically award confidence, respect, and degrees of accreditation to those who have not also achieved *demonstrable results* in their chosen fields. I would like the orthopaedic surgeon who operates on my trick knee to be the best or among the best in his profession, not simply someone who wants or tries to be the best – or who wants but does not try or know how to try, or possibly doesn't even want. I feel the same way about the dentist and the engineer whose bridges are expected to last, about the mechanic who repairs the brakes on my aging Subaru, the instructor who teaches me to use scuba equipment properly, the professor in whose course on James Joyce I recently registered, the poet whose book I just paid thirty-seven dollars for, the person whom we vote into office to govern the country. (Socrates in the *Republic* is not so wide of the mark here.) I presume Prof. Wilson feels exactly as I do in this matter. Is it not embarrassingly obvious, if we are interested in surviving as well as prospering in a reasonably well-administered country, enjoying what we can of life as fully as possible, and remaining or becoming intellectually vital, that we all subscribe to "elitist" principles? A working democracy is neither viable nor *conceivable* unless it is predicated on a determined and more or less successful attempt to nurture and produce both the educated citizen and the competent professional, and this is not possible unless we are willing to make certain hard sacrifices – at times, of our most cherished pseudo-egalitarian postulates. Why pretend otherwise? There is nothing more costly than an unreflected illusion – especially the illusion we cosset about ourselves. As John Gardner warns, "extreme equalitarianism ... which ignores difference in native capacity and achievement ... has not served democracy well."[12]

Finally – to return – it is apparently a moral lapse or even a form of criminal negligence to be "white, male, and middle-class," when one can no doubt remedy this state of affairs by taking large doses of melanin, undergoing a sex-change operation,[13] and filing for voluntary bankruptcy. I have no quarrel with the fact that I am male just as I do not deplore the correlative fact that my wife happens to be a woman, a plenary condition I cannot but applaud. But, alas, I am not quite as white as Wilson assumes, being of partly Hispanic-Sephardic descent and tanning toward the slightly shadier side of the spectrum. And as for being middle-class, the professor is welcome to inspect my bank account. I grew up poor and have remained faithful to my origins.

Joking aside, it seems to me that one of our besetting vices as teachers and academics is that we are far too comfortable with ourselves and tend, despite our confident presumption of good faith, our theoretical regard and moral concern, to take too much for granted. Our job is to furnish our students with the tools, habits, attitudes, and knowledge they require to survive and perhaps even flourish in the recalcitrant and competitive world they will be entering. To do this we need to be as critical and demanding as compassion allows, but we must not become as fatuous and blind as compassion predisposes.[14] Otherwise we remain as we are, heavy with the tainted grain of our subornments. We cannot assume that our students will always somehow be provided for or content ourselves by drawing attention to the resources and support systems they can always fall back upon. Our students require us not to be nice so much as *intelligent*. I am put in mind at this juncture of a story a colleague tells about finding a Mohawk child's school binder in a trash can where it had obviously been deposited by its owner. It contained an essay on the topic "What would you take with you if you had to spend a week in the wilderness?" The child had listed what to him were the essentials: a blanket, a knife, a gun, ammunition, some wire, matches. The white, male (and probably middle-class) teacher had given the project a passing grade but could not refrain from commenting at the end: What about food?

(3) Nobody with pretensions to self-respect (or is it job security?) seems to like J. Phillipe Rushton much. Prof. Wilson's cavalier linking of that notorious name with mine is a blatant example of sheer bad faith in the conduct of a supposedly professional debate. "Solway is prepared to allow," he writes, "with Phillipe Rushton, that the capacity of students to go beyond technology might be a matter of genetics ..."[15] Half a paragraph down, he reverses field and acknowledges, "Solway leaves it to others to decide, which is true ..." But the harm has already been done and the theatrical peripety, presumably in the name of "truth," cannot erase taint by association. I have been run out of town on a rail, bristling with Heideggerian feathers stuck in Rushtonian tar. I can only direct the reader to the passage(s) in question in chapter 6 of *Education Lost* in which I stay patently clear of facile or rebarbative conclusions regarding the priority of genetics or environment or the irreversible role of conditioning or the neurochemical substrate of intelligence in the formation of the mind. What I try to do there is call into question some of the pseudo-democratic postulates and shibboleths about the ostensibly aprioristic features of human intellectual development and to point out that it is illegitimate and even dangerous to transpose assumptions from one realm of being to another – what I call the "fallacy of transferred inevitables." That we are all born free – if indeed we are – does not mean that we are all born bright. It may not be possible to disentangle the genetics-environment nexus, especially as these two factors determine one another reciprocally, in the effort to discover why some students respond to their education and others – those whom David Hargreaves calls the "indifferent" and the "oppositional" – remain resistant despite our most dedicated investment of time, energy, compassion, and discipline.[16]

The now-common presupposition that environmental factors may be held responsible for most learning "disabilities," those aversions or inadequacies associated with poor students, simply cannot be verified. This manifestly does not mean that teachers, counsellors, and administrators should not make every effort to rectify obstructing or counter-productive situations where possible. It plainly does not imply that we should not do everything within our power – but also within the limits of the reasonable and the possible – to give those students, whether "disadvantaged" or simply "unmotivated," as many chances as we can afford to help them recuperate their latent or impeded capacities. But it does suggest, given this severely constraining world in which we live, that under no circumstances should our competent and eager students suffer a diminution of shared time, teacher sympathy, and classroom energy in the interests of the pedagogical reclamation of their less fortunate peers. I have seen too many good students, too many bright, devoted, and hard-working young people, left to their own untutored resources on the scandalous conjecture that quality can take care of itself. Meanwhile teachers and principals extravagantly spend their samaritan energies on remedial projects, proud of their democratic and charitable propensities, engaging in what Thomas Browne in *Pseudodoxia Epidemica* called one of "those encroachments which junior compliance and popular credulity hath admitted." How just is this? How democratic, ultimately? We see the results of such inferential charity all about us: good students stalled and idling, an Avogadro's number of poor or mediocre or frivolous students passing from one level to another with little to show in the way of accomplishment or conviction, far too many teachers surrendering to cynicism, indifference, and exhaustion as a consequence of pursuing their costly sacrament of the mundane, and an educational system in the throes of terminal disarray, blasted by the friendly fire of philosophists like Fred Wilson. Is this the kind of educational establishment, the kind of *society*, that satisfies our democratic ambitions? Is this the cultural product we are content to waste our lives affirming and underwriting?

The debate into which we are currently staggering, blinded by a fog of emotional pieties, really involves proprietary attitudes toward social amelioration and not vague proclamations about "genetic" superiority. The issue is not teleology but inclination, in particular the tendency toward favouring the dysfunctional at the expense of merit or just dessert which is now epidemic, the moral AIDS of our society. An article in the *Montreal Gazette* of 4 January 1994 reports the suffering of a six-year-old girl repeatedly raped by her twelve-year-old babysitter. The presiding judge, who describes the boy's intelligence as "borderline," has also "strongly recommended" that the offender receive immediate therapy "for his anger and sexual problems." But the agency involved in the proceedings, the Alberta Social Services department, has to this date refused to provide counselling or therapy for the young girl who, according to the director of the Edmonton Sexual Assault Centre, is badly in need of it. Despite the budgetary constraints under which our social institutions are struggling, resources are almost always allocated in the interests of those who disrupt, almost never in consideration of the innocent targets of abuse.[17]

This is a mindset, a social attitude or predisposition, that permeates every aspect of contemporary society and vitiates the "mandate" for so-called rehabilitation which forms the *raison d'être* of our cultural institutions. The contradiction is merely italicized in cases of violence and abuse, like that reported in the newspaper. The same *structure of response* is evident in the daily practice of our educational mandate (what Louis Althusser calls an ISA, or Ideological State Apparatus), in which those who abuse the privilege of education, for whatever reason – even one that may be regarded as socioeconomically or psychologically "legitimate" – receive prodigies of remedial attention while their more favourably endowed peers who demonstrate intellectual promise, desire to learn, and good discipline and working habits, are generally left to their own devices. (And a significant number of students who fall into this latter category do not necessarily come from privileged homes.)[18] Our efforts are increasingly devoted to remediation, which we mistakenly consider a function of enlightenment, but only minimally to the preservation, husbandry, and improvement of excellence, of what is either preferentially given or strenuously acquired or both. This is an infallible sign of a disintegrating civilization – which is, of course, the real issue.

My argument is that we have no choice, if we wish to survive both competitively and intellectually, but to make certain hard decisions. There is not that much crumple zone in front of us. As Hilda Neatby writes, those "experts in education," our "well-meaning men of restricted means" who refuse to meet the rigorous demands of excellence, are not educating but merely "conditioning for servitude." This is disastrous, she continues, "to the well-being of democracy which depends on the free development of the highest qualities of gifted individuals."[19] (We seem to have got our perception of our indispensable minorities hopelessly confused.) Similarly, Jacques Barzun affirms that in "the school system ... amicable stupidity is protected, being no threat; a pleasantly retarded mind contributes to everybody's ease."[20]

Thus I take vigorous exception as well to the conclusion of Wesley Cragg's aforementioned article (a more gentlemanly, certainly less gingival version of Wilson's thesis), which elaborates on "the Socratic insight (corrupted by Plato in the pages of the *Republic*) that genuine knowledge is within the grasp of anyone who can be inspired to make the effort." I presume Prof. Cragg is referring to the *Meno* in which Socrates performs his celebrated maieutic act, drawing out prior knowledge from the mind of the young slave boy and thereby demonstrating the validity of anamnesis. (I also presume that Prof. Cragg must believe this text was not "corrupted" by Platonic intervention.)[21] I would like to make two quick comments here. First, a close look at the Socratic technique in the *Meno* shows that the pedagogical transaction is flagrantly rigged and the teacher is merely prompting the student throughout the entire proceedings – to substantiate a theory. There is nothing in the operation that resembles genuine anamnesis. Secondly, and more to the point, to say that "genuine knowledge is within the grasp of anyone who can be inspired to make the effort" is to utter a non-falsifiable proposition. Perhaps what it affirms is so. Perhaps it is not. There is no way to tell. I have had many students whose performance would tend to corroborate Prof. Cragg's commendably liberal thesis, but then I have known at least as many others whose performance would appear to invalidate it. My argument in *Education Lost*, chapter 6, and once again in the present essay, is that so magnanimous a position is harmful and distracting if (a) it is held in a rigid and unreflected manner, since it is susceptible of neither empirical nor theoretical validation, being essentially an *expression of desire*, the pedagogical face of libido; and (b) if it is permitted to deflect us from concentrating on those who *are* inspired, who have made the effort, and who require our redoubled attention and concern to ensure the achievement now tantalizingly within their reach.

It is important to note that focusing on the capable as a pedasophical attitude or principle by no means rules out the practical recognition of the value of effort and discipline *as it applies to all students*. The question is plainly not whether one is born smart or gets smart through hard work: the distinction cannot be reliably demonstrated. The social psychologist Jeff Howard, who is also president of the Efficacy Institute in Lexington, Mass., persuasively argues that the belief in innate capacities operates as a demotivating factor, discouraging many students whose academic results imply a lack of inherent ability or prejudicing the achievements of those who are convinced of innate superiority and therefore consider hard work to be unnecessary.[22] But it seems sensible to assume that some people are indeed born bright and either fail through laziness and overconfidence *or* succeed through raw talent or a mixture of talent and effort, and that others, less bright, fail because they simply cannot deliver the goods *or* succeed through redoubled effort and old-fashioned stick-to-it-tiveness. Intelligence may function in an indeterminate number of ways. It may enter the academic lists as a given which is then frittered away, deteriorating through lack of use and application, or is preserved, sometimes against all odds. Or it may grow dendritically, responding to the pressures and catalysts provided by a favourable (Vygotskian) educational climate. The point I am trying to make is that there is no way to tell and that, as a consequence, the present controversy over whether children are born smart or get smart remains an empty and unprofitable distraction.

From the standpoint of the teacher dealing with students on a daily basis under classroom conditions, the prior emphasis must necessarily fall on continuous effort, hard work, high expectations, real demands, and rigorous practice. But there is a another issue as well which cannot be indefinitely evaded without undermining the educational imperative and bringing the scholarly environment into ruin or disarray. This entails the recognition that after a some passage of time – differently measured in different cultures

- scrupulous and often painful assessments of *realized* ability need to be made and certain decisive policies put into effect. By such policies I mean, quite bluntly, the filtering out of students whose academic performance does not finally justify the protracted investment of time, energy, and money which are always in short supply, and the corresponding solicitude or concern on the part of the teacher for those students who, for whatever reasons, exhibit a willingness to work and an aptitude for learning, that is, who show initiative and proficiency. For in the long sift these are the students on whose moral and intellectual vitality our survival as a society will depend. Their abilities must be monitored and nourished; they cannot be willed, wished, or legislated into existence.

The issue is philosophically focused once again by Agnes Heller. That men and women are born "equally endowed with reason and conscience is the foundational creed of the new, modern social arrangement," she writes. But "moderns, too, receive a *bagage* at the moment of their birth. One can draw better or worse in the genetic lottery ... by being better or worse equipped with certain endowments which can be developed." The only way of coming to terms with the brute "accident of birth" lies not in subscribing to the fiction of equal endowment, actual or potential, which leads to the educational quagmire in which we now find ourselves, but to *choose* one's life, address the "blank envelope" of one's existence, take responsibility for "the internal teleology of one's life." This is what Heller would call contingency thinking, a necessary first step and the only authentic possibility open to the modern individual, though we need not stop with contingency. "The object of choice is the letter in the envelope," and the envelope "is addressed to oneself." It is only in this sense that contingency can be transformed into destiny. From the standpoint of education, we can do no more than provide the student with the *conditions of autonomy* in the degree to which these are affordable and feasible. At the same time we must never lose sight of those students who, in Heller's terms, are busy addressing their own envelopes.[23]

One of my colleagues, objecting to my general approach, claimed during a pedagogical session that "the good students are precisely the students who don't need us." This is an attitude with which current educational thinking and practice is saturated, and its effects are little short of calamitous. *These are precisely the students who need us more than ever* if education is not to become rehabilitation by another name. Why should a generation of educators soft in the heart be permitted to produce a generation of students soft in the head? We are in danger of spreading ourselves so thin that we must eventually vanish from the scene of teaching and end up doing a little good here, a lot of harm there. For the problem with North American education is that it now operates as a levelling, not a leavening institution, as the cognitively gifted are increasingly neglected and de-meaned in favour of the cognitively disadvantaged. But we can no longer afford to treat our best students as a class of educational pariahs whose interests and welfare can be dismissed as a pedagogical or administrative distraction. They represent precisely those intellectual resources we must cultivate and invest if we are not to go into cultural receivership.[24] *Unreflected* liberalism leads to pedagogical evaporation. And once again it is the dedicated student who pays the price of our exorbitance and, in the broader context, our liberal, democratic society whose mortgage time threatens to foreclose.[25]

In any event, we cannot solve the nature-nurture conundrum, nor can we afford to lose the little time we have in so fruitless a pursuit. Meanwhile, we should not allow pity or compassion for the underprivileged, which we presumably all feel, to deter us from a real and working sympathy for the intellectually and affectively gifted – whether this "giftedness" is innate or earned is beside the point – who also need our attention if they are to realize their "gifts" in any meaningful sense.

For the most part we have failed as "educators" to realize that the central project in which we should presently be engaged is the renovation of the student *as student*,[26] by whatever means we can reasonably and effectively agree upon. These include our own re-education as teachers, the rigorous re-examination of the concept of education, the elevation of standards of admission, grading, and performance, the reduction of that portion of the education budget earmarked for administration by about 90 per cent, and the investment of that sum into teacher hiring and salaries, libraries, student fellowships, and the physical plant itself. The problem is that we lack the will and the candour to tackle the dilemma that our laziness, sentimentality, self-deluding oratory, and (fast disappearing) prosperity have created. For we must face the unpalatable fact that the students we are often condemned to teach are in large measure the pure reflection of our own theoretical blindness and incompetence.[27]

By all means, let us give *everybody* a chance – and a second and a third – but our reserves are necessarily limited, and we must function within certain inescapable "parameters." In order to escape teaching under the sign of a demotic aberration, to avoid cynicism (which Peter Sloterdijk brilliantly defines as "enlightened false consciousness"[28] and which in any case is merely the flip side of sentimentality),[29] and to keep the educational institution afloat, we must invest our capital wisely and enact certain discretionary refusals.

Finally, I might suggest that Prof. Wilson venture a little beyond his somewhat dubious and obviously sinister Solway-Rushton school of thought and struggle instead with the formidable Aldous Huxley who accuses our civilization of what he calls "reproductive delinquency." How long can a democratic society, Huxley asks, "maintain its traditions of individual liberty and democratic government [where] IQs and physical vigour are on the de-

cline?" Huxley sees no contradiction between "the facts of individual diversity and genetic uniqueness" on the one hand and the values of freedom
and tolerance on the other. He proposes an educational structure in which
the "values" of freedom, love, and analytic intelligence find a secure basis,
respectively, in the "facts" of human diversity, primary need, and conditions
of self-preservation. Since Huxley is no right-wing ideologue or vestigial
social Darwinist, I would imagine that Prof. Wilson is intellectually ob-
ligated to take his own argument a little further out from the shallows of
asalaminious sentimentality where he seems content to languish.

For example, why not take on Alfred North Whitehead who lays it down
as an unassailable principle that, in the "conditions of modern life ... the
race which does not value trained intelligence is doomed." And again, in
the "contest of races ... the victory will belong to those who are masters
of stores of trained nervous energy, working under conditions of favourable
growth." Whitehead, whose democratic credentials are unimpeachable, believed that the "sense of greatness is the groundwork of morals" and that
we were (circa 1929) at the threshold of determining "whether the equality
of man is to be reached on a high level or a low level."[30] (And this is
indeed the question – which looks increasingly as if it may have been answered.) Or why not try to board the redoubtable Northrop Frye, who in
his 1961 Massey lectures bluntly deposes: "In these days we're in a hare-
and-tortoise race between mob rule and education: to avoid collapsing into
mob rule we have to try to educate a minority that'll stand out against
it." Or fire across the bows of C.S. Lewis, who accuses modern educators
of "a sort of ghastly simplicity ... We remove the organ and demand the
function." (Lewis concedes acidly that our educational conditioners "are
not bad men. They are not men at all ... they have stepped into the void.")
And if he is still afloat, join the attack on Herrnstein and Murray's statistical
Cunard, just freshly christened, or grapple with the salty and abrasive William A. Henry III whose recent *In Defense of Elitism* argues that "the
core issue is our loss of faith in the right of every individual to fulfill his
potential, stretch his talent, and chart his own course."[31]

The anti-anti-elitist argument has been most recently launched by the
happily surnamed Mark Kingwell, whose *Dreams of Millennium* contends
that the principle of equality properly applies to questions of law, voting,
and opportunity, but that legislating "equality of outcome may palliate the
less able, but it also apparently works to punish the gifted and hardworking."
This, says Kingwell, referring to the popular movie *Forrest Gump* that promotes "the moral elevation of simple-mindedness," is nothing less than "a
virulent strain of Gumpism," which as I maintain has infected the educational institution to its intellectual and procedural core and paralyzed
most of its vital functions.[32] The issue thus requires hard, lucid, unsentimental thinking,[33] for the stakes are enormous. As Whitehead says, "there

will be no appeal from the judgment which will then be pronounced on the uneducated." De Gobineau is a quack, and Rushton must be approached gingerly and sceptically, but Huxley and Whitehead are accredited thinkers whose witnessing must be taken seriously. I am afraid that the kind of flaccid and nugatory (and, of course, politically correct) notions ventilated by the Wilsons of our world can only cloud our judgment and abet the slide into mediocrity and failure which the educational community seems determined to bring about.[34] For, in effect, education has become devastatingly ex-pensive: it costs far too much in every sense of the phrase and is largely devoid of thought. We are now saddled with a system dedicated to expanding socioemotional assets while yielding low to zero cognitive dividends. The main purpose of this system is to squander its diminishing reserves while producing, with exemplary skill and perseverance, the condition of moral bankruptcy and intellectual famine to which it must secretly aspire.

In summation, I wish to stress once again that it is imperative to think as clearly as we can at so critical a juncture in our history. The *pro forma* benevolism and cheap compassion of so many of our contemporary educators, which is my real target in this essay, is as perilous – if I may cite from my family annals – as my grandfather's obsessive charity, a legendary hunger for indiscriminate giving that gradually acquired pathological status.[35] He gave unstintedly to all who asked, becoming a local byword for imbecility and the victim of every needy petitioner and *clochard* in the neighbourhood. Bills went unpaid and rationing had to be introduced. Finally my grandmother was reduced to bribing the bank teller, standing guard at the door whenever a knock was heard, and monitoring all the socks and pillowslips in the house in order to continue feeding her family.

APPENDIX

(Cf. Michael W. Apple, *Official Knowledge: Democratic Education in a Conservative Age*, Routledge, London, 1993.)

In the halogen or Mandevillean light of the preceding (see note 33), one must take into account Michael Apple's sensitive and acute treatment of the issues and concepts that orbit around the term "excellence." I concur fully with Apple's contestation of what he calls "the conservative restoration" in education and in society, and, indeed, I have argued throughout these pages for the necessity of reallocating the educational budget toward schools, teachers, and students and away from the various entrenched corporate interests. But one must demur when Apple writes that "the current emphasis on 'excellence' ... has shifted educational discourse so that underachievement once again increasingly is seen as largely the fault of the student" and that

"Student failure, which was at least partially interpreted as the fault of severely deficient educational policies and practices, is now being seen as the result of what might be called the biological and economic market-place ... evidenced in the growth of forms of Social Darwinism." The issue is not so simple and clear-cut.

The causes for the undeniable decline in student capacity and perform-ance, even among the offspring of the Right,[36] are distressingly manifold and should be located in the larger, more pervasive practices and assump-tions of cultural life in general, which I have attempted to isolate in this collection. There is no question that "severely deficient educational policies and practices" lie at the "root," as Apple says, of our current malaise, but we must recognize as well that we are not dealing so much with a root as with a root system. This would include the infiltration of the media into the very subsoil of our thinking and desiring as well as the passion for technological bricolage that transforms mysteries into problems and there-fore ensures only delusional solutions that inevitably surface as new prob-lems. It also extends to the regressive policies of the "rightist agenda" that justifies and camouflages its monopoly of power and wealth by generating a therapeutic apparatus favouring the underachiever at the expense of the proficient student. It is precisely this complex and surreptitious dialectic that Apple and other like-minded educators, for the most laudable of rea-sons, persistently misunderstand. The "power elite," the avatars of political correctness, are not interested in fostering excellence, despite the empty cir-culation of the word in educational discourse, since a truly educated society capable of reflective lucidity and grounded in historical knowledge would rigorously oppose the essentially political agenda of the conservative res-toration and move to dethatcherize its social and educational brief. The doctrine of "teaching down" to the level of the student "clientele," of diluting the curriculum, and of depriveleging the dedicated teacher and the com-mitted student in the presumptive service of rehabilitating a vastly deficient majority works precisely to the advantage of an entrenched, propertied, and increasingly dominant minority, especially by keeping the deficient ma-jority in a state of continued dependence and intellectual stupor. The rein-fantilization of the student population, a clandestine operation that resists exposure by masking as charity, ensures the prolonged hegemony of the new master class even better than the reduction of subsidies – the other strategy in the war against enlightenment, to which Apple takes such praise-worthy exception.

My emphasis upon genuine "excellence" in the educational forum, re-flected in high standards and demanding course work as well as in generous fiscal allocations to the schools and decent salaries for teachers, does not argue for a resurgent Social Darwinism. Conversely, the refusal to recognize the debilitating influence of the home environment upon student performance in the current cultural situation, even among middle and upper-middle class families, works against the educational imperative, as does the primarily *moral* denial of the effects of individual talents and abilities, whether biologically given or socially acquired or both. It is vital that we unmuddle our thinking and see that the desideratum of "excellence," in the sense indicated above, far from collaborating with a privateering corporate structure, would actually in the long run destabilize the conservative restoration by favouring the development of an enlightened society willing to acknowledge the constraints imposed by "nature" as it would contest the limitations artificially – and often *deceptively* – established by a political and ideological agenda.

Finally, by advocating the need to "raise standards,"[37] I certainly do not support the disingenuous application of the phrase which, as Apple astutely contends, mandates "teacher and student 'competencies'" with the intention of centralizing methods and curricula for the sake of increased control. (See "Balnibarbian Architecture" for a stercoraceous critique of this manoeuvre.) Apple goes on to argue that the fears provoked by "falling standards and illiteracy ... are exacerbated, and used, by dominant groups" to their own advantage. That such fears may be "used" in order to reposition the educational debate on the terrain staked out by the right cannot be doubted, but that these fears have been "exacerbated" seems to me a rather eccentric account of the event. If anything, they have been systematically underassessed, and the "panic" over lax standards and rampant illiteracy is, in my reading of the situation, a displaced, vicarious, low-grade awareness of a cultural and social catastrophe of the first magnitude. These fears have not been exacerbated so much as misunderstood and grossly exploited.

By raising standards I mean, quite archaically, in the sense espoused by both Coleridge and Arnold, teaching the best that has been thought and written to the best of our perfected abilities in a learning environment that expects and demands best effort on the part of our students. Such a development requires not just another "national debate," which resolutely simplifies and misconstrues the issues, but an authentic, collective reappraisal of our cultural norms and preconceptions leading to concrete proposals for change; these would have to include the privileging of local centres of authority, an "inquiry"-based rather than "competency"-based pedagogy, a revised budget, and a new respect for the teaching function at the nonuniversity level. (As I argue later on, *all* education is higher education.) I realize that my argument is now breathing a rarefied ether, but at the same time one should perceive that there is really no alternative. The leveraged buyout of education in which so many of us are investing entails nothing less than the death of education and the collapse of communal life as we have known it.

· 6 ·

Script and Nondescript

Man has outdistanced the other animals because he has not one but
two languages: a thinking language for manipulating concepts inside
his head, as well as a speaking language ...

J. Bronowski, *The Identity of Man*

Varieties of intonation do not have universal value and remain a matter
of subjective evaluation. Only the predicative character of the statement
can thus have value as a criterion.

Emile Benveniste, *Problems in General Linguistics*

Addressing once again the familiar but increasingly problematic "scandal
of literacy" in contemporary culture, perhaps the primary issue in current
educational debate, I am put embarrassingly in mind of the exordium to
Lycidas:

Yet once more, O ye Laurels, and once more
Ye Myrtles brown, with Ivy never sear,
I com to pluck your Berries harsh and crude ...

Will we never have done with it? We struggle continually for fresh understanding without, it appears, ever arriving at a clear resolution or a set
of indisputable findings. But perhaps there is no other feasible way to proceed in a community as diffuse and logomachic as the teaching profession.
We circle endlessly around the same bordereau of topics and issues, hoping
by reiteration or accretion, to stumble in the direction of a gradual
consensus.[1]

Hence my repeated efforts in these pages to refocus our peculiar angle
of address, the critical parallax we adopt toward the scandal that refuses
to go away. At one point I regard the problem as a subset of a much larger
predicament, namely the catastrophic weakening of the temporal substrate
of experience, the collagen of memory, in the affective and psychological
life of the generation we are trying valiantly to educate, but with so little
evident success (cf. "Grammatical Fictions").[2] At another point I lament
that we find ourselves far too often tempted to re-foetalize the educational

transaction, teaching down to the level of our students and so reinforcing the habits and handicaps to which they have become accustomed instead of concentrating on emerging functions or latent capabilities to help them *reach beyond* the cognitive plane where they remain more or less trapped ("Teaching Down or Learning Up"). These two approaches are, of course, diagnostically related: encouraging students to aim higher than their present abilities would appear to allow, in the interests of sponsoring *qualitative* changes of the sensibility, is intimately connected to re-introducing students to the *grammatical force* of constituent temporality, the rediscovery of time as the medium of psychological integration and cognitive synthesis.[3]

In this chapter I wish briefly to reconsider the same subject from a slightly different camber, basing my discussion to some extent on the sensible and yet revolutionary theories of L.S. Vygotsky who, in the course of his experimental work with younger children, has investigated the complex relations between speaking and writing. But before studying this particular dynamic, we should begin by appraising how we normally respond to the concept, practice, and mystery of spoken language which, since we are constantly saturated in it, we rarely isolate and discriminate, *defamiliarize*, for purposes of inquiry and recognition.

Spoken language obviously starts with onomatopoeiac babble in the earliest stages of infancy, but as Vygotsky reasonably claims, it *evolves* as a function of symbolic representation in play.[4] The various forms of response in the play situation proceed deictically, predicated on the universal tendency to mimicry or gestural transcription, a kind of "writing in air" accompanied as the child matures by progressive verbal expression. Thus rudimentary forms of writing and speaking evolve in unison although this proto-writing bears only the most schematic relation to what will (or should) appear later as true graphological expression, while speech separates out of the play matrix comparatively early to predominate almost exclusively by the age of six. Although Vygotsky does not elaborate further, it would appear that spontaneous mimicry as such recedes into the background, without disappearing, of course, but functioning now as the accompaniment to that with which it was originally accompanied – a reversal of the syntactical order of precedence that prevailed at the beginning of the signifying process.[5]

What happens next in the normal course of development has been largely disregarded owing, no doubt, to its extreme obviousness. The mimicry function not only accompanies speech as a marginal illustration of the central text of expression or as a kind of somatic accessory to a preponderant verbalism, adding sinew and vigour to oral expression[6] but it is *taken up*, subsumed, transformed, and absorbed into the very rhythms of speech itself, that is, into the plastic or replicative tonality of the verbal event. When this happens, speech proceeds to signify on two levels: symbolically, deploying the sign-function in the mode of representational substitution; and *ostensively or analogically,* incorporating the field of gestural indication syn-esthetically *within* the medium of phonemic reproduction. Pointing becomes pointing out via stress and pitch; jumping with delight or exasperation man-ifests as degrees of tonal inflection; caressing or stroking appears on the phonemic plane as lilt or quasi-melody; signals of perplexity modelled on the physical plane as knitting or scratching the brow, sudden stasis, and a whole host of appropriate somatic activities re-emerge as culturally de-termined forms of pure vocality: pausing, holding the breath or letting it out slowly with phatic collaterality (the interjection of nonsense syllables which bob like fishing corks on the stream of expression to mark the place where we have cast our epistemic nets), and so on; surprise, delight, or, indeed, any deep or emphatic reaction reproduced in gesture as disruption associated with non-directional movement resurfaces on the vocal stratum as the phonomorphic array of both deflecting and commentative devices grouped under the single term, "laughter."

A recent example of what I am getting at is probably familiar to everyone: the infiltration of the interrogative pitch-rise into normal declarative speech. Young people have become increasingly prone to complete their statements as if they were asking a question rather than reporting or describing a state of affairs. A conversation I overheard in the hallways among a group of students is symptomatic:

"My teacher in Social *Studies*? [rise] He gave me a 92? [rise] I didn't really study very *hard for it*? [rise]"

"Well, what were you doing? [genuine question]"

"Well, I was so *nervous*? [rise] I just sorta did *nothing*? [rise]"

This sorta thing has become pervasive, even among adults. The rhythmic inflection associated with the interrogative mode when it is not warranted by the rhetorical context reproduces in the medium of speech tonality – in what we might call the *phonemics of address* – precisely the spatial and gestural modes of approach ensuring that one's interlocutor or playmate is fully present, attentive, implicated, *answerable* – that is, required to display what we might call the *proxemics of accessibility*, responsive to the tug of the question mark which operates like a little invisible hook. Thus speech is now working not only as representational substitution but as tonal analo-gy, restructuring the phonemics of address as the proxemics of accessibility.[7]

Once we recognize that speech functions not only as a first-order semiotic system based on the symbolic substitution of word for thing or event but also as an auxiliary, reflecting medium, a species of tonal mimicry and gestural subsumption, we find ourselves in a better position to come to terms (so to speak) with the plight from which our students are unable to extricate themselves. For what has happened since the utopian and ef-florescent sixties, with the vast expansion of the media and the gradual though inexorable decay of what Neil Postman ironically calls the Second

Curriculum – the discipline of mind founded on order, precedence, hierarchical patterning, delay of gratification, and the patient assimilation of progressively more complex topics, methods and principles of learning – is that our youngsters tend to remain for ever longer periods confined to the linguistic creche. When they eventually emerge they are barely able to toddle through a written sentence or to utter verbal sequences with even minimal lucidity. Life, thought, and education are regarded as a kind of extended saturnalia in which everyone enjoys the *right* to the gift of self-discovery, to the ludic reversal of the normative and the speeding-up of psychological processes of intellectual growth, and to the immediate gratifications of accomplishment – without having to suffer the inconvenience of *investing time*, undergoing the labour of application or experiencing the slow trial of achievement with all its attendant risks and imperatives. (As St Augustine warned in *On Order*, "Either follow this long itinerary or renounce everything" – "*Aut ordine illo eruditionis, aut nullo modo.*") We have come to expect and demand what reality will permit us to attain only fugitively and hazardously through the strenuous but rewarding ceremony of a lifelong apprenticeship. In short, *we have stopped working*.[8] But we have not stopped playing.

This peculiar indolence, our version of the long slumber of Rip Van Winkle and Sleeping Beauty the cultural library has always warned us about, is reflected in the linguistic routines of our students. For they have not managed to outgrow and leave behind the system of tonal mimicry, the analogue in speech of the mode of *gestural representation* in play, that permeates the medium of verbal expression like a phonemic dye. Such gestural seepage, when not controlled, produces a severe dilution of informational economies. As Roland Barthes notes, language requires that communication be doubly articulated, based on a *combinatoire* of digital units that eschews mere analogical plenitude. This latter form of skeuomorphic miming (i.e., the design of a similar artifact in another medium), operating as a form of displaced literalness, would lead to a paradoxical shrinking of the semantic and connotative field of expression after the original expansion initiated by the play mode. The order of development stalls and then effectively reverses.[9] So critical has this species of linguistic debasement become that the replicative function of tonal rhythm seems at times to overshadow, invade, and finally govern the field of symbolic representation we call speech. If we would only pause and listen carefully to what passes as conversation among our students, we would quickly discover the extent to which forms of play-mimicry, tonal duplication, and phonic reproductiveness have come to dominate ordinary speech. Adjusting the semiolect of Michel Foucault and Georges Bataille, we might define this analogic or replicative expression as *"exorbitated speech,"* when the tongue ceases to articulate and the eye of childhood swivels upward and back "to the nocturnal and starred interior of the skull."[10] A kind of collective autism supervenes in which the no-mothetic function of language – disambiguating the welter of events and promulgating laws to contain and discipline chaos – surrenders to the non-discursive realm of ecstasy, laughter, desire, and emotional contagion, the effect of which is to fracture the unity of discourse.

In the present situation, the play mode as a primordial form of "speech" has not been superseded in the normal course of events but persists in the guise of a largely unobserved but permeating stream of *tonal punctuation* which threatens to supplant the semantic content it is there to punctuate in the first place: laughter, gesture, pause, aposiopesis, modalities of contact in fragmentary or anaclitic phrases serving the phatic function of linking speakers in "dialogue" that paradoxically proceeds in chiefly non-discursive fashion. I hope it is understood that I am not some grim agelast like Jorge of Burgos in *The Name of the Rose* inveighing against laughter and spontaneity in the interests of canonical or ideological severity. Rather, I am suggesting that the staple ratio in speech between tonal facsimile and binomial substitution, between inflection and deputation, analogy and symbol, mimicry and representation, has altered dramatically in favour of the disproportionate hegemony of the former over the latter; increasingly, speech among the young has grown to resemble *vocal gesture* binding a closed society of neotonic communicators who continue to reproduce the modalities of the play function instead of rising dialectically to the plane of the re-presentational sign function.

Thus the word tends to become a vehicle or carrier of expressive tonality rather than a semantic token invoking the laws of symbolic exchange. And this is an important reason behind the general inability to master the complexities of literate communication, in speech as well as in writing, and to develop the *literate sensibility*, the coherent and unified self, so far as this is possible, which is the principal aim of education. At the basis of the prolonged and systematic effort associated with genuine education, we always find the *redemptive* (not the *remedial*) discipline of language which organizes the world given us to explore and in which the self acquires stability and duration. As Emile Benveniste deposes, "It is in discourse, *realized in sentences*, that language is formed and takes shape," generating discrete instances, units, and segments of meaning and reference which in turn constitute "all the coordinates that define the subject."[11]

The blurring of these coordinates is precisely the dilemma we are confronting. Our obliviousness to what is going on at the level of contemporary speech – that is, on the plane of first-order symbolic representation – renders our attempts at remediation improbable, to put it gently. We no longer begin, as we should – not only in the school but as early as possible in the home – to teach the conventions of good conversation, the elocution of the mind. To complicate matters almost inextricably, once the student embarks upon formal education, we do not teach writing as *written lan-*

guage, as a mode of thought and expression with its own laws of development, its own unique and autonomous manner of processing experiencing – that is, we do not teach writing as a *linguistic substance* differing in its essence from the usages of casual, unreconstructed, and reactive speech. As we know, early manuscripts tend to run words together, as if script were still very close to speech. But with the further development of writing, words became discrete, segregated items, generating the faculty of logical abstraction necessary to establish a "higher" non-affective synthesis of demonstrably analytic units into formal systems of representation. But if written language exists merely as the hydroponic or potted version of spoken language, formal systems of articulation must remain stunted and, as we may put it, deflorescent. There is no doubt that writing maintains a deep, genotypical relation with patterns of lucid speech, but it is absolutely distinct from what Vygotsky calls the "phenotypical idiosyncrasies" of merely reflex speech. Writing, in its fully developed form, must be treated *sui generis*, as a system of rules and structures for the re-organization of experience which cannot profitably be regarded as a mere echo or shadow of a precedent spoken language.

Writing is not a cloning device for reproducing spoken language. Script may be considered a transcription of verbal utterance only at the cost of its own devitalization. It is intimately related to speech in whose womb, so to write, it gestates; but after it comes into the world, the umbilical cord must be severed, and it must go on to develop independent life. Otherwise, as we see all around us, written language struggles into existence as a marginal and parasitic thing, a troubling grotesquerie unable to escape the foetal dependence on its source – instead of, to change the metaphor slightly, struggling from the maternal earth into single freedom like Milton's tawny lion at the Creation who "pawing to get free / ... then springs as broke from Bonds."

Walter J. Ong's notion of "secondary orality" is especially relevant in this context as it refers to the speech habits of those who, living in a hi-tech culture in which a new orality is sustained by telephone, radio, television, and cinema (Postman's First Curriculum), enjoy neither the familiarity with the mnemonic patterning devices and communal proverbiality that support a primary oral culture nor the ability to process experience chirographically. As a result, these young people continue in large measure dependent upon the instantaneities of expression associated with gesture, tonality, and reactive utterance, practising a kind of sonic calligraphy replete with expressive and redundant flourishes. But in linear, "historical" cultures, the organization of experience provided by the grapholect is essential: "To make yourself clear without gesture, without facial expression ... you have to make your language work so as to come clear all by itself." (This feat of prestidigitation Ong aptly calls "exquisite circumspection.")[12]

Thus we remain in the throes of what is by now an all-too-familiar pedagogical version of the double bind. We insist on trying to *impose* literacy, principally through grammatical remediation programs, upon a generation of students whose speech habits have not escaped the semantic radius of the nursery – that is, for whom spoken language functions extensively as a replicative or analogical medium – and whom *we* have failed[13] to properly introduce to the exigencies of written expression. The process unfortunately concludes in *resembling the gestural mode associated with contemporary speech* rather than establishing its own unique and heteronomous structure as an *independent form of graphic representation.*[14] This much is certain. The redoubling of effective writing courses, accompanied by the growing chorus of tragic lamentation, will have no significant effect on the verbal and lexical practice of our students whatsoever. The literacy crisis will persist as the litteracy crisis.

Furthermore, the consideration of speaking and writing and the complex, fluctuating relations between them would seem to require a theory of reading as well. I have analysed the phenomenon of reading in some detail in *Education Lost* and touched upon it throughout this collection. Geraldine Van Doren in *The Paideia Program* describes it in the following terms: "Reading is a major source of information and knowledge and promotes the understanding of ideas." Readers are "introduced to characters who may become lifelong companions; allowed to overhear conversations that say what no one has ever said before; invited to share feelings that deepen their own."

Nobody but the most inveterate cherrypicker could quarrel with this *summa*, certainly adequate as far as it goes. But reading would need additional theorizing if it were to be positioned in its mutual and symbiotic relations to speaking and writing, forming an equilateral triangle whose vertices would continue to rotate in the ongoing development of literacy. One of the essential functions of reading is to reinforce the inner sense of a linear, temporal continuum reflected both on the level of the sentence as a historical monad and on the level of narrative as a paradigm of identity, appealing to the memorial function that underwrites our ability to scan and connect, to render economical the unruly multiplicity of events impinging upon us. Reading helps to organize and to recollect: it is lecithin for the mind.

Obviously there is no culture devoid of writing and reading even if that culture is resolutely oral: predation and divination, tracks and omens both involve narrative decipherment. But in a truly literate culture the terms of the mnemonic system change. The proverb and the epic give way to a less fixed or hieratic mode of remembering, and the mythic or cyclic consciousness accedes to the force of temporal lineation, forming the more fragile and bewildering substratum of historical consciousness. The individual no longer listens to the stories of the wise or recapitulates the adventures of immemorial heroes in the lesser framework of his own life. Now he is constrained to assemble the diachronic units of a literate civilization developing in time and to establish a syntagmatic narrative sequence *for himself* if he desires to build and retain an identity capable of resisting the flux of anarchic event – the flood of impressions hourly rushing in upon him as well as the millennial terror of absurdity and cataclysm into which history dissolves if it remains unsubdued by syntax.[15] In a literate culture with a long and convoluted history, disciplined reading (or what we might today call power-reading), based on a sense of precedence, order, and hierarchical levels of meaning (as in Benveniste's theory of levels, yielding two types of relations, distributional and integrational) is a *sine qua non* for the development of the personality insofar as it reinforces the wavering structures of psychic temporality. Thus, with a little stretching, we might consider reading as a third representational system intimately and reciprocally linked to speaking and writing. (Though, of course, in order to read, something must first have been written, the inescapable text that, as Umberto Eco assures us somewhere, is "the human way to reduce the world to a manageable format.")

Moreover, the question would arise as to the difference between reading silently and reading aloud and whether these would form in turn two distinct semiotic systems or merely two sides of an identical phenomenon. For Augustine, who observed with astonishment that Bishop Ambrose read silently to himself, the distinction was palpable. The difference was equally apparent to Pliny the Younger who remarked in a letter to Fuscus Salinator that he read aloud and with emphasis "not so much for the sake of my voice as my digestion." I would suggest that both reading modes, for whatever purposes each may be undertaken, equally reinforce that inner tensorial continuum that enables us to interpret experience as inherently unified and meaningful.[16]

The inability to read consistently and with understanding, aggravated by lack of patience or poor habits of deferment, is a major cause of the epidemic of lexemia we are trying to combat and as critical a form of mental truancy as the deficiencies associated with speaking and writing. I am put in mind in this connection of one of my good students, a "wild talent" who scored respectable and sometimes very high grades in the several courses he took with me, and who displayed an impressive acuity of insight even when ill-prepared for the topics under discussion. Wishing to "upgrade his bibliography," he asked me to provide him with a list of essential novels. I suggested he begin with *Portrait of the Artist As a Young Man*, a demanding but by no means repellant text, and one that seemed to correspond to his own indomitable self-image. A week later I inquired into his progress only to be informed that he had fallen asleep somewhere in the first chapter and could not generate the interest to continue with the project. The problem seemed to be that the text drew too much attention to its own discursive practices and did not dish up "real adventures." Stephen Dedalus failed to measure up to the Young Indiana Jones. This scenario has occurred too often to be accidental. Even comparatively more promising students rarely possess the equipment that would enable them to pursue the intellectual dividends of a genuine literacy. It is this form of intellectual delinquency, this *corruptio optima pessimi*, that constitutes perhaps the most discouraging aspect of the crisis of competence defining the current situation, as if we were indeed, in the words of Sven Birkerts, "poised at the brink of what may prove to be a kind of species mutation.[17]

Once again Vygotsky provides us with an invaluable clue or conceptual insight to work with. A developed form of writing, he tells us, involves "the reversion of written language from a second-order symbolism to first-order symbolism." Written symbols are designations for prior verbal symbols and thus function as a second-order system of representation. Eventually, as the speaker-writer matures and acquires a "natural" facility with the production and manipulation of graphic signs, spoken language will begin to atrophy, not in itself, but as the intermediate link between script and referent. That is, written language is promoted to the level of immediate representationality and becomes a direct, first-order symbolic function perceived, Vygotsky says, "in the same way as spoken language." (Comparably, this is how one knows that one has mastered a foreign language, when one ceases to translate back into the mother tongue.)

This analysis strikes me as unassailable and helps to explain the semiotic disaster we are trying to understand. Applying Vygotsky's conceptual scheme to the dilemma of literacy in the current "American" milieu, it seems to me a warranted assumption that the contemporary student has by and large failed to complete the final stage of the literacy process, to *transform writing from a second-order to a first-order symbolic system*. In other words, for the contemporary student writing remains almost indissolubly tied to speech, which in turn interposes its linking function as a first-order system between the graphic sign and the object or referent when it should gradually be erased or cancelled from the semiotic equation. Instead of being equipped with *two* first-order symbolic systems, speech and script, our students approach the rich and tangled complexity of experience with a first-order oral symbolism, in itself weakened by the anachronistic persistence of the tonal duplicating function associated with early play-mimicry,[18] and a second-order graphic system of representation that has not been adequately refined or transformed into a first-order phenomenon.

To make matters worse, writing will frequently take on the form of a second-order mimicry system (script replete with iconic symbols, arrows, neatly severed hands with pointing index finger, boxes within boxes, little round smiling faces to indicate a happy thought, phatic interjections like "well" and "you know," etc.).[19] In this context it recuperates not the world but current speech, which in turn represents the world in large measure via the imitative or replicative mode correlative with play or infant theatre, giving us verbal-tonal facsimiles of reality that are perforce accented subjectively rather than symbolic substitutes for it that are objectively specifiable. Such is the nature of the predicament we are facing, which goes some way to accounting for the miserable failure of the remediation programs we continue to devise and support. These programs do not even remotely address the problem; they do not even touch it at a theoretical tangent.

You cannot teach writing to someone who has (1) failed to develop everyday speech as an adequate system of symbolic substitution but which instead retains its early, fossilized structure as a tonal and gestural imitative medium in proportions that weaken its surrogational function;[20] and (2) failed to achieve the consummation of writing as a second first-order representational system predicated upon a mode of symbolic substitution different from that associated with speech.[21] That is, you cannot successfully teach writing to someone for whom speech works as a kind of occultation, eclipsing the referent to which writing should make immediate and effortless appeal. Psychologically put, this means that writing will continue to be felt as a prosthetic mechanism, something alien to the sensibility, rather than as a "natural" or habitual mode of symbolic representation. Under these circumstances, we cannot reasonably expect that graphic and syntactical competencies will ever be effortlessly integrated into the so-called "expressive medium" of writing.

In order for true literacy to take hold, the individual must be supplied with two first-order symbolic systems. As the linguistic philosopher J.H. Uldall formulates the issue, "It is only through the concept of a difference between form and substance that we can explain the possibility of speech and writing existing at the same time as expressions of one and the same language."[22] Language is a *form*, its pure "glossematic" units (to use Hjelmslev's term) invisible to the eye or ear, a vast, mycelial system of potential *differences* inherent in the representational function *per se*. Speech and writing are *substances*, one phonic and the other graphic, that are related as linguistic manifestations of the same underlying form but, in the last analysis, must be understood as mutually independent signifying systems. As Uldall puts it, "in orthography, no grapheme corresponds to accents of pronunciation ... and ... in pronunciation, no phoneme corresponds to the spacing between written words." This interesting and remunerative line of thought receives further amplification in the work of the deconstructive theorist Jacques Derrida, who in *Of Grammatology* credibly reverses the accepted order of priority between speech and writing by claiming, with considerable philosophic power, that speech is already inhabited by the structure of writing insofar as it is constituted by the necessary absence of both the object (the referent in itself) and the subject (self-presence). Language is insecurely founded on what he calls "arche-writing" or "trace-structure" which, like Carroll's snark or Joyce's quark, never poses for the camera. For our purposes it is sufficient to recognize that speech and writing, though clearly related ontogenetically in the development of the signifying function in the individual's history of language acquisition, are also reciprocally distinct as orders of symbolic substitution for what is hyletically given in experience.[23] If they remain spliced together, with writing reproducing the dynamics of speech rather than attaining to its own peculiar and unique structure of representation, it follows that remedial instruction in writing will never entirely succeed in normalizing the written medium as a first-order surrogational system enabling the proper organization of thought and experience or, in Bronowski's phrase, as "a thinking language for manipulating concepts."[24]

What we therefore require in the current predicament is not a fresh onslaught of remedial and effective-writing programs, on the whole merely counter-productive clutter, but a thorough and analytically strenuous re-thinking of the literacy crisis, its origins, elements, stages, and momenta, and the realization that the problem must be attacked both at its roots *and* in our unreflected contribution to its continuation, indeed to its exacerbation. We can no longer rest content with Lilliputian answers to Brobdingnagian questions. We must first investigate and reform the speech-habits of our children, which means isolating the causes – not very far to seek – for the long retention of the mimicry modes complicit with early childhood and the corresponding dearth of good, protracted, and informative conversation in the cultural incunabulum we call the home.

Vygotsky, who is after all the founder of the Institute of Defectology, proves very helpful on this point as well. One of the central tenets of his cognitive theory, which has received independent confirmation and expansion by several contemporary thinkers, is the transformation of social or interpersonal processes into *intra*personal ones: "All the higher functions originate as actual relations between human individuals," as the latter engage, either consciously or involuntarily, in the internalization or refraction of the cumulative knowledge and history of the culture, including socialized speech.[25] But if this social process is an impoverished one, it follows as the night the day (and not vice versa) that the intrapersonal development of cognitive functions and emergent capabilities will correspondingly suffer. In the famine of books, conversation, directed studies, and "literate strangers" at the supper table (to quote E.D. Hirsch), can we profess surprise at the anorexic lack of verbal stamina and intellectual substance that cripples the development of our youngsters? Starvation does not generally produce anything like common health, let alone robust vitality.

Secondly, we must examine the reasons behind the failure of written language in the normal training of our children and students to shed its second-order status like the graphological snakeskin that it is and assume the function of a first-order, immediate, and autonomous signifying system in its own right.[26] For in the absence of this transformation, this causal decoupling, writing will continue to operate like a clumsy orthopedic device impeding our negotiation of the world; in other words, it will prevent rather than facilitate the complex and literate organization of thought. We would do well in this connection to elaborate what Vygotsky calls a "psychology of writing" that treats of that system of signs and symbols "whose mastery heralds a cultural turning-point in the entire development of the child." It is at this Vygotskian "turning point" or node of transformation that we may locate one of the defects of the increasingly popular "whole language" approach, which otherwise has much to recommend it. Proponents of whole language believe, as Kathy Toohy puts it, that "literacy skills are the best developed in the same way that spoken language is developed." In other words, whole language borrows its central principles "from oral language acquisition; learning to read and write can be as easy as learning to talk."[27]

While learning to read and write may be, and indeed should be, a challenging and delightful event in the development of the child, it remains a serious error in pedagogical judgment to downplay the element of *labour* involved in these sophisticated accomplishments. Reading, at least initially, is *work* and needs the sort of application that the child babbling its way into approximate coherence neither experiences nor requires.[28] Writing is even more laborious and while there is no good reason to treat it as a herculean task manageable only by heroes and demigods – it should certainly be made as relevant, interesting, and accessible as possible – it is inefficient and counter-productive to approach something so inherently formidable, perhaps the greatest single invention of the human mind, as if it were easy, effortless, natural, pure play. Writing is not natural in the way speech is, given normal conditions of practice and experiment. Writing is *artificial*, a second first-order system of representation that differs both structurally and materially from the plastic, informal, and perhaps instinctual impulse to turn an undifferentiated stream of sounds into isolable phonic semantemes. Learning to write can never be "as easy as learning to talk," just as learning to *converse* demands far more effort than merely learning to talk. And while I can see no reason that work should not also be enjoyable, I suspect that the fun-and-games attitude underlying much of the whole-language approach, when it addresses itself to the question of writing, actually sabotages the student's capacity to deploy graphic symbols with the rigour and competence indispensable for clear and rich expression. This may explain why many of my own students, nourished on whole-language pedagogy, still cannot write with even journeyman ability – despite the school's attempt to assist in developing "the student's own unique style in writing." Such originality is misplaced and premature and follows directly from the prelapsarian emphasis on play, naturalness, spontaneity, and a kind of Chiltonesque[29] assurance in the innate creativity of the growing child which regulation presumably deforms and stultifies.

Further, and far more apocalyptically, Vygotsky's "turning point" must now be sublimated into a cultural turning point in the development of civilization as we know it in the cis-Atlantic West where educational function is lapsing into a condition of terminal incoherence, declining in ways we have failed to analyse with sufficient clarity and rigour. One of these ways has to do with the failure to construct and promote an adequate model of functional literacy, which may be regarded in the light of our study as a metaphorical correlate of Milton's enigmatic "two handed engine at the door" in *Lycidas* or Derrida's image of the "two handed machine" in *Writing and Difference*[30] (which he introduces to explicate Freud's concept of memory as a mystic writing-pad: one hand to write, one to erase). I am proposing that we reconsider language as a kind of "two handed machine" or "two handed engine at the door" of literate experience we wish to open: one handle represents spoken language, with which we must come to grips (in order to rescue it from the realm of chromatic mimicry where we have allowed it to fall); the other handle betokens written language, which must be perceived and taught as an independent, first-order signifying system generating its own immediate relation to the world of experience in both its objective and subjective dimensions.

Invoking Jacques Lacan's definition of the metaphoric function as "one word for another," how convenient and even seductive it is to misconceive written language as a kind of metaphoric substitute for spoken language and merely apply the celebrated Lacanian algorithm for the transformation:

$$F \frac{S_1}{S} S = S (+) s$$

where F represents function, S the old term which stands for the signified of the new term S_1, which in turn yields a new system of representation S congruent with a plurality of local signifiers s that "crosses the bar," unblocking expression and providing for a semiurgical breakthrough to another level of representation (the plus sign as cross, with the vertical pole crossing the minus bar of metonymic horizontality into the realm of supervenient "difference"). *Thus written language would function deceptively as S_1, the new global signifier that signifies the spoken language S it has replaced* to become a new system S in turn – a change of levels but not, be it noted, of constituent substance. Pixilated as this partially idiographic notation might appear – an elaborate, pseudo-linguistic put-on – it does provide us with a formulaic description of our customary practice in treating script as a mere surrogate for speech rather than as an autonomous signifying system that objects to such algorithmic conscription.[31]

Consider, for example, the problem of spelling, now delivered into the mechanical care of the spell-check program (its dubious value in any case daily undermined by the phono-barbarism of commercial orthography). As Frank Smith argues in *Joining the Literacy Club*,[32] spelling has less to do with pronunciation or reproduction of sounds than with the maintenance of semantic consistency. Conventional spelling is a central function of the graphological system – we rarely pause to reflect that spoken words have no spelling – and exists primarily to stabilize meanings and to fix correspondences between words that are conceptually related and yet may be pronounced differently. (Smith gives the example of "medicine" and "medical" – but of course, the entire language works this way.) We teach spelling – or rather, we used to teach spelling – for the same basic reason that we once thought it necessary to inculcate the principles of grammar: to enable students *to think*, to relate ideas to one another, to connect meanings in a developing chain of sense-making, to ensure consistency, to prevent a kind of "functional" agraphia. One of the reasons our students by and large cannot think very well is that they do not know how to spell confidently and are sublimely innocent of grammar. But we should also recognize that grammatical rules *imposed* at a relatively late age are not very effective in the "war against illiteracy." Grammar, like charity, begins at home and in early schooling,[33] and like spelling, as Smith also contends, *comes from reading*. And the more abundant, precocious, and attentive the reading, the better the results.

In the light of these considerations, just to proceed with business as usual – that is, to continue to teach writing as a second-order system that reflects the instrumentalities of spoken language which in turn reproduces in its tonal substance the gestural codes collateral with the early stages of the play "matrix" – is not only to invite disaster but to spread the table. We now find ourselves in a condition of Albigensian innocence as to the cultural imperatives of the moment. It is vital, therefore, that we delve to the roots of the literacy predicament if we hope to liberate ourselves from the dreary, fruitless repetition of educational techniques and "strategies" that abet rather than avert the crisis in which we are both domestically and professionally implicated.

· 7 ·

The Bipolar Paradigm

To call for participation is to render "cognitive respect" to all those who cannot claim the status of experts.

Peter Berger, *Pyramids of Sacrifice*

The language of education ... must express stance and must invite counter-stance and in the process leave place for reflection, for metacognition.

Jerome Bruner, *Actual Minds, Possible Worlds*

GLOSSARY

Subject A	specific academic subject (chemistry, poetry, etc.)
Subject B	tacit subject (learning to learn)
Text A	class text (textbook, topic, experiment, etc.)
Text B	class-as-text
Bipolar teaching	the reciprocal and simultaneous presentation of a double subject; the teaching of learning *in the process* of teaching a given material.

THEORETICAL FRAMEWORK

Premises

It is the primary contention of this essay that, in any class irrespective of field or discipline, there should always be two subjects being taught concurrently: the specific subject under consideration (poetry, chemistry, philosophy), henceforth denominated Subject A, and the parergal, tacit, yet indispensable subject of learning itself (that is, of "learning to learn"), henceforth denominated Subject B. In an optimal classroom situation, both forms of teaching-and-learning proceed in implicit tandem, mutually reinforcing one another and developing over time in a cumulative fashion. The proper teaching of Subject A both facilitates and is facilitated by the proper teaching of Subject B, so that by the conclusion of a given semester the student should be not only *materially competent* but demonstrably a *better learner* as well. In a successful learning experience, the cognitive and the meta-cognitive elements should form an indissoluble whole, or to put it in experiential terms, task-competence should eventually coincide with process-competence.

This is as much as to say that education in the fullest sense of the term always occurs on two parallel levels or in two concurrent streams of reception and production. The first level or stream may be termed the noetic or cognitive; the second is the value dimension and is necessarily meta-cognitive, since values are best inculcated implicitly, by indirection, *anamorphically*, as it were (the "show" aspect of the "show and tell" process). The values we are concerned with here are not strictly moral or axiological but pedagogical, subtly reinforcing the "secondary" learning process as a function, aspect, or by-product of the "primary" didactic enterprise. *And this holds true for whatever the primary subject may happen to be.*

The second premise which underlies this chapter, then, is that what I have called Subject B, learning itself or learning to learn, cannot be operatively conceived as an isolable subject or academic discipline *per se*. (This is one of the fundamental errors of many training programs.) Subject B is always a function of Subject A, a spin-off effect, a parergon or *mise-en-abyme* of the primary discipline (in the same way that "critical thinking" cannot be a viable and coherent subject in itself but is rather an off-shoot of good, interrogative teaching). It depends upon the ancillary production of qualitative factors evoked, induced, or disclosed in the effective presentation of the course material by a teacher who is not only in command of his or her subject but who manifests *in situ* as a "carrier" of respect and enthusiasm for the discipline in question. If this second premise is correct, it follows that effective instruction (that is, the proper teaching of Subject A) derives in part from the communicable manifestation of a set of pedagogical attitudes toward both the discipline itself and the *act and process of learning* without which the course material cannot be maximally transmitted. The effective teaching of Subject B – that is, bringing to light what Michael Polyani calls "tacit knowing," employing the need to deobjectify and repersonalize learning – can never proceed artificially or mechanically, but always depends upon mobilizing, embodying, and radiating the pedagogical attitudes through which the primary subject is diffracted. In brief, effective teaching relies upon a synthesis or fusion of competent material-instruction (product) and shared pedagogical reflection (process).[1]

A third premise on which this thesis is based is that teaching students to learn (always in the process of teaching students a given material) is *productive* in the sense that the complex of attitudes, predispositions, and orientations toward learning that the students acquire is transferable and therefore cross-disciplinary. That is, students who learns about learning while studying a Survey of Fiction course will perform better when they go on to study chemistry, and vice versa.[2]

The fourth premise or tenet is a correlative of the previous three and should indeed be self-evident. Effective teaching, understood as *the reciprocal presentation of a double subject*, cannot take place without the creative intervention of the "good" teacher, one who is aware or who can be made aware of the fundamental *bipolarity* of the teaching function. The "good" teacher, as defined in my *Education Lost*, must satisfy two criteria: (a) mastery of the subject; and (b) possession of the delphic attribute we call "personality," the exhibition of *presence*, consisting of a set of qualities which, though they cannot be acquired, may nevertheless be cultivated and perfected.[3]

These "qualities of personality" may be variously denominated but would seem to comprise enthusiasm for the subject to be imparted, a certain mentorial individuality, intellectual amplitude and accessibility, narrative virtuosity, a command of the cultural encyclopedia, and personal authenticity. Such obligatory attributes cannot, as suggested above, be called forth by fiat or in a vacuum, but they can be developed, reinforced, modified, and "educated." In the absence of these pedagogical attributes, effective teaching will not be possible, precisely because what I have called Subject B (learning to learn) depends for its successful catalysing in the student upon the cognitive vitality of the teacher, the radiation of curiosity, interest, passion, and enthusiasm. A teacher who teaches only the subject and not the habits and attitudes that make for good learning is not performing well, for the simple reason that good teaching is always and infallibly a function of pedagogical bipolarity. (See appendix 1). As Alfred North Whitehead puts it in *The Aims of Education*, the teacher possesses a "double function." He or she must not only "create the environment of a larger knowledge" but should also "elicit enthusiasm by resonance from his own personality."[4]

Approach

It is important at the outset to recognize that bipolarity is not a "method" in the traditional sense of the term ("methods are dead research," as François Victor Tochon says) but a composite "approach" to both the material and the student on the part of the good teacher. (We are concerned here with values rather than magnitudes.) This approach can be summarized for the sake of convenience under three headings: textuality, narrativity, and dialogism.

Textuality. This involves a predisposition to regard the classroom situation itself *as a second text* apart from the actual text(s) under consideration.

That is, the classroom situation should be conceived as Text B, which is in process of being "written" as a collaboration between teacher and student at the same time as Text A (theme, topic, text) is being studied, analysed, or discussed. The class is consequently mediated not only by the given "text" (book, film, topic, experiment, etc.) but by its own discursive structures, constituting a new semiotic system, a kind of "overtext" in which the primary text is necessarily embedded. Gregory Ulmer approaches this idea when he proposes that the lecture, rather than merely conveying data, should approximate an actual text requiring student interpretation.[5] (Here I am suggesting that not only the lecture, but the entire class, should be regarded *sub specie textualis*.) Once this is conceded, it becomes evident that the class-as-text both demands and generates a certain creative élan on the part of the teacher as it does, *mutatis mutandis* and by a kind of intellectual contagion, on the part of the student as well. The class, then, should be regarded not simply as a forum for the analysis of texts, however these latter may be defined, but as a text in its own right, as something that is not only being "taught" but also written and interpreted, encoded and decoded, as a collaborative exercise between teacher and student. Text A and Text B, the given text and the class-as-text, are understood as constituting a reciprocal and isomorphic relation, thus providing for the sense of *creativity*, of collaborative authorship, without which most classes tend to degenerate into a condition of drill and rote, with the boredom attendant on passive reception.

The textual perspective that the prepared teacher adopts in such a classroom situation has much in common with the fruitful distinction drawn by Umberto Eco in his critical writings between the "closed text" and the "open text."[6] The closed text, which would correspond to "normal" class procedure, is one that elicits preordained expectations and is structured according to "an inflexible project." That is, it projects an "empirical reader" (read: average student), from whom it aims at drawing out an unexceptionable response. It tries, says Eco, "to fulfil the wishes of the readers already to be found"; it does not offer to *change* them in any radical or unexpected way. The open text, on the contrary, "seeks to produce a new reader" in tune with its *sui-generic* conditions. That is, it projects a "model reader" (read: dedicated student) who possesses what Eco calls "specific encyclopedic competence." In the same way as an open text seeks to produce a new reader, so the classroom regarded *under the aspect of textuality* seeks to create the model student who understands that she or he is not merely required to assimilate material, however competently, but to engage in a metacognitive process involving a change of the learning sensibility. The student is now expected to collaborate in the production of the classroom text as an interested and energetic co-author.

In practical terms this means that classroom material is not to be diluted or scaled down to the level of the student (as is all too often the case) but rather that the student, now actively implicated in textual production, is required to rise to the level of the material.[7] In other words, the student is expected to respond performatively, not merely assimilatively; he or she is not to be catered to but effectively challenged by the teacher's projective elicitations. What the principle of textuality demands is nothing less than a profound re-evaluation of pedagogic attitudes on the part of both the teacher and the student.[8]

Such re-evaluation would also require that an important part of the student's course work, irrespective of subject or discipline, would involve both occasional in-class discussion and specific written reflection on the elaboration of Subject B, the process of learning to learn. The teacher may set aside a portion of certain pre-designated classes to be given over to the subject of the learning protocol itself and solicit comments, observations, and suggestions with a view to improving the structural and dynamic aspects of the classroom situation, thus empowering students as *essential* contributors to the class-as-text. These occasions would be envisaged as integral units of class procedure. Similarly, written material on Text B topics (perhaps one major paper or several short papers per semester) would constitute one item of requisite class work and figure as a significant element in the overall grading scheme, thus establishing the learning protocol as an "official" component of the course syllabus.

The taxonomy drawn here with respect to Eco's semiotics would also correspond to Ilya Prigogine's distinction between closed and open physical systems.[9] The closed system is machine-like and predicated upon linear relationships; its final state is determined by its initial conditions. (In the same way, classroom homeostasis leads to no improvisatory surprises.) The open system involves a free exchange of matter, energy, and information with the surrounding environment and is predicated on non-linear relationships (i.e., "small inputs can trigger massive consequences.") In Prigoginian terms, all systems contain subsystems which are constantly fluctuating. At times a single fluctuation or combination of such may shatter the pre-existing organization, leading to a "bifurcation point" and producing in turn a new "dissipative structure." Similarly, the class-as-text (i.e., the *open* text) seeks in its own way to generate productive and unexpected, that is, *nontypical*, results in the student's performance-response, by co-opting the student into the textual structure of the class and thus requiring not only predictable sets of behaviours and scores but *an entirely new attitude to learning itself*, a new "dissipative structure." The student is expected not only to learn the material but to learn to learn, a process that is a function not so much of methodology as it is of attitudinality. The teacher (in Prigoginian terms) is looking to influence intellectual "fluctuations" with a view to initiating "massive consequences"; that is, to disengage the presuppositions of the typical "closed class" which does not address its intrinsic textuality and replace these with a new set of attitudes that allows for the production of the "open class" conscious of its own discursive and structural procedures.

Narrativity. The philosopher Richard Rorty recommends that in the course of scholarly pursuits and academic activities, theoretical discourse should be modified or reduced in the interests of "a general turn ... toward narrative." Theoretical material must be situated *personally* if it is to generate enthusiasm. A teacher who is anecdotally illiterate, who cannot regard himself or herself *sub specie fabulae*, who does not understand that the *act* of teaching must reflect a narrative procedure (re. class-as-text) in order to be effective, memorable, and response-productive, will be unable to establish and communicate what I have designated as Subject B – in other words, will be unable to teach learning over and above the teaching of course material.

Recent studies have persuasively indicated that the anecdotal function is essential to fruitful communication (this has nothing to do with the erroneously named "communications skills"). Narrative, says Fredric Jameson, "is the fundamental instance of the human mind"; or as Tzvetan Todorov argues, "Narrative equals life; absence of narrative is death." Thus Gregory Ulmer in his influential book *Teletheory* elaborates the notion of an "euretic" or inventive discourse (rather than a hermeneutic discourse) which he calls "mystoriography," a mode of thinking, writing, and teaching that opposes linear reflection in the analytico-referential register (standard methodological discourse) and proposes a new protocol that allows for private, popular, and disciplinary forms of address to be mapped unto one another. It is precisely this "new" form of discourse that stimulates the imagination of the learner by anecdotalizing theoretical material, appealing to vicarious involvement, to personal interest and curiosity.

As the critic and teacher Richard Ohmann writes, this is done by "incorporating the theoretical terms in a relaxed, conversational style ... it is important to fix my discourse in that key ... I want to project in the lecturing my own appropriation of these ideas, their integration into my whole outlook [and] I want to contest the routine segmentation of academic discourse into special languages." Obviously, such a procedure is not simply a question of having a large repertory of stories at one's disposal or some sort of nimble, pantomimic gift – though these are helpful – but of being able to recognize the *constructed* nature of the event in which one is participating – an event that resembles a macroscopic narrative whose subsidiary components include everything from rumination, questioning, and dialogue to anecdote itself. Those teachers who address themselves to Subject B, to the teaching of learning in the act of teaching the material, must also become learners: in other words, like Richard Ohmann, they must learn "to fix my discourse in that key."[10]

Dialogism. In the staple communications-theory schema, the classroom situation can be simplistically mapped as a "speech event" involving the transmission of a *message* from an *addressor* to an *addressee,* i.e., between teacher and student. The channel is open at both ends, of course, the student often assuming the role of addressor and the teacher of addressee, but the direction of the transmission is necessarily for the most part teacher-vectorial (from teacher to student). More fully rendered in the work of the communications theorist Roman Jakobson, the "speech event" is understood to include three additional factors: the *code,* the *contact,* and the *context.*

According to Jakobson, these six "fundamental factors" of communication are associated with six complementary "sets" or "basic functions": the addressor with the "expressive function" (attitude); the addressee with the "conative function" (urging, being urged); the context with the "referential function" (denotative orientation, the larger situation in which the message is embedded); the message with the "poetic function" (focus on language for its own sake); the contact with the "phatic function" (making sure the channel works); and the code with the "metalingual function" (glossing, checking that the same idiom or set of implications is in place). Thus diagrammatically:

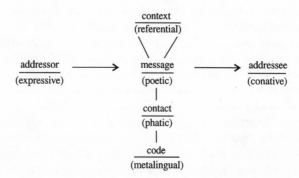

While it is obvious that all six functions of the communications schema must be invoked in operative teaching,[11] it is my profound conviction that the Jakobsonian model is not exhaustive. In order to account for all genuine communication, including classroom transmission, the model must be amplified to include the radical insight of the great Russian theorist Mikhail Bakhtin. Bakhtin contends that authentic dialogue (as I understand it, whether between two individuals, two groups, or, as in the classroom, between an individual and a group) demands the invisible presence of a "third" whom Bakhtin designates as the "superaddressee." This "third" may be an individual, a group of individuals, or a presence projected by either of the participants in the dialogue (each participant possesses his or her own proper "third").[12]

For example, the poet writing to or for a hypothetical audience may be, over and above that particular line of transmission, also writing to or for posterity, or a departed friend or lover, or God Himself (as is certainly the case with poets like Hopkins or Claudel). It is the invisible or absent superaddressee who establishes the validity, power, and meaningfulness of the communicative act. Similarly in the classroom situation, hovering over the addressor and the addressee (teacher-student; student-teacher), one must posit the invisible presence of the *author* of the specific text under consideration, dead or absent yet *essentially* present, in whose name the class is being "taught"; or of the *tradition of the discipline itself*, which confers authority and significance upon the dialogue in question. Such a re-cognition requires scrupulousness, respect, and perhaps even love on the part of the teacher, so as to avoid diluting or desecrating the subject which as "message" moves along the axis of communication.[13] If the student can also be disposed – indirectly, subtly, implicitly, by "contagion" – to sense or imagine the presence of the invisible third (the author, scientist, or group of scholars and researchers responsible for Text A), cognizant of that shadowy figure whom Jacques Derrida somewhere calls "the third party between the hands holding the book," they will already and insensibly have been inducted into the collaborative mode and actively engage in the production of Text B, the class-as-text itself in concert with both teacher-as-author and author-as-teacher. That is, it is only when the *imagination* is touched in reverence or respect that genuine learning, as opposed to passive recording, may be said to occur. Stated another way, true learning is first of all *productive* rather than merely receptive or reproductive.

But in order for such pedagogical symbiosis to occur, the teacher must assimilate the dialogical principle of the superaddressee, understanding that his or her attention must be directed not only to the student (as in the pupil-centred "progressivist" scheme) but to the author or authors of the material, to the tradition of the discipline, or to the over-arching cultural authority – if that personal enthusiasm, reverence, or respect necessary for genuine transmission and evocation is to "take" in the student. In Parker Palmer's words, the teacher may be regarded most fruitfully as a mediator between the learner and the subject, "the living link in the epistemological chain."[14]

It may also be noted that the Bakhtinian concept is capable of a certain dialectical refinement. Insofar as the teacher teaches *in the name of* the author or the tradition, drawing attention to the spirit of the discipline or to the cultural authority, she or he invokes the superaddressee. But insofar as the teacher teaches *as* the author, that is, as the representative or embodiment of the spirit of the discipline, the latter may now be understood as *active*, addressing the student through the medium or agency of what I have earlier called "the creative intervention of the good teacher." In this case the Bakhtinian "third" may be legitimately spoken of as the *"superaddressor"*: the cultural authority as the active and vital *sponsor* of the educational transaction. Whichever way we choose to regard the relation, Bakhtin's paradoxical formulation remains valid: in order for there to be two, there must first be three. Thus:

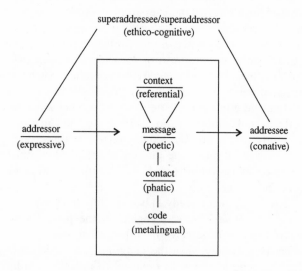

Consequently, in the terms of the proposed Jakobsonian-Bakhtinian model, textuality (in the *local* sense)[15] is subsumed in the expressive-conative axis between teacher and student; narrativity involves the effective diegetic arrangement of message, context, contact, and code; and dialogism introduces the triangular structure in which the "author" of the given text under discussion (i.e., a single individual, a group of scholars, or the tradition of the discipline conceived as a productive, historical force) presides at the ethico-cognitive apex of the classroom schema, as the "conscience" of the classroom event, the authority which, as Gadamer says, "has to do not with obedience, but rather with knowledge."[16]

This schema, of course, is offered primarily for the sake of diagrammatic convenience. The second pole of the bipolar class is in fact constituted by the effective amalgamation of the intrinsic terms of the new model into a dynamic classroom process. From the standpoint of the teacher, the induction of the student (through such devices as in-class discussion and assigned writing projects on the subject of the actual learning protocol) constitutes collaborative textuality; the framing of theoretical discourse within the personal or anecdotal mode (including historical contextualizing) fulfils the requirement of narrativity; and the directing of attention to the author, tradition, or cultural authority, thus assuming pedagogical responsibility not only *for* the student (progressivism) but *towards* the civilizing imperative, affirms the dialogical principle. From the perspective of the student, the progressive *awareness* of this process to which he or she contributes creatively (textuality), vicariously (narrativity), and ethico-cognitively (dialogism), comprises the *productive* dimension of his or her participation. This dynamic not only enhances the actual learning of a given material but also, in the growing *consciousness* of the pedagogical event that requires the student's assistance, stimulates the process of "learning to learn" by enabling the student to recognize, incorporate, and apply the three critical principles with respect to any given material and in any classroom situation.

Therefore, in the course of time, students moving through the educational system should come to expect and demand the right to contribute to the class-as-text; they will see the pedagogical "object" not as sterile and inert material but as situated in a personal and historical, that is, living process; and they will come to experience a growing interest in the larger cultural project that confers value and meaning on the private segmentations of individual life and study.

Comment: Corresponding Paradigms

In the same sense as Bakhtin foregrounds the dialogical principle in communication, so for Jacques Lacan the mutual recognition of subjects (subjectivities) precedes the cognition of objects. Another way, then, of regarding the Bakhtinian concept is by enlisting the Lacanian distinction between the *énoncé* (statement) and *énonciation* (utterance), between the object that is communicated and the fact *that* it is communicated by subjects. No *énoncé* is a pure content, a semantic substance, a simple message; it is also an invocation, an address to another subject, a continuous *signifiant* that can never come to rest in a fixed or final *signifié*.

In the classroom context, the *énonciation* must be considered as bearing equal weight or importance with the *énoncé* itself. Style, process, and self-awareness cannot be divorced from the content to be imparted and in fact should be regarded as an intrinsic and necessary aspect of that material in the larger sense of constituting a double subject. Contemporary semiotic theory would appear to reinforce the validity of this insight as applied to the development of pedagogical protocols. For example, in the work of

Jacques Derrida and Michel Foucault, the psychological subject is considered to be an effect of the text, *a function of discourse*. If this is indeed
the case, the communicant (as well as the communicator) is structured and
articulated as a "by-product" of the actual discourse in which she or he
is engaged.

Since knowledge necessarily presupposes predication, the semiotic thesis
suggests, pedagogically, that the learning protocol itself should function as
an integral and essential component of the dynamic of material instruction
and should therefore be conceived as the second pole of any specific learning
context: in effect, it must be treated *consciously* as an ineluctable part of
the total subject under consideration and included *veritably* within the curriculum of instruction.

Such basic repositioning of the communicative forces within our modular
schematism is, if not overtly proposed, at least implicitly suggested in, for
example, J.L. Austin's original privileging of the "performative" mode of
discourse over the "constative" and in Jurgen Habermas's determination
of the speech act as possessing an "interactive" dimension, establishing a
revelation and revealing an intention over and above the claims of the cognitive truth-function. My notion of pedagogical bipolarity, influenced as
it is by Bakhtinian speculation, owes something also to Austin's distinction
and in particular to Habermas's concept of the "dual structure of speech":
every speech act communicates simultaneously on two levels, conveying
a propositional content as well as a metacommunication (this latter consisting of the system of reciprocal expectations of the participants in
dialogue.)[17]

These reflections permit us to consider *standard* educational procedure
as involving a one-way transmission of semantic commodities and
"discipline-skills": what we might refer to as predetermined data-packages.
This form of transmission (or exchange, but only in the sense that data-
packages may be sent back the other way) would lead – as it inescapably
does – to the anonymity and indifference associated with the commodity
form, to the incessant unrolling of what Jean-François Lyotard calls the
"*grande pellicule éphémère*" as a conductor of disassociated attentions. What
is needed, on the contrary, is an awareness of the *process* of transmission/
exchange, elaborated as a part, function or aspect of the "skill-and-
information commodity" itself, in order to render the class sensitive to its
own communicative conventions. One of the two major subjects of a class,
apart from the instructional material, is always the class itself, the act of
teaching-and-learning, in which case the class must be understood as what
Roland Barthes has called a "second-order signifying system" constructed
on the basis of a semiotic structure that exists before it, but that it paradoxically modifies, re-focuses, and eventually incorporates.

Thus what I have called Subject B entails an empirical focus upon the meta-dimension of learning, disengaging information about how we transmit and receive information or, alternatively, refining and strengthening the so-called "learning-skills" with which students acquire and develop their "discipline-skills." The way in which students come to terms with modes of experience, systems of meaning and objects of knowledge in the learning situation must itself be made *to emerge into awareness* within the classroom dynamic as *another form* of experience, meaning, and knowledge. This implies that the fundamental criterion of the successful learning situation, put as simply as possible, is the fostering of an epistemic and evaluative *pluralism of the subject*.

If, as Gregory Bateson has argued, skill is a coding of largely unconscious information, then what we may call "skilled" or "skilful" performance is the integration and exhibition of repressed or subliminal knowledge, its translation into practice leading to its refinement, improvement, flexibility, and appropriateness. The teaching of Subject B consists, in these terms, *of expressing primary process content in the form of secondary process grammar*, enabling the learner to focus, structure and organize the actual learning process to his or her advantage, thus promoting better learning.[18]

From a structural or morphological standpoint, the "moment of learning" occurs at the intersection of two complementary modes or "textual" forces: the transmissive and the self-descriptive. That is to say, it is inefficient, pedagogically speaking, to equate the classroom scenario with its purely "phonetic" content: message, lesson, topic, theme, "subject" – the classroom *what*. A second impulse or "dimension" is co-present with the first. The location of this second factor is not in any particular topic or theme but in the "phonemic" systems and devices by which the material is structured and imparted – the classroom *how*. Effective learning occurs at the intersection of the what and the how, the phonetic and the phonemic, the class as a forum for the analysis of texts and the class-as-text itself, self-descriptive and transparent to its own discursive practices and techniques. And it is precisely this element of class reflexivity that engages, motivates, empowers, and *authenticates* the student as co-responsible for the overall effectiveness and viability of the class as a learning theatre, as a functional medium of reception *and production*.[19]

Concluding Remarks

A. My concept of bipolarity will be seen to share certain features with the principles of experiential learning, especially as the latter envisions "a paradigmatic shift from the transmission model of teaching toward a process-oriented, experiential model seeing learners as active agents of their own learning" (cf. Viljo Kohonen, "Facilitating Self-Direction in Language Learning," University of Tampere, Finland, 1991). But the distinction between bipolarity and experientiality (the latter in some respects the ambsace of contemporary educational theory) is crucial. The experiential model entails the promotion of (1) self-directed learning and (2) collaboration between learners, to be facilitated by specific and formal phases of instruction whereby much of the responsibility for learning devolves from the teacher onto the student. The bipolar concept attempts, rather, to generate (1) the appropriate cognitive attitudes toward learning and a certain metacognitive awareness of the learning process acquired in the act of learning a given material, and (2) collaboration between *learner and teacher*, under the auspices of the "superaddressee," in the overall textualization of the classroom schematism.

Succinctly, experientiality is a matter of aptitudes, bipolarity of attitudes. It is not only a question of facilitating learners to manage their own learning but of assisting them to acquire that set or complex of attitudes, assumptions, and orientations that enable them to learn willingly, appetitively, and integratedly. Again, bipolarity is not to be identified with the constructivist school (Piaget) in which text, subject, or protocol is presumably *reproduced* or reinvented by the student. In most cases (except with young children) such a procedure is manifestly impossible. To revert to our prior terminology, bipolarity entails not the reproduction of Text A but the collaborative production of Text B (in which Text A is embedded). In other words, it facilitates and enables the mutual *authorship* of the classroom schematism itself, which both requires and generates the creative excitement, the productivity of self, from which all genuine learning flows.

It is curious to note that bipolarity works by combining and modifying various aspects of what are generally considered to be antithetical paradigms, the "behavioural" which is concerned with the transmission of knowledge and the "experiential" which is concerned with the transformation of knowledge, into a new pedagogical composite which both transmits and incites, conveys and provokes. Text A comprises knowledge of facts, hospitality toward ideas, and development of abilities, focusing on content and product. Text B involves an emphasis on process and the metacognitive awareness of the learning situation itself. Bipolarity sees both dimensions as mutually implicated in the sense of being reciprocal functions of the same pedagogical event.

This is not only a question of encouraging learners to regard themselves "as increasingly competent and self-determined, assuming an increasing degree of responsibility for their own learning" (Kohonen), but more to the point, to view themselves as engaged with the teacher in the production of the collaborative classroom text under the aegis of a mutually recognized superaddressee. Students come to understand themselves as *writers* in the larger sense, upon whose active intervention in the learning situation the success of the enterprise depends. That is, what they are meta-learning is responsibility in the form of *response-ability*.

B. Bipolar pedagogy takes radical exception to the current fashionable emphasis on "learning skills" as such and *in vacuo*, and to techniques of "memory management," "data acquisition," "storage," and "information retrieval" increasingly associated with experiential learning. It affirms that the technological and cybernetic model that governs much contemporary thinking in education is both misguided and harmful and that the deployment of "learning strategies" does not lead to pedagogic autonomy but rather to pedagogic dependency and intellectual demoralization.

As Max Dublin argues in his recent book, *Futurehype*,[20] most contemporary pedagogical techniques "are blunt instruments when pitted against the rich complexity of human individuality and the many kinds of subject matter." Teaching and learning involve the *human being* and not that hypothetical construct so dear to many current theorists, the hypostasis of programmable circuitry that reacts to predesigned input to yield predetermined results. Bipolarity is based on the following working assumptions:

- learners *respond* rather than react;
- learning is not a pure skill, like juggling or typing, but a mysterious and not altogether analysable process having more in common with hunger, desire, love, and curiosity than with task-oriented strategies of accomplishment – it is a "skill" only in Gregory Bateson's sense of a (partial) "codification" of unconscious information;
- the teacher must therefore appeal to the *person* and not to the abstraction inhabiting the pedagogical monographs, deceptively referred to as the "learner";
- the best way to negotiate such an appeal, and thus enhance *actual* learning, is by applying the principles of textuality, narrativity, and dialogism;
- as a consequence of the above, teachers must be exposed to these principles, invited to reflect upon their import and practicability, and develop through guided reflection and attendant practice that productive state of mind (as well as its empirical classroom correlate) which enables genuine learning to take place;
- genuine learning comprises not only the transmission of material but the metacognitive awareness of the learning process;
- such metacognitive awareness can be stimulated or provoked only by engaging the student (no longer an abstraction) in the collaboration of the classroom text, regarded as an ongoing narrative, under the beneficent auspices of an acknowledged superaddressee whose "presence" generates

the respect, deference, love, or gratitude without which genuine learning must remain elusive, partial, or improbable.

What is required on the part of the teacher is nothing less than a Kuhnian "paradigm shift," that is, a new set of premises, problems, and procedures, which in the case under consideration entails moving away from technicity with its stress on rule, program, method, and system, and toward intentionality with its stress on nuance, detail, context, and history – as previously stated, from aptitude to attitude, from reaction to response, and from learning as such to learning to learn while learning the material.

C. While it is important to note that "learning to learn" is not a mere placebo-statement selected for its tautonymic sonority, it should also be recognized that its unfolding and translation into the sphere of praxis by no means entails a series of recipe-dominated *étapes*. This would simply be one more technological delusion. Learning to learn, it cannot be sufficiently re-emphasized, is a by-product of learning the material and is, moreover, a reflex or function of the teacher's attitude towards the act of ransmission-evocation which in turn generates in the student the process of assimilation-production. It is based jointly on the "pedagogical principles" and the "working assumptions" designated above. Teachers should not be *trained* to elaborate a "method" – as often as not pedagogically counter-productive – but sensitized to adapt and interiorize an "approach" to the classroom situation involving a relationship between addressor, addressee, and superaddressee in the narrative exposition of the material. And it is precisely this educational process that constitutes the second, metacognitive pole in the theory of *didactic* bipolarity, corresponding on the side of the teacher to what we might call the second, metacognitive pole in the theory of *mathetic* bipolarity on the side of the student, learning to learn while learning the material.

D. What constitutes a "successful" class remains a vexed question. In a typical college English class of forty students, the teacher who regards care-and-catering as "top priority" will define a successful class as one in which only five students or so are lost as drop-outs; the surviving thirty-five generate a grade average of approximately 75 per cent – grading is always lenient and numerically manipulated to satisfy a pre-ordained criterion. The course work, never too demanding, consists of a stipulated number of "writing projects," low-level discussion of texts, a couple of films, and ample opportunity for grade-recovery in cases of dereliction. There are no complaints or grievances, and students move along through the system, impaired but without impediment. The whole enterprise is founded on a paramedic attitude to the student and resembles the operations of a higher or transcendental daycare.

In my estimation, such classes are nothing less than resounding failures and are symptomatic of a profound betrayal *of the student*. I regard a successful class as one in which (let us say and hope) fifteen students respond with growing delight and interest to the complexity of the material, experiencing not only a renewed conviction of the importance of education but also a demonstrable change of the sensibility (naturally, the extent of this change will vary from student to student). Another fifteen, as the reality principle dictates, will probably fail to meet the challenge of the bipolar paradigm based on the principles of textuality, narrativity, and dialogism, thus representing the inevitable class erosion. The middle ten will proceed to muddle through, denizens of Dante's Vestibule "whose lives knew neither praise nor infamy." The grade average, with luck, will likely hover between the sixty to sixty-five per cent mark. This is by no means the ideal scenario, the longed-for utopian class – Thomas More's Raphael remarks, "with such students I knew I wouldn't be wasting my time" – but no teacher ever expects the irruption of miracle. A realistic teacher will accept class losses in the range of thirty-five to forty per cent and a miscellaneous stratum of twenty-five per cent who perform neither badly nor well, in the interests of the "sacred remnant" who are redeemable, educable, willing to work, and susceptible of a desire to learn – who are what I have called "response-able."

Although these remarks will no doubt strike many readers as repellently elitist or archaically aristocratic, I believe that a *viable* democracy cannot prosper, let alone survive, if it neglects the principle of excellence in its educational procedures. As Hilda Neatby, no pedagogical fascist, trenchantly observes in *So Little for the Mind*: "The 'democratic society' in the name of which education is being steadily watered down lives only in the creative efforts of the gifted few ... and on the ability of the majority in varying degrees to inspire, support, and use them." And both Neatby (in *A Temperate Dispute*) and Jacques Barzun (in *Teacher In America* and again, later, in *The House of Intellect*) bolster their arguments by referring to Thomas Jefferson's plan for education in Virginia, that "the twenty best geniuses be raked annually from the rubbish" and be sent to the University. Barzun remarks, "No one can accuse Jefferson of harbouring undemocratic feeling," and Neatby comments, "What Jefferson desired ... was not that a new kind of democratic education be devised for the common man, but that the essential values of the old aristocratic education be made available to the common man." *Res ipso loquitur*.[21]

APPENDIX ONE: THE GOOD TEACHER

The concept of the "good teacher" is subjected to thoroughgoing analysis in *Education Lost*, chapter 2. The notion is by no means as self-evident as it may initially appear, and Carl Rogers's celebrated definition of the good teacher as one who possesses an "unconditional positive regard" for the child takes far too much for granted.

It is probably more useful to work within the terms of the recent philosophical debate on the subject of the good. As is well known, G.E. Moore claims that goodness is a simple indefinable property like yellowness, but that, unlike yellowness, it must be conceived as non-natural, and there the matter appears to rest. But as philosophical commentators such as P.T. Geach and Bernard Williams have pointed out, Moore's apodictic assertion errs in confusing predicative adjectives with attributive. "Yellow" is predicative since it admits of the analysis: "That is a yellow bird" = "That is a bird and it is yellow." But "good" is attributive since the affirmation "He is a good hockey player" does not yield the constituent or embedded statements, "He is a hockey player and he is good."

An attributive adjective is one, as Bernard Williams points out, that is "logically glued" to its substantive. In other words, the sentence "She is a good teacher" does not justify the logically connected assertions, "She is a teacher and she is good." Thus what is intended by the phrase, "the good teacher," turns out to be an attributive problem and demands for its analysis, from a grammatical standpoint, an inquiry into precisely what it is that makes an adjective attributive, and from a moral-epistemological perspective, an investigation into that set of qualities and attributes that modify the vocational essence of the pedagogical sensibility.

The concept of attributiveness (rather than predicativeness) strongly suggests that these qualities are neither *detachable* from the personality nor *derivable* from external sources, which accounts for the tenor of my argument in *Education Lost* that the necessary properties that determine the "good" teacher *cannot be acquired.* They are attributive and therefore "glued" to their substantive, being intrinsic and essential. But that does not mean they cannot be perfected, cultivated, refined, reinforced, "educated," if they are already inherent – which is precisely what the bipolar paradigm assumes and attempts to achieve with the properly prepared "good" teacher. Or in the words of Henry Fielding, albeit in a somewhat different context, "It is much easier to make good men wise than to make bad men good."[22]

APPENDIX TWO: THE METACOGNITIVE POLE

The superaddressee at the apex of the communications model, functioning as the "conscience" of the speech event, represents the ethico-cognitive dimension of the dialogical transaction. Its presence is vital for the success of the pedagogical event. The reason is not far to seek. Genuine learning is always in some measure a function of the *desire* to learn, and it is this very desire, this awareness of lack, upon which – as Hegel established, to be followed by Jacques Derrida, Jacques Lacan, René Girard, and many other semioticians – the sense of self depends. But the consumption of the object that temporarily satisfies that lack is also understood as a *negation* of it, i.e., a denial of dependency, which would partially explain why that which is learned (the consumption of the pedagogical object) is so often forgotten. Hegel concluded that genuine self-consciousness can only truly emerge when desire is no longer oriented toward a perishable object but rather toward another sentient subject. "The long peregrination of consciousness toward an adequate concept of itself" (as Peter Dews puts it), which is one of the major desiderata of education, can only begin when reciprocity becomes possible without coercion.[23]

Thus the teacher (or addresser) must also be regarded as surrogate, deputy, or embodiment of the "author," now understood, in a further extension of the Bakhtinian insight, as *both* superaddressee and superaddressor. That is, the teacher teaches both *towards* the author (in the name of the tradition) and *as* the author (representative or embodiment of the tradition), thus providing the student not only with a pedagogical object to be consumed (Text A) but with a model of reciprocal subjectivity (author/teacher: a tradition represented by the individual at the head of the class) towards which the student is cognitively and imaginatively oriented. The class is then a learning site in which the faltering but questing subjectivity of the student comes to a progressively more adequate concept of itself, or in which the student recognizes that *his or her identity is a function of continuous learning.* And such learning, once again, entails far more than the mere passive consumption of a pedagogical object, which is always partially negated or forgotten, but involves the strenuous and imaginative *adequation of the self* in the eventual correspondence with another approbative subjectivity.[24]

Similarly, for the social philosopher Jürgen Habermas, the truth cannot be established by an appeal to ultimate evidence (Text A). There must always be a consensus basis for the articulation of truth, an engagement to provide grounds. This requires the assumption of what Habermas calls the "ideal speech situation" (Text B), in which dialogue is free of external constraints and internal distortions. Although this situation will always be improbable, we must *presuppose* the ideal conditions of dialogue to be ultimately realizable, even as we know simultaneously that such cannot be the case. We cannot evade the structural limitations of "communicative reason." Yet in order for authentic dialogue to occur, the meeting of mind with mind under conditions of respect, reciprocity, and at least partial transparence must be, if only asymptotically, both postulated and attempted. But this can only be done, it seems to me, under the benevolent auspices of the surperaddressee, the "absent presence" of the cultural authority whose recognition evokes the assumption of continuity and mutual implication in the historical field, as well as the reverence, concern, and interest without which education degenerates into parody or resentment. And insofar as the teacher manifests as the representative of this authority (author, discipline, tradition), the superaddressee will also manifest as superaddressor.

It is for this reason that the Paideiac theory that classifies teacher and student as *equals* is so misguided and counter-productive. Teacher and student are not equals, they are *friends* (sometimes) – but one necessarily takes precedence, incorporating *the respect for* as well as *the presence of* the cultural authority, without which the learner cannot experience that combination of delight and deference on which all genuine learning depends. And only when the student is made conscious of this reciprocal dynamic will he or she have interiorized the metacognitive pole of the learning context which, apart from the assimilation of material, signifies the other, crucial dimension of what we intend by "education."

APPENDIX THREE:
APROPOS THE CRISIS IN CONTEMPORARY EDUCATION

The bipolar model is text-and-author centred, that is, *learning*-centred, rather than, as in the reigning progressivist paradigm, programmatically *learner*-centred. The rationale behind this shift of emphasis is that learner-centred pedagogy, especially at the secondary levels, leads to the "progressive" (read: regressive) re-infantilization of the student and the insensible refunctioning of the educational apparatus into a kind of monstrous kindergarten. The inevitable result of years of progressivist pedagogy is the gradual erosion of responsibility and autonomy on the part of the student and the formation of a counter-productive attitude toward the learning protocol itself: an attitude of *waiting to be helped* which in many students is inescapably transformed into an attitude of *expecting to be helped*. And this despite the fact that progressivism, associated with the illustrious names of educators like Froebel, Pestalozzi, Thorndike, and Dewey, was originally conceived as engaging the learner actively. The paradoxical results of this enlightened pedagogy are now pervasive.

While I have no quarrel with the standard perception of the teacher as a provider of assistance and encouragement – this is, after all, one of the teacher's many roles – I grow increasingly sceptical of the institutionalizing of the teacher-student relationship as a specification of the parent-child relationship, that is, of the "politically correct" consideration of the student as helpless, victimized, deficient, the necessary recipient of pedagogical charity and the object of surrogate parental love – an attitude which in the long run merely serves to confirm the student in his or her congenial inadequacy. This is not to imply that the contemporary student, generally speaking, is not under-equipped and poorly prepared to pursue an education: such is plainly more often the case than otherwise. Rather, I am suggesting that the ubiquitous tendency to regard the student as disabled and blamelessly incompetent reconfirms the attitude of passive expectation that undermines the pedagogical will and renders effort and intelligent application more and more unlikely.[25] These presuppositions which have infiltrated the educational milieu at all levels are little short of catastrophic as students are progressively disburdened of personal responsibility for their choices, comportment, and development.

Furthermore, in the present context such perceptions or considerations tend to be reinforced by brute economic factors. One of the most resonant rallying cries in the current situation is that of "student retention," which means the retaining of students in our classes and colleges so as to preserve a competitive edge vis-à-vis other institutions and thus to protect our jobs. I had always assumed that "student retention" had something to do with teaching in such a manner that the student would be trained and encouraged *to retain the class material* in memory as well as practice. At present, the latter translation appears somewhat naive. But the problems introduced by rampant progressivism are merely aggravated by the new retention psychology, which requires that teachers *conciliate* their students by lowering standards, relaxing evaluative procedures, and practising a kind of socio-professional condescension. This desideratum requires not that we teach our students as rigorously, effectively, and professionally as possible but rather that we keep them in our classes as long as possible or at least insure against premature drop-out by whatever means we can mobilize. Nevertheless, it is clear that many students are unready for the educational demands legitimately placed upon them and would benefit from either extensive, *extra-collegial* remedial work (which would entail *rethinking* the educational apparatus and perhaps inserting a make-up year between high school and college) or from several years spent outside the educational institution, during which time they might be expected to acquire the experience and maturity to prepare them for the exigencies of learning.

The bipolar teaching-and-learning model I have adumbrated in these pages (an elaboration of the "dramatic paradigm" proposed in *Education Lost*) is based upon the working assumption that text-and-author-centred pedagogy does not dismiss or neglect the student's best interests but, on the contrary and in the long view, serves them most faithfully and effectively. As Shaun Gallagher argues, the I-thou model of teacher-student relation is unable "to capture the hermeneutical situation of educational experience ... because such a focus explicitly leaves the subject matter outside." The subject matter itself "is the thing that must elicit interest and demand effort."[26] The student is brought to understand, implicitly and through actual practice, the necessity of *taking responsibility* for his or her education, of moving away from the temptation to passive consumption and toward the desire for active production. Similarly, the teacher arrives at the understanding that the *act* of teaching cannot be *merely* improvisatory, impres-

sionistic, oracular, or culturally unreflected. Without this sea change in pedagogical attitudes, genuine learning will remain an *ignis fatuus* leading
teachers and students in an endless chase for results that somehow always
fail to materialize. And it is much too late in the day, as well as naively
self-indulgent, to affect surprise.

In the terms of the Jakobson-Bakhtin template proposed above, the renewal of the sense of responsibility would require bringing the student within
the cultural radius of the "third," which is anathema not only to student
indolence but to teacher sentimentality as well. But this "third" may also
be regarded from a Lacanian perspective as the Other, the structural frame
and inhibiting factor that relativizes the subject and enables *relation* to occur
without fusion, imaginary dispersal, or narcissistic indifference to the world
beyond and around the self. The Lacanian diagram invariantly rotates the
triangular schema we have been using to locate the privileged perspective
at vertex C:[27]

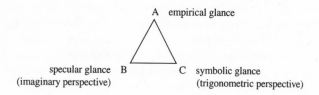

The "symbolic" (Lacan) or trigonometric perspective (as I will call it) at
vertex C, where we would now locate the super-addressee, is precisely what
rescues the empirical student at A (suffering an incapacity for difference)
and the deluded teacher at B (suffering a progressivist, imaginary fusion
with the student) from revery and encapsulation – provided both A and
B can be brought into the locus of substitution at C, that is, can valourize
the redemptive identification. Thus, if we like, we can propose a quasi-
Lacanian triangular representation of the classroom schematism, as follows:

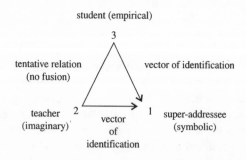

The theoretical impact of this schematism reproduces that of the previous Jakobson-Bakhtin classroom model, but brings out perhaps a little more clearly the danger inherent in teacher-student smeltdown envisioned by the progressivist model of pedagogical relationships. The mutuality of teacher and student along a single axis of relation, refusing subsumption in the symbolic totality represented by the super-addressee as Other, would result, to apply Lacan's terminology, in the construction of an "imaginary relationship." As Jane Gallop explains: "In the imaginary mode, one's understanding of other people is shaped by one's own imagoes" (i.e., unconscious images or clichés).[28] *"The perceived other is a projection," a specular double.* This is precisely how the teacher in the progressivist paradigm, which has in effect *saturated* the pedagogical sensibility, tends to regard the student, that is, in the mode of specular reproduction and *in loco parentis*.

It is, in other words, precisely this saving convergence in the "third," the establishment of a condition of intellectual unity under the auspices of the cultural authority, which so many educators remain incapable of effecting – either because they do not have the competence that comes with knowledge and discipline or because they are subject to the orgiastic enthusiasms associated with the unreflective personality. Mem Fox, the influential Australian children's writer and language teacher, is a case in point. For her the good teacher is one who "aches with caring" – a platitude repeated so often in her text the reader aches with embarrassment – who subscribes to the fairy tale of instantaneous transformations (the teacher Mrs B. in the space of half an hour breaks down in tears and experiences a wholesale change of the sensibility), who seems to spend a lot of time "weeping" and "bonding" with her charges, and whose maudlin and roseate attitude to teaching may be summarized in one sentence: "I am unashamedly present in my classroom as a pseudo parent of my vast student family because of the evidence of effectiveness of families in allowing children to learn."[29]

This is teaching founded squarely on the fusion, the melding, of the "first" and "second" along the axis of communication, invoking the model of the ideal family bathing together in a jacuzzi of intimacy and contentment. Intellectual rigour remains a scarce commodity, judging not only from Fox's gung-ho prose but from the dreary specimens of adult student writing she so copiously and jubilantly provides. But the family is clearly the wrong educational paradigm. As Jerome Bruner warns in his sceptical reflections on the linking of education with the community and family, the school is not merely "a transition zone from the intimacy of the family to the life of the community,"[30] an insight further developed by Richard Mitchell who lays it down that "Our proper business is with the Good, the True and the Beautiful, and this business can be conducted not through arousing pleasant feelings, but through working the mind." Otherwise education be-

comes little more than "the consolidation of the mundane through the accumulation of the trivial,"[31] a fair assessment of Memfoxian pedagogy or
any form of teaching that disregards the demanding requirements and the
authentically unifying effects of the cultural authority, our larger and historically sustaining "family," in which we consciously participate. It is vital
for the success of the educational project in the largest sense that we recognize the difference between the genuine participation of minds in the
culture and the raw and immediate fusion of selves in the classroom.

These considerations, I reiterate, should not be misinterpreted as pejorative or prejudicial. It is important that the student be given the chance
to develop capacities that are routinely ignored or even suppressed. The
student's assessed or attributed potentials should neither be taken as fixed
nor as inevitable once preventive circumstances have been removed. Rather,
as Israel Scheffler affirms,[32] these potentials must be stimulated and en-
hanced through the application of certain contingent variations in curricular
practice, namely "influence" (one subject area or discipline facilitating another) and "effort," which he defines as "the design of appropriate studies,
the provision of suitable training or experience, the will to learn and practice." Moreover, insofar as potential is a function of conditional prediction
and also betokens the *capability of acquisition* dependent upon individual
choice, to increase learning potential also entails putting "the means of
learning within the person's *own decision range*, to provide the basic skills,
the prerequisite knowledge and *attitudes for learning*" (italics mine). It is
my contention that the setting-in-place of a bipolar schematism in the normal
class environment constitutes precisely the contingent variations of influence
and effort and contributes as well to the faculty of acquisition-capability
that empowers the student as a progressively more autonomous and confident learner.

A class which thus takes into account what I may paradoxically call the
"reality of potential" conforms via the mode of bipolarity – the progressive
enfranchising of the student – to the structural properties of the Prigoninian
"open system" discussed earlier. The distinction introduced by Lawrence
Halprin in his important book *The RSVP Cycles*[33] between closed and open
scores is also pertinent here. A "score" is a paradigm, plan, or set of rules
for accomplishing a task, e.g., a shopping list, computer program, or agenda
of any sort. A closed score succeeds if the objective is achieved in the manner
specified in advance. An open score fails if a specific, pre-allocated objective
is achieved *without variation*. The open score allows for the spontaneous,
intuitive, innovative, and surprising in optimal classroom procedure and
may only in this attenuated way be said to comply with a prior intention,
which can never be entirely spelled out in advance. Consequently, teaching
according to a *specific* plan or agenda devoted exclusively to the assimilation
of Text A, as in the current competency-based or criterion-specific programs

that deform and mutilate teaching into the application of a set of algorithms, forecloses on the development of the student who, by contributing to the class schematism as a co-producer of Text B, assumes an equal responsibility with the teacher in the "open score" structure of learning to learn.

APPENDIX FOUR: THE PROBLEM OF TEACHER-EVALUATION.

Teacher-evaluation has recently come to the fore again as a serious and troubling issue vigorously debated in a number of competing forums. Student organizations have grown more and more inclined to develop their own protocols and questionnaires which are sometimes applied unilaterally and independently, occasionally to the chagrin and discomfiture of teachers who feel that such critical instruments are insufficiently planned, codified, and tested. The results they yield therefore tend as often as not to cloud rather than clarify the issues involved. Within departments themselves, teacher-evaluation has become a principal item on the agenda of discussion, raising a host of vexing and inconclusive questions and proposals. Should evaluation be voluntary or enforced, individual or collective, semestrial or semi-semestrial, gauged via multiple-choice score sheets or written essays or a combination of the two? What specific questions should the apparatus pose and how should they be framed? Are recommendations to be binding or merely advisory? Should the information generated by these instruments travel throughout the department or remain in the private custody of the teacher concerned? Should a para-grading system be devised to take its place alongside normative evaluation of students, so that the teacher is equally exposed to the pass-or-fail threat? Or is teacher-evaluation finally an unworkable scheme, leading to disruptions in parietal life, invasion of privacy, and various forms of invidious discrimination? May the student, often unprepared for the exigencies of collegial performance, unfledged, and self-elected, be regarded as a competent authority in such matters?

The advantage of the bipolar schematism with respect to the question of teacher-evaluation should be obvious. In this new context such evaluative procedures are integrated into the textual nature of the class as a fundamental aspect of the learning-and-teaching protocol itself. Formal questionnaires become unnecessary. The issue of confidentiality ceases to exist as a social and political abrasive. A systematic program requiring departmental unanimity, levied from outside the classroom and therefore recognized as an *imposition*, an external constraint limiting or compromising academic freedom, no longer applies. Instead – and this cannot be sufficiently over-emphasized – both teacher-evaluation and course-evaluation enter into the learning situation as *intrinsic* features of the classroom scenario, functions of a supervening textuality (Text B), with the result that learning-to-learn and learning-to-teach (the continuous modification of context, method, and approach) operate in a complementary mode. Classroom practice, both didactic and mathetic, is constantly being *adjusted* to take into account, through discussion and written input, the dynamic and *component* nature of the classroom situation.

The installation of a working bipolar model should therefore lead not only to better learning but also to better teaching (assuming, of course, the sincere and conscientious contribution of the teacher as well as of the student). When regarded as non-extraneous and uncoercive, that is, as an *inherent* unit of class procedure *per se*, both teacher-evaluation and course-evaluation are assimilated into the discursive transparency of the local class structure, where I believe they have always belonged.

POSTSCRIPT

Some of the issues I have focused on in this essay are also addressed in David Perkins's *Smart Schools*, in particular chapter 5 which deals with the creation of the metacurriculum.[34] This, Perkins suggests, "should be blended in rather than added on ... infused into the usual teaching of the subject matters, enriching and amplifying them." The metacurriculum includes among its several components the desiderata of "learning to learn" and "teaching for transfer." Transfer means that students are enabled to use "in other subject matters and outside of school what they learn in a particular subject matter."

The ability to transfer knowledge from one subject area of life to another is certainly one of the objectives of a decent education and should almost go without saying, since the alternative is mere encapsulated expertise, which is the intended result of what we usually call training. The essential structure of genuine education is always and necessarily metaphorical: the renovation of the familiar and the domestication of the unfamiliar by carrying a particular content or meaning from one dimension or experience over into another. In this sense education has always been predicated on the dynamics of metaphorical transfer, and the concept of "teaching for transfer" adds nothing to the staple educational procedures. Moreover, the ongoing debate about whether so-called thinking skills are discipline-specific or transferable across disciplines, a major preoccupation among educators since the time of E.L. Thorndike, remains a cul-de-sac. It all depends on how we define or classify "thinking." If thinking is a generalized function involving curiosity, the ability to make analytical moves in a linear and cumulative fashion, the seeking of analogies, and scepticism about immediate or apparently demonstrable results, then it is certainly transferable under conditions of enlightened instruction. (As Harriet Vane puts it in Dorothy Sayers's *Gaudy Night*: "If you learn how to tackle one subject – any subject – you've learnt how to tackle all subjects.") But if thinking is more narrowly defined as entailing specific procedures and operations required by certain disciplines and turning, so to speak, on different pivots of verifiability, then it probably is not.

I am concerned with here neither metaphorical transfer (which should be standard practice) nor transferability of "thinking skills" (which remains problematic) but the shift or displacement of the proper pedagogical attitudes freely across the curriculum and into the region of habitual experience as well. If one learns properly in one subject, in large measure by interrogating the natural process of query and assimilation and by developing an interest both in the subject being studied and in the nature of the performance required for mastery, then one will learn better not only in the discipline under consideration but in other disciplines too. What we are dealing with here is not the debatable transplantation of mental operations but a sort of *affective convection*, a willingness to adopt the catechetical view (sometimes and rather weakly called a "thinking disposition") which manifests as curiosity, wonder, desire, effort, and openness to the new and the difficult. This assumption is based on the following premises:

a. Any and every subject is inherently interesting if it is nontrivial (and even the trivial may be interesting if investigated from a higher-order or cultural perspective). Even a poorly taught subject is *intrinsically* interesting. Boredom is in the student, not the subject.[35]

b. Metacognitive attention and inquiry stimulates interest and enhances learning ability across the curriculum by indicating the kind of *stance or attitude* that favours the assimilation and integration of new material.[36]

The point is not whether certain forms of problem solving, decision making, or causal reasoning – what we habitually misconceive as thinking "strategies" or "skills" – are exportable from one discipline or context to another: it is the extent to which students are capable of developing a passionate attitude toward knowledge, a desire to appropriate the new *on its own terms* as well as its enabling assumptions and methods into the stuff of one's own experiencing. And even if the new subject is perceived as alien to one's talents and aptitudes, one can still learn something about these talents and aptitudes (or apt études) via the mode of their proprietary resistance which may eventually lead to their partial modification. My basic thesis is wholly commonsensical: *Good learning is founded on the education of desire to a far greater degree than it is on the refinement or manipulation of thinking "strategies."* And this entails kindling a respect for the "cultural authority" under whose aegis we collaboratively study and work. I doubt very much that there exists somewhere in the pedagogical empyrean a set of miraculous "systematic methods to help students to think and perform more effectively," as the blurb to *Smart Schools* promises.[37] Many of these putative "methods," if examined dispassionately, turn out to be little more than teased, distilled, enumerated, and docketed principles of common sense. The answer to our predicament will not be found here but only in the substantial renovation of the moral and intellectual character which the home in particular and the culture in general are responsible for providing.

This goes some way, perhaps, toward explaining why some of our so-called advanced proposals for new educational paradigms merely beg the question they so earnestly seek to answer. I am thinking in particular of Lewis J. Perelman's *School's Out* which, while legitimately taking exception to moribund educational structures and policies, trades in the vision of a technotopian future in which archaic learning habits will be superseded by something called "hyperlearning" mediated through information technology.[38] This new venture is predicated on the abandonment of the school as we have come to know it and the pedagogical tradition associated with it in favour of a learning environment nomadically extended throughout a cultural economy based on corporate modes of exchange and informational circuitry. "We have the technology today," Perelman exults, "to enable virtually anyone ... to learn anything, at a 'grade A' level, anywhere, anytime." Perelman is guilty of the same mistake as Perkins and so many other Erewhonian educators who fail to realize that *learning is not in the technology but in the learner* and who succumb to the siren temptation of equating information with knowledge and technique with ability, listening to the seductive harmonies of capital and data humming through the soundcard of the millennium.

I would be willing to give odds that both Perkins and Perelman are the privileged recipients of a strong traditional education, linear, conservative, cumulatively sequenced, and energized by the occasional powerful teacher cast in the ancestral mould, and that anyone educated according to the revolutionary models they recommend would be unable to compose such initially persuasive books as these. For both *Smart Schools* and *School's Out* are passionately argued and undeniably intelligent works, even if they are wrong-headed and infected by a kind of superfuture virus, a strange flu of technoleptic infatuations, to which these authors should, perhaps, have been immune. I remain convinced there can be no "progress," no improvement in our deteriorating situation, no accession to something demonstrably better until we recognize that all the "strategies," aids, techniques, media, postmodem devices, and curricular modifications in the world are merely ancillary phenomena which may certainly impinge, at times dramatically, upon our learning performance but cannot substitute for the slow and temporal development of the irreducible self nourished by a rich intellectual culture.

But the chances of such a collective change of heart and mind are negligible. Still, so long as we are constrained to manage and control the symptoms of intellectual decay – that is, to work backward from the school to the home – we should try to resist the seduction of method and technique, ultimately mere placebos. Learning to learn is all very well, clearly one of the over-subjects we must address. But how does one learn courage and faith: the courage to proceed with so hopeless a task and the faith in the power of honest and disinterested intelligence? For this is the real issue, nothing more. But plainly nothing less.

· 8 ·

Charlie Don't Surf

PREAMBLE

A few years ago while vacationing in Puerto Vallarta, I decided to initiate myself into the mystery of body surfing. The early results were drearily predictable. On my first venture into the heart of the cliché, I was unceremoniously manhandled, tossed a hundred yards further down the beach, and stripped of my expensive pair of goggles. On the second occasion the surf whipped my bathing suit off and deposited me naked on the pebbles in the full glare of amused publicity. Later on during the same instructive day I noticed a young woman bleeding from the ears and nose being attended to on the sand where she had been flung by the waves, and toward nightfall I joined a group of fishermen contemplating the prostrate form of a middle-aged man disgorged by the surf, apparently dead. An inveterate tourist, living on what Browning calls "the dangerous edge of things," I began to understand belatedly that such powerful forces are not to be trifled with but demand the respect born of disciplined foresight and intelligent effort. As one of Patrick White's characters says, "It's the edgercation that counts."

The next day I struck up an acquaintance with two experienced surfers from Hawaii who agreed to tutor me in the intricacies of my subject: the preliminary gauging of the height, velocity, and distance of the incoming comber, the noting of its colour and shape, and the sensing of the current as one swam out to meet the growing wall of turbulence. One had to judge precisely the moment just before the enormous wave crested and plunged twenty-five feet above one's head and throw oneself into it with sublime assurance. If one calculated aright, the upshot was a half-mile ride at three-storey altitudes toward a paradisaical shoreline. If one faltered at the critical instant, there was nothing for it but to dive immediately under the great masonry of water and surface on its yonder side to await the next wave on its journey in from the Pacific. If one guessed wrong or hesitated, especially when a long way out, the sequel did not bear much considering.

There is a surf in the affairs of men which needs to be studied, gauged, respected, and mastered if one is to be carried toward the comparative haven envisioned by the conduct of our education.[1] This surf is what the Catholic philosopher Paul Virilio calls "embodied time,"[2] the great prenoetic force that imparts the gift of a direction and a destination, a potential identity, upon our lives but that, if unrecognized or misapprehended, leads inevitably to dispersal, confusion, anarchy, despair, *zerstreutsein*. The *awareness* of this interior state, of the dismemberment of self that follows upon the hubris of mere indolence or the confident assumption of privilege, constitutes the *preliminary stages* of education, as chronicled in the following uncollected poem written shortly after my thalassic misadventures.

Surf

The sea collects its miles one by one,
gaining power from distance;
hoves up like a chest of drawers
in a child's nightmare,
gathers in bulk and muscle as it approaches
tearing seagulls wing from wing
and scattering plumage all about,
shoves its hummocks on
paunch by shoulder
peaking to avalanche,
combs, crests, and

sends its miles crashing down
in roiling rack and spew and thrashing havoc.
It strips the seamask from the face,
lifts, slams
you down upon the underwater tarp,
loops you through its hollow suddens,
batters breath,

and with a queer tropical fastidiousness
peels you like a fruit.

So, picking gold from the finger,
modesty from the loins,
it spits you naked on the beach at last
like a little plum pit,
then with a parting kick
that turns your ribs to mush
rolls its haunches to the sealine
without a backward look,
like the oldest father
leaving you nothing but an education.

The progressive negotiation and mastery of the temporal dimension of
our existence – the assimilation of history into one's structure of response,
which, in the words of Agnes Heller, transforms "contingency into destiny"[3]
– comprises the *ultimate purpose* of education, an idea I tried to capture
in a poem I wrote several years later.

Windsurfing

It rides upon the wrinkled hide
of water, like the upturned hull
of a small canoe or kayak
waiting to be righted – yet its law
is opposite to that of boats,
it floats upon its breastbone and
brings whatever spine there is to light.
A thin shaft is slotted into place.
Then a puffed right-angle of wind
pushes it forward, out into the bay,
where suddenly it glitters into speed,
tilts, knifes up, and for the moment's
nothing but a slim projectile
of cambered fibreglass,
peeling the crests.

The man's
clamped to the mast, taut as a guywire.
Part of the sleek apparatus
he controls, immaculate nerve
of balance, plunge and curvet,
he clinches all component movements

into single motion.
It bucks, stalls, shudders, yaws, and dips
its hissing sides beneath the surface
that sustains it, tensing
into muscle that nude ellipse
of lunging appetite and power.

And now the mechanism's wholly
dolphin, springing toward its prey
of spume and beaded sunlight,
tossing spray, and hits the vertex
of the wide, salt glare of distance,
and reverses.

         Back it comes through
a screen of particles,
scalloped out of water, shimmer
and reflection, the wind snapping
and lashing it homeward,
shearing the curve of the wave,
breaking the spell of the caught breath
and articulate play of sinew, to enter
the haven of the breakwater
and settle in a rush of silence.

Now the crossing drifts
in the husk of its wake
and nothing's the same again
as, gliding elegantly on a film of water,
the man guides
his brash, obedient legend
into shore.[4]

In short, what our culture seems to have forgotten or consigned to perilous neglect is the indispensable problematic of temporal surfing.

WADING OUT

Time is reduced to presence, the content of a series of discontinuous moments.

                                      Ronald Sukenick

If memory stands as the interior analogue of the surrounding and pervasive dimension of time that controls and disposes, then it follows that the contempt or indifference with which time is regarded must have a corresponding effect on memory as the medium in which identity coheres or out of which it gradually crystallizes. As memory decays, identity grows ever more ephemeral and capricious, becoming merely reactive in nature and turning education, as the school of the self, into nothing so much as a parody of its declared intentions and its own historical development. That is, education becomes a species of induction into a trade or profession demanding a specific set of skills, facts, and rules, hard enough to acquire yet completely detachable from the self which it is presumably intended to qualify or redeem. The agenda of education today envisions and even sanctions the erasure of time and the ensuing cancellation of the temporal, reflective, and coherent self, which can now only react to the challenge of a task or extend itself anonymously into a series of procedural applications.

Regarding this dilemma from the standpoint of Wilhelm Dilthey's celebrated "three categories of thought," i.e., value, purpose, and meaning, associated respectively with present, future, and past, one might say that the static or fundamentally discontinuous self is certainly able to isolate values and to project these from within the bubble of the present into a featureless or deceptively hopeful future. But values and purposes may exist paratactically, in a kind of patternless assemblage, without attaining to definition and cohesiveness. As David Carr writes, "Only the category of meaning overcomes the chaos of this array and brings order. Under this category belongs the notion of the development of a life." In other words, it is the category of meaning, founded in the past and in the deep sense of the temporal current in which we move and which moves through us, that "encompasses and orders the things we value and the purposes we pursue," enabling us to connect event, act, and memory into an integrated and conscious structure.[5]

But this linking of parts and fragments into a conceptual and experiential unity depends upon immersing the potential, reflexive self into the stream of temporal continuity. This stream differs from the mythic parabolas of "circular" time (as analysed by Mircea Eliade and Claude Lévi-Strauss) as well as from the mere segmentations of linear time that increasingly characterize the nature of contemporary experience. Neither circular nor mechanically linear, *continuous time* carries us toward the syntactical and dynamic parsing of the truly historical world in which we occasionally live. As John Ralston Saul remarks, "We may remember the event of two days ago, but we cannot remember the passage of the two days ... Without an ordered memory, civilization is impossible."[6] (Saul denominates as "linear memory" what I believe is more accurately rendered as "continuous memory.") Further, by "continuous time" is also meant – if it is not already self-evident – the ability to make distinctions in relative temporality. For many of my students there seems to be no distinction between events that occurred in the fourth century – say the Christianizing of the Roman Empire under Constantine – and in the eighteenth century – say the French Revolution. The past exists as a kind of formless amalgam in which events tend to have all occurred simultaneously. The past is simply a single, external "then" as the present is a single, eternal "now" which almost immediately joins the amorphous and largely irrecoverable "then" of a yesterday that remains virtual, flat, uni-dimensional, and irrelevant.

The opposite of continuous time is not extinction but the poor man's eternity, the world of discrete and serial instantaneities, a form of static movement, the succession of non-incremental "nows" in which so many of our students live and move and have their flickering, hyphenated beings. If one does not live securely in continuous time, in its gradual distillations from the prenoetic to the teleological, then one cannot formulate a credible syntax of existence predicated on the integrated, *synthesizing* relation of parts along a temporal axis. For it is only in continuous or *contextual* time that one can establish an identity that is both uniquely personal and authentically historical.

The relation we are investigating, then, holds between the "categories" of time, memory, and identity and, depending on its strength or lack of it, is responsible for the construction or disintegration of the self. *Time is the medium of emergence*, which Emmanuel Levinas defines as "a dynamism which leads us elsewhere than toward the things we possess" (or, we might add, the things we do not possess).[7] Memory may be construed as both the faculty that grammaticizes time – shaping, organizing, editing, and synthesizing the flood of featureless event in the direction of narrative coherence – and also as the interior *analogue* of time (much as the conscience internalizes a set of external macroscopic norms – the superego, so to speak, of temporality. Interestingly, Sir Thomas Browne in *Christian Morals* defines conscience as the "the punctual Memorist within us"). Identity is a kind of temporal thickening which resists the forces of dispersal and randomness that constantly threaten.[8] Where the relation no longer holds, or obtains only in a fluctuating and unpredictable way, we find ourselves confronting what Agnes Heller refers to as a swarm of "thin identities," a world growing increasingly uneducable.[9]

It is precisely here, in the failure of memory or retrocognition, that we may locate the irruption of *gratuitous* violence. The individual for whom history carries no particular urgency – or for whom time is merely a burden that oppresses the inchoate sense of absolute freedom incarnated in the moment – can blithely and impenitently deny *anything*, on any scale of magnitude. Thus the Holocaust never happened, despite the crushing weight of historical testimony and the poignant testimony of living survivors. Thus Charles Manson may be reappropriated as a cult hero since the brutal murders he committed occurred in 1969 and therefore, from the perspective of the dystemporal sensibility, are no more than figments, ciphers, non-events. Thus the individual on the level of ordinary domestic time forgets or violates the inner laws of his or her own moral and intellectual development that establish the *person* as a responsible agent in the dimension of emergence and continuity, that is, in the world of *humanized* time or radical – rooted – temporality. Charlie ain't the only one who don't surf.[10]

The recognition of radical temporality is what is always being forgotten by professional educators, a lapsus common to the western philosophical tradition as a whole. Even Kant backed away from the notion that the subject is constituted in time through the synthetic unity of the transcendental imagination, revising the concept of radical temporality out of the 1781 edition of the *Critique of Pure Reason* and replacing it in the second edition of 1787 with the idea of the *atemporal* realm of pure thought as the condition underlying the possibility of experience. Western thinking has always had trouble with the theory and experience of time, which is why antinomian thinkers like Bergson, Heidegger, Whitehead, and Derrida have become so important to us today. "For it is time," as Ned Lukacher writes, "that is at the very root of our capacity to feel and to think. The categories of sensory and conceptual experience are rooted in the primordial time-sense of the imagination."[11] And educational thinking, as the most critical and pertinent branch of epistemology, can least afford to succumb to the crippling theoretical amnesia that has beset the philosophical tradition since its official beginnings in the work of Plato. We are in fact the victims of a double forgetting, for until recently radical temporality was always assumed in practice though rarely disengaged as a theoretical principle. Today it is no longer even assumed, as the conduct of liberal education proceeds at almost every level in a historical vacuum, in a *discretum* rather than a continuum.

SURFING

Long for transformation. O be fervent for the fire
in which something boasting of changes escapes from you

Rainer Maria Rilke

The rediscovery of time on which contemporary education stands or falls (or rather, sinks or swims) depends in part upon finding, developing, or disambiguating appropriate metaphors from within the turmoil and ferment of our experience. In fact, not merely the judicious application of metaphor but the *living out of one's experience through the conscious agency of metaphor itself* serves as one form of temporal rehabilitation. For our purposes, the four basic rhetorical tropes that organize the linguistic architecture of experience – metaphor, metonymy, synecdoche, and irony – may be understood as reducing to two, since synecdoche is really a specification of metonymy (part for whole as an aspect of contiguity and association) while irony, like the Fourth Gospel, differs from the original synoptic three in terms of negative complexity and the introduction of an external context. Moreover, from the perspective of temporality, we may plausibly regard the metonymical series of parts and functions as falling under the aegis of metaphor precisely because metaphor *constitutively* embodies or incorporates the stream of temporal development in its intrinsic mode of operation. That is, metaphor is the central tropological function not only because it is based on the principle of transformation but also because it *incarnates and performs* within its very *modus operandi*, as a linguistic motor or transformer, the activity on which it is theoretically predicated. Metaphor practises what it preaches.

Perhaps it would be more accurate, though no doubt a trifle clumsy, to propose a new term for the hypostasis of the temporal continuum within the operation of the trope. Since metaphor works by developing transformations and metonymy by generating sequences, and since both figures of speech combine in the production of *sequences of transformations*, we might designate the primordial *ur*-trope as *metaphoronymy*,[12] the primary or central rhetorical device that mirrors and reproduces the process of temporal development. But it does even more. Not only does metaphoronymy *take time* to develop in itself as a spool of signifiers unravelling across a sentence or an utterance, it also generates the *inner sense of temporality* by virtue of the presuppositions embedded in its epistemological structure. That is, the first term in what is essentially a knowledge generator requires to be completed or matched by a second term that unfolds or discovers or elaborates the implications contained potentially in the opening gambit of the trope and that may even be said to propagate novelty.[13] The initial term launches or catalyses an internally emergent effect that, in lexical or symbolic form, arrives to fill in the epistemic blank. Metaphoronymy schematizes and reproduces the temporal code inherent in the workings of logical presupposition or narrative implicature – *it tells the story of time itself* as it amplifies its semantic plot and completes the expectant emptiness at the heart of tropological implication. All speakers by virtue of the free gift of language are subsumed into the temporal process of psychic emergence; but where the metaphorical transaction is reduced to the level of unreflected cliché and language becomes merely reactive, fragmented, unconscious, and almost entirely *reproductive* rather than generating new possibilities of meaning and fresh tropological substitutions – in other words, where renewal collapses into repetition and attendant expectation into apriori satisfaction – then the deep sense of temporal continuity, founded in the operations of language, is weakened and dispersed. The linguistic surfer does not so much arrive at an intended destination as find himself or herself thrown up widdershins and akimbo on the beach.[14]

The metaphoronymical function, the "mechanics" of generative implication, may be (somewhat whimsically) schematized as follows:

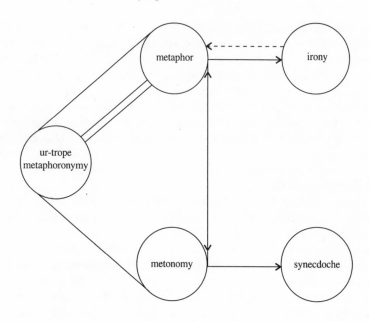

The Tropological Machine

   The ur-trope is perhaps best visualized as a temporal vector inherent in
the psychic structure that grounds the operation of linguistic implicature.
We are not here considering the naming or referential function of language,
our Adamic inheritance, which is no doubt primary, but the secondary function of *rhetorical displacement*, of one name presupposing another that
substitutes, completes, modifies, or extends its predecessor. When language
refers to things or events in the world, it performs in the referential mode,
and even here the temporal dimension is invoked through the medium of
absence; that is, when the named element is missing, it is recuperated inwardly through fear, anxiety, hope, or the primitive sense of possibility.
But such temporality is comparatively crude and internally undifferentiated.
When, however, the reference is autotelic, that is, when a part of language
refers not to thing or event but to *another part of language* (which may
itself be referential in the primary sense), or when the element that is designated remains *initially* unspecified but is nevertheless *required* by the
maiden term to realize its potential, the process we have called metaphoronymy comes into play and the tropological machine is activated. The workings of implicature or rhetorical displacement, its psychic structure one of
expectation and necessity, of semantic intention, generates the deep sense
of coherent, meaningful, developing time – even prior to the stage of
sensitivity-to-narrative and without which the narrative chain could not be

forged. The metaphorical transformation, sparked into existence, as it were, by the linguistic solenoid or current of intention at the source of communicative desire (or is it necessity?), is then diffused through metonymical (and synecdochic) sequencing and, at a more sophisticated level of verbal process, reversed or dissembled by irony (which, like metaphor, is based on the principle of similarity in difference and difference in similarity – but this is another story.) For our purposes it is sufficient to recognize the essential relation between tropology and temporality, rhetorical displacement and the sense of cumulative, "historical," *meaningful* time. (And whether this operation is itself metaphorized as a "machine," a game, an athletic activity, or in any other way remains indifferent, provided it refracts the sense of a *developing* temporal process.)

As for "education," which is itself an extended metaphor in both its etymological and operational aspects, this requires from its practitioners and beneficiaries a healthy and vivacious sense of metaphorical (or metaphoronymical) involvement.[15] A conscious and deliberate hospitality to the exigencies of basic metaphorical thinking remains the *sine qua non* of all educational practice, far more than the application of pedagogical methods and contrivances to the teaching protocol or the introduction of the latest technological inventions and refinements into the classroom. It is poetic metaphor and not instructional science that makes for an authentic teacher. Similarly it is the educational metaphor itself, as well as the deployment of rich and pertinent metaphors as such, that allows the recipient to presuppose an evolving and increasingly complex self and that makes for the genuine student.[16] Education is essentially a metaphorical process that works through the transformation of the given and the consequent projection of the new.

But once the teacher has acquired or developed what we might call metaphorical competence, the inner disposition to regard the teaching event *sub specie translationis* – thus building temporality into the very structure of presentational assumptions that underlie the act of teaching-and-learning as a transformation of the sensibility – the next step is to disengage the appropriate set of metaphors, those intended to counteract the baleful effects of stasis and discontinuity afflicting the educational scene today. And these would have to be *temporal metaphors*, in other words, metaphors that not only schematize the process of logical presupposition and narrative implicature but also *focus* on the crucial topic of gradual development in time. For the major casualty of modern education, which creolizes our awareness of temporal relation and accidence, is time itself – which has suffered both dilution and compression at the hands of the technological paradigm. As Jean Baudrillard claims, technology is about disappearances, of history into simulacrum, objects into images, reality into virtuality, ends into means, and time itself into a scattergram of serial instantaneities.[17] And one of the ways in which this apocalyptic cancellation proceeds is through the worship of pure velocity, the apotheosis of impatience. Technology as the productive application of the human mind to the solution of "problems" may be expected to produce benefits we would be foolish not to welcome and pursue. But as a *paradigm* of human thought, feeling, and activity, an ideal that we strive to approximate in our intellectual and affective lives, it is nothing short of cataclysmic, since it tends to marginalize or cancel the deep, interior, prenoetic current of emergent temporality.

This is because technology works towards the collapse of the interval between input and output, the erasing of the distance not just between means and ends but between beginnings and ends. In an era of "dromocratic technology," as Paul Virilio argues, we have become "speed flesh," "bodies without wills," and "metabolic vehicles" waiting to be boarded by sheer virtuality.[18] The notion of speeding-up is crucial, as we continue to accelerate into the self-contained and ideally static moment.

Virilio claims that the technological project is dedicated to the disappearance of the self, seducing us to identify with the neutralizing transparency of pure velocity, the "ideal vector" of acceleration that relieves us of the imperative of concrete existence, of the slow exfoliations of identity, and the stringent obligation of continuous presence. The individual, subject to the demands of technological instantaneity, grows distressingly "picnoleptic," that is, becomes the victim of frequent time lapses, gaps in the memoried continuum of conscious life. As Virilio sees it, the individual ceases to pray or converse, activities dependent on the expressive sublimity of patience, but rather stutters, curses, falls back on the automatism of jargon, or simply remains silent, living out a technological parody of religious transcendence, entering "a technical beyond, finally as mysterious as that of the old religions."[19] Or in the words of Milan Kundera, "Time becomes a mere obstacle to life, an obstacle that [has] to be overcome by ever greater speed."[20] We have entered the realm of the quantum sensibility, emitting transient photons of gestural utterance, as we vanish from one orbit of our experience and reappear in another without having crossed the intervening distance.

Consequently, to return to the subject of metaphor, the highway has superseded the road or the path as a favourite symbol of human endeavour, which is now conceived as a line that leads directly from one point to another and, what is more, as a line that shrinks proportionally to the increase of pure, insensate, life-eclipsing speed. How far we have come from the redemptive and propitious metaphor of the anabasis, the gradual odyssey of learning, whether imagined as a winding road or a sea journey that does not just traverse a distance but explores (and even suffers) a timescape! Consider, for example, the celebrated poem of Constantine Cavafy, which we could do worse than adopt as an emblem or prototype of the educational adventure.

Ithaca

When you start on your journey to Ithaca,
then pray that the road is long,
full of adventure, full of knowledge.
Do not fear the Lestrygonians
and the Cyclopes and the angry Poseidon.
You will never meet such as these on your path,
if your thoughts remain lofty, if a fine
emotion touches your body and your spirit.
You will never meet the Lestrygonians,
the Cyclopes and the fierce Poseidon,
if you do not carry them within your soul,
if your soul does not raise them up before you.
Then pray that the road is long,
that the summer mornings are many,
that you will enter ports seen for the first time
with such pleasure, with such joy!
Stop at Phoenician markets,
and purchase fine merchandise,
mother-of-pearl and corals, amber and ebony,
and pleasurable perfumes of all kinds,
buy as many pleasurable perfumes as you can;
visit hosts of Egyptian cities,
to learn and learn from those who have knowledge.

Always keep Ithaca fixed in your mind.
To arrive there is your ultimate goal.
But do not hurry the voyage at all.
It is better to let it last for long years;
and even to anchor at the isle when you are old,
rich with all that you have gained on the way,
not expecting that Ithaca will offer you riches.

Ithaca has given you the beautiful voyage.

Without her you would never have taken the road.
But she has nothing more to give you.

And if you find her poor, Ithaca has not defrauded you.
With the great wisdom you have gained, with so much experience,
you must surely have understood by then what Ithacas mean.[21]

The teacher teaches by slowing down, stopping often, rediscovering time on the way to Ithaca.[22] The results of this slow and variegated journey, enriched by progressive deferrals, are educational in the true sense of the term because they generate an inner process of transformation, a species of metamorphosis that brings the traveller into harmony or, failing so elusive a goal, at the very least into productive tension with the great temporal forces that encompass our existence: history and nature. I will ask the reader to consider one more poem in the little anthology I have assembled here, a sonnet by Rainer Maria Rilke which refocuses the metaphor of the journey as self-transmutation.

Archaic Torso of Apollo

We did not know his unfamiliar head
Where hung the ripening apples of his eyes,
But still his torso candelabra-wise
Glows, where his gazing, screwed back from the dead,

Holds itself back and gleams. The bow of the breast
Could not else blind you, nor in subtle turning
Of loins could a smile break that goes there yearning
To that mid-place which held the seeds at rest.

Else would this stone, short and disfigured, cower
Under the shoulders' dropped, transparent power
Nor shine like sparkling skins of beasts of prey
And would not from all contours of the knife
Break starlike out: for there is no place, nay,
Which does not see you. You must change your life. [23]

TOWELLING DOWN

Factically the existent Dasein has forgotten the prius.

                                                    Martin Heidegger

Such metaphors as I am proposing here with their defining temporal content seem to me to yield rich dividends for educational thinking. But whatever set of metaphors one decides to work with, they must be chosen with a scrupulous eye for context.[24] Israel Scheffler in a recent book devotes an important chapter to the consideration of some of the most common metaphors governing our way of thinking about education in general, of which he identifies four: horticulture, ceramics, sculpture, and organic function. (See appendix.) Frank Smith isolates five such proprietary metaphors, which he dismisses as "misleading": information, process, skills, levels, and stages.[25]

For my own part the metaphorical constructs I find most congenial, as they apply both to general considerations and to actual classroom practice, inevitably entail the dynamics of process and development. Sometimes, for example, I regard the grammatical sentence in the active voice as not only a syntactical apparatus for the production of meaning but as a small metaphor for education itself, with the subject representing the unformed or inchoate self (a collection of drives, wants, fears, and unreflected assumptions), the predicate as the learning transaction which processes the raw material by gathering and directing it toward a coherent future, and the object as the momentarily realized self which may now enter into a new and more complex sentence as a more developed subject.

In facetious moments I turn to the metaphor of champagne making, which strikes me as enormously appropriate to the educational process. The first step is critical, the cuvée of chosen wines to be blended, since the quality of the blended wines is all-important for the eventual result – something that wine-makers know but educators would prefer to forget. The second step, the addition of special yeast and sugar, completes the primary stage. There follow three subsequent procedures, roughly co-terminous with secondary education, namely the second fermentation, the bottling to retain the carbonic pressures, and the "schooling" of effervescence into a stable component of the wine. Finally, at the highest levels, we find the double process of *remuage* or riddling, that is, dislodging the sediment, and of *dosage*, the addition of rock-crystal sugar and brandy to determine final sweetness or dryness. The champagne metaphor, with its temporal substratum and inherent complexity, is eminently suited as a model of the educational project.

But I return to the metaphor with which I began, riding the surf, *riding time*, as an expressive analogue of the process that genuine education incorporates and enacts, as I have ridden a surf of temporal metaphors to carry me to my conclusion in this chapter. Memory, the educational desideratum, should be understood not simply as the faculty that reassembles the world into which we are obscurely thrown[26] but also as the *interior dimension of time itself*, as that which carries us toward a possible future, "elsewhere than toward the things we possess," as well as away from the moral peonage of an unillumined past. "To be free," as Terry Eagleton reminds us, "you have to remember."[27] To be a person and not a mirage, a mere fluctuation of the virtual zero, one must recognize that the past is not negotiable and the future is not an extravagance. But this is only conceivable if we are disposed to honour time as the dimension in which forgetfulness of the self and of others, the daily forfeitures of moral and intellectual cohesion, can find no purchase or nourishment.

APPENDIX

Israel Scheffler, in *In Praise of the Cognitive Emotions* (Routledge, London and New York, 1991), distinguishes some of the most common educational metaphors influencing our way of thinking about the subject. I recite them here and offer a moderate critique.

Growth. The teacher as gardener. But adults "do more than simply facilitate the child's development toward a unique stage of cultural maturity." The course of the student's cultural, social, and moral development is not divided into natural stages on a strict analogy with plant growth. Moreover, in this case, the plant is required to develop the ability to make autonomous choices.

Moulding (forming, shaping). The teacher as potter, the child as clay. But in ceramics there "is no *independent* progression toward any given shape, as there is with respect to the growth of acorns." Clay is passive, given its inherent limitations or resistances; and the potter is wholly responsible for the final outcome, as the teacher is not.

Sculpture. "The artist exercises real choice in its production; yet his initial block of marble is not wholly receptive to any idea he may wish to impose on it ... [Also] the artist's initial idea is not ... fully formed in advance, remaining fixed ... It gets the process started but is modified by the process itself, during which the artist in continually learning as well as creating." All this corresponds to education, but "the growth metaphor at least acknowledges the continuing development of the object in question after the departure of the gardener."

Organic. Its function is to preserve cultural continuity. The term "function" refers to the contribution to the normal or satisfactory biological working of the organism. However, to say that education is indispensable to the normal or satisfactory working of the culture begs the question and fudges the issue, since *moral issues* are not stressed in social "function" statements. Is education to contribute to the preservation of cultural continuity – its social function – or is it rather to disrupt the normal or satisfactory working of the culture where the latter is open to charges of immorality, violence, and fraud? (Hence Postman's "thermostatic" function of education, rather than organic function.) Social function statements are often "confused by the socially irrelevant connotation of value surrounding the term 'function.'" That is, as Dewey suggests, perhaps it is society that should serve the school rather than vice versa.

The problem with Scheffler's formulations, which are apposite as far as they go, is that they do not go far enough, stopping short of the dialectical perspective that the subject would appear to require. Scheffler conceives of education, at least in his discussion of controlling metaphors, on a strictly binary or dyadic model situating the teacher as gardener, potter, or sculptor on one side of the slash and the student as plant, pot, or statue on the other. One is active and the other receptive, and although he indicates that this paradigm is liable to break down on precisely this account, since the student must also be regarded as capable of expressing independent choice (at least in the sequel), nevertheless the metaphorical complementaries remain in place as explanatory tropes that assume an *external* encounter between those involved in the process. But the sculpture metaphor, for example, seems much less frozen and intractable once we grant that the opposing terms of the pedagogical relation are to be found ultimately *in the student*, who in this view is both sculptor and sculpture. The student is in a fair way towards acquiring an education once he replaces the binary function with the mitotic and accepts the idea of self-bifurcation, which permits him to regard the process of learning as both self-referential and self-transcendent. At this point the self splits in two in a kind of healthy, productive schizophrenia, the vital and demanding teacher-self taking in hand the lazy and insubordinate student-self, shaping it toward literacy, competence, and the psychical economy that Yeats, following Dante, called "unity of being."

For, as Freud stressed, there exists a fundamental aspect of the self which is refractory and mineral, which continually *resists* the civilizing impulse, which would rather play or dream or forget. True education recognizes the appetitive principle as one of the most basic manifestations of the self and attempts to counteract or neutralize or at least modify what is most insistent and voracious within us by introducing the teacher, who represents the other basic principle of the self, the desire for order and coherence, into the psyche of the student. The latter gradually assimilates the teacher, opposing will to wilfulness, bringing what is lithic or static to life by imposing form and by discarding as far as possible mere hyletic excrescence, all that is redundant and inhibiting. The sculpture metaphor, on this argument, works dialectically, once we are willing to admit that we are never as autonomous, initially at any rate, as we like to suppose, that we are never wholly alive to begin with, that some (we hope diminishing) part of us always remains shapeless and violent, like the figure of Death in *Paradise Lost*, "if shape it might be called that shape had none" – requiring precisely the demiurgical and preceptorial hand to keep the chaotic in check. Education re-enacts in limited compass the great iconographies and tensions of myth, poetry, and religion: the same battle is constantly being fought.

Thus the sculptor within struggles with the block of stone which is equally within, wielding the heavy-grit sandpaper, then the lighter-grit, next the black emery, laving the stone in water till it bleeds milk, drying it, polishing with heated beeswax, and finally submitting the block to endless buffing. This is one of many appropriate metaphors. The important point is that in choosing our metaphors we must remain subtle and flexible, knowing that in order to do justice to the ritual of metamorphosis that is true education, we must be suspicious of spatializing or reifying or exteriorizing our terms. For the teacher's duty is to dematerialize: in other words, by a reciprocal process of projection and osmosis, of intellectual and moral displacement, to *re-locate* as a disciplined presence in the mind and heart of the student, sponsoring the temporal process of renewal, that is, of increasing differentiation leading to paradoxical unity across a trajectory of "instruction." And the student for his or her part must know how to welcome that presence, must be willing to recover the sense of "embedded time" on which the process of self-transformation depends, however we inflect it metaphorically.[28]

· 9 ·
Teaching Down or Learning Up

Human history becomes more and more a race between education and catastrophe.

H.G. Wells, *A Short History of the World*

"Gossip," quoth the wolf, "wat nou?
Wat harvest thou imunt – wedder wolt thou?"
"Wedder Ich wille," the vox sede.
"Ich wille oup, so God me rede!"

Anonymous (thirteenth century)

Perhaps the only agreement to be found among the various competing schools of thought in the teaching community today is that we are embroiled in an educational catastrophe of the first magnitude. Beyond this initial certainty we find ourselves in a state of growing bitterness and seemingly endless discussion sinking inexorably into various forms of factional strife. We have come to resemble Poe's narrator in "A Descent into the Maelstrom," whirling around in a vortex that threatens to overwhelm us and seeking desperately for a "cylindrical object" that offers "resistance to its suction" – an approach, an attitude, a hope, a conviction, a theory that will keep us afloat or at least reduce the speed of our descent.[1] But a general consensus appears to be forming in the approximate (though non-cylindrical) shape of a *theory of condescension* that assumes that the best way of dealing with the mass of incompetent and dysfunctional students inundating the schools is to develop a *therapeutic* pedagogy that regards the student as a hybrid of innocent victim and helpless infant. This entails the core assumption that everyone is equally retrievable, the re-installation of the social niceties (avoid failing or offending anyone; cf. the now-familiar pedagogical poster that reads: "There is no such thing as failure: only feedback"), the privileging of busywork over performance, the staging of short-term reclamation projects, the parodic dilution of course content, and the consequent reduction of mentorial expectations.[2] That is, the general spirit or attitude now emerging recommends that teachers, with a mixture of realism and charity, "teach down" to the level of the student in the hope of gaining some rudimentary purchase on the unprepared and ill-furnished minds we

wish to inform and cultivate, completely reversing Matthew Arnold's celebrated dictum in his Oxford valedictory lecture that culture "does not try
to teach down to the level of inferior classes" but rather to reclaim them,
"to make the best that has been thought and known in the world current
everywhere."3 But Arnold, after all, is usually considered to be lecturing
in usum delphini. As a colleague of mine insisted in one of the conferences
that increasingly clutter the pedagogical horizon, the dilemma we face will
eventually yield to a pragmatic assessment of student abilities and the adop-
tion of an appropriate method and syllabus, which latter are to be tailored
to the current measure of inadequacy. Afterwards, according to this authority, "you just line 'em up and teach 'em."

It is my abiding fear that such a pedagogical theory, if that is what we
can call it, or that so lax and remissive an attitude to negotiating the maelstrom, will do nothing but compound the disaster. To begin with, I should
stress that I do not believe *any significant solution* is feasible in the contemporary educational environment and that what we are discussing is really
one or another way of minimizing losses that are in any case inevitable.
Too much harm has already been done – too many temporally fixed opportunities, as I will argue later, have been allowed to slip unobservedly
away – to shore up the utopian dream of *present redeemability*. But we
may perhaps recoup some of these losses and at the same time prepare
for a more sanguine future *if* we can bring ourselves to resist the seductive
hope of short-term effectiveness and to adopt a rigorous, sceptical, and unsentimental approach to the predicament of education in the present
moment.

This is why I regard the *teaching-down ethos* as delusionary, despite the
appeal it makes to the ostensibly practical or charitable teacher, and propose
instead a *learning-up model* which commends a carefully maintained severity, a kind of ascetic predisposition to the exigencies of teaching and
learning, not in order to conduct punitive raids into the field of education
but precisely to act in the long-term interests of the students whom we
wish to benefit, those we meet on a daily basis and those who will be entering
the learning institution in the years to come. Learning up means – at least
at the secondary and especially the collegiate levels – that we do not shrink
from treating students as responsible adults capable of coming to terms
with the *va-banque* wager that education represents,4 that above all things
we refrain from condescension, that we visibly expect our students to work
diligently and hard and to strive for self-transcendence – that is, to respond
to pressure-treating – and that we do not adulterate course material under
the assumption of student inadequacy, turning education, as Richard Mitchell laments, into "the consolidation of the mundane through the accumulation of the trivial."5 We will assuredly suffer heavy casualties along
the way, but it is better to lose some, even many, of our students in the

interests of the survivors than to mediocritize the entire student population for the sake of retaining intact our therapeutic ideals and our sense of diagnostic virtuosity. For this point must be grasped in all its unpleasantness: condescension to the student is merely the other face of self-flattery.

Such advocacy, I am aware, flies in the face of the vigorous "retention campaign" currently being fought in schools, newspapers, and ministries (See appendix 1). In Quebec the high school and college drop-out rate hovers around 40 per cent, which is considered patently unacceptable if not cataclysmic. For my part I fail to see what the fuss is all about. Recuperating this "lost constituency" into an educational system that ensures nothing so much as failure, incompetence, and subsequent unemployability is at best a bitter joke and at worst ... I leave the reader to complete the ellipsis. What is required before anything else is a pervasive and significant *upgrading* of the quality of education at all levels, a thorough reconsideration of what education entails – and by that I do not mean more and more "reform" – if the "lost" are eventually to be saved and the "saved" not to be inevitably lost. What is the point of reducing the drop-out rate to 5 per cent, a figure much bruited about by our elysian authorities, if retention serves as little more than a passport to apathy, ineptitude, and one or another form of bankruptcy?

But if we really wish to improve education and to do something positive and meaningful about the crisis we are all so busy normalizing, then the time has plainly come for re-thinking the educational apparatus and the set of proprietary attitudes we bring to bear on it. This means reconsidering *everything*, from our penchant for over-administration to the habitual ways in which we regard the classroom itself. With respect to the latter, I would even go so far as to propose developing the classroom analogue of Antonin Artaud's "theatre of cruelty," which is by no means "sadistic or bloody" as the name suggests but involves a form of staging illumined by the unsparing light of conscious principle. Cruelty, says Artaud, means "strictness, diligence, unrelenting decisiveness and absolute determination." And again: "Cruelty is very lucid, a kind of strict control and submission to necessity." It may prove beneficial to accustom ourselves to regard the classroom as a sort of Artaud theatre in which mere psychologizing and intrusive topicality are ruthlessly expunged, the audience is taxed to the limit, and what may be called the stigmatics of production leave a profound imprint on the minds of the observer-participants. Better this, at any rate, than the kind of street theatre currently in place, the lax productions that look so good on printout paper but generally translate into supervised mayhem.[6]

And if the true function of the classroom has something to do not with the school's retention of the student on the census – which really means job retention for the teacher – but with the student's retention of the matter on the syllabus, then we would do well to remember the Freudian-Derridean analysis of memory as a form of *resistance* offered to the stream of incoming material.[7] Memory is a double system, combining both freshness of surface (or permeability) and depth of retention (or the resistance), which allows traces to be inscribed and preserved. But there is no "breaching" or "path-breaking" (Freud), no resistance and subsequent preservation or retention without what Derrida calls "a beginning of pain" (which, in Freud's words, "leaves behind it particularly rich breaches"). This is what Nietzsche has called the science of "mnemotechnics"[8] and what Artaud, a votary of the goddess Mnemosyne, refines into the "theatre of cruelty." There is no complex learning without struggle, effort, and, yes, even a little suffering, as attested by no less an authority than the apostle of loving-kindness, Parker J. Palmer, who writes: "Good teachers know that discomfort and pain are often signs that truth is struggling to be born among us."[9]

Under the aspect of the classroom of cruelty, we would have to acknowledge that students are capable of more than we give them credit for (though often less than we give them credits for), despite the intellectual disadvantages under which they labour, *once they can be made aware* precisely what is at stake and that they are expected to take a major share of the responsibility for their own literate future. An encouraging number of my own students have approached me for extracurricular help and have undertaken various reading programs I have prepared for them, ranging from a summer's browsing to a more comprehensive multi-year syllabus. These are the students who have realized the magnitude of the issue they must address and have come to see that no single class, semester, or remedial project is sufficient to recapture the territory they have inadvertently lost. What we need to teach our students, in devising ways for them to learn up to the level of the material, is, first, the *recognition* of their predicament – which means refusing to cater to their assumptions of adequacy or innocence – and, secondly, the *conviction* that something serious has to be done and that, with energy, discipline, and humility, they are more or less capable of doing it.

Their condition of deprivation, though not their economic psychology, curiously resembles that of the students I once met in Casablanca sharing the few textbooks they could procure and studying into the small hours of the morning in the public parks where electric light was freely available. The seriousness of purpose which these students manifested in their self-directed efforts shows not only what is possible but puts to shame the indulgent attitudes and preoccupations of many of our own students for whom the cognitive requirements and constraints of genuine education seem as likely to provoke resentment and evasiveness as humility and desire.

"Without transportation, you are left to the resources of your own feet," writes one of my students in another improbable term paper. There is an important truth embedded in this ingenuous and bathetic sentence. Pramming students about from one day to the next, from one course to another, from public school to college to university, merely contributes to the habits of evasion they are in danger of entrenching. We must on the contrary give them something to reach for, and the assurance that it is worth reaching for, if they are eventually to stand up and walk. Or even better, I sometimes feel, in what remains a depressed environment in every sense of the term, to enable them at least to perform the intellectual equivalent of metro-surfing in the favelas of Rio, rather than being shunted through life by the displaced and residual momentum of an educational system fast running out of power and authority.[10]

The teaching-down syndrome (buckwheat field as opposed to burdock hut, see note 10) enjoys a very respectable pedigree, of course, and is perhaps most incisively formulated in the work of Edward Thorndike which insists that general laws of instruction be adapted to the peculiar needs of individual learners,[11] and which received its most thorough and systematic development in the "progressive," learner-centred pedagogy associated with the name of John Dewey. But in the current situation, this apparently enlightened and unexceptionable theory of instruction has led not to effective teaching, as its numerous votaries continue to claim, but to the worst forms of defective teaching. *Corruptio optima pessimi.* For we now operate in a therapeutic environment which envisions the progressive re-infantilization of the student. "The reason children are the future," writes Milan Kundera in *The Book of Laughter and Forgetting*, "is not that they will one day be grown-ups. No, the reason is that mankind is moving more and more in the direction of infancy." It is this program that constitutes the subversive agenda of "our entire technological age ... with its cult of youth and child-hood, its indifference to the past and mistrust of thought." For this reason, he suggests, those equipped with "memory and irony" come to feel like lone adults abandoned on an island of children.[12] Current pedagogy merely abets the continental drift that carries the island of children further and further away from the mainland of historical and intellectual continuity: the more we proceed to teach down, the further the island recedes with its cargo of temporal displacements. But the obligation of our profession allied with the urgency of the moment requires nothing less than a heroic and unsentimental effort to re-attach the island to the mainland, to build causeways and bridges of reinforced historicity: of memory, discipline, ability, erudition, and contextuality. (Education may be thought of in this respect as exerting a peninsular force.)

Thus the responsible teacher today must, it seems to me, do everything in his or her power to avoid the condescension and counter-productiveness implicit in teaching down to the student and invest both energy and attitude in trying to bring the student dendritically up to the level of the material.[13]

In Lacanian terms, the teacher is engaged in writing and sending a letter
to the student – the letter of education, the message that everything is at
stake in the serious reception of the material and its gradual transformation
and incorporation into the sensibility. What Lacan in his Seminar on "The
Purloined Letter"[14] calls "the time for understanding" required by the epistolary transaction may extend into the indefinite future: the destination of
the letter cannot in the nature of things be established in advance of the
pedagogical event, very much like Tom Sawyer's fragment of bark on which
he writes a message that is not so much delivered as discovered – at a
later time.[15] The sending of the letter of education entails the recognition
of the two essential Lacanian constraints: one must first presuppose a "necessary interval between the sending of the letter and its arrival," so that
the effects of reception and incorporation are not always immediate and
may in fact emerge only when it is no longer possible to test for results
(one should note Jacques Derrida's contestation in "The Purveyor of Truth"
that the letter, regardless of one's best intentions, may indeed never arrive
at its destination);[16] and secondly, the educator should realize that certain
discourses paradoxically yet necessarily produce their own addressees, that
the letter may create its destination, or in the terms I will be using further
on, that the classroom transaction is a device for creating the "model student." In the pedagogical sense this means that education needs to be regarded not merely as transmissive but, far more to the point, as metamorphic, transformative, that is, as fundamentally *creative*.

To put this in rather more clinical or diagnostic terms, one would say
with L.S. Vygotsky that there are two developmental levels in the learning
process that need to be distinguished: the *actual* developmental level, which
defines functions that have already matured and which misguidedly serves
as the basis or starting-point for most formal educational procedures; and
what he calls the "zone of proximal development," which defines functions
that are still embryonic or in the process of maturation and depend upon
assistance and collaboration. Learning "which is oriented toward developmental levels that have already been reached is ineffective from the viewpoint
of the child's overall development." It results in lag and sluggishness. On
the contrary, in concentrating on the *potential* to formulate and solve problems that students would have been unable to do independently, and by
initiating learners into domains of complexity that transcend their unaided
efforts, the teacher enables them to anticipate and so command their otherwise elusive futures, to perform what we might designate as a category
jump. The concept of the zone of proximal development enables us, says
Vygotsky, "to propound a new formula, namely, that the only 'good learning'
is that which is *in advance of development*"[17] (italics mine). In other words,
in learning up to the level of the material as well as to the set of expectations
embodied in the discipline and reflected by the teacher, students are in

effect *learning up to the level of their own proximal development*, given its larval or potential presence.

Reverting to the more effusive idiom I employed earlier, one may suggest that students, in learning up to the level of the task, become in the course of time other than, different from, what they were in the period of the actual epistolary process (*selon* Lacan and Derrida) – always assuming that students are *potentially* able and receptive. Teaching down leaves students pretty well where they were before the encounter with the teacher in the privileged scene of education. And to put it bluntly, where there is no change in the exchange, no strenuous repatriation of a primordial possibility, then there is no education. For there is a sense in which *all education is higher education*, involving the love of difficulty in the recognition of the difficulty of love for the achievable self which is at once the promise and the trial of what we call education.

The learning up approach is often condemned as a haughty and unbending form of mandarin practice, as a sign of "elitism" – a term of which I am inordinately fond as it inscribes phonetically the cognomen of the great contemporary Greek poet, Odysseas Elytis, whose "philosophy of life" is summed up in one of the cyclic headings of *The Little Mariner*: "Anoint the Ariston." Good teaching in this sense is always *Elytist*. Surely, one would think, it is about time one summoned an exorcist and rid the word of its demonic connotations.[18]

Strangely enough, Mortimer J. Adler writing in the introduction to *The Paideai Program* considers American education as already infected by the bacillus of elitist practice[19] and recommends its thorough asepsis by a single-track system that ignores individual differences and aptitudes – precisely what Huxley in *Brave New World Revisited* regards as the basic fact on which sound education rests.[20] Adler illustrates his thesis with a wholesome dairy metaphor that conceals and distorts the real nature of the situation. All containers, whether of pint or gallon measure, should be filled with the same high-quality cream, "not skimmed milk for some and cream for others." What he fails to consider is that quality is not only a function of the substance to be poured *but of the container* in which the educational cream froths and settles. Size – pint or gallon – is not the apt (or at least not the only) metaphorical correlate here but rather (and also) the quality and nature of the substance of which the container is made and which necessarily imparts some of its own intrinsic properties to the flavour, consistency, and nutritive value of its contents. After all, the cream may clabber on the instant. The mind that receives determines the quality of the final product as much as any other factor one may wish to isolate in the complex process of education. The mind that conveys, the materials conveyed, or the medium in which the conveyance occurs are null without appropriate reception, that is, without the suitable preparation and treatment of the receptacle. Cream for all, certainly, but if the cream continues to sour despite the best intentions and precautions of the dairy, then the container must be carefully inspected and, if necessary, designated for another use or function. Otherwise, the dairy may go into receivership.[21]

The dilemma is chronic and, as we recall, informs the classical debate on the subject of education as well. For example, the conflict between the two forms of pedagogy in Aristophanes' *The Clouds*, the greater Logic entailing modesty, discipline, respect, and what we would today call individual accountability, and the Lesser Logic enjoining the practice of indulgence and the same system of "instruction" for all, with a view to the exploitation of the marketplace.[22] Similarly, Terence in *The Brothers* (second century B.C.) weighs the relative merits of the traditionalist mode, associated with the conservative Demea, and the progressivist bent, championed by the libertine Micio, arguing finally for a reasonable armistice and a combination of what is best in both pedagogical attitudes.[23]

In the current environment, however, the terms of the debate seem to have hardened almost beyond the possibility of reconciliation or mutual subsumption. Line 'em up and teach 'em, as if education were only a trumped-up form of execution by firing squad, or Anoint the Ariston, teaching students to draw as best they can the strenuous Miltonic bow. For as Milton writes in his evergreen 1644 essay *On Education*,[24] "These ways would try all their peculiar gifts of nature, and if there were any secret excellence among them, would fetch it out and give it fair opportunity to advance itself." And such is, I remain convinced, the only way in the current situation of unscrambling the anagram of intellectual potential, of discovering and nourishing the "secret excellence," the latent talent for which we are also responsible.

Admittedly, nothing we attempt to do at this point is going to work very well. We are wandering aimlessly about in an apocalyptic hiatus, very much like Matthew Arnold in "Stanzas from the Grande Chartreuse,"[25] who finds himself "Wandering between two worlds, one dead, / The other powerless to be born." But one thing is certain. Teaching down to the student is becoming increasingly untenable. We must teach the student first to learn up to the material and to the level of the teacher's expectations. Learning up will generate its own spate of insoluble and near-insoluble problems, but the losses and derelictions it will produce are, in my estimation, consolingly less alarming than those brought on by the teaching-down syndrome. Difficulty is redemptive. As Whitehead cogently argued in *The Aims of Education* with respect to educational materials, a textbook of "real educational worth ... will be difficult to teach from ... If it were easy, the book ought to be burned; for it cannot be educational. *In education, as elsewhere, the broad primrose path leads to a nasty place.*"[26]

Once again, as so often in the long history of western thought, we do well to heed the anti-demotic critique implicit in the educational theory of the great Greek philosophers. Aristotle warns us in the *Metaphysics* against the danger in educational practice of *apaideusis*, the inability "to distinguish between that which requires demonstration or proof and that which does not." (The source text would appear to be the *Gorgias*, especially the peroration, in which Socrates denounces *apaideusia* – the un-cultured state – as a profound evil. The same idea receives further amplification in the Seventh Book of the *Republic*.) In the modern context, *apaideusis*, as George Steiner translates the term, is the "want of schooling, a fundamental lesion in education ... an indecency of spirit and understanding."[27] Teaching down is the contemporary form of apaideusis, of trickle-down or voodoo pedagogy, and its effects of adulteration and reductiveness will continue to be felt not only educationally but socially as well – unless we can bring ourselves to examine our proprietary assumptions and embark upon our own re-education before the class bell tolls.

One of the principal ways in which we have decided to deal with the apaideutic deprivations from which our students suffer is the brute proliferation of remedial writing and grammar courses. But such courses, as Richard Ohmann argues, are "notoriously ineffective."[28] How is it possible that it never occurred to us, experts in the field, that writing is not something that happens in a Hoover bag? Grammar abhors a vacuum. Let us consider briefly the pre-conditions for learning to write coherently.

a. Writing requires reading. Teaching writing to those who do not read is a utopian proposition. From the denial of the book springs the very cacographic excesses we are trying to purge and rectify. As Frank Smith contends, the ability to write coherently is not learned by rote or the assimilation of specialized procedures: "Everything points to the necessity of learning to write from what we read." Mere diagnostic or remedial intervention is largely innocuous: "the knowledge that writers require resides – in existing texts."[29]

b. Writing requires articulate speech. Teaching writing to those who have scarcely been exposed to conversation and who do not speak in approximate sentences is a thirteenth Herculean labour. "Literary education proceeds," as Frye argues, "by intertwining a speaking style and a writing style. No written style will be any good unless it is based on a good speaking style."[30]

c. Writing requires the ability to listen, which in turn requires both patience and the ability to discriminate nuance or connotative implication.

d. Writing requires a minimal familiarity with ideas. Teaching writing to those who can seldom remember being excited by an idea or who react to the introduction of ideas with embarrassment generally leads to the tedious assembling of paratactic fragments rather than the production of coherent sentences (which requires the teacher to become proficient in a new discipline, the study of segmantics). This is because the sentence is not only a grammatical structure but an ideational unit which, through devices such as clause subordination on the one hand and semantic linkage on the other, generates relations of contiguity and distribution between the basic segments of linguistic organization. That is, a felicitous sentence, through processes of ideational cohesion and syntactic transference, generates meaning by functioning as an integral part of a supersentence, itself the visible manifestation of an *idea*.

e. Writing requires (at the very least) a rudimentary sense of history, that is, of exigent temporality. Teaching writing to those who have only the most tenuous sense of historical process, both communal and personal, leads inexorably to the epidemic practice of *tautology*, the major tendency of contemporary student writing. Tautology is neither rational nor linguistic; it is a form of stasis, removed from the flow of process, and – from a psychological point of view – comes to be out of a sense of resentment against the demands of logic and expression.

f. As a corollary of (e), writing requires memory. Teaching writing to those whose memory is thin and discontinuous, who live in intermittence, cannot accomplish more than inculcating a facility with simple sentences. A sure sign of such inadequacy is the phenomenon of bad paragraphing (see also (d) above), the desynchronization of narrative units or constituent frames of expanding discourse. As Jeremy Campbell argues, "The construction of psychological time is as complex as the construction of a spoken sentence; both linguistic intelligence and temporal intelligence share in common the ability to represent real experience in symbolic terms."[31] Putting together a sentence and then another sentence in such a way that they constitute the small, coherent narrative sequence we recognize as a paragraph depends upon the operation of what is called "episodic memory" – that which binds events in subjective time into the construct of personal identity. Precisely this sense of interior or subjective time is both reflected by and stabilized in the core grammatical system that enables us to negotiate a temporal world.[32]

In sum, what is needed for education to "take" on any level, including the grammatical, is a serious and holistic emphasis on the larger *context* in which education occurs, and the awakening in the student of a profound *conviction* of the importance of the educational project. This is what Max Dublin denominates as *cultivation*, which is "respectful of context" and pays close attention to detail. "Most goals are not achieved by single acts of will, that is, by change of habit, of custom, and of culture. Cultivation takes time. Its effect or its failure are cumulative."[33]

Geraldine Van Doren, one of the contributors to the Paideia Program[34] attempting to refine and upgrade language instruction in the schools, informs us that "Language is an instrument for shaping, ordering, evaluating, and appreciating our thoughts and feelings." As it is on the basis of this distinction that language instruction generally proceeds, we can locate one of the central problems in current remedial and instructional practice precisely here. The statement is exemplary in revealing the pervasive misapprehension about how language works which is shared by both reactionaries and revolutionaries in the field of current pedagogical debate. For it shows no awareness of the most important developments in linguistic psychology and philosophy over the long and chequered history of the subject, from the Modistae of the thirteenth century to the profound and suggestive insights of contemporary semiotic analysis. Put plainly, there are no "thoughts" and few "feelings" containing structure and complexity without the genetic intervention of language. Language is not only an expressive and representational medium, as the quoted statement takes serenely for granted, but the *productive and configurative principle of human experience itself.* Nor can language, (as Jacques Derrida has argued throughout his *oeuvre*) recuperate a prior origin – a pristine and inviolate, pre-existent "thought" or "feeling" – since this is necessarily and "always already" mediated and structured by linguistic articulation. That is, according to Derrida, there is always a linguistic supplement at the epistemic source, a differential trace of something that infiltrates and subverts a presumedly anterior mental substance; there is always the testamentary echo of the Word.[35] We can never arrive at the primal "thought" which language ostensibly shapes and orders; on the contrary, language is always at the ever-receding source of our discretionary experience of the world. It does not merely express the self: it structures and articulates the self from which it cannot be disengaged and from which it should not be considered in theoretical isolation. I do not *use* language; I *am* language. The sooner we succeed in dispelling the instrumental "heresy" at the root of so much speculation on our so-called language skills, that is, the sooner we recognize what is really at stake in the inculcation of both linguistic facility and felicity, the more effective we will become as teachers *re-enacting the very function of language itself* but at the level of conscious intent: in other words, as *mediators* of the literate sensibility exercising a *creative* influence on the lives of our students, as providers and transmitters of "cultivation."

In the more immediate and empirical context, we need to take particular note of the *nature*, the etiology of the linguistic anorexia from which so many of our students suffer. The students with whom we interact in our classes have by and large failed to master what is now somewhat flexibly called "pragmatics," a term I adapt here to designate an elementary cultural accomplishment involving the ability of interpreters to contextualize the multiple implications of the signs the language requires them to deploy in order to augment communicative potential. It is "background information" they are lacking – a term we find pervasive in Hirsch but which was apparently first introduced by Yehoshua Bar-Hillel in the 1960s and applied by researchers in the field to signify those general schemes of world knowledge assumed to be part of our linguistic equipment (or what we might call the *language package*). That is, the schematic paradigms that permit us to draw more or less detailed cognitive maps of the world are an inherent part of the lexical information we carry about with us, of the very language we habitually speak and write. As Hilary Putnam claims, background knowledge must be understood *as intrinsic to the semantic competence of the speaker or writer.*[36]

Therefore, it is reasonable to assume that if the language package is deficient in range and content (or in Chomskyean terms, if the "semantic component" that provides information about the meaning of lexical items is impaired), then no amount of "enriched" or accelerated grammatical instruction is going to have much of an effect on our students' ability to write or think coherently. "Students characterized as 'low achievers' in school," says Frank Smith, "usually have limitations in their *prior knowledge* rather than defective learning abilities."[37]

Another way of theorizing the effect of linguistic deprivation is to focus on the phenomenon of *implicature*, something we generally take for granted. Umberto Eco defines implicature in a neo-Gricean manner as the positing of a presupposition as if it were already assumed as the case, that is, of using a verb-term, when it is not felicitous to do so, as part of a "prelocutory strategy" obliging the addressee to accept the verb-term *as if* felicitously uttered and therefore engaging him or her to activate "the whole of the presuppositions the term postulated.[38] (Colin MacCabe similarly refers to presupposition as the means "whereby discourse produces within one domain of thought another domain of thought *as if* this other domain had already been introduced.")[39] Eco adduces the following example:

John: Smith loved my paper.

Tom: Oh, I sympathize with you.

A certain level of semantic competence is required if John is to correctly parse Tom's "rhetorical strategy" as implying that Smith is an academic dumbbell – a feat of interpretation a surprising number of my eighteen-year-old students are incapable of performing with any degree of consistency. When implicature succeeds, it does so because it posits as communicationally questionable – or is *understood* as doing so – "a presupposition that the signification system had registered as unquestionable in all the other cases in which a given ... term was used felicitously."

In other words, if the language package is inadequately filled, *if lexical context is too shaky to sustain presupposition*, implicature is very likely to fail, and its failure is a sign of precisely that prior semantic incompetence that obviates time-intensive grammatical instruction in default of that larger cultural environment *by* which constituent lexicality is informed and permeated (and *of* which lexicality serves as both its semantic and pragmatic support). Presupposition, the stuff of implicature, may be regarded as a kind of phantom syntax by which language is always haunted, a ghostly chain of inferences and assumptions that link our linguistic expressions to one another and allow for those multi-dimensional and polyvalent units of sense without which surface grammar has little to gain purchase upon.

This also explains the tenuous status of irony in the current lexical climate (as well as the bewilderment often experienced in the attempt to supply lawful alternate readings of partial or enigmatic phrases).[40] Irony may be regarded as one of the forms of what Otto Jespersen calls "indirect negation," which includes a variety of linguistic deflectors such as interrogatives, conditionals, hortatives, and ellipses.[41] Now if *direct negation as such* functions not as a primary reality or an initial proposition but rather as a *modality* that dialectically qualifies a *prior* event or proposition, then its formulation requires a second-order process of mental abstraction that works like a derivative in mathematics, presupposing something that comes before, a fundamental unit on which it operates. Thus negation would be understood as a function of a rule of transformation, its formula, as Ray Jackendoff derives it,[42] reading "A sentence ($_sX$-neg-Y_s) is an instance of sentence negation if there exists a paraphrase 'It is not so that ($_sX$-Y)'." Simply put, a negative sentence is one that can be transformed to take the form: "It is not so that X is Y." But what counts for the argument I am developing here is that a transformation works as a sort of higher-level extrapolation from a given state of affairs ("Negation is first acceptance," as Emile Benveniste has it),[43] and consequently, being a more complex, deuteronomic procedure than immediate positing, demands a certain sophistication and a differentiated psychology.

The linguist T. Givon, carrying the theory of negation a little further, comments on "the *presuppositionally* more marked status of negative sentences."[44] Thus, to return to Jespersen, when negation is *indirect*, we may assume that a more complex operation of third-level abstraction, that is, a *double prescinding* in which a supposition has become a presupposition (or more accurately, if clumsily, in which a presupposition has become a pre-presupposition), has intervened in the act of awareness and its verbal expression, and this would account for its relative scarcity in the current environment characterized by linguistic malnourishment and cultural backwardness. Implicature has fallen on evil days. (Analogously, Freud argues that negation does not exist in the unconscious, and must therefore be worked up, sublated, embodied in its *effects* through feints, countermoves, and displacements.)[45]

Irony, negation, and presupposition rely on the prior existence of adequate background information,[46] which Eco divides into two subtypes: the background information conveyed by the linguistic expression (e.g., presuppositional sentences, negative entailment in ironic expressions), and the background knowledge of the participant in discourse (whether as sender or addressee). That is, the speaker (or listener) who is deficient in background information experiences great difficulty in deploying (or recognizing) the felicity conditions and alternative contexts which control the meaning of expressions, and suffers as well from an epistemic deficit in general information and discursive capacity. (In connectionist terms, there is a marked reduction in "content addressable memory" or associative recall, the synecdochic faculty that reproduces a whole by activating a part.) Thus, for a substantial number of students, one must come *to terms* with speakers and listeners for whom the background informational frame, *on the syntactic as well as epistemic levels*, is distressingly thin, which accounts for the perilous status of irony, indirect negation, presupposition, implicature – what we may call in a general way *the hospitality for alternatives* – in the present situation. (See appendix 2.)

An immigrant woman with as yet little English whom I overheard recently in the kitchen-appliance section of a hardware store asked the shop assistant for "luminal oil" to wrap foodstuffs in. She was clearly looking for aluminum foil. Only two of thirty-eight students in my Theory of Interpretation class solved the conundrum, despite the obviousness of the cultural and pragmatic markers – hardware store, kitchen department, wrapping of foodstuffs, the fact that the shopper was of another culture – which contextualized the unctuous radiance of the phrase.

Another way in which we have decided to deal with this predicament, apart from the proliferation of remedial language courses, is to increase the number of so-called introductory courses. These offerings do not clearly distinguish between the historical, methodological, and thematic forms they may variously take, but we soldier on despite the attendant confusion and ambiguity. Essentially, an introductory course tends to become a watered-down version of what we used to call a survey course and involves either the elimination or the expurgation of texts we were once required to read as standard fare. (One of my colleagues now refuses to teach anything by Joyce. Golding seems to represent the upper limit.) But dilution of content may simply exacerbate the "problem" we benignly assume that we are addressing. What we are really doing, though we are not given to articulating the process, is back-shifting to a presumed earlier stage of intellectual development the student has skipped along the way, and then accelerating into the present without making untoward demands upon the student's inner resources. The hidden assumption behind this pedagogical agenda is that the long, gradual absorption cycle (ages six to sixteen) can be reproduced in a comparatively short, compressed period of time (ages seventeen to nineteen). But there is no evidence to justify this assumption, and downsizing content may rectify little while producing only boredom, frivolity, and a false sense of accomplishment.

My own children, like most Canadians, were avid hockey players. As infants they began with Christmas-gift board games which they referred to as "twiddly hockey." Later on they took to the street where they devoted themselves to what they called "piddly hockey," graduating eventually to the rinks where they continued to ply their obsession with "Ridley hockey" (after a certain Mike Ridley who played with the Washington Capitals). This sequence, despite some overlap, was reasonably strict and pedagogically sound in a practical sense. Given the "hidden agenda" of current educational procedure, and drawing on the above terminology, we might say that today we are in the unenviable position of having to teach Ridley hockey to those who have not yet enjoyed the full benefit of twiddly and piddly but for whom twiddly and piddly at this late stage are no longer very effective. Gored on the horns of this dilemma, many, perhaps most of us, have decided that there is nothing for it but to return our charges to the level of the board game, unaware, it seems, that our tendency to therapeuticize education is becoming increasingly costly as we succeed in recuperating fewer and fewer students. Our insistence on twiddly pedagogy or piddly discipline is little short of catastrophic. In the words of Philip Rieff, a new kind of community is now being constructed that does not "generate conscience and internal control" (what he calls a "renunciatory moral demand system") but desire and the safe play of impulse.[47] To put it another way, students habitually enter their classrooms with the same half-earnest, half-frivolous prophylactic attitude with which they frequent the condom dispensers in the washrooms.

As teachers we must be especially stringent and critically aware of these pervasive Asclepian tendencies in order to resist the progressive banalization of our "mandate." As Max Dublin deplores in *Futurehype*, "How hungry we are today to trivialize our problems ... in order to be able to claim mastery over them, no matter how petty that mastery may be."[48] Rieff uttered a similar lamentation a quarter of a century ago: "That such large numbers of the cultivated and intelligent have identified themselves deliberately with those who are supposed to have no love for instinctual renunciation suggests ... the most elaborate act of suicide that Western intellectuals have ever staged" (i.e., siding with the unreconstructed individual). He continues: "The anti-cultural predicate upon which the modern personality is being re-organized" is taking us to the brink of a radical disorganization of the self. "To change the dynamics of the culture, the analytic attitude would have to become a moral demand." The problem may be expressed in the following terms. Ascetic culture, the analytic attitude, the modalities of control associated with the old moral demand system, now confront a vast "deconversion experience," which has produced the therapeutic being who replaces the dialectic of perfection, based on a renunciatory mode of being, with a dialectic of fulfilment, based on the appetitive mode.

The therapeutic attitude is "remissive" rather than "ascetic." Moreover, a culture of releases rather than controls ensures that the remissive modality in turn becomes controlling, that the counter-interdictory is installed as the new interdictory. Cultural life in general and education in particular appear to be inexorably subsiding into the kind of psychotropic utopia envisioned by Stanislaw Lem in his mordant analysis of eschatological anaesthesia. "The grim prospect of becoming benignimized seemed inevitable."[49]

It is clear that we must begin to detherapeuticize education, and one of the ways in which we can proceed is via a renewed consideration of the rhythms inherent in the educational process. Alfred North Whitehead's analysis of the issue bears directly upon current problematics.[50] To start with, Whitehead claims that it "is not true that easier subjects should precede the harder ... The postponement of difficulty is no safe clue for the maze of educational practice." We must avoid the false psychology of the pupil's progress as "a uniform steady advance" in the asymmetric periodic scale of intellectual progress.

The same point is made in a somewhat different context by Vygotsky, for whom "child development is a complex dialectical process characterized by periodicity, unevenness in the development of different functions, metamorphosis or qualitative transformation of one form into another."[51] Moreover, for Vygotsky as for Whitehead, difficulty is an essential function of the learning process, and both regard the larger cognitive scheme as constitutively dialectical. For Whitehead, education in the broadest sense proceeds in accordance with a sequence of three intellectual stages, predicated on the Hegelian dialectic. These are:

STAGE 1: *Romance* (thesis), which generates a ferment in the mind, absorbing ideas with "possibilities of wide significance" and experiencing the wealth of "unexplored connections" between things. (See appendix 3.)

STAGE 2: *Precision* (antithesis), the setting in order of the ferment "already stirring in the mind." But the stage of precision is barren without a prior stage of romance. This second, analytic stage, which subordinates the romantic flux to exactness of formulation, is the stage of grammar, language instruction, and the stricter forms of science.

STAGE 3: *Generalization* (synthesis), defined as "a return to romanticism with the added advantage of classified ideas and relevant technique."

The main point is that "the development of mentality exhibits itself as a rhythm involving an interweaving of cycles, the whole process being dominated by a greater cycle of the same general character as its minor eddies." The larger, over-arching cycle covers the whole of life, the stage of romance stretching across approximately the first twelve to fifteen years, that of precision consisting of the entire period of secondary and tertiary education, and the third stage of generalization comprising the experience of later adulthood. Within this grand parabola of learning and development, each particular stage itself comprises an orderly series of three cyclic steps or periods. The same holds true for each faculty or discipline and each subject in the curriculum.[52]

Further, the various disciplines develop in their cyclic rhythm at different rates. The third period of generalization in language study, for example, correlates with the second stage of precision in science, just as the stage of precision in language corresponds temporally to that of romance in science. Education consists in the continual repetition of such periodicities, each lesson or subject forming what Whitehead calls an "eddy cycle" – so that education remains deeply archaic and approximates the Ptolemaic system of universal order with cycles and epicycles in a sequence of theoretically endless repetitions.

Two other factors must now be noted. The first or romantic stage is not necessarily *easier* (i.e., vague, diluted, reductive) than any other. The contemporary attitude to education, which is remedial or therapeutic, reverses both the complexity factor and the periodicity cycle by diminishing and trivializing content, and by placing the second or precision stage before the primary or romantic one, introducing elements of rule and procedure prior to the "encouragement of vivid freshness" of ideas without which education is a dead letter. A further problem, if Whitehead is correct, is that mid-adolescence constitutes a second major cycle and so begins with a wider romantic stage following the synthesis of later childhood. Thus in focusing on grammar too insistently – i.e., back to basics – in the student's college years, we find ourselves in the position of trying to install a First Rhythm Stage 2 cycle into a Second Rhythm Stage 1 period. The romantic stage in adolescence should ideally follow on "the generalization of capacity produced by the acquirement of spoken language and reading." But the customary and natural sequencing of accomplishment has been perilously skewed, leading to what Whitehead calls "a block in the assimilation of

ideas." When one stage, say the discipline of precision in grammatical concinnity, is imposed before the logically prior stage, in this case that of romance, has run its course – and when the stages are also vertically incommensurable (not only does 2 come before 1, but A2 comes before B1
rather than before A3) – one cannot hope for anything resembling the orderly, progressive, and lucid assimilation of ideas.

And there is still one further complication that renders our congenial
methods almost hopeless. *There is no evidence that the rates of absorption
and mastery can be accelerated and compressed,* that is, that students can
reproduce *intensively* between the ages of seventeen and nineteen what they
have failed to adequately produce *extensively* between the ages of six and
sixteen. Once again Vygotsky's ideas may prove helpful in our efforts to
reposition the dilemma we are considering. Revolution and evolution in
the cognitive dynamic "are mutually related and mutually presuppose each
other ... Leaps in the child's development are ... no more than a moment
in the general line of development," but leaps and lines of development
are reciprocally determined. Certainly one cannot have the former without
the latter. These leaps or early "reconstructive processes," as Vygotsky calls
them, enable human beings to achieve increasingly complex modifications
of their intellectual behaviour.[53] It follows by extrapolation that the omission
or scanting of certain stages in cognitive advancement in the "general line
of development" will have serious implications for the long-term cognitive
itinerary of the learner. The "leap" requires the "line," a process which,
to borrow a Gouldian phrase, resembles a kind of "punctuated equilibrium,"
short bursts of dramatic change in a context of general stability or gradual
development. The pupil cannot be expected to elide some of these processes
in the course of his or her education and then mechanically reproduce them
in hypertrophic or speeded-up form at a later stage of development without
experiencing some degree of epistemic distortion. As Jane Healy remarks
in *Endangered Minds* (see note 53), since the current trend among the young
is toward the use of less elaborated codes of discourse, "How successfully
these [language] skills can be taught to brains that may have passed a 'sensitive period' for syntactic development is unknown" – although she makes
it pretty clear that stutter-stepping students through linguistic circuits they
should have negotiated many years before, when the critical gates were open,
is not an altogether sanguine prospect. "In development," she warns, "missed
opportunities may be difficult to recapture." It is precisely this species of
pedagogical grotesquerie that permits a student at the age of eighteen to
take several make-up or remedial composition courses for which he or she
receives first-class grades based formatively on previous inadequacies, and
then to produce the following sample in response to a short-essay question.
(This example, one of a daunting myriad, is excerpted from an examination
paper in my Interpretation class. Judging from his grades the student had

done remarkably well in the effective-writing classes he took prior to registering in my course.) The specimen is a truncated reply to a question asking the student to compare two short texts, Kafka's "On Parables" and John Barth's "Glossolalia."

Well, the Parables talks about two people who are having a discussion, betting and gamibeling and he refers to the parables, defined as explaining differently, in other words, like the encyclopedic book their are alot of parables, in Glossolalia is a story of confusion of definitions, alot of discussion. The both have more discussion between people.

What is the *teacher* to do in his or her near-terminal plight? Backtracking and rectifying, our customary response to the dilemma, is as absurd as it is ineffective, a retrograde and belated procedure as desperate in its way as recommending Preparation H to shrink facial wrinkles. Once again Whitehead may help us as he discriminates the double function or obligation of the teacher: "to elicit enthusiasm by resonance from his own personality," and "to create the environment of a larger knowledge and firmer purpose." We must take this concluding recommendation seriously. The ultimate motive power must come from within the student, he says, in the sense "of wonder, of curiosity, of reverence ... of tumultuous desire for merging personality in something beyond itself ... Apart from it life sinks back into the passivity of its lower types." I would add that the motive force must also come from within the teacher who must, as Thomas More would say, inform his conscience correctly. How is the teacher to continue with so improbable and depressing a task as teaching in the current situation, informing his or her own conscience, eliciting enthusiasm, and creating a larger cognitive environment for students who are not likely to willingly "merge personality in something beyond itself" unless the motive comes from within the "autonomous" self? The need to think clearly and unsparingly is the prime desideratum today.

It is important for us to understand the situation in which we are all implicated, if theory and argument are to have any basis in reality. We live in a society that, while democratizing the educational institution and making it accessible to everyone whether qualified or not, has by that same token entrenched education as a value-deficit experience, a *betagam* phenomenon moving us down the alphabet of learning and away from the origins of productive achievement toward the psi-omega of mere information without structure or resonance, a noetic economy with all its constituent features under threat of collapse. Teachers, as members of the tribe of Medvedenko (see Chekhov's *The Sea Gull*), remain overworked and underpaid, pedagogical chars performing a cross between babysitting duties and janitorial functions. Students, for all the lip-service paid to the sanctity of the category they occupy in the cultural hierarchy, are routinely infantilized and relieved of the burden of responsibility and labour without which education degenerates *ad placetum* into parody or farce. Theories go on proliferating with lurid abandon, repeating one another with cosmetic modifications across the generations, so that some educational thinkers come to resemble nothing so much as humans diligently imitating parrots, imitators copying the imitations of other imitators.[54] And as the educational plant is progressively updated with new power-priced, feature-packed gimmicks and gadgets improperly understood and assimilated, the paradigm for learning that these represent and implicitly lobby for continues to subvert the relation of authenticity between teacher and student upon which true education is predicated. The result is (so to speak) cab-forward technology in place of the lotus sutra of the mystical law of inner development. Why affect surprise that such unreflected practice should produce a graduate society of digital communicators and half-baked emoticons incapable of reflecting upon their experience, of inhabiting the structures of memory, or of finding their place in the historical continuum that endows experience with meaning and direction? Even Caspar Hauser, very much a synecdoche for contemporary education, was capable of historical nostalgia, as his original statement would appear to suggest: "I want to be a rider like my father."[55]

The position I am adopting here may appear somewhat paradoxical or contradictory. On the one hand I seem to be arguing on behalf of the postulate, associated in various ways with the names of thinkers like Piaget and Binet, that asserts that development is prior to learning, that cycles and stages of intellectual growth must be plugged into at the proper time if students are to assimilate the material we require them to master. Otherwise we are condemned to playing catch-up pedagogy, offering accelerated forms of intellectual rehabilitation in the vain hope of repairing deficits that continue to increase and to undermine our best efforts at reclaiming what has been lost. On the other hand I am strenuously advocating with thinkers like Vygotsky the need to pitch our subjects, methods, and requirements, like a quarterback leading his receiver, ahead of the student's actual capacities, to goad, tempt, and exacerbate the will to learn as if under the aegis of Browning's great line "A man's reach should exceed his grasp," to teach by *projective elicitation*, and to mobilize a supervening difficulty in order to challenge response. (What Toynbee says of civilization is equally applicable to education.) This latter notion reverses the terms of the earlier position, in the belief that learning may indeed precede development.

The muddle is not theoretical but derives from and reflects the almost impossible situation in which we now find ourselves. If these cycles of learning and assimilation do indeed exist, programmed genetically into the structure of the brain, then the educational project must take them formally into account in the construction of the curriculum. But nothing prevents the architect of the curriculum or the teacher in the classroom from, *at the same time*, devising methods and approaches to stimulate the learner to aim at higher levels of complexity and degrees of attainment *within* the given cycle, eddy, or temporal unit appropriate at the given moment. And if the existence of these cycles should prove undemonstrable or unpersuasive, then activating "the zone of proximal development," which by definition is always in advance of any given developmental stage, remains the only theoretically sound practice we have. The important thing is to resist the temptation to backtrack, returning students to an earlier stage of development of which they have been defrauded *but which may be largely irretrievable in any event*, since we are very likely dealing with a variant of the so-called critical period effect.

The truth is that we are facing for the most part an Esau-like generation that has been cheated of its birthright by parent and pedagogue alike, but which, as it approaches maturity, shows little desire, will, zeal, or ambition to recoup the contents of its deprivation. Thus the pervasive slogan or buzzword we hear all around us which does nothing so much as camouflage the barrenness of our thinking: *motivation*.[56] The student must be motivated to learn, as if learning under undistorted conditions were not one of the most natural and inevitable functions of the organism and among the greatest of experienceable joys. To stress constantly the need for motivation, to elevate it to the status of a chief pedagogical desideratum, to give it pride of place in the teacher's methodological pharmacopoeia, shows just how far we have fallen from the level of plain good sense. Do we consider it necessary to motivate our children to play, to eat, to breathe, to be curious about the world, to make connections between things, events, and ideas?[57] In the sphere of education, motivation comes by itself (assuming no irreparable damage to the mind of the learner) if two broad conditions are satisfied: that the teacher is competent, and capable of radiating by virtue of his or her comportment the rich delight of intellectual attainment, that is, if the teacher can address the student in order to stimulate what is there rather than to motivate what is not; and that the student is potentially capable of accepting the wager of the self, of acknowledging in some way his or her own basic drive to both differentiation and cohesion. We may continue to theorize about the requisites and vicissitudes of education, indulging in the excesses of teacher talk with its lexicon of "competencies," "strategies," "accessibility," "nurturing," and all the other pedagogical borborygms, and congratulate ourselves on the depth and purity of our moral commitment to the welfare of our students, but I can see no way of successfully detouring these two related imperatives. And that is precisely why we must accept the logical paradox in which we are embroiled, by no means

giving up completely on remedial programs and methods but recognizing
that at present they will have only a limited value.

At the same time, instead of catering to our students with the familiar
battery of nostrums and placebos, awarding them high grades for doubtful
accomplishments, measuring their work formatively against initial achievement or lack thereof, and emasculating the curriculum of its genuine substance so that it becomes an epicene parody of all that was once intended
by the word "education," instead of proceeding on the dogmatic conviction
that a plethora of foundational courses, lab "ponderations," and technical
programs, relieved by a dusting of cultural cosmetics, are going to do the
job for us, we had better avoid the Gadarene plunge by affirming the
reciprocal need for maintaining standards in teaching and learning. We may
do this by setting our students as well as ourselves laborious and authentic
tasks, refusing to teach down, and remembering that nothing less is at stake
than our individual and collective survival.

To put what I am saying as simply and bluntly as possible, education
will continue to be a dead letter, a misspent effort and a hopelessly muddled
farrago of ineffective theories and programs unless the following improbable
events should miraculously occur:

- a cultural revolution starting in the home and culminating in the restoration, in Theodore Roszak's phrase, of the "Homeric interlude" – what
  Jacques Barzun calls the "priming coat" of early education;[58]
- a change in social thinking that would accord tangible recognition to
  the importance of the educational function, elevating the public school
  and college teacher to the approximate salary and prestige levels of the
  universities and the higher professions;
- the long-deferred awareness that the mind develops in rhythms and patterns of assimilation that should be reflected in the curriculum.

Even should the three previous conditions be met, education will continue
to stagger from failure to failure as it does from conference to conference
unless teachers recognize that teaching down to the student is a pedagogical
posture that ensures intellectual bankruptcy and must be replaced by a
learning-up model if disaster is to be averted. To quote Whitehead once
again, as we approach the great Cretaceous of current educational policy
and practice, "in the conditions of modern life the rule is absolute, the
race which does not value trained intelligence is doomed ... there will be
no appeal from the judgment which will then be pronounced on the uneducated." Jefferson said it too, of course, long before Whitehead and the
rest of the prodromic sodality: "If a nation expects to be ignorant and free,
it expects what never was and never will be."[59]

I write the above fresh, euphemistically speaking, from my morning Survey of Fiction class[60] in which the topic under discussion was the peculiar nature of the "open" (Eco) or "writerly" (Barthes) text which challenges readers to confront and modify their habitual assumptions about reading and interpretation. To illustrate the point I brought up the related notion of the conversion experience and its roots in the ordeal of Saul of Tarsus on the road to Damascus. None of my students had heard of Saint Paul. None had ever come across the idea of the conversion experience in their reading or classwork. None, it appeared, had ever done any serious reading voluntarily, although a few had read *The Hitchhiker's Guide to the Galaxy* and *The Belgariad*. But what I found truly dismaying, after further discussion with my students on the degree of their preparedness for education, was their tranquil satisfaction, amounting almost to ineffable content, with this state of affairs.

An important caveat needs to be registered here. One should beware of falling into the postmodernist trap of claiming that such students have proleptically managed to subvert and reinscribe the centre/margin hierarchies of knowledge associated with postcolonial forms of domination and the rigid exclusivities of the Eurocentric tradition. They have, *at best*, merely succeeded in enacting a parodic reversal of the privileging categories of western thought, marginalizing the central while centralizing the marginal. This new hegemonic centralization of the dispersed and peripheral, the introduction of small personal, regional, or parochial narratives to replace the grand narrative of emergent meaning, and the canonizing of the spirit of immediate gratification along with the structures of iconic instantaneity at the expense of a trans-historical coherence reflected in myth, philosophy, literature, and the rigorous consistencies of humble grammar, suggests that we are dealing with a dysfunctional and self-indulgent constituency that needs our help. We are clearly not confronting a cohort of rapidly advancing postmodernists coming to free us from the totalizing explanatory systems that presumably blinker and oppress us. To regard the student as deprivileged Other amounts to pedagogical suicide – apart from the distressing tendency of the Other, once having expropriated the centre, to become the Same, a new locus of power and exclusion, in effect, a neo-ideological dominant.

There are, as I have tried to indicate in the foregoing, a plurality of ways in which to conceive or imagine the learning-up approach. One of the most fruitful is to regard the classroom event as a species of parable, a fundamentally *literary* encounter between teacher and student with the purpose of effecting a radical displacement of the sensibility. The point is to lead the student out of an empirical or undifferentiated state of being to a more complex, heteronomous, and self-possessed condition of mind – as Gonzalo says in *The Tempest*, to rediscover his potential self in a time "when no man was his own." This involves convincing the student of the crucial importance of education in itself as a form of upward metamorphosis, as a procedure that transforms the common, lexical "reader" of ordinary experience into a competent, hermeneutical "reader" capable of analysis, reflection, and historical connectedness – in Umberto Eco's phrase, into someone willing and able to take "inferential walks in the cultural encyclopedia."[61] Consider in this context Kafka's provocative – both insightful and inciting – parable, *On Parables*, which I reproduce in full.

Many complain that the words of the wise are always merely parables and of no use in daily life, which is the only life we have. When the sage says: "Go over," he does not mean that we should cross to some actual place, which we could do anyhow if the labour were worth it; he means some fabulous yonder, something unknown to us, something too that he cannot designate more precisely, and therefore cannot help us here in the very least. All these parables really set out to say merely that the incomprehensible is incomprehensible, and we know that already. But the cares we have to struggle with every day: that is a different matter.

Concerning this a man once said: Why such reluctance? If you only followed the parables you yourselves would become parables and with that rid of all your daily cares.

Another said: I bet that is also a parable.

The first said: You have won.

The second said: But unfortunately only in parable.

The first said: No, in reality; in parable you have lost.[62]

The enigmatic quality of the piece is only apparent, depending on what Ogden and Richards in *The Meaning of Meaning* called "the utraquistic subterfuge,"[63] the unfair use in argument of diverse referents for a single term – in this case, the term "parable" which the second man uses to denote something like "nonsense," "frivolity," "impracticability," and the first, clearly the author's representative, to signify the opposite, the condition of "higher reality," of coherence, order, self-integration, and awareness of essential values. In this light, the primary function of the parable is to educate. It wants to persuade its recipient of the importance of intellectual and spiritual transformation, of *going over* from a state of mind marked by narrowness of vision, exclusively practical concerns, easy self-satisfaction, daily experience, and the mere absorption of relevant information (Plato's realm of Necessity) to one with a different set of properties entailing the condition of epistemic readiness, the awareness of the mystery, grandeur, and *demandingness* of existence (Plato's realm of Reality). And the very act of deciphering the parable, going from an initial state of perplexity or irritation over to one characterized by active enlightenment and understanding, mimes the parable's message as it does the classroom scenario and the larger pedagogical encounter as well.[64]

More particularly, the parable nature of the classroom event may be specified as a function of what Seymour Chatman calls the narrative chain of textual communication. Intervening between the real author and the empirical reader, the text operates as a little world of deferred encounters between an "implied author," whose discourse is shaped and edited to distinguish it from everyday haphazard or unreconstructed speech, and an "implied reader," the ideal correlate of the empirical reader, who is already inscribed in the text as the desired recipient and collaborator, the one who actualizes the text by participating in its discursive "strategies," who, as Wolfgang Iser says, embodies those "predispositions laid down, not by an empirical outside reality, but by the text itself." Although the meeting or convergence between these twin mirroring idealities may be mediated by an indefinite series of internal narrators and narratees, as in any reasonably complex novel, the fundamental dynamic remains that of an engagement between two imaginative projections, two ideal selves implicated in the process of mutual self-transcendence.[65] Thus Chatman's diagram:

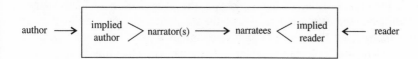

The reader is not expected to remain passive or uninvolved but in responding to the various pressures and manipulations exercised by the text is gradually nudged in the direction of an identity different from his or her customary, unexamined self – perhaps not so far as Joyce's "ideal reader suffering an ideal insomnia," yet far enough to experience even a slight modification of daily character, which corresponds in some measure to the lineaments of the implied reader sketched by the text. Similarly, there is nothing to prevent the teacher from considering the class as a diffuse, open-ended text in its own right, projecting an implied or model student to whose partly discernible profile the real student is expected to conform. Thus:

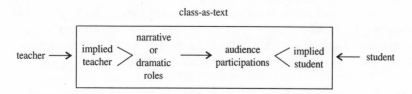

The teacher in shaping a pedagogical self appropriate to the occasion plays any number of narrative or dramatic roles which anticipate the participatory responses of the implied student, the latter "placed" as the ideal correlate of the raw, untutored sensibility that enters the textual space of the class at one point and leaves it, one would hope at least moderately influenced, at another.[66] But in the process of going over from the sphere of actuality to that of implication, from the quotidian to the textual (entering a world Jacques Derrida describes as "neither a *non-place* nor an *other* world, neither a utopia nor an alibi" but a "sure and certain consciousness ... upon whose basis all speech can be brought forth"), the student has performed precisely the parable function envisaged by the pedagogical imperative, that is, in Kafka's terms, has entered "some fabulous yonder," has "become parable." Or in the terms proposed above, has "learned up" to the level of the text – in effect by entering the textual milieu represented by the class and taking up the position, the stance and deportment, already prepared or adumbrated therein.[67]

The perspective of parable we have adopted here is mutable and polyvalent, depending on the theoretical parallax we find most suitable to our talents, premises, or sense of the occasion. To repeat, I am assuming it is pre-eminently educative to regard the presentation of class material, often dismissed as mere didactics or the sterile transfer of dead information, as a *literary* act that approximately resembles a parable, which can in turn be divided into three sub-types or paradigms. The teaching-down approach will coincide on this hypothesis with the (1) *conventional or rabbinical view of the parable* as a pedagogical device for disseminating truth to the simple and uneducated (the parable as an early version of the now ubiquitous audio-visual aid). The teacher is then required to *promote* understanding by making the material as accessible as possible: simplifying, providing glosses and explanations by the gross, leaving nothing to chance, soliciting responses by sympathetic probing and enthusiastic reinforcement, and conveying data in the mode of what Edwin Honig calls "analogical baiting"[68] so that all complexity and doubt is resolutely banished. Ostensibly like Christ preaching to the multitudes or a parent telling bed-time stories to a child, the teacher ensures that least-effort understanding or low-investment pleasure remains the paramount consideration of classroom dynamics.[69]

"Elitist" pedagogy, in the *dyslogistic* sense, may be compared to the (2) *hermetic theory of the parable* as a code meant to be deciphered by the elect. Its function is to *prevent* general understanding, to ward off encroachment by the uninitiated, the ill-prepared, and the unmeritorious. Paradoxically, this is the view occasionally endorsed by Christ himself, who replies to the disciples when asked why he teaches in parables,

Because it is given unto you to know the mysteries of the kingdom of heaven, but to them it is not given.

For whosoever hath, to him shall be given, and he shall have more abundance: but whosoever hath not, from him shall be taken away even that he hath.

Therefore speak I to them in parables: because they seeing see not; and hearing they hear not, neither do they understand.

And in them is fulfilled the prophecy of E-sai-as, which saith, By hearing ye shall hear, and shall not understand; and seeing ye shall see, and shall not perceive (Matthew 13: 11–14).

Christ's reference is to Isaiah 6:9–10, in which the Lord instructs his prophet to speak to the people in such a way as to "make their ears heavy, and shut their eyes; lest they see with their eyes, and hear with their ears, and understand with their heart, and convert, and be healed." Seeing, hearing, and understanding are, it would seem, educational outcomes that must be systematically short-circuited in the case of the multitude – it is caviar to the general. There can be no misconstruing Christ's intent, reiterated in Luke 8:10 – "Unto you it is given to understand the mysteries of the kingdom of God: but to others in parables; that seeing they might not see, and hearing they might not understand." And ditto Mark 4:11–12, which discriminates the elect, here the disciples, who are fit to receive the good news and pursue their education, from the masses whom Christ presumably condemns as idolaters no different from the idols they fabricate and worship. (The source passage may be located in Psalms 115:5–8: "They have mouths, but they speak not; eyes they have, but they see not; They have ears, but they hear not ... *They that make them are like unto them.*" and similarly Psalms 135: 15–18 as well as Isaiah 44:18. The allusion is to idolatry, idol-makers, and idol-worshippers.)

This parabolic attitude – teaching so as to thwart, impede, and prevent easy understanding or accomplishment – would make someone like Howard Nemerov, the distinguished American poet, an excellent teacher, if the well-known story about his post-class autopsy is not apocryphal. Nemerov was observed emerging from a creative-writing seminar chuckling and rubbing his hands with delight. Queried by a colleague, he replied: "Another budding talent bites the dust!" Elitist or hermetic teaching deliberately makes everything as difficult and rebarbative as possible, presumably to separate the tares from the wheat. So stringent and uncompromising is this form of pedagogy that even the disciples, anointed and privileged, occasionally find it necessary to approach the Master for an *explication de texte* (Matthew 13:36). But not many of the uninitiated will survive the ordeal.

What I have called Elytist teaching or learning-up pedagogy attempts to find a middle ground between the rabbinical and the hermetic theories of parable, and corresponds to the (3) Augustinian or patristic view which requires that decipherment stimulate desire.[70] (For as Augustine was aware, Christ, the master of paradox, also espoused an anti-hermetic conception of parable. See, for example, Mark 4:22 – "Nothing is hid except in order to be made manifest; nor is anything made secret but that it might become plain.") The parable is meant to excite curiosity, challenge interest, ultimately to *provoke* understanding, neither to promote it unduly nor rigorously to prevent it. Thus Christ spoke in parables, says Augustine in the *Sermons*, not "in order to prevent [the essential truths] from being communicated, but in order to provoke desire for them by this very concealment"; and again, in *Against Lying*, with respect to these essential truths, "For they are more joyfully discovered." (Augustinian teaching in this sense resembles Derridean writing where meanings struggle for embodiment, "preventing, but calling upon each other, provoking each other too.")

This point is so important for Augustine, who is after all one of the great teachers in the western tradition, that he lets no opportunity pass to renew and reconfirm it. "What is sought with difficulty," he pronounces in *On Christian Doctrine*, "is discovered with more pleasure ... Those who do not seek because they have what they wish at once frequently become indolent in disdain." Augustine was acutely aware of the scandal in the Christological doctrine of the parable and tried to reconcile it at least partially with the rabbinical view by siting "difficulty" as a *pedagogical catalyst* and not as a narrow-meshed filter: neither teaching *down* to the incapable nor rejecting the undeserving but teaching through difficulty in such a way that desire and potential are stimulated and the hearer is invited to learn *up* to the parabolic level exemplified by both the teacher and the material.[71]

Of course, Augustine was providentially spared having to meet Howard Nemerov's students, or mine for that matter, and one may legitimately wonder how he would have reacted to the affective gradients and intellectual orientations of the Ninja Turtle generation. Augustine presupposes the imminent possibility of conversion and conviction, a concern with the welfare of the soul, a seriousness of mind largely absent in the contemporary ambience. He did not pause to reflect, it would seem, on the undecidable effect of difficulty – *any* difficulty – which in certain situations may just as readily alienate as recruit the wavering sensibility. Nevertheless, I submit that the patristic conjecture, in attempting to strike a balance, however problematic, between the rabbinical and the hermetic, is the only plausible approach in the crisis of deterioration afflicting contemporary education. Even should the casualty rate in the average class exceed the norms we have come to regard as acceptable – and many teachers, it should be said, play limbo under a high-jump bar – anything less than the Augustinian synthesis in the context of education at all levels represents an evasion of responsibility. Difficulty must on no account be avoided.

Regarding this dynamic from a constructivist perspective, the education scholar Mario Désilets argues that an important factor in influencing motivation in learning – though I would prefer the term "desire" – is "the degree of difficulty."[72] Students who do not respond to difficulty, who will not make the effort to transcend the limitations we all begin with and which threaten continually to foreclose, or who for one reason or another prove over time inadequate to the task, incapable of surviving in the hardiness zone in which all genuine schooling is situated, must not be permitted to live off the scraps of pedagogical catering we so guiltily purvey. Let us make no mistake about this. In teaching down, we take the bottomless plunge, relying only on the bungee line of putative resilience to avoid critical impact, ultimately to find ourselves, educationally speaking, wambling about in that parody of I Corinthians 2:9, Bottom's discombobulated dream:

The eye of man hath not heard, the ear of man hath not seen, man's hand is not able to taste, his tongue to conceive, nor his heart to report ... It shall be called "Bottom's Dream," because it hath no bottom.[73]

APPENDIX ONE

Perhaps those teachers and administrators suffering from retention neurosis might learn a valuable lesson from the snowy owl which, as William Calvin informs us, in a bad year for lemmings, will not lay too many eggs, "whose successors will starve to death later in the season." The snowy owl, with the wisdom of Athene, "conserves resources so there will be several well-fed offspring rather than a half-dozen weak ones which may all die. *Less is more, when the forecast is poor.*" Analogously, what we need to do is ensure a more promising environment for our hatchlings rather than cram the nests with future Humpty Dumpties. As Calvin advises in his discussion of the q-Q spectrum (quantity versus Quality as competing evolutionary strategies), it is important that we "get control of the situation and encourage quality as the preferred strategy."[74]

I think it is generally understood, though rarely confessed, just what is meant by quality in the field of education: for starters, the earlier introduction in the curriculum of the so-called "hard" or "advanced" subjects, especially the maths and sciences; a thorough study of grammar and a workable familiarity with a second language by the age of twelve; and at least a cursory knowledge of some of the "classics" of literature as well as a synoptic knowledge of world history by high school graduation. This does not mean that we should engage in the systematic forcing of prodigies on the order, for example, of Hester Thrale's five-year-old daughter, Susanna, of whom she writes in her diary of 1775:

Her Improvements more than equal my hopes, my Wishes, nay my very Fancies. She reads even elegantly & with an Emphasis, says her Catechism both in French & English: is got into Joyn hand with her pen ... She knows the Map of Europe as well as I do, with the Capital Cities, Forms of Govt. & the Lines Circles & general Geography of the Globe She is Mistress of; & has a knowledge of the Parts of Speech that She cannot be ensnared by any Question.[75]

But it does mean that as parents and teachers we should be positively rubescent with shame at the spectacle of eighteen-year-old, middle-class students routinely producing such rubbish as the following (despite the occasional *felix casus*):

When Christ was at the stake and had nails in certain places.

The main characters in the story are talking among themselves by using language.

In these days, war is but a small piece of the world pie in which seems to really stink these days.

Thomas More wore a thorn shirt and was very much into the Roman Catholic religion.

In analising such a book one must lick your way to the center of the Tootsie Roll-Pop.

This book is alot about mid-evil times and the monk-persons in ministories.

(from a collection of student term papers now on my desk. See my *Education Lost* for other, rather chastening examples.)

These instances of graphic deficiency proliferate like grackles at the feeder and range perilously close to "normative production." The question poses itself: why retain students in mass institutions dedicated to preserving standards of unabashed mediocrity, their victims pretty well crippled for the rest of their intellectual careers? Why not instead do something substantial, scrap these Procrustean beds that go by the name of schools, admit we are stuck in a pedagogical cul-de-sac, start ratcheting up our entrance and performance standards, and reconsider the issue of educational *quality* that we so glibly conspire to avoid in our senseless infatuation with newfangled terminology, "advanced" methods, and the latest "reforms" that offer an eternally receding salvation? Why not, in other words, become truly revolutionary and "progressive" by rediscovering the wisdom inherent in the western intellectual tradition we have been so resolutely betraying over the last fifty years until we have reached the current impasse? For honesty does pay *in the long run*. It is time, then, that we confessed, if only to ourselves, that our preoccupation with numbers, quotas, graph curves, continuous assessment, theories of evaluation, process/product approaches, criteria-based learning, elusive "competencies," lab "ponderations," collapsible structures, designated coverage, and the rest of our educational supercargo has little effect on the issue we are allegedly addressing.

I admit that the predicament we are in is so vast, so complex, pervasive, and intractable, that there are days when I feel stunned with hopelessness; for what our culture lacks at present is not only quality schools but quality homes. Legions of children, even among the comparatively privileged, whose intellectual lives have already been blighted by neglect and indifference enter an educational institution that, from grade school to grad school, merely puts the finishing touches on the debacle. For the teacher, principal, and administrator in the serenity of their enlightenment effectively consummate a process that only time and systematicity have prevented the parent from completing.

I believe the moment has come to recognize that we do not have a "problem" on our hands – problems are specific, localizable, and soluble through the application of appropriate methods and techniques – but rather that we are rapidly approaching a cataclysmic watershed in the course of our civilization as we have come to know it over two millennia. In this context the educational crisis may be considered not only as the sickness itself but also as a kind of thermometer on which we read the progress of the fever. A better thermometer is certainly preferable to an inferior one, and we are well advised to perfect our instruments, especially as the instrument affects that which is to be measured. But what we need to do, with an urgency that admits of no delay, is to analyse and come to grips with the nature of the infirmity that we seem paradoxically content to suffer and discount. We need to recover our bearings, to find our history and recuperate our language. We need principally to redefine the individual in relation to the community, to re-invest in our children, not simply salving our consciences by registering them for scholarship funds but by diligently monitoring their distractions, and by setting aside large tracts of time for conversation, reading, directed study, and informative travel (which does not mean Disneyland) – that is, by contending stubbornly and at considerable personal expense against the strong cultural drift toward dispersal, violence, insensate entertainment, and what we might call the desire for private sufficiencies. Formal education in itself is no longer the only issue, unless, of course, we conceive of education in the largest possible sense as that which "society," whether by contract or evolution, was initially designed to serve. But as long as we euphemistically contrive to misapprehend a general catastrophe as a specific problem, to misread cultural collapse as educational decline, and to surrender the responsibilities of family and home to the expertise of the educator and the bureaucrat, we will have truly out-Heroded Herod in the slaughter of the innocents to which we have consigned our future.

Education, in effect, is both a symptom we must correctly decipher and an aspect of the disease we must learn to control, that which needs to be read as well as that which needs to be re-written. But one thing is certain. Zero teaching in the home followed by teaching down in the school must eventually produce the hollow man, lost somewhere between the essence and the descent, whom T.S. Eliot warned us about more than two generations ago, and whose attributes are now everywhere to be seen:

> Shape without form, shade without colour,
> Paralyzed force, gesture without motion.[76]

Naturally, the insistence upon quality entails that we revive in our own minds a humble respect for the reality principle that we tend to find immoral. Which it is, like death and taxes, and just as inevitable. In education this means that single-track systems like those recommended in the Paideia Program are likely to fail. What is even worse, they are bound to complicate the threadless labyrinth in which we have become lost. All children may be educable, as Paideia unobjectionably claims, but if so they are educable at different – sometimes incommensurably different – *rates of educability*.[77] Moreover, students often come equipped with different – and sometimes absolutely different – *limits of educability*. In an ideal society with infinite means and resources, such inbuilt rates and limits might be safely ignored with the reduction of the teacher-student ratio toward tutorial manageability and the expansion of education time to occupy a significant portion of the actuarial lifespan. But in a society that dedicates the larger proportion of its education budget to administrative waste and futility, and that suffers at the same time both an intellectual and competitive disadvantage vis à vis Europe and Japan, mere survival indicates at least a moderate degree of theoretical astringency. We must accept the stubborn, unpleasant fact that individuals arrive in the schools pre-equipped with variable *rates and limits* of educability which are only relatively accessible to "treatment," and that the scale of collective progress in any given class or program generally conforms to the overall parameters imposed by the LCD (lowest common denominator) factor. We need to modify our theoretical postulates and the practical behaviour that flows from these in strict accordance with the reality of the situation, despite the cost to our most cherished egalitarian sentiments, if we are to salvage some part of an education for those students whom we are systematically defrauding.[78]

The current situation reminds me of the old Jewish joke about the golf game in heaven between God, Jesus, and Moses. God achieves a hole-in-one by creating under the arching golf ball a brand-new universe that conforms to the laws of the divine stroke. Jesus summons a dove out of the blue which lifts the golf ball tenderly in its beak and deposits it for another hole-in-one. Moses leans on his club and irritably remarks: "All right, you guys, do you want to screw around or do you want to play *golf*?" God is the American progressivist educator. Jesus is his Canadian counterpart. Moses is the only realist around.

APPENDIX TWO

In the words of Paul Simpson,[79] "what an utterance implicates in a particular context may even be the opposite of its semantic entailments." His example runs as follows:

A: You've just failed your philosophy exam.

B: Terrific.

Implicature rests on the speakers' recognition that the entailments of a sentence – core propositions that are context-free – may diverge, reverse, or "defease" in dialogical or illocutionary situations, a process that implies an imaginative distance between the semantic base of a sentence and its non-truth-conditional components. The contemporary student has considerable difficulty determining meanings *not* directly and immediately deriving from the context-free semantic base of a sentence or an utterance. That is, the problem resides in a failure to *contextualize* adequately. This should not come as a surprise since context is, so to speak, itself contextualized in the larger encyclopedic system of implicit conventions and background information.

Precisely this lack of contextualization ability in so many of our students goes a long way to explaining why most silver-bullet, remedial programs are mainly a waste of everybody's time. One cannot acquire a facility in grammar management, lexicality, or mentation by a species of technomagic – abstract rules applied in an environment of decontextualized practice – as if learning to write and think were simply a question of stepping into a benzel dodecahedron and being whisked off to another star system in twenty minutes.[80] One needs a certain exposure to or saturation in the historical and cultural database over a period of many years, however random and unsystematic the process may be. What Shaun Gallagher says about problem solving is equally true of handling implicature. Both capacities depend "not just on the use of skills, but on a certain amount of background information organized in corrigible schemata for easy and efficient access."[81]

Gallagher continues: the student's preparation "is not simply the accumulation of information, but includes the development of abilities to project certain schemata which translate the unfamiliar into the familiar." So far so good. But Gallagher weakens his case when he goes on to argue that the success of the dialogical "interchange of interpretations" that constitutes the classroom event depends to a great extent on the teacher's tailoring the pedagogical presentation to the measure of the student's *Vorhabe*, that is, the latter's resources, background information, or fore-conceptions that schematize the acquisition of new knowledge. What Gallagher fails to realize here, carried away as he is by gusts of phenomenological enthusiasm over Husserlian horizons into Heidegerrian valleys, is that there is little a teacher can do when confronted with students whose "fore-structures" of knowledge and "prepredicative experience" would require a plethysmograph to detect. (Or put in more clinical language, how is *indexation* – the linking of new concepts with prior knowledge in order to establish an epistemic net and a taxonomical structure of ideas – to proceed if there are too few appropriate nodes in the mesh of pre-accumulated knowledge to provide for suitable linkaging?) One can enter the classroom armed to the teeth with hermeneutic subtleties and deploy a formidable battery of sophisticated concepts treating of the scalene relations between fore-structures and subject matter, the teacher's understanding, the facilitation of learning, and the student's comprehension, only to find that Hans-Georg Gadamer is no match for Roseanne Barr. Teaching becomes faking it, going through the motions, practising what I have elsewhere called the higher karaoke. To put it plainly, there is no substitute for *education*. One must begin more or less like Henry Adams if one is to conclude with some degree of appropriateness, as Adams does: *Nunc Age*.[82]

APPENDIX THREE

Closer to home (if I may be permitted another of my innumerable parentheses), the intuitive "feel" for the importance of the romantic stage may go some way to accounting for the enormous popularity of Bill Watterson's Calvin and Hobbes comic strip. From the empirical perspective, Hobbes is nothing more than a commonplace stuffed tiger, the typical *vade mecum* of the fearful child, the psychological hot-water bottle which in various forms we have all needed to cuddle into. But Hobbes in his transformed state is also the romantic embodiment of Calvin's rich and curious imagination through which the otherwise unreconstructed urchin is driven to the recoding of his everyday experience. Hobbes, who seems to be composed in equal parts of Blake's tyger and Milne's Tigger, at times loftily reflective and at others bouncedly mischievous, operates as Calvin's interlocutor and confidant, engaging productively in the experiments Calvin performs upon his world. Hobbes is precisely the imaginative agent seamlessly implicated in generating that ferment in the mind to which Whitehead refers, which leads to experiencing the wealth of "unexplored connections" between things, the internal preceptor and, in the largest sense of the phrase, the romantic collaborator who, when awakened, represents the initial stage of education so many of us have inadvertently skipped. Without the Hobbes factor coming into play, precision degenerates into repetition and generalization remains sketchy and lacking in substantial content.

Hobbes may also be regarded as a sort of mobile grammatical correlate which underwrites the "striped" or alternate mapping and formulation of experience, with the emphasis falling on the interrogative and conditional functions too often scanted in the early development of our students – the missing "Homeric interlude" to which Theodore Roszak points.[83] This is also what Gary Snyder intends in his recent *The Practice of the Wild*,[84] especially the chapter in which he elaborates Thoreau's provocative notion of "tawny grammar," the re-writing of the prosaic world to express the "wild and dusky knowledge" that relates us, tiger-fashion, to nature and stimulates our hunger for the infinite possibilities of experience – that allows, in Snyder's words, "the subtle and many-layered cosms of the universe [to find] their way into symbolic structure and ... [give] us thousands of tawny human-language grammars." Given this stress on the interrogative and conditional functions characterizing the stage of romance in the educational process – in other words, the freedom to query, explore, and propose options to the "real" – it is no accident, I think, that the names work ironically and "under erasure," the totalitarian Hobbes and the predestinarian Calvin subverted by their self-inscribed and friskily homonymous antonyms. Part of the pleasure of Watterson's comic strip lies in the way these historically resonant names self-destruct and form themselves anew in the course of each improbable escapade, bearing witness to the core of freedom contained in the husk of the drearily inevitable – that is, to the primary romantic desideratum in what we call "education."

We may note in passing that such forays into the *paranautical* realms of the strange and exuberant – like the voyage of Maurice Sendak's Max in his natty wolf costume sailing to Where the Wild Things Are – are predicated on the realization that the world would remain semiotically opaque, a mere banal datum despite its quota of hot suppers, without a connective grammar of event and possibility. The romantic impulse, as Heidegger saw, springs "from dissatisfaction and deficiency, as a wanting-to-be-away-from-oneself" – from the ordinary, decent or indecent, unrehabilitated self.[85] But this requires that the axial or longitudinal grammar of possibility around which the imagination rotates tilt away from the declamatory and the imperative towards the insistent framing of questions, the vocative of surprise and the odd syntactical modifications of conditionality that occur in our re-writing of both the world and ourselves. Only thus can we be expropriated and dispossessed from the quotidian self to become the radically other, a self founded in a romantic grammar of logical impropriety which tests and orders the illimitable, a Jumanji self. Nature herself appears from time to time to indulge in such bursts of the improbable, probing the limits of Creation, as the trove of unlikely metamorphic forms embedded in the Burgess Shale would seem to attest.[86] There is a sense in which education should perhaps also seek to explore the "wonderful life" of human potentiality in the intellectual correlatives of the Burgess Shale.

Notes

1 "Whence followeup with endspeaking nots for yestures, plutonically
pursuant on briefest glimpse from gladrags ..." See the passage on the
creative use of marginalia and footnotes in James Joyce, *Finnegans
Wake*, II, 2, Penguin, London, 1967. For a more "scholarly" approach
to the tremendum mysterium of the footnote and its lamentable slide
into the reduced status of the endnote, see Gertrude Himmelfarb's *On
Looking into the Abyss*, Vintage, New York, 1995, which dedicates an
entire chapter to the subject. The endnote makes it easier, she claims,
"to give a faulty or incomplete citation, or to parade one's erudition (or
conceal one's ignorance) by citing a dozen sources rather than the single
pertinent one." The reader will quickly discern that I am, by temperament as well as by intention, a dozen-source endnoter, but I will extenu-
ate the practice by deposing that I am neither trying to parade erudition
nor conceal ignorance. Rather, this endnoting practice, which I find personally congenial, reflects my saturation in the prose writers of the later
English Renaissance, particularly Robert Burton and Thomas Browne,
whose compositions effectively incorporate into the principal discourse
itself what was subsequently sieved out into the small print at the bottom of the page or at the end of the chapter or the book. I regard the
endnote, then, as an equivalent or alternate world, a place where I can
range freely among my sources and the reflections they engender without jamming the traffic of the central argument (or being perceived as

doing so) in the so-called "main body" of the text. This is not so much a scholarly practice as a necessary concession to the early but accelerating Denaissance in which we now write and read.

INTRODUCTION

1 See T.M. Amabile, *The Social Psychology of Creativity*, Springer-Verlag, New York, 1983; and David Perkins, *Smart Schools*, The Free Press, New York, 1992. Mullen is cited in Borg, W.R., & Gall, M.D., *Educational Research*, Longman, New York, 1994, originally published as "A Self-Attention Perspective on Discussion" in *Questioning and Discussion: A Multidisciplinary Study*, ed. J.T. Dillon, Ablex, London, 1988. For the report on reading, see Anderson, R.C. et al., *Becoming a Nation of Readers: The Report of the Commission on Reading*, National Institute of Education, Washington, DC, 1985. In particular, Amabile's study of motivational orientation, relying both on "empirical demonstration" and on the work of previous scholars, strikes me as little more than jargon-infested mystification calculated to occlude the obvious, and in this sense it is symptomatic of most of the literature in the field. But sometimes the obvious breaks through with such startling banality as to anaesthetize incredulity. Thus Amabile informs us that motivation "may change considerably over time, depending on the initial level of intrinsic interest, the presence or absence of social constraints, and the individual's ability to deal with those constraints effectively." To paraphrase Milorad Pavic in his *Dictionary of the Khazars* (Random House, Toronto, 1988), educational researchers generally tend to be about a hundred pepper fields west of Constantinople. (Pavic's definition of reading also seems far more suggestive and potentially fruitful than the ponderous conclusions of the Anderson report. "Reading," says the novelist, "is really like trying to hit one tossed stone with another.")

I might also note that when the research is not redundant it is often just plain wrongheaded or even perverse. For example, Lewis J. Perelman in *School's Out*, Avon Books, New York, 1992, drawing on the work of Eric Hanushek, claims that there is little or no evidence of improved learning resulting from smaller classes and higher teacher pay. But can any reasonable person with a healthy distrust of "expert" research – even if he or she has had no practical experience in the schools – entertain the slightest doubt that the increased sense of self-respect and leisure/study time attached to higher salaries would make for improved pedagogical performance? Or, as noted above, that smaller classes correlate with better teaching and learning? (As an ironic parenthesis, I would point out that Perelman, pushing hard for distance-delivery systems, satellite classrooms, mediated instruction, games and computers, recommends establishing a National Institute of Learning of whose acronym he seems blissfully unaware: NIL.) Such writings must be contested. As Martin Amis puts it in *The Information* (Random House, Toronto, 1996): "Don't be steamrollered: show your own quiddity in the field where the mad contend."

2 With respect to my loping and ubiquitous analogy, one must return, as Ned Lukacher argues, to the primal site of our epidemic metaphors, that is, to the core experience that legitimates them, if one is to understand staple behaviour and practice, whether private or institutional. Lukacher incidentally remarks on Paul de Man's French transliteration of his name – *Loup cacher*, or hidden wolf – which suggests a paronomastic relation to our present thesis. (Ned Lukacher, *Primal Scenes*, Cornell University Press, Ithaca, 1986.) We may find a similar paronomasia at work in the name which Aristotle gave to his school, the Lyceum or Place of Wolves whose meaning we have disastrously forgotten. See Camille Paglia, *Sexual Personae*, chapter 3 (Vintage, New York, 1991) for a short discussion on the Olympian derivation of the term. Barry Lopez, also aptly surnamed, takes us through the same derivation in *Of Wolves and Men*, Charles Scribner's Sons, New York, 1978. (With respect to Lopez and his important book, I should mention here that the wolf I am metaphorizing in these pages is precisely the imaginative projection of myth, fable, and folktale Lopez is trying honourably to defang. My aim, I hope it is understood, is not to rehabilitate the wolf as it is found in nature, noble as this ambition may be, but to recruit a cultural stereotype in order to substantiate an argument, that is, to pursue what Freud in *The Future of an Illusion* called our "education to reality." The wolf may be said to reflect an essential aspect or component of our own human nature that many of us have systematically forgotten or repressed, a thesis elaborated in the most recent book on the subject of wolves and men, Peter Steinhart's *The Company of Wolves*, Vintage, New York, 1995).

3 Of course, the "strategy" of Maurice Sendak's Max (see "Teaching Down or Learning Up," appendix 3) might also be considered: don a wolf costume to impress the Wild Things. We may translate this gesture into our field of interest as the development of a focus and directedness, an energy and dedication, comparable to the wolf's – or, put plainly, the shedding of sentimentality – quite unlike the wolvish toge of Coriolanus. In any event, because the wolf cannot be defeated does not mean that one should give up the struggle and retire into destructive resentments, helpless inactivity, the indulgence of clinical depression, or a Candidean garden of private delights and sufficiencies. The terms of the conflict are not victory and/or defeat, but *the continuation of the struggle* and/or defeat.

4 We no longer know, apparently, what Christopher Lasch's generation –
   or at least his kindred intellectual circle – knew: "We had no great confidence in the schools; we knew that if our children were to acquire any
   of the things we set store by – joy in learning, eagerness for experience,
   the capacity for love and friendship – they would have to learn the better part of it at home" (Christopher Lasch, *The True and Only Heaven*,
   W.W. Norton & Co., New York and London, 1991). With respect to our
   children today, perhaps the best that may be said is that the degradation
   of home life prepares them for the terminal debacle of their school careers by a kind of negative homeopathy.

CHAPTER ONE

1 Richard Ohmann, *English in America*, Oxford University Press, London, 1976. As Hilda Neatby remarks in *So Little for the Mind*, Clarke
   Irwin, Toronto, 1953, Canadian educational thinkers are generally
   twenty years or so behind their American counterparts. Small dogs pee
   where big dogs poo. This means that sometime soon we too will make
   the momentous discovery that composition courses aren't what they're
   cracked up to be. Meanwhile we continue to ply our aspirin pedagogy,
   trying to control the symptoms while leaving the infirmity intact.
      We should remark an exception to Neatby's principle of pedagogical
   lag in the work of Northrop Frye, for example, his essay "The Beginning
   of the Word" (1981), collected in *On Education*, Fitzhenry & Whiteside,
   Toronto, 1990, in which he proposes that learning to write starts with
   poetry, "the most primitive and powerful way of stylizing utterance,"
   moves toward prose, and only later confronts the specialized and peripheral "forms of jargon known as communication skills." He continues: "Trying to reverse the procedure by starting with the kind of gabble
   fostered by textbooks in 'effective writing' and working one's way in a
   vaguely literary direction does nothing ... I do not trust any way of
   teaching writing except composition from models, feeling one's way into
   the idiom of cultivated prose." In fact, we have got it all wrong in today's neogrammatical and rehabilatory climate: "The English teacher's
   ideal is the exact opposite of 'effective communication' or learning to become audible in the marketplace."
      To make matters worse, the "skills" of reading and writing normally
   inculcated, whether early or late, are primarily "passive skills" which
   lead "to reading such things as traffic signs, to learning how to do what
   one is told." We do not teach grammar in order to enable students to engage in what I have elsewhere called "the literate scansion of the universe" but, as Frye implies, so that students will themselves become
   grammatical units in the larger, sentential process determined by the

ideology they are constrained to serve. The relation between standard grammatical instruction and the politico-economic imperative is a subject that has yet to be fully explored. Interestingly enough, on the Frigian theory of social docility, we would be logically required to view the illiterate student who has not benefited from grammatical training as a carrier or harbinger of freedom, as one unamenable to socio-grammatical processing, the Viconian barbarian, whether of sense or of thought, who contests the homogenizing principle. On Frye's own terms, such individuals would have to be supported and maintained in their condition of communicative inadequacy. But perhaps the dilemma is only apparent. The illiterate is a revolutionary *malgré lui* and poses a threat to genuine social life based on mutual respect between unique individuals as grave as that associated with the averaging-out tendencies of ideological candling. Active literacy predicated on scrupulous reading, clear thinking, and the capacity for critical judgment remains an essential condition making for social peace and cultural productivity.

One should also note that Frye's ideological caveats are given impressionistically and merely occasionally and thus lack the cogency to be found in the systematic critiques of thinkers such as Louis Althusser (who regards education as among the most powerful ISAs or Ideological State Apparatuses), Antonio Gramsci (who developed the notion of the cultural hegemony), and Michel Foucault (for whom education functions like an interior panopticon, a means of internalizing social control). Frye's contestation finds perhaps its fullest development in the critical hermeneutics of the Frankfurt School, especially in the work of Jürgen Habermas which recognizes and tries to subvert the structures of ideological power and authority that educational institutions, among others, reflect and embody. Sound educational thinking requires that we adopt the standpoint associated with the hermeneutical approach of these "masters of suspicion," to apply Paul Ricoeur's celebrated phrase.

The reader interested in pursuing the hermeneutical critique of the hegemonic and authoritarian structure of educational discourse may also wish to consult Paulo Freire's *Pedagogy of the Oppressed* (Herder and Herder, New York, 1970), Michael Apple's *Ideology and Curriculum* (Routledge and Kegan Paul, London, 1979), and David Kolb's *Postmodern Sophistications* (University of Chicago Press, 1990), among a burgeoning literature on the subject. Shaun Gallagher argues in one of the most recent and valuable entries into the hermeneutic field (*Hermeneutics and Education*, SUNY Press, Albany, 1992) that it is precisely because educational situations are less than ideal and never strictly reproductive that emancipation from repressive and distorted structures of discourse is possible. But at the same time, such emancipation can never be absolute and must reflect to some degree the distorting power of ideological relations.

2 See Jacques Barzun, *The House of Intellect*, Harper, New York, 1959; and E.D. Hirsch, *Cultural Literacy*, Vintage, New York, 1988. (Italics mine.) While I cannot agree with Hirsch's strange, perhaps aberrant insistence on the need to memorize lists of decontextualized facts in order to achieve the desired state of cultural literacy, he is certainly persuasive in his analysis of the importance of schematic templates and general-information packages in the coherent scansion of experience. His main argument is fundamentally sound. It would be unfortunate if we permitted his theoretical excesses – the result, I suspect, of unreflected enthusiasm – to distract us from his kernel insight. And as I indicate now and later in the text, Hirsch is by no means the first to propose the notion of cultural literacy but only one of the most recent and bluntly contentious in a line of illustrious predecessors. The pedantic nature of his *recommendations* for learning has opened his work to damaging attacks by his critical adversaries. See for example, among many others, Lewis J. Perelman (*School's Out*, Avon Books, New York, 1992) who, scenting a weakness with adrenal ferocity, accuses Hirsch of "triviaphilia" and of peddling "brain-dead 'facts'" in his construction of an "artificial" curriculum.

3 I recall a few years back boggling over the results of a poll conducted among college-level students. By the age of eighteen, these students had read, on an average, six books *voluntarily*, aside from their required course work.

4 See Theodore Roszak, *The Cult of Information*, Pantheon, New York, 1986; and Umberto Eco, *The Role of the Reader*, Indiana University Press, Bloomington, 1984.

5 Edward Sapir, *Selected Writings in Language, Culture and Personality*, University of California Press, Berkeley, 1949. (Italics mine.)

6 Benjamin Lee Whorf, *Language, Thought, and Reality*, MIT Press, Boston, 1956. See also David Rumelhart *et al.* who argue convincingly for "the important synergistic role of language ... in shaping our thought" (*Parallel Distributed Processing: Explorations in the Microstructure of Cognition*, vol. 2, MIT Press, Cambridge, MA, 1986). Even though many forms of human classification turn out to be motivated rather than arbitrary, there is no doubt that language determines in large measure the ways in which we conceptualize the world of mind and culture.

7 I say reality as "sensed," not as captured, to avoid the undecidable conflict over referentiality.

8 See Judith Greene's *Psycholinguistics*, Penguin, New York, 1972, for a lucid account which is also an unsparing critique of Chomsky's transformational grammar. What is at stake here, of course, is the relation

between "competence" and "performance," the former regarded by Chomsky as an a priori linguistic universal. Subsequent research has tended to indicate that competence and performance are not as readily separable as Chomsky's formulation suggests, a finding that in part underwrites my own thesis in these pages. See also Richard Rorty, *Contingency, Irony and Solidarity*, Cambridge University Press, Cambridge, 1989, for an extensive discussion of the subject. Extrapolating from the work of Donald Davidson, Rorty claims that the "idea that there are nonlinguistic things called 'meanings,' which it is the task of language to express, as well as the idea that there are nonlinguistic things called 'facts,' which it is the task of language to represent" must now be discarded. Language is too deeply seamed and sutured into the subject-object matrix to be treated as severable and re-implantable. All this goes back, of course, to Ferdinand de Saussure's revolutionary thesis: "Language is not a nomenclature."

9 Jonathan Culler, *Structuralist Poetics*, Routledge, London and New York, 1975. I should indicate here that I use the word "grammar," cognate with "glamour" (cf. the two meanings of "spell") in a non-technical sense to denote not the formal study of morphology and syntax but the partly mysterious way in which disparate items of thought, language, *or* experience, as well as the amalgam of thought, language, *and* experience, are distinguished and connected to form integrated structures of meaning reflected in acts of recognition, expression, and behaviour. Grammar has to do with the ability (1) to distinguish between different orders of event or alternative worlds, whether virtual, textual, or actual, and (2) to construct seamless, diachronic wholes from isolable, synchronic constituents, whether epistemic, semantic, or experiential – a process that always retains a flavour of magic as it simultaneously relies on the exertions of discipline and the acquisition of knowledge.

10 Michael Harris, *In Transit*, Signal/Véhicule Press, Montreal, 1985.

11 Examples abound. At present I am grading my way through a new batch of term papers, in the first of which, a study of Frost's "The Road Not Taken," I find the following: "He compares life to a walk in the woods, and arrives at a fork." This sentence is plain, unobjectionable English, devoid of "grammatical" errors. The problem is that it suggests the poet is composing his poem, engaged in drawing comparisons, *while at the same time* enjoying a walk in the woods. There is nothing in the narrative of the poem to certify the assumption. Here we have another category mistake or mixing up of discrete levels of experience, with its prepositional unawareness of both the world to which the poem refers and the world in which the reader and writer of the paper encounter one another. In the next paper, treating of Eco's brilliant novel, my student writes: "In the abbey, where *The Name of the* Rose took place." Same

business. It is almost with relief that I come across a fragmentary identification a little further on that yields to immediate and obvious "grammatical" analysis (apart from its onomastic nonchalance): "Rosa Pristina is the girl's name who slept with Adso before she was burnt at the steak." What strikes me as most interesting about this phrasing, however, is the lexical unawareness of temporal relation, since Adso could not have slept with Ms Pristina* *after* she was grilled (though the orthography does open the possibility of cannibalism). Such discrepancies or infelicities cannot be explained away as a form of syllepsis (i.e., a grammatical construction in which a single word is used to modify two words with only one of which it agrees, a common stylistic procedure) but as a kind of amphibology (i.e., ambiguity arising from uncertain grammatical construction). Student writing is not sylleptic but amphibolic, not a taking of grammatical liberties but the result of structural incoherencies *which are themselves the product of a failure of the temporal imagination*, an inability to distinguish clearly between time strata, grammatical mood, and conditional worlds. This is the deeper amphibology we need to come to grips with, a basic uncertainty in time-world construction.

12 A certain Aristides Mastoras, resident of the Greek island of Paxos, whose self-proclaimed object in life is "to fantasize experience." In a delfinian world, a new and different grammar of complexity is permitted, one that may perhaps be described as *sinusoidal* insofar as the latitudinal grid and longitudinal curve remain perpendicular to each other, proper and unskewed. Thus, like Arion's or Antony's, the delights of the poet Mastoras "were dolphinlike, they showed his back above / The element they lived in" (*Antony and Cleopatra*, V, ii). The latitude of the language crosses the longitude of the self in precisely the spot where one is visible to others.

13 Neil Postman, *Technopoly*, Random House, New York, 1992.

14 I am here referring to and citing from my *Education Lost*, OISE Press, Toronto, 1989. For an illuminating study of the different kinds of time which in their differing proportions make up the cultural perspective, see Edward T. Hall, *The Dance of Life*, Doubleday, New York, 1983.

---

*The allusion is to the Latin conclusion of the novel, from Bernard of Morlay's twelfth-century *ubi sunt* composition, *De contemptu mundi*: *Stat rosa pristina nomine, nomina nuda tenemus.* (The rose survives because of its name, we have only names.) After the publication of *The Name of the Rose*, Eco discovered an alternate reading of this line: *Stat Roma Pristina nomine.* "Had I come across this version before, both my life and yours would have changed." (Umberto Eco, personal communication, 20 Nov. 1991). Certainly my student's analysis would have changed, though in what way it is beyond mortal prescience to know.

What we are speaking of here under the rubric of "prenoetic temporality" would, in Hall's terminology, consist in a conflation of "personal time," "micro time," and "metaphysical time," classified under the categories of "individual-physical," "individual-cultural," and "group-cultural," respectively. Cf. Hall's temporal mandala or map of time, p. 17. (*Beyond Culture*, Doubleday, New York, 1976, is an important reference text for anyone interested in the deplorable state of modern education, which double-digs the ground for the later work in its analysis of both culture and time. The ur-text is, of course, *The Silent Language* (Doubleday, New York, 1959). The study of spatial proxemics, *The Hidden Dimension* (Doubleday, New York, 1966) bears upon our subject only proximately. I regret that neither space nor time permit me to develop a high-context relation with Hall's oeuvre.)

15 Roman Jakobson and Morris Halle, *Fundamentals of Language*, Mouton, The Hague, 1956, and especially Jakobson's essay included there, "Two Aspects of Language and Two Types of Aphasic Disturbance."

16 Ferdinand de Saussure, *Course in General Linguistics*, McGraw-Hill, New York, 1976. (Saussure developed and presented his ideas at the University of Geneva in the first and second decades of the century.) According to the *Course*, the sentence operates under syntagmatic constraints (parts can occur only in conjunction with certain designated elements – thus syntactic and grammatical rules) and out of consideration for paradigmatic contrasts (parts can be *replaced* only by certain designated elements – thus substitution or commutation rules). In the formulation of Robert Scholes (*Structuralism in Literature*, Yale University Press, New Haven, 1974): "The meaning of a single word is determined partly by ... the word's syntagmatic (linear, diachronic) aspect, often conceptualized as a horizontal axis along which the sentence is spread out ... [and partly] by its relation to words *not* in the sentence but present in a paradigmatic (or 'vertical,' synchronic relationship ...)." Apart from Scholes's lucid contribution to the subject, noteworthy studies include Terence Hawkes's *Structuralism and Semiotics*, University of California, Berkeley, 1977, and David Lodge's *The Modes of Modern Writing*, University of Chicago, Chicago, 1977.

17 David Lodge, ibid. It is no doubt advisable to avoid the temptation toward neurological speculation. The sort of dysfunction I am considering here may be said to *resemble* the symptoms of Broca's aphasia which, as Jay Ingram informs us, cannot handle or reproduce connectives, "words like 'but' or 'when' or 'if,' the words that make grammatical sentences possible." Ingram alludes to Helen Neville's well-known experiments which "seem to show that we use one part of the brain for 'grammar' words and another for concrete words like nouns and verbs." Much of our students' *writing* is manifestly deficient in grammatical or connec-

tive tissue, although their *speech* is not, and in fact often seems to suffer from connective overload. This suggests the intriguing possibility that we are dealing with *two* distinct, representational systems whose relation to one another is asymmetrical, an idea I address in chapter 6, "Script and Nondescript." The *physiology* of aphasia is broached here only as a metaphorical equivalent, although one cannot a priori rule out some form of physiological substratum as a correlate of the dysfunction. See Jay Ingram, *Talk Talk Talk*, Penguin, New York, 1992.

18 For example, "blue" in the phrase "blue eyes" generates meaning in part *differentially*, insofar as it is not "brown," "green," "grey," etc., colour-words that are implicitly present even though the selection has already been made.

19 Paul Virilio, *The Aesthetics of Disappearance*, Semiotext(e), New York, 1991. (Italics mine.)

20 Edward T. Hall, *Beyond Culture*.

21 In today's online, web-browsing world, time is experienced mainly as a shortcut through or around the thickets of demanding temporal application. Which is to say it is scarcely experienced at all. As Cliff Stoll remarks in *Silicon Snake Oil* (Anchor, New York, 1995), "Good research, like good art, good cooking, good teaching, and good whatever, requires patience, creativity, multiple approaches, time, and work. Lots of work."

Looking at the same issue from another perspective, François Peraldi, prescinding from the three Lacanian registers of the imaginary, symbolic, and real orders of existence, distinguishes three corresponding levels of time. Imaginary time is time held in suspension, unmeasurable and monotonous, akin to undifferentiated revery. Real time is alien to the subject's integrative fibre of recollection, a sudden irruption of the totally different periodicity proper to the outer, unknown, irreducible world of the Other. "Confronted with the unbearable aspect of the non-representable and nonsymbolized real," Peraldi writes, "the subject can either escape into the imaginary world ... or can symbolize ... [the] nameless 'Thing.'" As soon as the real is symbolized or named and its name linked into the signifying chain of discourse, the individual enters into *symbolic time* marked by signifiers with a specificity (for example, dates) that establishes a coherent and predictable relation between memory and anticipation, fact and speculation, historical traces and future probabilities. The value of the humanistic disciplines (and language studies) resides precisely in this initiation of the subject into the order of symbolic time which provides the only workable alternative to the stasis provoked by the real or the fantasy of existence induced by the imaginary. (Cf. Francois Peraldi, in *The Purloined Poe*, ed. John P. Muller and William J. Richardson, Johns Hopkins University Press, Baltimore, 1988.)

22 Todorov's structural analysis of the *Decameron* in terms of basic grammatical and syntactic categories, as consisting of propositions and sequences whose constituent parts of speech contribute to the narrative process (characters are nouns, their attributes, adjectives, and the actions in which they engage, verbs), touches upon the notion I am broaching here. (See Tzvetan Todorov, *Grammaire du Decameron*, Mouton, The Hague, 1969). The historical "text," too, may be seen as a narrativizing of grammatical categories, that is, in Terence Hawkes's phrase, as "a kind of sentence-structure writ large," with historical personages subbing as nouns, their attributes comprising states of being, interior properties, and exterior conditions, and their actions clearly readable as transformations of a situation. By the same token, the sentence may be understood as *the historical dynamic writ small*, involving contexts, properties, and conditions participating in a sequence of semantic transformations. For an extensive and thoroughgoing analysis of narrative structure, see Gerard Genette, *Narrative Discourse*, Cornell University Press, Ithaca, New York, 1980, especially chapter 5 where he discusses "metadiegetic narrative," a form of storytelling in which, like Ulysses among the Phaeacians, one tells the story of the past as if it were occurring in the *narrative* present. For the relation between the basic tropes of language (metaphor, metonymy, synecdoche, and irony), and the parsing of the historical continuum, see Hayden White's *Metahistory*, Johns Hopkins University Press, Baltimore, 1973, 1987.

23 George Steiner, *Real Presences*, University of Chicago Press, Chicago, 1989.

24 Gerard Manley Hopkins, *Poems and Prose*, Penguin, Hammondsworth, 1953.

25 In a class of thirty-six students, to whom I had assigned "Hansel and Gretel" as a study project in the light of Bruno Bettelheim's interpretive analysis in *The Uses of Enchantment* (Vintage, New York, 1977), it turned out that only seven could boast of prior familiarity with the story. Another nine had "heard of it." (Five of my students hailed from different traditions and could supply the deficit with similar tales from their own "encyclopedia," but the results of my soundings were still sobering.)

26 Jacques Derrida comments on Rousseau's *Emile* as follows: "We know what importance *Emile* gives to time, to the slow maturation of natural forces. *The entire art of pedagogy is a calculated patience.*" (*Of Grammatology*, Johns Hopkins University Press, Baltimore, 1976. Italics mine.)

27 Hilda Neatby, *So Little for the Mind*. For an extensive analysis of this phenomenon, the epidemic lack of autonomy, the missing sense "of individual responsibility for individual achievement," see Philip Rieff, *The*

Triumph of the Therapeutic, Harper, New York, 1966. Peter Sloterdijk, writing along the same lines in *Critique of Cynical Reason* (Fitzhenry & Whiteside, Markham, 1987), puts the matter in his typically ammoniac way: "In the end, one will have to attend urological classes to learn how to piss correctly." In Edward T. Hall's terms, this is a classic instance of "informal learning" – what is learned without the knowledge that it is being learned – being programmatically misconstrued as "technical learning" – information transmitted explicitly and in coherent outline form. He cites as an example of this ludicrous technolatry the case of a couple of children, noticing a neighbour's child clambering up a tree, wanting the name of her instructor in tree climbing. (*The Silent Language*, Doubleday, New York, 1959). Gerald Graff also comments interestingly on the diffusion of "therapeutic man" in contemporary society: "One's very selfhood is understood as a problem, if not as a grievance, a condition of acute vulnerability ... requiring permanent administration and 'caring.'" It is a very small step from "the victimized self-conception of the therapeutic type" to the problems and grievances of the contemporary student and the concomitant tendency of teachers to therapeuticize education (*Literature Against Itself*, University of Chicago Press, Chicago, 1979).

28 See also John Simon, *Paradigms Lost*, Penguin, New York, 1976, Christopher Lasch, *The Culture of Narcissism,* Warner Books, New York, 1979, Frank Smith, *Insult to Intelligence,* Heinemann, Portsmouth, 1988, and Max Dublin, *Futurehype,* Penguin, New York, 1990, for detailed and extensive documentation of this thesis. I have also found Lincoln Barnett's *The Treasure of Our Tongue* (Mentor, New York, 1962) and Jeremy Campbell's *Grammatical Man* (Simon & Schuster, New York, 1982), extremely useful in contextualizing the problem. As for Postman, who comes carrying the message, his critique of the depredations of the First Curriculum can be found fully developed in *Teaching As a Conserving Activity* (Delacourt, New York, 1979) and *The Disappearance of Childhood* (Delacourt, New York, 1982). In a recent foray into the field of cultural analysis (*Technopoly*), this valiant Quixote of the classical curriculum, with whom I confess to a profound sympathy, tilts instructively with cybernetic giants – or, rather, tries to infect them with a moral virus. For a less apocalyptic treatment of the same material, see Stephen Toulmin, *Cosmopolis*, Macmillan, New York, 1990.

29 And avoid what Béralde in Molière's *The Imaginary Invalid* castigates as "specious babbling which offers words in place of sound reasons and promises instead of results." And results are certainly at issue. I have taught and tested large numbers of students over the years who had presumably benefited from the writing-skills programs into which their

placement scores directed them. Yet most of the time, after considering
their work, I could just as well have quoted Theseus's pronouncement
on Peter Quince's prologue: "His speech was like a tangled chain; nothing impaired, but all disordered," or sympathized with Alice trying to
make sense of the Mad Hatter's remarks, which "seemed to her to have
no sense of meaning in it, and yet it was certainly English."

30 What they would want to hear is something like Jerome Bruner's dictum that "the lesson ... depends upon the attunement of the teacher to
the expressions and intents of members of a class." (*Actual Minds,
Possible Worlds*, Harvard University Press, Cambridge, MA, 1986). But
eam fortasse vidit in Vtopia. Scholar-teachers like Bruner, working in
the graduate departments of patrician universities, comfortably aging to
pink like subsiding trilliums, can affect proletarian attitudes, indulging
with impunity in Elysian meditations. What are the "expressions and intents" of the average high-school or college class? Attuning oneself as a
teacher to this level of performance and expectation is tantamount to
committing pedagogical suicide. In giving students what they want to
hear, education is in danger of becoming, like cooking, sophistry, and
the beauty trade, one of the forms of what Plato in the *Gorgias* calls
kolakeia, that is, flattery.

31 And the ghost-writer is already with us in the guise of the latest cybernetic phantom, a monstrosity that goes by the name of Rightwriter. This
grammar-checking software is by and large "not very effective," spot-
ting on an average "only about 45% of the errors" in any given sample
of student writing, apart from being intrusive, confusing, awkward, and
on the whole user-unfriendly. More to the point, Rightwriter is completely oblivious of the interior or underlying dimension of prenoetic
temporality and refuses to speak to the central issue of cognitive anorexia from which too many students routinely suffer. As a result, its influence is in the long run merely pernicious, distracting its manipulators
from the real problem they need to confront and resolve while catering
to the educator's misguided sense of technical effectiveness. One teacher,
reporting on his encounter with the reified ectoplasm, finds that it "has
helped me to reduce my use of the passive voice, and to shorten the
long, convoluted sentences I used to favour." (These citations are from
the "Language across the Curriculum Bulletin," John Abbott College,
Spring, 1992.) Rightwriter would plainly have demolished Proust and
chopped up Joyce into bite-size gobbets, but it is no kinder to ordinary
mortals for whom the epitome of good writing appears to be the effortless production of short, active, colourless sentences from which all traces of personality have been diligently scraped away. (Note the passive
construction.) The basic conceptual flaw on which Rightwriter rears
and strides is the attempt to modify external "performance" while ignor-

ing the reality of internal "competence" (if I may apply Chomsky's categories here). But Rightwriter continues to strike with gathering ferocity and soon the Sons of Rightwriter will begin to haunt the educational establishment, producing an increasingly zombified clientele. I suspect that unless we intervene quickly and decisively, we will have on our hands a job for Ghostbusters – who, despite what the movies imply, are not infallible. Jacques Barzun's recommendation of the proper way of going about the incommensurable job of teaching students to write seems far more sensible than mobilizing the usual array of recipes and techniques: "There may be a better target than 'effective communication,' with its implied guessing at the mind of another. A preferable aim ... is 'fit expression.'" In other words, if the writer's "word portrait is a good likeness, he will automatically communicate." (Jacques Barzun, *A Word or Two Before You Go*, Wesleyan University Press, Middletown, CT, 1986). Clifford Stoll puts the matter with characteristic terseness in *Silicon Snake Oil*: "The emphasis on writing tools – outliners, hyphenators, spell checkers, laser printers – takes the students' minds off the main task: to think. And then to write."

32 Bruno Bettelheim, *The Uses of Enchantment*.

33 Benjamin Bloom, *Stability and Change in Human Characteristics*, Wiley, New York, 1964.

34 Torsten Husen, *Present Trends and Future Developments in Education*, OISE Press, Toronto, 1971.

35 Lionel Trilling, *Sincerity and Authenticity*, Harvard University Press, Cambridge, MA, 1972.

36 Pierre Bourdieu and Jean-Claude Passeron, *Reproduction in Education, Society and Culture*, Sage, London, 1977.

37 Naturally, even the best students cannot be expected to organize themselves in a vacuum. It is precisely here that "good teaching" may also intervene to provide the impetus and the supervision that enables such programs to get off the ground. The Writing Project in the English department at John Abbott College would have been a dead letter without the contribution of teachers like Penny Ross, Shan Evans, and Adrienne Elliott. Still, in the absence of the "habitus," even such well-intentioned and well-administered programs can have only a Parthian effect. In the words of Simeon Potter, "A child's acquisition of language depends largely upon the quality of the family life ... the boy or girl who hears lively conversation and discussion among people of all ages within the family circle over a long period of years enjoys untold advantages" (*Language in the Modern World*, Penguin, Baltimore, 1960).

38 Richard J. Herrnstein and Charles Murray, *The Bell Curve: Intelligence and Class Structure in American Life*, Free Press, New York, 1994. (Italics mine.) There is no doubt that this is one of the most important

and controversial books to appear in recent years in the field of cultural studies. Here I wish only to register a certain scepticism about the appositeness of the authors' underlying premises regarding the nature of intelligence, which they understand for the most part in its instrumental and pragmatic aspects, as mere verbal facility or spatiovisual performance. As Alan Ryan remarks in an unfavourable review of *The Bell Curve*, entitled "Charles Murray's IQ," in *The New York Review of Books*, 17 November 1994, "The only thing with which IQ correlates very closely is our performance on tests that measure the same skills that IQ tests measure ... [I]n a world full of lawyers and economists and scientifically trained professionals ... [i]ntelligence tests test for just that kind of intelligence." Ryan concludes his article on a *fortissimo* note: "In short, *The Bell Curve* is not only sleazy; it is, intellectually, a mess." My own sense of the book is that there is much in it that merits respect and that many of its arguments are indeed persuasive, especially with regard to education. The Ryan review on the whole must be taken *cum grano*: anyone reading the review and not the book would remain unaware of the robust good sense and close argumentation that rescue the latter from some of its more problematic speculations and propositions. And it should be said that Herrnstein and Murray do temper their definition of intelligence by noting the obligation to marry it with a "kind of wisdom [that] does not come naturally with a high IQ."

Ryan focuses, unfairly as it seems to me, mainly on the weaknesses and discrepancies in the text, which in a work of such ambitious scope and passionate purpose are bound to crop up, but fails to consider its manifest strength, its honesty, courage, and evidential force. Ryan would no doubt argue that its flaws are symptomatic of its underlying premises, which I find to be sound. Where the authors seem to go astray is in some of the recommendations that flow from these premises, as, for example, the suggestion that some sort of *cognitive* screening test be applied to potential immigrants. Ryan is perfectly correct in taking exception to such easily abused and misconceived practices. But *The Bell Curve*'s essential thesis here is that *competency rather than nepotistic principles* should be brought to bear in assessing whether immigrant applications should be approved or not, which strikes me as eminently reasonable. In my estimation, if an applicant promises to become a liability rather than an asset to his or her adoptive country – that is, if the applicant cannot show that he or she is (a) financially stable, (b) sufficiently educated, or (c) possessed of skills and abilities that may legally contribute to the productivity of the nation or serve some recognized need – then refusal would seem entirely justified. The Swiss seem to have no problem with far more rigorous screening procedures.)

39 John Ralston Saul, *Voltaire's Bastards*, Penguin, New York, 1992.

40 Gregory Ulmer, *Applied Grammatology: Post(e) Pedagogy from Jacques Derrida to Joseph Beuys*, Johns Hopkins University Press, Baltimore, 1985, from which I quote in the ensuing.

41 Ulmer cites the powerful critique of Regis Debray, delivered at the Estates General of Philosophy, Paris, June 1979, which insists (in Ulmer's words) that "no real thinking ... can occur by means of television for reasons inherent in the medium." Television "(1) is a communication without reciprocity; (2) replaces the value of truth with the pursuit of seductive effects; and (3) is ephemeral, prohibiting verification by the inhibition of memory." But Ulmer argues that Debray is in error. His mistake, "from the point of view of [Applied Grammatology], is to imagine that the traditional mode of philosophizing ... is the only kind of philosophy possible, instead of considering that the philosophical project, in order to operate with film/video, should be rethought, redefined, redesigned to exploit the virtues specific to these media." I would argue in turn that Ulmer is mistaken, that the very word he uses, "rethought," implies the ability to reason in a linear, sequential, and non-analogic way that can be promoted and distilled only in the traditional, print-oriented pedagogy of which he himself is an obvious beneficiary, and that the supposed "virtues specific to these media" – presumably electronic instantaneity and pictorial structuration – have yet to be demonstrated as virtues favourable to diachronic thinking, even when that is erroneous thinking. And as for *philosophic* thinking, I cannot do better than quote from Vincent Descombes (*The Barometer of Modern Reason*, Oxford University Press, 1993), who very sensibly claims that philosophy "cannot allow itself the luxury of not being *difficult*." (Italics in text.) Debray's critique remains intact, as does Annie Dillard's simple and comprehensive summing-up in *The Writing Life* (HarperCollins, New York, 1990): "We watch television and miss the show."

Further, I find it a trifle bizarre, to say the least, that the polemic in favour of the filmic paradigm or cinetext model as furnishing the organizing principles of the "new pedagogy" is based to a large extent on the theoretical writings and production examples of Sergei Eisenstein (and Bergman, Godard, *et al.*) which appeal chiefly to a small, highly educated gentry (people who read Sontag and Barthes, for example). My students on the whole appreciate movies like *October* and *Last Year at Marienbad* mainly for their sedative properties and find the theoretical principles they embody far too wiredrawn and *raffiné* to generate much interest. Their idea of a good film is something like *Tango and Cash*, as rich in explosive violence as it is poor in character motivation. *Tango and Cash* provides them paronomastically with the appropriate objects of desire, dancing and money, but Eisensteinian theory, which dissociates the image from the thing it ostensibly reflects or imitates, thus relying on abstruse, cerebral manipulations and values, leaves them cold. Class performance predicated on the filmic paradigm would have to adopt *Tango and Cash* and not *October* as its structuring score or template: lots of jokes, flip banter, rudimentary development of ideas, one-dimensional plot line (no double inscription here), heaps of teacher acrobatics (like Mr Keating pirouetting on the desk in *Dead Poets Society*) – and, it should be noted for the benefit of our cismundane theorists, scenic representation stuck with Krazy Glue to the reality it appears to reproduce.

Andrei Codrescu puts the matter with characteristic directness in *The Disappearance of the Outside*, Addison-Wesley, New York, 1990. "The image," he writes, " is the enemy of the word: the two issue from different places ... are located in different regions of the brain ... The Reader and the Viewer are not the same creature ... they are now two competing strains of humanity." For Codrescu, those who are nourished by the image tend toward a shallow, collective, simulated existence, absorbed into the featureless horizon of spectacle and simulacrum in which mutual resemblance overrides individual uniqueness. It is in the private act of reading, mediated by a complex grammar that provides the distance in which *judgment* may develop, that the self is formed.

Similarly, Jacques Ellul cogently remarks, "Teachers who work out illustrations and make use of films to make knowledge more accessible ... are convinced that the mode of thinking that involves images and intuition can fit in perfectly with the traditional mode of thinking by reasoning and discourse ... Yet ... they are *opposing* mental attitudes." There is no doubt for Ellul that these two modes of response are mutually inhospitable: "The dominant use of one means prevents our valid use of the other." Images eliminate the epistemic distance between subject and object and reinforce cognitive instantaneity, promoting a global, intuitive reaction that bypasses the mental apparatus. Ellul does not mince words here. Audio-visual techniques "are comparable to ancient idols, which required human sacrifice." The image devours the word, the fragile vehicle of truth, by reducing its laborious, involuted, deferring character to the dimension of a "displayed, fictitious, and simulated reality." The teacher should not become an audio-visual specialist but a dedicated iconoclast. See Jacques Ellul, *The Humiliation of the Word*, William B. Eerdmans, Grand Rapids, MI, 1985. David Cronenberg in his film *Videodrome* has articulated the psychic danger the TV screen poses as a permeable membrane allowing the unreal or virtual world of pure spectacle to leak into and contaminate the real world whose laws, despite our resistance or neglect, remain inexorable. Reality becomes hallucination, infected by the mediagraphic virus, once we accept, as the character Prof. O'blivion remarks, that "the television screen is the retina of the mind's eye ... television is reality, and reality is less than television." (For an interesting study of Cronenberg's work, see Douglas Kellner writing in *The Canadian Journal of Political and Social Theory*, vol. 13, no. 3, 1989. For an analysis of "telematic being," which is disastrously innocent of history because it has "the power to collapse distance instantaneously through image and information processing," see Arthur Kroker and Michael A. Weinstein, *Data Trash*, St. Martin's Press, New York, 1994.)

42 Paul Fussell, *BAD, or the Dumbing of America*, Simon & Schuster, New York, 1991.

43 The issue is not really very complicated. Television, if it is not rigorously controlled and time-censored, is bad for you for two reasons. Its *content* pedestrianizes the mind, since its presentation of human psychology must be ruthlessly simplified and resolutely cliché-driven regardless of format: sitcom, soap opera, news, commercial, late movie, prime-time programming. Otherwise it quickly dies the Nielson death. Secondly, as Postman has persuasively argued, its *form* changes (perhaps "distorts" is a better word) the mind's structure of expectation and apperception, promoting a generalized response which is discontinuous, analogic, anti-hierarchical, nondiscursive, iconic, and instantaneous, that is, which works against the symbolic displacements of the educational imperative. The kind of "attention" which television promotes is akin to hypnosis or mesmerism, an involuntary eclipse of the waking, analytic faculty, or quite bluntly, another form of unconsciousness. Its real effect is to loosen or sever the fibres of disciplined attention, to detach the retina of the introspective eye, disrupting inner, epistemic vision. To put it another way, *all television is violent* regardless of its content. The social problem of violence *on* television is really the cognitive problem of violence *in* television. (To give belated credit where it is due, I would note here that the anti-TV argument has been forcefully and comprehensively made in Jerry Mander's ground-breaking *Four Arguments for the Elimination of Television*, Quill, New York, 1978, to which the reader is emphatically referred.)

44 Matthew Hodgart, *A Voyage to the Country of the Houyhnhnms*, Gerald Duckworth, London, 1964. This novel is a true prolepticon. Another of its serendipities is evident in the name of one of the most popular search engines in today's Web-browsing world: Yahoo, whose Web guide for kids is known as Yahooligans!

45 Derek Attridge, *Peculiar Language*, Cornell University Press, Ithaca, 1988.

46 What Jacques Derrida writes in "Fors," with respect to the ongoing saga of the "Wolf Man," applies precisely to the conduct of the postmodern: "the tale of a tale, of its progress, its obstacles, its interrup-

tions, its discoveries all along a labyrinth." And see Eco's *The Name of the Rose* for a more popular staging of the same idea, a novel that constitutes the very labyrinth it describes. "So what else is new?" Joyce might have yawned. Interestingly, many of my colleagues are deeply sceptical of the plausibility of introducing such material to the contemporary college student, who is, presumably, insufficiently advanced to consider the kind of fiction that has been with us since 1760 (the publication date of *Tristram Shandy*). It is, apparently, the kiss of death to broach *ideas* in the contemporary classroom. At what point, then, one is inclined to ask, are ideas supposed to impinge upon the life of the student? Intellectual deficits, as I have argued here, are precisely the negative quantities we will have to positivize if we intend to do anything meaningful about the literacy scandal. But the emphasis on ideas is what many critics righteously dismiss as *elitist* or Carriage Trade education. The alternative, I am afraid, is to continue in the direction we appear to have taken, depriving students of the discipline they need in order to *learn* in any meaningful sense of the term – pursuing, if I may be permitted to so phrase it, the usual *delitist* curriculum. The best I can say about this sort of pedagogy is that it does yield from time to time some interesting sand-tray work.

I realize the position I am taking up here is bound to be an unpopular, perhaps even an offensive one. It will be rejected by many critics as reactionary and anachronistic or as fanciful, illusory, and "metaphysical." But the Gramtech ideology grows increasingly more powerful. Linked to the current paramedic attitude to the student, the dilution of course material, and the ritual awarding of inflated grades for effort, presence, and other entelechial reasons, its influence may soon become irresistible. As a marginal comment on this entrenched and composite ideology, I quote from a student paper on the subject of the relation between ideological authority and carnival subversion (cf. Mikhail Bakhtin):

"The ones who do not follow must be destroyed as heretics or traitors because if left to live they would influence the others who accept and might be able to turn them from the ideology thereby disrupting the society which is based in the centre of and the outer margins are surrounded by the difference who sometimes threaten the central."

I note here (once again) that this student's work, which is symptomatic of current neophyte efforts, will not be rectified by increased grammatical instruction at the secondary levels but only by a change in scholarly attitude and study habits, augmented reading, a massive reduction in TV watching coupled with a growing awareness of the cultural brownout that affects our vision, and by what I have called the rediscovery of time – if indeed recovery is possible at this late hour.

47 Such forms of agraphia are by no means unique to our age, though different sets of causes may be adduced to account for these phenomena in
different periods. Henry Craik, in *The State of Education* (London,
1884, cited in Lionel Trilling, *Matthew Arnold*, Harcourt Brace Jovanovich, New York and London, 1954) provides instances rather similar to
those I have cited. For example, to the question, "What is thy duty towards thy neighbour?" we might find an answer like: "My dooty toads
my nabers, to love him as thyself, and to do to all men as I wed thou
shall and to me; to love, onner, and suke my farther and mother; to
onner and to bay the Queen and all that are pet in a forty under her; to
smit myself to all my gooness, teaches, sportial pleasures, and mars-
ters." Craik indicates that such responses are not anomalous but typical
productions of average students. This situation was addressed and at
least partially rectified in the early years of the twentieth century, but is
now clearly re-emerging in the new age of instant childishness or
infantaneity.

An important point needs to be made here. The universal panacea
that is often proposed in such situations, the teaching of grammar in its
superficial and belated forms rather than embedding early grammatical
instruction in a cultural propaedeutic, is not only generally ineffective
but may actually perform a socially repressive function rather than an
intellectually consolidating one – especially when it works to distract the
mind from basic and even explosive questions. For example, in the battle between scholastics and humanists in the early Renaissance period,
one of the former wrote that proper university education should consist
in "deliuering a direct order of construction for the releefe of weake
Grammacists, not in tempting by curious deuise and disposition to conte
courtly Humanists" (quoted in William Manchester, *A World Lit Only
By Fire*, Little, Brown, Boston, 1992). While the point is well taken *in
itself*, it must be understood *in context* as a reactionary argument intended to hedge and constrain the development of the imagination, always a threat to a closed society or to, in contemporary terms, the
"guardians of gridlock."

Finally, we need to recognize that it is not merely the written English
that is off; we only like to think that this constitutes the "problem." But
what is really disguised by these defective grammatical surfaces we insist
on treating on the level of the symptom is something else entirely,
namely, a linguistic and intellectual bankruptcy so profound, extensive,
and resistant that it would require nothing less than a heroism of mythological proportions – or the insouciance of the ironically hopeless – to
confront directly and attempt to resolve. Nor, in the current milieu, is it
the exclusive obligation of the harassed and benighted teacher of English to provide grammatical instruction in the teeth of a culture whose

customary practices and assumptions ensure the failure of such remedial efforts. We are all equally responsible: parents, corporate and media interests, teachers of other disciplines, and the students themselves. As Simeon Potter argues (in *Language in the Modern World*), "Literacy is precarious: there is no guarantee that it will survive in a community without constant vigilance and toil."

48 The sense of disquiet or even uncanniness occasioned by such productions, which are legion, seems to me at times to have something to do with an uncanny reversal of Freud's definition of the "uncanny" as the emotion one feels when that which ought to remain "secret and hidden ... has come to light." Here something which ought to come to light remains secret and hidden. (Cf. *The Pelican Freud Library*, 14, Penguin, Hammondsworth, 1973, 1987.) But the fundamental secret, as if downloaded from a Henry James short story, is that there is no secret.

49 Paul Feyerabend, *Against Method*, Verso, London, 1988.

50 David Hume, *An Enquiry Concerning the Human Understanding*, Clarendon Press, Oxford, 1984. See I, iv, 6.

51 And it is precisely this "deep structure" – prenoetic, hypotemporal, schematic, and requiring to be filled, as it were, with conceptual and empirical matter (compare Kant's notion of the "schematism of the imagination") – that underwrites as it is written over by the surface grammatical system we blindly continue to regard as self-sufficient and autotelic. Such blindness is what Neil Postman calls "superstition," defined as "ignorance presented under the cloak of authority ... for example ... the belief that students who are given lessons in grammar will improve their writing" (Neil Postman, *Conscientious Objections*, Vintage, New York, 1992). See also G. Hillocks Jr, *Research on Written Composition*, National Conference on Research in English, Urbana, IL, 1986. Hillocks determined that grammar teaching as a "focus of instruction" in itself is not nearly as effective as what he calls the "inquiry" method drawing on the personal and social, that is, the meaningful experience of the student. Hillocks is cited by John Willinsky (*The New Literacy*, Routledge, New York and London, 1990), who mordantly alludes to "a half century of research demonstrating that the teaching of grammar does not facilitate better writing."

52 We are here in quest of a deeper understanding of grammar as quintessential, uninhibited, extrasensory, subliminal, and telepathic (though Marlowe in Raymond Chandler's *The Little Sister*, acronymizing the surname Quest, ends rather typically with "toots" rather than "telepathic." I am indebted for this reminder to Nicholas Royle, *Telepathy and Literature*, Basil Blackwell, Oxford, 1991).

53 My two subjects are technically adults, old enough to drive, vote, marry, or die on the battlefield. The author of the first exhibit is nine-

teen, the second a year younger. They manifestly need time in order to develop, but my fear is that they will continue living as quasi-temporal beings for whom time (to paraphrase Andrei Codrescu) will remain an idea whose time has not yet come or whose time has irretrievably passed. Such issues may appear trivial or paradoxically ephemeral to the very students whose intellectual and spiritual growth depends upon a clear-sighted consideration of them, but obviously we cannot scant the importance of time merely because it is temporary (although in a certain sense, of course, time is the one thing that is not temporary).

CHAPTER TWO

1 As for example the wonderful line, made more poignant by the poet's love of a young woman, "backing tooth by tooth into the grave." But see W.D. Snodgrass's well-known "April Inventory":

> The girls have grown so young by now
> I have to nudge myself to stare.
> This year they smile and mind me how
> My teeth are falling with my hair.

Aside from the Thomas persona and maybe the Snodgrass *aperçu*, does one detect as part of the Conti-figure the perambulating erotic lyricism of Leonard Cohen, the ever-present bottle of Charles Olsen (that indispensable heraldic prop), and, of course, the jaded innocence, humour, and near-undifferentiated lust of the Romantic archetype governing the common perception of the poet, Lord Byron, the poet as perpetual adolescent, always on the scent of the ladies, like Byron's own Don Juan who "... went forth with the lovely Odalisques / And though he certainly ran many risks ..." etc., etc.

2 A film sharing in the same illusory quality as the one James Dickey imagined being made of the life of Robert Frost: "despite the authenticating of whatever settings the film might choose for its backgrounds, despite the rugged physical presence of Frost himself, any film made of such elements would have to partake of nostalgic visions" (James Dickey, *Babel to Byzantium*, Grosset & Dunlap, New York, 1971).

3 To the film's credit, it should be noted that our teacher-hero is not intended to be swallowed whole. A caveat to the ecstatic pedagogy practised by Mr Keating is registered by a sympathetic colleague who considers himself a "realist," and Mr Keating is portrayed at one point as a trifle naïve (in accepting without question the transparent evasions of Neil Perry in the matter of his father's permission). Nonetheless, apart from these two qualifying instances, which in the event tend to get passed over, Keating is clearly intended to be acknowledged as hero and martyr (in the Structural Analysis of Etienne Souriau, he performs the

dramatic function of the Lion – desire, will, nobility, intelligence) and the style of pedagogy he represents as far superior to the competing forms. The film's advocacy cannot be doubted.

4 If use value is an indication of the amount of socially necessary labour required in the production of any article, we might say that the "labour" inherent both in writing a poem and in its interpretation and analysis (as well as its recitation) constitutes one aspect of its essential value (the other, of course, involves its literary merit or quality) and is to be understood as constant. Exchange value is variable and depends upon the relationships that obtain within different systems of exchange, for example, the systems represented by the class test, by the literary cenacle, or by the cocktail party (the social value of educated reference), none of which has anything to do with the labour (or merit) embodied in the poem and existing there as a constant. Judging from some of Mr Keating's remarks and the function which poetry is regularly made to assume by some of his students, its exchange value is impressively high in the market system represented by seduction. It would seem that even the noted pedagogue has failed to distinguish properly between inherent content and phenomenal form, between the constant and the labile, and has presided a little too insouciantly over a kind of "tropological" reduction of use-value to exchange-value. That is, by means of his intervention the reality of lived experience and especially literary experience succumbs to a certain manipulative irony for the purpose of an expected profit, as if in unwitting confirmation of Paul Ricoeur's reflections in *History and Truth* (Northwestern University Press, Evanston, 1965) on the alienation of the word which, as a form of degraded labour, "does not seem to realize that it too is negotiated on a market of services."

Moreover, for critical readers interested in this line of inquiry, we might add that the aspect of labour subsumed in the aesthetic, the principle of play, leisure, art, or non-alienated work – although regarded by Herbert Marcuse in *Eros and Civilization* (Beacon Press, Boston, 1966) as "unproductive" and by Jean Baudrillard in *The Mirror of Production* (Telos Press, St Louis, 1975) as resistant to the Marxist dialectic with its "double ideological expression ... of ... repression and sublimation" – provides the theoretical basis for understanding aesthetic phenomena as *intrinsically* inimical to violation by exchange. Even if, as commodities, aesthetic objects can be made to enter into one or another system of exchange, they remain, as embodiments of immanent freedom and self-authentication, outside the scheme of equivalents that controls whatever sort of market economy we might care to imagine. The teaching of literature must begin with the consideration of aesthetic transparence or of the freedom embodied within the aesthetic artifact as an expression of the freedom experienced by both the producer and consumer (or as recent literary theory has it, the producer-consumer and consumer-producer) *as human subjects*. Freedom, of course, is not anarchy or libertinism, and only comes to be within a structure of constraints – the freedom of the pianist on the keyboard, for example, as a function of extensive knowledge and interminable practice. Marx observed in *Capital*, "Labour is man's coming-to-be for himself ... the self-creation and self-objectification of man," a formulation that applies equally well and perhaps even more aptly to aesthetic creation. The brand of pedagogy practised by the Mr Keatings of this world dispenses with both the consideration of genuine freedom and the emphasis upon the determining function of necessary constraints in the production of the artifact as well as the self.

Thus the role Mr Keating plays within the school, that reflection of society at large, is by no means adversarial but, for all his charismatic personalism, entirely if subtly complicitous. Once again, as Marx wrote in *The German Ideology*, "As individuals express their life, so they are. What they are, therefore, coincides with their production, with what they produce and how they produce it."

5 David Hargreaves distinguishes "four types of pupil": the committed, the instrumentalists, the indifferent, and the oppositionals. The two central categories far outnumber the first and fourth, and in schools catering largely to middle-to-upper class students, the instrumentalists are in clear ascendancy (David Hargreaves, *The Challenge for the Comprehensive School: Culture, Curriculum and Community*, Routledge & Kegan Paul, London, 1982). The majority of the film's viewers, if they were candid, would have to confess: "Cameron, c'est moi."

6 We have as well a soupçon of Cowley, a bit of Herrick, a little Shakespeare, a drum roll of Vachel Lindsay and (of course, though himself not a poet) the indispensable Thoreau. As Cameron explains, the class covered the Romantics and the post–Civil War poets, but has not yet arrived at the Realists in its chronicle of progress – possibly the non-encounter with Hamlin Garland does not constitute a serious loss.

7 Mr Keating is copiously prone to uttering sententious maxims such as "Language was invented to woo women," "Sports is a chance to have other human beings push us to excel," "You must trust that your beliefs are unique, your own ..." (this last precept would justify the treacherous behaviour of the "bootlicker," the Judas-like, red-haired Cameron, who betrays his teacher to the authorities), and defines poetry as the embodiment of "beauty, romance, love."

8 The film is set in 1959, forty-three years after the date of the poem – a substantial interval in itself – but it was released in 1989, in effect catapulting Mr Keating into the immediate present and inviting us to consider him a strict contemporary. In any case, the director had a plethora of, shall we say, less conventional material to choose from.

9 Good poets, like good teachers, are acutely aware that the expressive vitality of literature is based on a kind of ascetic discipline and rigour. This freedom/constraint axis is constantly undergoing reformulation, e.g., the notion of "rule-governed creativity" and "recursive processes" elaborated by Noam Chomsky to reconcile the systemic imperative with performative freedom on the level of ordinary language use. The apparently paradoxical nature of aesthetic creativity bears a strict analogy to the implicit process of generating new sentences. In both cases, "competence" is internalized. Extrapolating from language to pedagogy, one might say that Mr Keating is teaching "performance" but not inculcating "competence."

10 The reference here is to the condition of genuine choice – a condition the direct opposite of ritual choice, that is, of the choice that has been made for one in advance of the conflictual moment. Many of those events we erroneously consider "choices" bear a close structural resemblance to the decisive non-decisions associated with Sir Galahad in *The Quest of the Holy Grail*: "With Galahad, hesitation and choice no longer have any meaning; the path he takes may divide, but Galahad will always take the 'good' fork." (Cf. Tzvetan Todorov, "The Quest of Narrative," in *The Poetics of Prose*, Cornell University Press, Ithaca, 1977.)

But as Edward Howard Griggs writes in *The Use of the Margin* (a quaint little book published by Huebsch in 1907), "In all our living is an unavoidable element of experiment. If we wait until we know how to live before we begin, we never begin ... If we do not choose a vocation until we know all the laws determining the active expression of our capacities in some avenue of work, we fail to find our call." The roads between which we must choose radiate outwards into the unknown, bending away "in the undergrowth"; scanned *before* the moment of choice, they are equally not taken, which is to say that they are *inwardly* obscure and indeterminate, requiring a commitment that is always to some extent founded on guesswork, "experiment," conjecture. This is the major theme of the poem.

Its minor theme obviously identifies the road not taken as that which remains untrodden *after* the decision has been taken, after all the wave functions but one, so to speak, have collapsed. Then the road not taken is simply and tautologically the road not taken, and the poem comments sadly on the ineluctable nature of time, the medium of choice:

Yet knowing how way leads on to way,
I doubted if I should ever come back.

(The speculation is in some respects like that of Henry James's Spencer Brydon in "The Jolly Corner" – which appeared six years before Frost's poem – who wishes to discover what would have become of him had he taken the other fork of a major decision.) Hence the ambiguity, that doubleness again, of "sigh" in "I shall be telling this with a sigh," which expresses both *regret* that the other path, the one really not taken, can never be explored, and *relief* at having made the choice that *was* made despite the inner obscurity of law and motive and the outward uncertainty of result.

At a certain level, all choice is laborious, snarled, labyrinthine, as Hamlet and Sophie knew better than most. Of course, this does not cancel the self-evident truth that the experience of choice may be rendered even more difficult if the individual at the crossroads intuits one of the possibilities as more perilous and anxiety-laden than the other, thus leading to a greater sense of heroic endeavour. But the traditional interpretation of the poem that Mr Keating falls back upon stops precisely here, ignoring the negative ambiguity of the title, the contradiction at the centre, and the existential complexity of the subject.

11 Not to mention another conceivable irony: Frost's "yellow wood" calls to mind the first line of Tennyson's *Tithonus:* "The woods decay, the woods decay and fall" (just as its closing lines recapitulate the conclusion of Tennyson's "Ulysses"). Tithonus chose the less travelled path, taking not a human wife but becoming instead the consort of a goddess, with catastrophic results. The unconventional way has led more or less directly to his downfall. These decaying or yellow woods of choice are always with us, of course – another irony. One decision leads inevitably to another, and we must always decide to choose, resisting the insidious temptation to withdraw from the confrontation and allow events to decide for us. So Wordsworth writes in "The Prelude":

> The immeasurable height
> Of woods decaying, never to be decayed.

12 This procedure structurally reproduces the function of the hysteric within the confines of the family that is at first challenged and disrupted only to absorb the alien component in the interests of a renewed and reconfirmed solidarity. (See Freud's "Fragment of an Analysis of a Case of Hysteria" (*Dora*), *The Pelican Freud*, vol. 8, Penguin, New York, 1977.) The same role may also be assumed by the maid, seduced, seducing, and abandoned. Derrida's analysis of the pharmakon also relies on the same binary logic. The pharmakon is both the ill and the remedy, the disease that functions as a cure, the scapegoat that, like Mr Keating, is necessarily banished and yet remains inscribed in the very centre of the society dependent upon that which it appears to repudiate. "The city's body *proper* thus reconstitutes its unity, closes around the security of its inner courts ... by violently excluding from its territory the representative of an external threat or aggression ... Yet the representative of the outside is nonetheless *constituted*, regularly granted its place by the community ... in the very heart of the inside." (See Jacques Derrida,

"Plato's Pharmacy," *Dissemination*, University of Chicago Press, Chicago, 1981.)

Similarly, Stanley Fish argues with his usual mischievous relish that "Professionalism cannot do without anti-professionalism, it is the chief support and maintenance of the professional ideology ... The ideology of anti-professionalism – of essential and independent values chosen freely by an independent self – is nothing more or less than the ideology of professionalism taking itself seriously." So there! one would like to add. But there is little doubt that Mr Keating stands to the institution employing him as the embodiment of "the ideology of anti-professionalism" that allows that institution to take itself seriously. (See *Doing What Comes Naturally: Change, Rhetoric and the Practice of Theory in Literary and Legal Studies*, Clarendon Press, Oxford, 1989.)

Finally, compare Umberto Eco's hypothesis that language, the repressive parallelogram of forces that limits our freedom, defends itself against the revolutionary and liberating thrust of literature "by reciting the literature, which questions the given language's position, in certain set places" (*Travels in Hyper Reality*, Harcourt Brace Jovanovich, Orlando, 1986).

13 See Thomas S. Kuhn, *The Structure of Scientific Revolutions*, University of Chicago Press, Chicago, 1962, 1970.

14 The four pillars of Welton School are tradition, honour, discipline, and excellence. In the students' parodic reinscription, the fourth pillar, excellence, emerges as "excrement."

15 This "deceptive authenticity" also characterizes the more recent and very popular *Renaissance Man* (1995), starring the cuddly Danny De Vito as Bill Rago, a civilian instructor hired by the army to preside over a collection of misfits and troublemakers. Although Mr Rago signs up for another tour of duty after being commended by his employers, capping the schmaltz with a happy ending, the view of education promoted by the film does not differ in any significant way from that of its celebrated predecessor. It is true that Mr Rago has neither training nor experience as a teacher – he is an out-of-work advertising exec with a Masters degree – but his warmth, accessibility, endearingly fallible nature, and a belated gift for personal empathy qualify him as another in the cinematic line of charismatic preceptors (whose template may be found in the 1987 *Stand and Deliver* and perhaps in *Lean on Me*, also 1987, these in turn predicated on Sidney Poitier's 1967 *To Sir with Love*; for a more problematic version of this paradigm, see *Waterland* [1993]). Moreover, the reality principle is carefully trimmed, hedged, shaped, and monitored so that it rarely intrudes to disrupt the pedagogical equation. The class is agreeably small, enabling the teacher to develop and maintain personal relationships with his students; the stu-

dents, despite their apparent unruliness, are eminently redeemable
(Dirty Dozen fashion) and, as it turns out, immensely talented as well
(cf. the rap version of *Hamlet* they effortlessly stage); and the lesson
plan, such as it is, orbits safely within the Shakespeherian ragius
(*Romeo and Juliet, Henry V,* and *Hamlet*, including an inoffensive, socially acceptable interpretation of the incest motif in the latter). As with
the Neil Perry episode in the earlier film, reality makes a homeopathic
guest appearance with the arrest of the promising young Hobbes for
various felonies, a scene with the obvious purpose of building a certain
theoretical immunity against the counter-kitsch I am recommending
here. The most pedagogically acute moment in *Renaissance Man*, to
give the film its due, is the short and trenchant analysis of contemporary
American education offered by Mr Rago's immediate superior, Tom:
the collapse of the home environment, followed by the inevitable failure
of commitment on the part of the insecure and underpaid teacher, leading to the issuing of worthless certificates, and culminating in the intellectual mediocrity of a nation bent on its own destruction. But this telling *aperçu*, which occurs during a reflective interlude in a bar, is
nowhere developed and is in fact effectively neutralized by the tepid and
saccharine rhetoric of subjective perfectibility without benefit of scholarship deployed throughout the film. Perhaps the most moving instalment
in this genre of the fallible-heroic pedagogue is Lina Wertmuller's *Ciao,
Professore* (1994), in which failure to achieve educational purposes,
though glazed with a caramel of humour and sentimentality, forms the
subject of a bitter rumination. The *most* one can hope for in the relation
between teacher and student in a socioeconomic world hostile to genuine education is a slight, reciprocal influencing for the better – maybe.
(Since this writing, a new slew of educational or quasi-educational films
has flooded theatres and video outlets – most notably the insidious *Mr
Holland's Opus* (1996) – but I must obviously make a quietus
somewhere.)

CHAPTER THREE

1 See Jean-François Lyotard, *The Differend* (University of Minnesota
 Press, Minneapolis, 1988). The "differend" is defined as "a case of conflict between two parties (at least) which could not equitably be decided
 for lack of a rule of judgment applicable to both argumentations." A situation may then develop in which a "plaintiff" can present the case only
 in the language of the more powerful adversary if it is to be effective –
 thus admitting ultimate defeat, for it is precisely the terms of reference
 adopted by the adversary that the plaintiff wishes to overcome. As a result, the latter may win a temporary judgment, for which he pays by losing the case. This is like arguing the validity of retaining Shakespeare

on the curriculum because such study promotes the effective use of English for instrumental or commercial purposes. It is doubtful whether Derrida's writing "*sous rature*," the strategy of using the established vocabulary while not subscribing to its premises, is a sufficiently antiseptic device. One probably has no choice but to mobilize a blunt, agonistic discourse and hope for the best, relying on the theory of education which, in the words of R.S. Peters (*Education and the Education of Teachers*, Routledge and Kegan Paul, London, 1977), "consists in seeing things under certain aspects which constitute intrinsic reasons for engaging in them ... intimately connected with caring about something and ... not ... a case either of 'knowing how' or 'knowing that' which are the usual alternatives offered." More likely, however, we will continue to register the tedious reiteration of the usual blahtitudes and technologemes – "skills," "goals," "competencies," and the rest – like the metronomic ringing of garage tire pumps. Meanwhile our administrators see to it that we are kept in a state of peonage, both intellectually and fiscally, through the agency of superficial tampering, usually called "reform," which absorbs all our interest and resources.

2 Richard Mitchell, *The Gift of Fire*, Simon & Schuster, New York, 1987.

3 Some of these "variables" would be: Are evaluations disguised popularity contests? Students may know what they like or want, but can they plausibly be expected to know what they need? Can a teacher's *personality*, the source of his or her teaching, be effectively modified without producing blatant hokiness? How may questions be devised that do not embody the ideological claims of belief systems? Are such instruments means of administrative control? Can a good evaluation reconfirm a teacher in bad pedagogy? Do such assessments create the illusion of democratic process in order to facilitate more subtle forms of persisting domination? Does the evaluation format trigger a certain prestructured response?

The question of evaluation is in all respects and in every category of pedagogical activity a complex and troubling one, but when it comes to teacher evaluation it remains even more difficult to determine what precisely is being evaluated in the first place. I suspect that the *results* of the process are themselves in need of further evaluation, considering that these will often betray not only a hidden structure of desires and assumptions on the part of the student that have little to do with educational purposes but also reflect a *conceptual agenda* that equates education with entertainment and learning with organized distraction. In the idiom of current French scholarship in the field, the question of evaluation is regarded as essentially an *epistemological* issue. As Louis-Marie Ouellette cautions us in a recent and valuable study of the subject: "*il import de préciser l'objet de l'évaluation ... parce que l'objet de l'ac-*

tivité d'évaluation influence et détermine la definition même au concept." (See Louis-M. Ouellette, *La Communication au coeur de l'évaluation en formation continue,* Presses Universitaires de France, Paris, 1996.)

4 Parker J. Palmer, *To Know As We Are Known,* HarperCollins, San Francisco, 1993 (orig. publ. 1983). Of course, Palmer's "desert teacher" would find it next to impossible to flourish today, especially in the desert. As Andrei Codrescu writes in *The Disappearance of the Outside* (Addison-Wesley, New York, 1990), "it is increasingly difficult to live Outside in the contemporary world. The desert once available to the saints is a testing ground for nuclear weapons." The Inside desert of the contemporary classroom is not all that far behind.

What I have above called "mere indifference" may express itself not only in boredom or disobedience but also in self-righteous adherence to "mere opinion," as, for example, in the context of the current creationism-evolution debate in the high schools. A recent CBC television interview with a group of students in a Christian fundamentalist community focuses on a teenage girl who, representative of her peers, claimed that she had as much right to her "views" as Charles Darwin did to his. Darwin, of course, did not have "views" but a reasoned and analytically scrupulous set of convictions built up laboriously over a lifetime of painstaking research. The student's views, on the other hand, consisted only of a set of dogmas instilled in the home and ventilated in the middle of a biology class with an unfounded assurance devoid of reflection, curiosity, or the search for evidence. Thus even the problems that exist *within evolutionary theory* remain unremarked. (See, for instance, Mark Ridley (so aptly named), *The Problems of Evolution,* Oxford University Press, Oxford and New York, 1985, 1990.) What I find most interesting here is the neophyte tendency to assume equal authority with the teacher, coupled with a pervasive disrespect for scholarly procedure – a phenomenon by no means confined to this particular debate but in fact epidemic. Teachers may decide to go on talking, but their words are effectively "taken away." (What Palmer, a devout Christian, would have to say about evolution is a moot question.)

5 See Arthur Kroker and Michael A. Weinstein, *Data Trash,* St. Martin's Press, New York, 1994, for more on Crash theory and the dead hand of the recombinant sign. Henry Giroux "reproblematizes" the issue in the now-standard (and largely unreadable) idiom of critical pedagogy in claiming that "None of the many recent reports about educational reform even scratches the surface of this problem," which is really about the "relationship between pedagogy and power." We should, rather, be moving away from "the mapping of domination toward the politically strategic issue of engaging the ways in which knowledge can be re-

mapped, reterritorialized, and decentered." (*Border Crossings*, Routledge, New York and London, 1992). This distinction was originally made, crisply and unpretentiously, in the middle of the nineteenth century by Orestes Brownson, who deplored the tendency of certain educators to seek reform "without disturbing the social arrangements which render reform necessary." (Cited in Christopher Lasch's *The True and Only Heaven*, W.W. Norton, New York, 1991.) For more on the subject, see the discussion on educational reform between Gilles Deleuze and Michel Foucault, reported in the latter's *Language, Counter-Memory, Practice* (Cornell University Press, Ithaca, 1977). Foucault proposes not reform but what he calls "revolutionary action" defined in part as "aggressive inquiry formulated ... by those who are being investigated." Deleuze addresses the following remarks to Foucault: "The notion of reform is stupid and hypocritical. Either reforms are designed by people who claim to be representative, who make a profession of speaking for others, and they lead to a ... new power which is consequently increased by a double repression; or they arise from the complaints and demands of those concerned ... If the protests of children were heard in kindergarten, if their questions were attended to, it would be enough to explode the entire educational system." (In a similar vein, Agnes Heller suggests with regard to "reform-minded minor utopians" that there are certain limits beyond which the utopian imagination should not trespass; in particular, she lays it down as an ethical maxim that "dreams of other persons' happiness should not be forged without them." Cf. *A Philosophy of History in Fragments*, Blackwell Publishers, Oxford, 1993.) As far back as 1929 Alfred North Whitehead was already writing against the reform prepossession. He comments in the course of an anti-reformist argument conducted in his *The Aims of Education* (republ. Macmillan, New York, 1967) on the ineffectiveness of "formal alterations" since "the very nature of things ... will see to it that the pea is always under the other thimble" – precisely the truth that reformspeak is designed to suppress. The passion for reform still needs to be defetishized. Almost sixty-five years later we find Andrew Nikiforuk writing in *School's Out* (Macfarlane, Walter & Ross, Toronto, 1993): "Every change is presumably for the better, but little improvement in the quality of instruction or organization of the school actually takes place. Indeed, the quality of education, I would argue, has been in decline." The specific cast and behaviour of the reformist state of mind is very similar if not identical to the *modus operandi* of the Paris police as explained by Poe's Dupin in "The Purloined Letter": "at best, when urged by some unusual emergency ... they extend or exaggerate their old modes of practice, without touching their principles ... What is all this boring, and probing, and sounding ... and dividing the surface of the building into registered square inches ... but an exaggeration of the application of the one principle or set of principles ... to which the Prefect, in the long routine of his duty, has been accustomed?" This is not "acumen," says Dupin, but "cunning," which may be "persevering" and even "ingenious" but never leads to the attainment of its object. What is lacking, Dupin intimates, is empathy and imagination, the ability to identify sympathetically with others – and also glaringly absent (to quote from "The Murders in The Rue Morgue") is "the quality of the observation." Without empathy and perceptiveness, imagination and acumen, all we can expect to get are exaggerations of old ideas and practices, never a new set of principles.

6 Paolo Freire, *Pedagogy of the Oppressed*, Herder and Herder, New York, 1970.

7 Marc Tucker, director of the American National Center on Education and the Economy, in a lecture attended by David Perkins (cf. *Smart Schools*, Free Press, New York, 1992), compares the relationship between "direct workers" – those who assemble products or provide services – and "indirect workers" – administrators, etc. – in prosperous countries like Denmark and West Germany on the one hand and the declining United States on the other. In the former, Perkins reports, "the ratio of indirect workers to direct workers is substantially lower." With respect to the education industry, if we compare certain European countries and the province of Quebec, the ratio, as we have seen, is *apocalyptically* lower. Andrew Nikiforuk is also scandalized that there are more education adminicrats in New York State or any large Canadian province than in all of western Europe.

8 Elliot Eisner contends in *The Educational Imagination* (Macmillan, New York, 1985), one of the most important books in the recent literature, that "one should not feel compelled to abandon educational aims that cannot be reduced to measurable forms of predictable performance." In the ongoing debate between what we might call the reverent and the Promethean schools of pedagogy, Eisner comes out plainly on the side of the former, taking strong exception to objectives pedagogy, which states that purposes should precede activities and that criterion levels of competency must be specified in advance. On the contrary. The teacher's real aims are not instrumental, list-oriented, or empirical but "implicit and contextual." Rather than focusing narrowly on outcomes, "it is perfectly appropriate for teachers and others involved in curriculum development to plan activities that have no explicit or precise objectives." Cognitive flexibility is all. In a neat, summary phrase: "To expect all our educational aspirations to be either verbally describable or measurable is to expect too little." Similarly, David Perkins in *Smart Schools* dismisses the behavioural objectives movement, presumably be-

ginning to recede in the US as it rises to increasing prominence north of the border, as having "trivialized the behaviours [it] aimed to cultivate."

From the perspective of J.J. Apter and K.C.P. Smith, the distinction is one between alternative states which they designate as telic and paratelic. "In the telic state, behaviour is chosen to achieve goals, in a paratelic state, goals are chosen ... to provide a *raison d'etre* for the behaviour," as in play, mountain climbing, and so on (quoted in Stuart Sim's *Beyond Aesthetics*, University of Toronto Press, Toronto, 1992). Again, James Carse discriminates usefully between finite games that are played within strict demarcations and infinite games in which the rules and boundaries are themselves subject to change. (See James P. Carse, *Finite and Infinite Games*, Macmillan, New York, 1986.) We might then argue in accordance with Eisner's counsels of wisdom that education is preferentially a paratelic phenomenon or a kind of infinite game. When it becomes insistently telic or grimly finite, we find ourselves in the present barren landscape trapped between a desert of inflexible demands on the one hand and a mountain of trivial procedures on the other.

Meanwhile we proceed with busywork as usual. The classroom itself is in danger of becoming like Pee Wee Herman's Rube Goldberg kitchen in which a multi-stage, elaborately sequenced process is activated to produce a slice of toast. As Michel de Certeau warns in *The Practice of Everyday Life* (University of California Press, Berkeley, 1984, 1988), "the means of diffusion are now dominating the ideas they diffuse." It is not, as McLuhan argued, that the medium is the message but that "the medium is *replacing* the message" (italics mine). The form of education is now "eliminating the very content that made it possible."

9 The *réforme pédagogique* apparently derives in part from the British industrial system which begins by analyzing a working situation in terms of its components and goals – which may be fine for industry but raises the issue of appropriateness for education. In any event, the reform apparatus is clearly the educational bastard of an industrial sire, namely the archaic behavioural model or gunboat pedagogy associated with Clark C. Hull, K.W. Spence, and especially B.F. Skinner, whose emphasis on "task analysis" and "programmed instruction" has been decisively weakened by Frank Smith's powerful attack in *Insult to Intelligence* (Heinemann, Portsmouth, NH, 1987) and *Joining the Literacy Club* (Heinemann, Portsmouth, NH, 1988). (The concluding chapter in the latter, "How Education Backed the Wrong Horse," is rapidly acquiring "classic" status.) Interestingly, Ralph Tyler, the father of Educational Objectives – and one of the first, in the words of Russell Osguthorpe ("Instructional Science ... ," *Educational Technology*, Englewood Cliffs, NJ, June 1989) "to define educational objectives clearly in terms of

overt student behaviour ... that is, given a certain content area, how the student should think, feel, or act" – has been passionately repudiated by his former student and leading American exponent, Cyril Clark (who will also have necessarily repudiated his own influential book, *Using Instructional Objectives in Teaching*, Scott, Foresman, London, 1972). The work of Michael Scriven as well, who back in the sixties gave us "formative evaluation" as opposed to "summative evaluation," now finds itself on perilous ground.

But perhaps the most effective misericorde to the reform mindset is provided by Richard Gibboney's trenchant paper "The Killing Field of Reform" (University of Pennsylvania, Graduate School of Education, Philadelphia, 1991), in which the author interrogates the dismal record of the reformist prepossession across the United States between 1950 and 1990 and shows how progressive reformism has led inescapably to confusion, banality, and demoralization. Summarizing his findings, Gibboney writes: "The characteristic fragmentation of the technological mindset is evident in these programs in their passion for incoherent detail, in their emphasis on decontextualized technique, and in their stoic indifference to seminal ideas." Should we affect surprise that one of the major casualties of reform is "the intellectual and democratic quality of school life"? For additional confirmation, see Max Dublin (*Futurehype*, Penguin, New York, 1990), who informs us that in New York City alone, in the period 1979–81, 781 innovative programs were introduced into the educational system, with predictably negligible effect – except, obviously, to create more employment for administrators. One needs to be chalcenterous to swallow what is going down now. As David Perkins cogently argues in *Smart Schools*, "one of the most misleading premises of educational reform [is that] we need a new and better method ... the most powerful choice we can make concerns not method but curriculum – not how we teach but what we choose to try to teach." What is perhaps even more "misleading" or deceptive is *the way in which method invades the territory of curriculum* – methodological "innovation" passing itself off as curriculum reform – as exemplified in the competency-based programs of that unduly influential reactionary outpost, Alverno College, whose brand of decaf pedagogy is guaranteed not to prevent the academic mind from enjoying its slumber.

(Note: A selective Objectives bibliography would include Hull's *Essentials of Behaviour*, Yale University Press, New Haven, 1951; Spence's *Behaviour Theory and Conditioning*, Yale University Press, New Haven, 1956; Skinner's *Science and Human Behaviour*, Macmillan, New York, 1953; and Tyler's *Changing Concepts of Educational Evaluation*, AERA Monograph Series on Curriculum Evaluation, no. 1, Rand

McNally, Chicago, 1967. One might also wish to consult Michael Scriven's "The Methodology of Evaluation" in the same series. See Osguthorpe, 1989, for an encyclopedic cowcatcher. It is astonishing to contemplate the extent to which the most "advanced" model in education is merely a gentrified version of a behaviourist relic.)

I conclude this excursus with a most interesting letter sent me by my colleague, Edwin Holland of the Department of Social Sciences at John Abbott College, as a follow-up to an informal discussion on Alverno-style reform, which he regards from the perspective of Turing-computability.

April 26, 1995

My Dear Solway

Since you have been so kind as to express an interest in my notion of Turing-computability and the critique of the behaviourist schema of education, I will attempt to outline it for you.

My notion developed rather specifically in response to a course in educational methodology in which I was presented with the practice of designing "learning hierarchies" for student instruction. These hierarchies were based on the idea that the "learning outcome" would best be achieved by identifying the sequence of steps (hierarchy) through which a student would proceed to arrive at the desired end. Inherent in this approach is the assumption that learning any specific objective is, in fact, a *method* and can be stated as an algorithm.

Given that an algorithm is a mechanical procedure that can be completed without benefit of "creative intervention" and can be described as a sequence of simple steps, this model of learning seemed very effective in dealing with the "outcomes" presented to illustrate it. To teach a student to change a flat tire, to use one example, one would break down the process into the sequence of actual and simplest separate tasks needed to accomplish the change and instruct the student to follow the given sequence. The same procedure would be used, then, to develop learning hierarchies for the more complex tasks which we required our students to perform.

However, when I attempted to devise such a model for one of my class assignments, I found it exceedingly difficult to identify all the "steps" and began to wonder if it were really possible. It could have been simply a problem of size: perhaps I had an infinity of steps. If this were the case, the hierarchy would be impossible to describe from a practical point of view, but, since it was presumably computable, it would be theoretically accomplishable. If, however, it were not computable, then it would be impossible. This suggested a look at Cantor's identification of non-countable infinite sets and the Turing test of computability.

In brief, if the elements of an infinite set cannot be paired one-for-one with the set of whole numbers, then that set is not countable. One such set is the set of all the functions of the positive whole numbers that take on integer values. Since there are more such functions than there are whole numbers, it follows that not all the functions are computable.

In a very real sense, it is a set such as this upon which we ask our students to draw when we ask them to write papers. In effect we are asking them to identify a sub-set of relationships from the non-computable set of all possible relations ("functions") in constructing a literary or social scientific analysis. It would be impossible, therefore, to write an algorithm of such a "learning outcome": not only is it non-computable, it requires "creative intervention" to identify and select such a sub-set.

In addition, our expectations raise questions of relative computability. It is generally the case that we set "outcomes" for which, even if they could be computed, both P and *not*-P are equivalent and for which both P and *not*-P are not equivalent. There are many cases of this in our field. In Anthropology we first noted this when Oscar Lewis presented his ethnography of the same community that Robert Redfield had described earlier. Lewis' community was poor and mean-spirited while Redfield's was comfortable and cooperative. Both propositions were equivalent "computations" for the assignment, "write an ethnography of this village," and not-equivalent for the same assignment.

To the extent, then, that we wish to teach our students to think inventively on the things of this world, and to draw on all that they know and can discover in order to find relationships among whatever may contribute to our understanding of these things, then we must logically reject behaviourist ideas of teaching methods.

Collegially yours,
Edwin Holland

10 Jacques Barzun, casting a jaundiced glance from his position of eminence, writes: "At the moment, it seems to me that anything sober and well-reasoned has no chance against the flood of vague pieties and mechanical nostrums" (personal communication, May 1993). Perhaps all that remains to us is the dubious satisfaction of the Pyrrhic critique. Or perhaps the time has come to stop talking and writing books like this one and to take to the streets. I sometimes feel that nothing less than a genuine revolution, a prolonged May 1968, a blunt refusal to continue with things as they are, is going to have any effect on a society whose *raison d'être* is to provide moral support and fiscal nourishment for its entrenched and parasitic bureaucracies. (As Lawrence Cremin says, whenever America needs a revolution, it just gets another curriculum.) I find myself in profound sympathy with Alain Touraine's argument that history has withdrawn from the rigid, "crystal-like" structure into which

our society has been transformed, that "[c]alculations seem to have replaced action ... We must take this crystallized society in our hands and
shatter it against the wall of our silence and our anger." (See "From Crisis to Critique," *Partisan Review*, 1976, no. 2; quoted in Edith Kurzweil,
The Age of Structuralism, Columbia University Press, New York, 1980.)

11 I owe the phrase to my colleague Barry Reynolds with whom I remain
in cordial disagreement. Technique, as differentiated from style, would
apply to *specialized* forms of writing, for example, lab reports or accounting protocols, which presuppose a prior, more generalized capacity
for expression. Grammar is not a technique but a foundation on which
technical writing is predicated and which cannot be disengaged from the
temporal and epistemic categories of experience. *Formal* grammar does
not generate content, any more than technique *per se* does, but relies
upon a prior content that comes already pre-schematized, so to speak,
by the temporally ordered sensibility. As Simeon Potter argues, "good
writing, least of all in practical affairs, is seldom a matter of technique
that can be detached and isolated from other facts of human behaviour
and experience." (See Simeon Potter, *Language in the Modern World*,
Penguin, Baltimore, 1960.)

12 The simile is from Paul Fussell's *BAD, or the Dumbing of America*
(Simon & Schuster, New York, 1991). See his chapter on restaurants,
which complements his section on the poor nourishment provided by the
educational establishment.

13 Robert Nisbet, *The Social Philosophers*, Crowell, New York, 1973. Of
course this line of thought enjoys an ancient pedigree going back to
Aristotle's *Politics*, the primary source of the decentralist option. The
German sociologist Ferdinand Tönnies at the end of the nineteenth century clearly articulated this seminal distinction as one between
Gesellschaft or "society," based on contractual relations between isolated individuals and an abstract, over-arching authority, and
Gemeinschaft or "community," based on affection, kinship, and mem-
bership in small, associative units. The current tendency in education
stresses *Gesellschaft* at the expense of *Gemeinschaft*, which is, quite
frankly, the Balnibarbian option.

But what about those cases where consultation and consensus *do* appear to have occurred? From whatever angle we take on the question,
reform remains the sugar shack of academic politics. At the university
level, especially in the United States, reform is effectively thwarted by
rhizomatous administrations and a reactionary professorate unwilling to
surrender its research perks for actual classroom teaching. As Charles J.
Sykes puts it, "Reform may be the most popular leisure activity of the
American university." Here, not surprisingly, it is precisely because they

are designed, approved, and implemented by professors safeguarding the sugar taps with buccal proficiency that reforms "end up ratifying the same values that created the problems in the first place." See Charles J. Sykes, *Profscam*, St. Martin's Press, New York, 1990.

14 Teacher evaluation by students may readily fall into the same category of insidious control. Though students exercise a certain nominal effect on the performance of the teacher (as often as not, inauspicious), the evaluative instrument furnishes a "higher" authority, whether the already propagandized conscience of the teacher or the administrative apparatus itself, with the power to determine pedagogical conduct in the absence of rigorous cultural reflection. This is simply another brick in the edifice of political correctness, another lens in the Foucauldian panopticon. (For a thorough analysis of panopticon psychology, see Michel Foucault, *Discipline and Punish*, Vintage, New York, 1979.) It would seem to me far more appropriate to reverse the procedure and have teachers evaluate students, not only in terms of scholastic ability but in terms of character, attitude, maturity, willingness to participate, and so on. (How to apply the results is, of course, another question.) In any case, the teacher cannot do better than consult Nikiforuk's *School's Out* on this question. Many educators, he writes, "believe they are delivering a product ... to a specialized market, a body of consumers known as students. The quality of the product and its delivery can be gauged only by its popularity, by how good it makes the students feel ... [But] viewing education as a consumer product defeats the historic notion of schooling as a community enterprise." Evaluation should proceed "not on the basis of feelings, but on the quality of individual performance measured against standards of excellence."

15 See Kenneth Bruffee, "Collaborative Learning and the 'Conversation of Mankind,'" *College English*, 46, 1984. For more on this subject, one might consult the work of Michael Oakeshott, Frank Smith, Viljo Kohonen, Carol Nicholson, and David Hargreaves, among many contributors to the field.

16 "You cannot profit from small techniques ... Examine your environment." See the chapter "The Fire Book" in Miyamoto Musashi's *A Book of the Five Rings*, on the philosophy and practice of Kendo, originally written in 1645 (translation by Victor Harris, Overlook Press, Woodstock, 1974). But small techniques and neglect of the parietal environment are a speciality of the technomorphic school of educators.

17 As Hans-Georg Gadamer argues in *Truth and Method* (Crossroad Press, New York, 1989), which adapts a Platonic epistemology to a modern problematic, the paradigm of thought that currently holds sway subdues both *episteme* (theoretical knowledge) and *phronesis* (moral

knowledge) to the rule of *techne* (instrumental knowledge). With respect to *phronesis*, we should recognize that moral knowledge has not only declined to the condition of mere problem-solving or technical know-how but also and ironically now carries with it in its new career the emotional concomitant of self-esteem, an unearned feeling of ethical propriety. For an interesting discussion of the ways in which the phronetic has yielded to the frenetic, see Shaun Gallagher, *Hermeneutics and Education*, SUNY Press, Albany, 1992.

18 Andrew Nikiforuk, *School's Out.*

19 Recent studies in comparative education have elaborated on Geertz's original proposal (see *The Interpretation of Cultures*, Basic Books, New York, 1973) and have given us the case-study method, *qualitative* analysis, and "phenomenological" research – aspects of ethnographical thinking – in contradistinction to so-called epochal thinking which seeks to establish a relationship between, in Vincent Descombes's words, "a particular configuration of human existence" and an anterior proposition. (See Vincent Descombes, *The Barometer of Modern Reason*, Oxford University Press, London, 1993, for an *explication de texte*, and Frank Smith, *Whose Language? What Power?*, Teachers' College Press, New York, 1993, for a practical instance of ethnographicity.

20 As the poet Eric Ormsby writes, one must welcome the way "a chance felicity / silvers the whole attention of the mind" (*Coastlines*, ECW Press, Montreal, 1993). According to some educational scholars, such flexibility of adaptation is a characteristic feature of the practice of *expert* teachers. Novices tend to stick to lesson plans and timetables, their energies cannibalized by *didactics* – the anticipation of events. Experts, on the other hand, tend to alleviate the discordance between planning and immediacy by "deliberately avoiding rigid plans" and developing a more flexible time epistemology to account for the concrete teaching instance (pedagogy triumphing over or at least not succumbing to didactics); that is, they establish a balance, a "wave function," between the "two aspects of the double agenda" of teaching. (See "Novice and Expert Teachers' Time Epistemology: A Wave Function from Didactics to Pedagogy," François Victor Tochon and Hugh Munby, in *Teacher & Teacher Education*, vol. 9, no. 2, 1993.)

But I would suggest that the alleged inflexibility of novice teachers, their anxious devotion to didactics, is not only and certainly not entirely a function of inexperience but rather one of the baleful results of teacher-training programs which systematically drain the postulant of all spontaneity, exuberance, and mettlesome self-confidence. I have known many beginning teachers at the college level, for example, who have not had to sacrifice their individuality on the altar of the certificate and who have demonstrated a rich and protean vitality in the classroom; and conversely, I have suffered as a student under the yoke of too many experienced teachers who aspired to nothing so much as the condition of rigor mortis, perfect monsters of the didactic.* The difference between pedagogy and didactics, despite what cluster analyses appear to tell us (perhaps experienced teachers simply learn how to lie better), may correlate not only with the expert/novice dyad but also with the *fundamental* disparity between energy and paralysis, attributes of personality as well as reflections of its condition – healthy or unhealthy, untrammelled or tyrannized, talented or pedestrian, supple with joy or deformed by institutional constraints. As Michael Brian of Concordia University once remarked in class, a good teacher should be able to discourse for two hours on a stone at a moment's notice. I would only add that a good teacher, expert or novice, is one who enjoys the prior disposition, the opportunity having been provided, to drop the lesson plan and pick up the stone in the first place. Similarly, Camille Paglia writes: "I would like to liberate classroom teaching, to free it from the iron yoke of the prefab daily syllabus and allow more room for improvisation, especially in lectures" (Camille Paglia, *Sex, Art, and American Culture*, Vintage, New York, 1992).

21 Descartes may have begun in radical doubt but quickly relapsed into certainty, invoking the rules of logical inference, the standard metaphysical categories and, to top it all off, a benign creator. The temptation to practise such *escamotage* is almost irresistible, even in the secular domain. (With regard to the phrase "Descartes before the horse," of which I was inordinately proud when I "coined" it in 1994: I have since come across it twice in the same week in October 1995, first in Paul Theroux's *The Happy Isles of Oceania* (1992) and a few days later in W. Lambert Gardiner's *The Psychology of Teaching* (1980), requiring me to cede double priority and put Gardiner before Theroux and Theroux before Solway.)

22 "Consciousness is not a strictly linear system, but one in which circular causality obtains. Attention shapes the self, and is in turn shaped by it." There is no a priori recipe or menu for the emancipation of conscious-

---

*I am relying for my "data" chiefly on my own experience as both a student and a teacher. Much of this experience is recent: I am still a teacher, and am currently a graduate student as I was during the period 1987–89. During this time, as in my earlier student days, I have noticed no statistically appreciable difference between novice and expert teachers with respect to the flexibility factor. More to the point, over half the "expert" teachers whom I have observed closely remain strangers to improvisation. The fact that my "study" is non-parametric does not shake my confidence in its revelatory power.

ness, only attention, being in a state of "flow." The same is true for the rheomatic act of teaching. See Mihaly Csikszentmihalyi, *Flow*, Harper-Collins, San Francisco, 1990.

23 John Ralston Saul, *Voltaire's Bastards*, Penguin, New York, 1992. Few books have provided a more penetrating analysis of the Aceldama of modern education than this one. One should be aware, though, that Saul is using the word "rationality" in a special sense, roughly synonymous with Habermas's "Instrumental Reason." Agnes Heller, who takes note of Habermas, objects that the "rational Imagination of the mind" is not the lone villain of the piece but works hand in glove with "the irrational Desires and devices of the unconscious soul." She concludes in the mode of *Macbeth*: "they did the bloody work together" (Heller, *A Philosophy of History in Fragments*).

24 The issue is far more complex than may at first appear, and the promiscuous assignment of blame is more likely to lead to resentment than amendment. But the fact obstinately remains that we are all and equally responsible for the catastrophe in which we are all and equally foundering: parents who neglect to provide their children with the early, *cultural* instruction that serves as a *sine qua non* for later achievement; administrators in their sublime indifference to reality and their obsession with mere programmatic reform and *rational* constructs; teachers who trade in suspect goods like student retention, faculty evaluation, curriculum busywork, and all the other nonessentials of genuine teaching; and the students themselves who, at a certain age and ostensible maturity corresponding to secondary levels of education, must take themselves in hand and recognize that they too are implicated in the vast catering industry that education has become. Any student interested in acquiring a real education today has no choice but to rely to an ever-larger extent on his or her own resources and initiative, that is, to become an autodidact. How students may be expected to realize their own intellectual shortcomings and inherent unsoundness of attitude when scarcely anyone else seems to know or care in any meaningful sense remains a moot and perhaps insoluble question. Nevertheless, self-knowledge is the last court of appeal. The teacher's central function in the present moment (a function that may be suicidal in the Nielson-rating climate we have constructed for ourselves) is to alert students to certain basic and doubtlessly unpopular givens: their TV-saturated expectations; their short, parallel attention spans (an analogue of manic channel switching or "zapping," as Thomas Pynchon calls it in *Vineland*) which nullify the psychic structures, the prolonged and linear bestowals of attention necessary for learning; and their immense good fortune compared to their Third World counterparts who would regard as a privilege what they themselves experience as boredom. Proposing more and more reforms

instead of embarking on a sober, protracted, and intense inquiry into the cultural predicament itself, of which both the educational institution *and* the proposed reforms are only manifestations, amounts to little more than installing a new starter coil when the entire engine has seized.

25 I owe this formulation to my colleague Ruth Taylor. The relation between administration and teaching today is perhaps most aptly summarized by analogy in Swift's pamphlet "A Short View of the State of Ireland" (1727), in which the great satirist writes: "Thus, we are in the condition of patients, who have physic sent them by *doctors at a distance*, strangers to their constitution, and the nature of their disease" (italics mine). Our disease, of course, is the system in which we teach, which has sapped our will and contaminated our thinking to the point that we have become its unwitting carriers.

We should also be aware that the reform prepossession is not always pedagogically motivated but follows from certain economic decisions. As noted above, what we have been brainwashed to call "outcomes pedagogy" is really little more than cutback economics. What this actually means on a *collective* scale is less money and more real work for teachers, less real work and more money for administration. As a case in point, in my home province of Quebec, which does not differ markedly in this respect from other regions of the country, the current government has cut its budget for educational services by 3 per cent and trimmed other areas of the education system by as much as 10 per cent while negotiating pay increases for senior school administrators. See the *Montreal Gazette* for 24 April 1996.

One must remain alert for disingenuous arguments here, as for example Lewis J. Perelman's invidious claim that education bureaucrats are "selling the myth that teachers are underpaid" (*School's Out*, Avon Books, New York, 1992). As for the bureaucrats, they aren't; as for the teachers, they are. The truth of the situation should be indelibly clear to anyone who has worked in the system for any length of time. From the perspective of the typical bureaucrat, which is of course never openly articulated, the teacher is the enemy or the traitor, and the student is the victim or the pretext. And as for teachers' salaries (I speak from hard experience), the currency in which we are paid seems to generate the buying power of the zero-inch Glazunkian porpuquine nose, as Douglas Hofstadter reports in *Metamagical Themas* (Basic Books, New York, 1985). Maybe Perelman is thinking of university professors, in which case his thesis is veridical, but unfortunately he does not make the distinction.

26 Our obsession with technique is only a modern displacement of a basically theological sense of architecture. Hugh St Victor, writing in the twelfth century, lays it down in his *Didascalion* that "Divine scripture is

like a building. The foundation is in the earth and it does not always have smoothly fitting stones. The superstructure rises above the earth, and it demands a smoothly apportioned construction." Although the learned doctor acknowledges the necessity of firm foundations, and is thus somewhat in advance of most contemporary theorists, it is nevertheless evident that the foundation counts for little in comparison with the glory and magnificence of the superstructure.

This sort of thinking, perhaps most clearly exemplified in the writings of the fifth-century theologian Dionysius the Areopagite (cf. "Of Divine Hierarchies"), has survived into the present moment despite the belief that we have emancipated ourselves from superstition and retrogradation. Our reliance on abstraction and our conviction that, by virtue of its articulation and its numerical reinforcement, abstraction is *ipso facto* real, keeps us labouring in the Dark Ages, all the darker for our presumption of clarity and progress. In education we are diligently building a new cathedral that does not promise to resist its internal stresses and the buffetings of weather, since it is really nothing but an elaborate Meinongian object. The logician Alexis Meinong held that one can extend the definition of an object by stipulating that to every list of properties there corresponds a particular object, be it existent or not. Meinongian objects can be associated with any set of properties including contradictory sets. The educational institution today is such a Meinongian object, which appears rational and internally consistent insofar as it corresponds to a prior theoretical construct – but which, even so, may be perfectly non-existent. Once it becomes too *weightily* non-existent, the entire edifice – or what there is of an edifice – collapses. The plaster started falling at least twenty years ago, an early warning signal we sublimely failed to heed. The actual physical plant of most Canadian schools, in various stages of decay as maintenance budgets are cut back, serves as an eloquent analogue of our predicament.

The central fact is that in the contemporary cultural and educational contexts, top-downing has become counter-productive and must be balanced or generously supplemented by a real investment in bottom-upping. Recent organizational theory, as Kenneth Gergen argues, shows that top-down leadership is often stultifying and inefficient and that the health of an organization "depends on its susceptibility to multiplicity of voice," that is, on its hospitality to a plurality of constituent dialogues. (See Kenneth J. Gergen, "Organizational Theory in Postmodern Culture," in Michael Reed and Michael Hughes, eds., *Rethinking Organization*, Sage, London, 1992.) What George Devereux says about the quantifiability of the behavioural sciences applies equally to the rationalization of education: "It is not possible to hasten the advent of that millennium by bypassing the construction of an appropriate conceptual scheme, to serve as its foundation, and by building instead from an inappropriate, ill-fitting and borrowed roof downward." See George Devereux, *From Anxiety to Method in the Behavioral Sciences*, Mouton, The Hague, 1967. Linda Hutcheon on modernist architectural theory, especially the social failure of its housing projects, seems particularly appropriate in this context: "Although Gropius and Le Corbusier both designed workers' housing, neither seems to have felt the need to consult those who would live there: it must have been tacitly assumed that the intellectually underdeveloped would allow the architects to arrange their lives for them." See Linda Hutcheon, *A Poetics of Postmodernism*, Routledge, New York and London, 1988.

27 Simeon Potter, *Language in the Modern World.*

28 The first citation is from *Teacher in America*, Little, Brown, Boston, 1945. The subsequent Barzun citations in the paragraph are from *The House of Intellect*, Harper & Brothers, New York, 1959. I would draw attention to the ugly and rather scary word "strategy" which proliferates in educational writing today as if we were preparing for war, not school. The same applies to "target" as in the oft-repeated phrase "target performances" or the double whammy "decision-targeted systems." Jerome Bruner and others are fond of the word "trigger," as in "presuppositional triggers." David Perkins speaks of "the last bulleted item" – another ballistic term, here inflected through the lexicon of print terminology. Such metaphors are especially beloved by cognitive scientists who bullet their target words strategically in important-sounding agglutinating phrases such as "hypothesis identification strategies" and "hypothesis evaluation strategies." This is plainly a form of military address which ultimately generates what John Willinsky has called "the executive-class language of these times" (John Willinsky, *The New Literacy*, Routledge, London and New York, 1990). The educational world is bursting with instructional *cognoscenti* – "the whole sick crew," to quote from Thomas Pynchon's *V* – whose influence, I am convinced, grows more pernicious every day as their language and thought-patterns infest the scholarly milieu from the most austere theoretical papers to the most informal encounters in the staff room. We have embraced the language of the master replete with its proprietary techniques of domination – or, in the words of Michel de Certeau (*The Practice of Everyday Life*), with "categories and taxonomies that conform to those of industrial or administrative production." It is, in fact, the military-industrial complex all over again plying its conscriptions in another sphere which should by rights have resisted its conceptual subversions.

Perhaps one of the worst offenders in this recent blitz of gonzo rhetoric is Lewis J. Perelman (*School's Out*), who cannot refrain from mobilizing military analogies and references by the truckload. Hyperlearning systems, we are told, will in the future "bear less resemblance to old-fashioned classrooms than the MI AI Abrams tank bears to a Roman chariot." His example of hypermedia learning involves a young girl sampling the Battle of Fredericksburg via computer graphics or even viewing "simulated troop movements" through smart eyeglasses while touring the real battlefield. (The complete passage is cited for effect in Sheldon Richman's *Separating School and State*, The Future of Freedom Foundation, Fairfax, Virginia, 1994.) One of the important applications of cognitive science is to "military combat information centers." Information technology is – you guessed it – "exploding." The virtual instance from *Macbeth* duplicates Birnham wood and Dunsinane castle. We jeep into Kuwait and the Gulf War for an isomorphic visit. And so on throughout. The choice of metaphors and ostensives in such writers indicates a pervasive vulgarity of spirit that should make us deeply sceptical of their visions and proposals.

29 See Frank Smith, *Joining the Literacy Club*, Heinemann, Portsmouth, NH, 1988. The problem with all these procedures and "strategies" (as Smith also argues in *to think*, Teachers College Press, New York and London, 1990), these locutions bristling with commands such as "identify the nature of the problem," "define and clarify essential elements and terms," "judge and connect relevant information," and so on, is that they are too obvious and vague to be of any practical assistance. The difficulty is usually that "we do not know enough about what we are trying to think about. *We lack knowledge rather than skills*" (emphasis mine). Without a general understanding of the circumstances in which the topic is embedded or to which it applies, literacy remains a will o' the wisp. (Or as Dr Johnson puts it in Boswell's *Life*, overstating for effect, "a man must have *extensive views*. It is not necessary to have practised, to write well upon a subject" (italics mine)). This is not to diminish the importance of phonic instruction but to suggest that the unreflected skills-premise upon which the customary approach is based leads to only two possibilities: defective pedagogy or adiabatic pedagogy. That is, we either make things worse or stabilize the infelicitous.

Moreover, we not only disregard the force of context and application in the larger semantic configurations of writing, we have signally failed to reflect upon the complex *layerings* of the grammatical organization of experience itself. We habitually treat grammar as an arrangement of the surface components of *sentences* while remaining oblivious to the prior function of grammar as a way of schematizing an otherwise-undifferentiated temporal flux, an operation of which writing may be regarded as both an embodiment and a *representation*. As Jacques Derrida puts it in *Writing and Difference* (University of Chicago Press, 1978), "The 'objectivist' or 'worldly' consideration of writing teaches us nothing if reference is not made to a space of psychical writing." We have neglected both ultra-grammar and infra-grammar, structure and context, the psychical and the social, in our pedagogical obsession with the merely superficial and mechanical, that is, with the realm of immediate manifestation. Instead we should long ago have concerned ourselves with *mediacy and irradiation*, the ultra and the infra, in the "teaching" of grammar, through early exposure of our children and students to the modes of indirect instruction: story-telling, reading, and informed, suitably tempered discussion of the many things the world presents to our attention, conducted in an atmosphere of respect, joy, and curiosity. There is no other way of proceeding if we want genuine "results." Small wonder our students cannot write.

30 For more on the defensive purposes behind what we might call the elaboration of the semiolect, of which this last word is a good example, see Michel Foucault, *The Archaeology of Knowledge*, Pantheon Books, New York, 1972.

31 We should never forget the luminous obscurity of that inner dimension in which moral and intellectual values flicker, flare, phosphoresce – eventually, with luck, grace, and incessant labour, attaining clarity of outline. Or, if we prefer to apply a technological metaphor, we can say the mind which must always be re-minding is like a darkroom in which the photographic negative of the self posing against the background of history is developed. As Vladimir Nabokov writes: "Memory is a photo-studio de luxe on an infinite Fifth Power Avenue" (*Ada, or Ardor*, Vintage, New York, 1990).

32 W. Lambert Gardiner, *The Psychology of Teaching*, Wadsworth, Monterey, 1980. This is one of those rare books, crammed with specialized and technical detail, yet offering a vision of teaching-and-learning that is humane, enlightened, and genuinely "progressive." It should be reprinted a.s.a.p.

33 The proliferation of tree diagrams in the current milieu might make a good case for clear-cutting. Such topiary excesses are now the norm. See, for example, J.D. Novak and D.B. Brown, *Learning How to Learn* (Cambridge University Press, New York, 1984), a veritable kit of pedagogical scrabblings like Vee heuristics, instructional planning diagrams, tentacular scoring models, you name it. But all this is just more canoodling around. What the teacher requires today is some sort of internal scamscan device and renewed confidence in common sense. (For a passionate, extensive, and bituminous critique of this species of idolatry, see – or hear – Jacques Ellul, *The Humiliation of the Word*, William B. Eerdmans, Grand Rapids, Michigan, 1985. In today's world, Ellul writes, "Anything human is considered negligible. But statistical documents, curves, and graphics are convincing." Language assumes mere

auxiliary status, factotum to the image.) As for the desire to plant bra-
chiating tree diagrams in the minds of our students, pedagogical arbor-
ists might do better to consult Deleuze and Guattari, who think that
"the spreading rhizome might be a less repressively structuring concept
than the hierarchical tree." (See Gilles Deleuze and Felix Guattari, *A
Thousand Plateaus*, Minuit, Paris, 1980.) Of course, rhizomes have a
way of running off the page and thus confounding diagrammatic
representation.

34 Sven Birketts provides a telling critique of this "access characteristics"
epistemology. "Once it dawns upon us," he writes, "that our software
will hold all the information we need at ready access, we may very well
let it. That is, we may choose to become the technicians of our auxiliary
brain, mastering not the information but the retrieval and referencing
functions." (See Sven Birketts, *The Gutenberg Elegies*, Fawcett Columbine, New York, 1994.) This point is taken even further in the following
passage from an anonymous letter by an Ontario high-school teacher,
which appears in Andrew Nikiforuk (*School's Out*): "Just because a student knows how to retrieve something doesn't mean he will know what
to retrieve. If you don't know that you don't know ... then what?" Moreover, since what you know is what you are, person-plussery may actually undermine the literate and temporally coherent self. As Jacques
Barzun claims, the educated judgment is "buttressed ... by the great
piles of octavos incorporated into one's fabric." (Jacques Barzun, *A
Word or Two Before You Go* ... , Wesleyan University Press, Middletown, CT, 1986). The dilemma is aptly summarized by Kenneth Gergen, who claims that "the technologies of social saturation are central to
the contemporary erasure of individual self." These proliferating technologies "engender a multiplicitous and polymorphic being who thrives
on incoherence, and this being grows increasingly enraptured by the
means by which this protean capacity is expressed. We enter the age of
techno-personal systems." (See Kenneth J. Gergen, *The Saturated Self*,
Basic Books, New York, 1991.) The person-plus network is just such a
techno-personal system, which in our field I have referred to as cyborg
pedagogy, and which may be more broadly understood as the latest
stage in the ongoing process of the virtualization of the self. In the
words of one of our most important philosophers, "the Object has become the subject's mode of disappearance" (see Jean Baudrillard, *The
Ecstasy of Communication*, Semiotext(e), New York, 1988). This is the
condition Arthur Kroker has called *technotopia*, which "is about disappearances: the vanishing of the body (into a relational data base), the
nervous system into 'distributive processing.'" What we are witnessing
is "the endocolonization of the unwired world" of time and history by
the technologies of mediated presence. (See Arthur Kroker and

Michael A. Weinstein, *Data Trash.*) In fiscal terminology, one might say
with George Soros "that the 'real' economy is being sacrificed to keep
the 'financial' economy afloat," a judgment which now applies not only
to economic activity but to the formative basis of an entire cultural
world. (See George Soros, *The Alchemy of Finance*, John Wiley, New
York, 1994.) Robert Frost's lines from "Build Soil" seem precisely apposite here:

> At present from a cosmical dilation
> We're so much out that the odds are against
> Our ever getting inside in again.
> But inside in is where we've got to get.

To conclude this lengthy excursus: the notion of distributed intelligence elaborated by Perkins and others plainly originates in AI research
– a very dubious source that should deter us from taking the notion seriously – and probably derives specifically from Marvin Minsky's *The
Society of Mind*, Simon & Schuster, New York, 1987, which contends
that intelligence is not a centralized phenomenon but the cognitive re-
sultant of a cybernetic collectivity. See also Nicholas Negroponte's *being
digital*, Vintage Books, New York, 1996, especially chapter 12, for a
preferential treatment of the subject, including favourable commentaries
on Minsky and on Mitchel Resnick's recent work contesting "the centralized mind-set." I will only remark here that the gap between artificial intelligence and real intelligence is very likely unbridgeable and that
a distributionist network cannot experience the world or the flavour of
mortality or the sensuous ground of all real thinking in the same way as
a conscious agent precariously balanced between anxiety and joy, fear
and desire, indolence and discipline. "There are only two things that can
interest a serious mind," said the poet W.B. Yeats toward the end of his
life, "sex and the dead." Tell that to a distributed intelligence.

35 One must realize that a significant number of our administrators know
little or nothing about *education*, have not read their Plato, Piaget,
Postman, or Perkins, practised no theory and theorized no practice: in
short, flourish impenitently in the ignorance of their ostensible discipline. They are not "educators" but pure administrators, running
schools like teaching factories, book-keepers but not book readers who
infect the collegial atmosphere with their unproductive and self-
justifying bustle. They form part of what I have elsewhere called the immense etcetera of teaching and learning, nullifying the teacher while
quantifying the student. Their influence on education, because they do
not possess the understanding, sympathy, and knowledge required by
their mandate, is almost wholly destructive. Genuine reform or meaningful progress remains impossible unless this class of parasitical manipulators is either diminished – or educated. There are, of course, redeem-

ing exceptions, and I count myself fortunate to know one or two, but the general condemnation holds. Administration increasingly inundates the scholarly milieu in an access of pure redundance, defeating the purpose of the real enterprise, like rain during a student carwash.

Thus we find ourselves wandering ever more aimlessly in the gap that has widened between the various constituencies of the educational project – administration, teaching, studying – which resembles the space that Camille Paglia laments has opened up between the disciplines themselves, "a wasteland where wolves run free" (Camille Paglia, *Sex, Art, and American Culture*).

36 Jacques Barzun, *Being Here*, University of Chicago, 1992.
37 H.I Marrou, *A History of Education in Antiquity*, Mentor, New York, 1964.
38 David Hitchcock, *A Guide to Evaluating Information*, Methuen, Toronto, 1983. See also Smith, *to think*, where the polymentorial OMSITOG is regarded with bemused incredulity, as befits. To Professor Hitchcock's initiating question, "Have you critically examined your grounds for this belief?" (p. 5), my reader must supply the answer.
39 Jacques Lacan, *Le seminaire, livre XX: Encore*, Seuil, Paris, 1975.
40 This species of advocacy is also marred by the lack of basic grammatical reflection, in particular on the relation between linguistic structure and sensed reality as mediated by grammar and syntax. It is a serious mistake to regard grammatical concinnity as a mere phenomenon of the surface, as a *means* or device for expressing pre-existent ideas. Thus teachers will often commend a student for the "basic thoughts" detectable in a piece of writing while deploring its grammatical deficiencies. But grammar presides at the very foundation of thought itself past a certain level of crude response. One does not first have ideas and then proceed to formulate them. These ideas are themselves structured by a grammatical architectonic already imbued with constituent temporality. If the prenoetic and temporal grammar is absent or defective, the so-called basic thoughts can never be adequately formulated despite a belated crash course in the rules and conventions of standard practice. Ideas come pre-formulated, as it were, and *already* grammaticized; what we call "formulation" is really secondary elaboration and implies a certain degree of conscious structuration But what Husserl called "prepredicative experience" and Heidegger "fore-having" (*Vorhabe*) constitutes a prerequisite of all organized thinking and writing. (Similarly, as Gregory Ulmer writes in his explication of Derrida, the constituting operations of language usage – the paradigmatic moments of selection and the syntagmatic process of combining elements – "are carried out on preformed material." See *Applied Grammatology*, Johns Hopkins University Press, Baltimore, 1985.) This is one reason that the indiscrimi-

nate reliance on decontextualized rules or the continuous intervention of grammar machines always produces unsatisfactory results. Such techniques usually kick in far too late in the process of grammar acquisition (or acquisition *by* grammar) to do much good and, besides, do not go to the root of the dysfunction in current student writing. (See chapter 1, "Grammatical Fictions," for a more detailed analysis of the problem.)

Thus the essential fatuity of most software programs for teaching reading and writing, like the Princeton College Board's recent entry in the field, disingenuously called *Guides*, which is designed to improve the student's "reading and study skills" and to facilitate "written communication." One look at the tabular summaries with their arbitrary "topics," "diagnostic" and "follow-up" components, and bifurcate charts linking judgment "skills" to developmental "units" is enough to freeze the spirit of all except the most dedicated roboprofs, who presumably do not have one. I have yet to meet a student whose writing has improved demonstrably as a result of these irrelevant and lifeless interventions. A major cause of the ongoing literacy crisis is precisely the increasing reliance on cybergogic programs and techniques, a classic case of the cure collaborating with the progress of the disease. In fact, the cure is really only one of the manifestations *of the disease itself*, or in Washington Irving's phrase, "it doubles the evil instead of redressing the wrong." We have completely lost sight of what it means to be thinking human beings moving in the pellicle of historical time.

41 The central character in Frank Smith's as yet unpublished novel, *In Respect of the View*, an insecure personality who compensates for his weakness by trying to dominate his environment, explains the new technology of education which he enthusiastically supports: "Management, planning, accountability. It's starting slowly, of course. Teachers are terrible traditionalists. But the structure is being put in place – the core curriculums, specifications of basic skills, continual monitoring and testing – of teachers as well as students. Things aren't allowed just to happen in schools anymore; they can be rationalized, justified and implemented ... And centralized control will specify what the results will be ... All we have to do is plug in the new objectives." This is the same character who, in danger of a Humpty-Dumpty-like fall, clings desperately to the roof of a newly raised barn, plainly misapprehending its principle of construction.

This form of pathological thinking, to which our educators are especially prone, is beautifully satirized by James Hogan in *The Genesis Machine* (Ballantine Books, New York, 1978), in which a cadre of government administrators is trying to urge a group of scientists to produce creative breakthroughs according to timetable. All the latter need to do, apparently, is plan methodically toward specified objectives and "wrap the whole thing up into a practical implementation framework." There is a very real danger, as I have earlier argued with respect to teachers themselves, that they will be insensibly conscripted or even forced into this twisted conceptual world. As one of the characters reflects afterwards, "the very people who are capable of finding out the ways of solving the real problems are being muscled into making the problems worse." What is happening in education is only an instance of this larger syndrome afflicting the entire culture, perhaps most tersely expressed by Alain Touraine in *The Post-Industrial Society* (Random House, New York, 1971), in which he argues that *occupational* systems of work are gradually being transformed into *technical* systems of work, that is, organizational structures now tend to assume greater importance than the actual work being structured or restructured, at a crippling cost to the development of the individual. In the words of B.W. Powe in *a tremendous Canada of light* (Coach House, Toronto, 1993): "What systems, polls and corporate strategies deny is the *aspiring* individual, the source of purpose and value. *Systems always push things downward*; their method is one which imposes structure, freezes meaning" (italics mine).

The current *réforme pédagogique* in Quebec simultaneously provides both an excellent example and an unwitting but nitric indictment of the systemic obsession that nullifies the mandate of most educational ministries. It should also be pointed out that these ministries, huge consortiums motivated by self-interest masking as public concern, tend to suppress the results of unfavourable studies or fail to commission objective and longitudinal studies in the first place. As Andrew Nikiforuk has recently written with regard to the Year 2000 educational program in British Columbia: "In the ... flurry of innovation, the ministry also neglected two tenets of good school reform: quality control and control groups ... Without such controls the ministry will never be able to say with any accuracy how well the progressive theories embedded in Year 2000 really serve the interests of children or society." It is curious how the imperative of continuous assessment (whether formal or anecdotal) generally lodged in such documents never applies to the reform apparatus itself. (See Andrew Nikiforuk, *If Learning Is So Natural, Why Am I Going to School?*, Penguin, Toronto, 1994.)

For a heuristic version of the *modus operandi* of the education establishment, stripped of the aura of social responsibility and professional enlightenment which conceals its real nature, see the film *Robocop* 3 where we find a powerful corporation by the name of Omni Consumer Products levelling an entire neighbourhood and evicting its residents to prepare for a presumably utopian future intended only to serve its own corporate interests. It is true that our ministries do not resort to the

gross violence and brutality favoured by Omni Consumer Products, but
there is more than one kind of savagery at work in public life. Increasing teacher workload while reducing the number of teachers as well as
their salaries, applying shallow technological solutions to resolutely
human predicaments, systematically raiding the curriculum of its substance and history, and thus defrauding students of a meaningful education in any sense of the term is as cruel, grim, and destructive a project
as anything envisioned by the producers of grade-B movies. As Nikiforuk testifies in his most recent book (cited above) with reference to
the cadre of educratic "profiteers and careerists" who flourish at the expense of their constituencies, the school system they control "has become just another complex committed to its own growth and aggran-
dizement," another massive industry polluting the social and
pedagogical environments.

42 The maps of Borges and Korzybski call to mind the famous Spring
Carpet of the Persian king Chosroes I (A.D. 531-79), which was so large
the king could promenade along its woven paths and flowerbeds – ap-
proximately what we are doing in the counterfeit groves of academe.
(The Jorge Luis Borges story, "Exactitude in Science," concludes his *A
Universal History of Infamy*, E.P. Dutton, New York, 1979.) This syndrome in its modern proliferation is what Jean Baudrillard has called
the *precession of simulacra*: "it is the map that engenders the territory ...
It is the real, and not the map, whose vestiges subsist here and there."
We can no longer even say that we are living in a mimetic or secondary
world, but only in a world constructed on the principle of "substituting
signs of the real for the real itself," in a kind of dream characterized by
the miraculous correspondence of the real to the model (Jean Baudrillard, *Simulations*, Semiotext(e), New York, 1983).

Whatever metaphor we deploy, perhaps we should just fess up and
admit that we are the victims not of a problem but of a contradiction or
paralogism. The architectural metaphor remains probably the most apposite. When a problem becomes a contradiction, the roof caves in: that
is, in the words of Francis Fukuyama, the issue "not only cannot be
solved within the system, but corrodes the legitimacy of the system itself
such that the latter collapses under its own weight" (*The End of History
and the Last Man*, Avon Books, New York, 1992). What is happening in
education today merely reproduces the affliction from which the larger
culture is suffering, and surely cannot redress the balance via mere innovation and reform. "No efficient organization of education," writes
Simeon Potter in *Language in the Modern World*, "can compensate us
for the loss of culture itself." As Christopher Lasch explains in his commentary on Henry George's historical theories, advanced civilizations
inevitably "had to devote more and more of their resources to the main-

tenance of an idle ruling class ... they finally collapsed, top-heavy, under their own weight" (*The True and Only Heaven*). The architectural and cartographical figures coalesce in David Kolb's possibly utopian assurance that we "can care for the whole without a map of the whole ... There is a difference between being above and being amid it all" (David Kolb, *Postmodern Sophistications*, University of Chicago Press, Chicago, 1990).

I conclude with another map that comes to mind when considering the temporal panorama of cisAtlantic education, that of Dr Astrov in Chekhov's *Uncle Vanya*, which charts the relentless deforestation over a half century of the district he loves: "On the whole it is a picture of gradual and unmistakable degeneration, which in another ten or fifteen years will be complete." This degeneration is due, quite bluntly, to "stagnation, ignorance, complete lack of understanding."

CHAPTER FOUR

1 Gregory Ulmer, *Teletheory: Grammatology in the Age of Video* (Routledge, London and New York, 1989). All subsequent citations from Ulmer are from this book.

2 The source for this "new" style of thinking is obviously McLuhan's *The Gutenburg Galaxy*, University of Toronto Press, Toronto, 1962. The locution "analytico-referential," seems to have originated with Timothy J. Reiss in *The Discourse of Modernism*, Cornell University Press, Ithaca, NY, 1982.

3 Ulmer speaks of "the prominent display of anecdotes" in the composition of John Cage's *Mushroom Book*, and claims that the anecdote serves "as the basic unit of composition in all his scores, lectures, and essays."

4 I owe this example to the inimitable Count Duckula, his lootbag crammed full of such melismatic embellishments.

5 See Roland Barthes, *The Rustle of Language*, Hill and Wang, New York, 1986. Ulmer's "third meaning" may owe something to Barthes.

6 *Interchange*, vol. 21, no. 3, OISE, Toronto, 1990.

7 It is this form of time that Henri Bergson meant by *la durée* and that Walter Benjamin was getting at in his famous distinction between "homogeneous, empty time" and time "filled with the presence of the now." See also Max Horkheimer's analysis of mass culture as depriving man of his *durée*, especially the succinct reference to the problem in a letter to Leo Lowenthal: "You will remember those terrible scenes in the movies when some years of a hero's life are pictured in a series of shots which take about two minutes ... This trimming of an existence into some futile moments which can be characterized schematically symbol-

izes the dissolution of humanity." This and other letters of Horkheimer
on similar subjects may be found in Martin Jay's *The Dialogical Imagination* (Little, Brown, Boston, 1973).

8 See Ann E. Berthoff, *The Sense of Learning*, Boynton/Cook, Heinemann, Montclair, 1990.

9 See both Fredric Jameson, *The Political Unconscious*, Cornell University Press, Ithaca, 1981, and Tzvetan Todorov, *The Poetics of Prose*,
Cornell University Press, Ithaca, 1977, for extended discussions of the
subject.

10 In Rene Girard's formulation, the narrator "makes his way to the novel
through the novel" (*Deceit, Desire, and the Novel*, Johns Hopkins University Press, Baltimore, 1980.)

11 It is probably needless to say that this procedure has nothing to do with
that current bromide, the provision of character or role models.

12 Fiction is essential, writes Louis Marin in *Utopics* (Humanities Press,
NJ, 1984), because the "characteristics and signs" it contains are "placed
outside a logical system in which they would have been judged according to a true-false system. [Compare Cela, n. 13] Fiction also makes it
possible to give this complex totality ... the density, force, and 'presence'
of a transcendent object or part of reality." The function of narrative,
whether mythic or diegetic, is what he calls "transformation-in-the-
telling," since it "explains and clarifies what normally, in lived experience, would remain opaque." In terms of my thesis, the individual is
constituted and rationalized in "the time of narrative discourse" which
smooths out the tensions, contradictions, and small destabilizing anar-
chisms of unworked experience. (In Marin's terminology, classroom/
textual practice would be conceived as a species of "utopic discourse,"
blending the "discursive and narrative modes" to produce a hybrid form
with close ties to "mythic narrative.") Or to take a page from Italo Cal-
vino, the teacher, like the writer, must attend the school (located in
Cerro Negro) of the Father of Stories, "who uninterruptedly tells tales
that take place in countries and in times completely unknown to him"
(*If on a Winter's Night a Traveller*, Harcourt Brace Jovanovich, New
York, 1981). In the pedagogical context, it is important to recognize,
with Frank Smith, that thought "flows in terms of stories – stories about
events, stories about people, and stories about intentions and achievements. *The best teachers are the best storytellers*" (Frank Smith, *to
think*, Teachers College Press, New York, 1990. Italics mine).

Page Smith, extrapolating from the writings of William Lyon Phelps,
deprecates the customary classroom manner of "the modern professor,"
for whom the "real things are the abstractions; the personal, the individual, the anecdotal are all distractions and indulgences." It is precisely
here, among these putative distractions and indulgences, that effective

teaching is to be found. (See *Killing the Spirit*, Penguin, New York, 1991.)

13 Camilo Jose Cela develops precisely this point in his 1989 Nobel lecture, "In Praise of Storytelling." "By thinking we can detach ourselves as much as we wish from the laws of nature ... in thought, the kingdom of nonsense lies next to the empire of logic, for we can conceive more than what is real and possible. The mind is capable of shattering its own machinations and then recomposing them in an image that is novel to the point of aberration ... Free thought, in this restricted sense, opposed to empirical thinking, is translated into stories." But storytelling is not a matter of being like gods in perfect indifference to the laws and constraints that shape our existence, not only physically but morally as well. Rather, what storytelling has to teach us is "that with effort and imagination, we could be like human beings."

14 "*Il n'y a pas de hors-texte*" – arguably Derrida's most famous utterance, but one still requiring some qualification. It is by now a critical truism that what we are in the habit of calling "identity" is situated at the crossroads of innumerable textual "forces" or "inscriptions," but we must also introduce a salient distinction here. Self and textuality are mutually implicated, given. Instrumentally, however, in the mode of the so-called *aufhebung*, the act of transcendence or sublimation carried out by consciousness, the self that becomes aware of its productive or textualized nature is in a position to actively shape, modify, and reconstruct itself to accord with its own self-proposed narrative project. "The category of the real," as Stephen Greenblatt writes in his analysis of Thomas More (in *Renaissance Self-Fashioning*, University of Chicago Press, Chicago, 1980), "merges with that of the fictive" – if, that is, one consciously determines to live one's historical existence as a narrative fiction, subject to constant revision and diegetic patterning of the structure of identity.

15 Peter Brooks, *Reading for the Plot*, Harvard University Press, Cambridge, MA, 1992. This is a much more tolerant way of regarding the inveterate narrativity of old age than Jacques Derrida's callous dismissal of "the garrulous and tenacious hypermnesia of certain moribunds" (Jacques Derrida, *Writing and Difference*, University of Chicago Press, 1978). Narrative desire, whatever form or malformation it may assume, is precisely that which defines and establishes our human resistance to the erosions and dispersals of time, domiciling what Georg Lukacs calls "the transcendent homelessness of the idea" in the struggle against the merely featureless and interminable (Georg Lukacs, *The Theory of the Novel*, MIT Press, Cambridge, MA, 1971).

16 Richard Rorty, *Contingency, Irony and Solidarity*, Cambridge University Press, Cambridge, 1989.

17 Paul Feyerabend, *Against Method*, Verso, London, 1988, 1990.

18 Richard Ohmann, *Politics of Letters* (Wesleyan University Press, Middletown, 1987). I might also note that although Ohmann is talking
   about classroom technique, what he has to say pertains equally to
   pedagogical writing, as his own congenial practice makes abundantly
   plain.

   The narrativizing of theory as a program for educational discourse
   has also acquired the influential backing of Jerome Bruner (*Actual
   Minds, Possible Worlds*, Harvard University Press, Cambridge, MA,
   1986). In Bruner's words, "the narrative and the paradigmatic come to
   live side by side." Unfortunately, Bruner's advocacy is seriously compromised by a disabling misconstruction of narratological theory. For example, in attempting to trace the sources of polysemous reading, he attributes the four-level hermeneutic ("*litera* [sic], *moralis*, *allegoria* and
   anagogia") – popularized by Dante in his famous letter to Can Grande
   della Scala – to Nicholas of Lyra (1265–1349). In fact the principles of
   allegorical exegesis in the post-classical world were first formulated by
   Philo of Alexandria (A.D. first century), whose binary distinction between the literal and nonliteral (or ethical) levels of scriptural meaning
   was expanded by Clement (d. 216) into the threefold system of the mystic, moral, and prophetic components of theological interpretation, refined by Origen (d. 254) into the literal, moral, and spiritual, and finally
   restructured by Augustine into the famous quadratic schematism of the
   literal, etiological, allegorical, and anagogical. (Eucherius of Lyon, d.
   449 – himself influenced by the *Collationes* of John Cassian, 370–435 –
   was instrumental in shifting the etiological category over into the moral.)
   Nicholas of Lyra, arriving late in the hermeneutic game, actually
   stressed the importance of the literal level to the detriment of the other
   three, which renders him narratologically suspect. (See Susan A. Han-
   delman, *The Slayers of Moses*, SUNY Press, Albany, 1982, for a brilliant
   and comprehensive account of these matters.)

   Further, Bruner errs in associating the celebrated *sjujet/fabula* distinction far too intimately with Frank Kermode who is only elaborating
   a concept proposed by the Russian Formalists more than two generations ago; moreover, Bruner compounds the scholarly discrepancy by
   misconceiving *fabula* as "the timeless, motionless, underlying theme,"
   which it manifestly is not. (The *fabula* is the undifferentiated temporal
   sequence of events which the *sjujet* or plot rationalizes and orders.)
   E.M. Forster makes a similar distinction between story and plot in
   Aspects of the Novel (E. Arnold, London, 1927), giving as an example
   of the former the phrase, "The king died and then the Queen died," cited
   by Bruner without attribution in the course of his argument on narrative causality. But in fact the quoted phrase exemplifies mere succession,
   that is, *story*; causality is a function of *plot*, epitomized in another phrase
   offered by Forster: "The King died and then the Queen died of grief."

Or again, in Bruner's discussion of the top-down determinants of discursive forms, we find a reference to "Vladimir Propp's analysis of 'characters' as functions of the plot." But Propp's morphology of the folktale yields thirty-one "functions" which are defined as *acts* of the characters regarded as units of narrative syntax; the characters themselves are not so much associated with functions as distributed among seven "spheres of action" distinguished by Propp as Villain, Donor, Helper, Sought-for Person, Dispatcher, Hero, and False Hero.

These are only a few examples of Bruner's dubious literary scholarship, which largely invalidates what might otherwise have been an important contribution to the field of narratology. When it comes to psychology – the discipline that undertakes, with variable results, the laborious verification of the self-evident – Bruner is usually trustworthy, but in literary-critical analysis the maxim of Apelles would apply: *Ne sutor ultra crepidam.*

19 The practice of questioning or of soliciting questions as a systematic educative device is an integral aspect of the anecdotal function, since anecdote may also be conceived as *analogical response*. This response is not necessarily or always an *answer* but a taking up of the question, especially if it is posed by the student, into a larger cycle of query, response, and reflection, all abetted by the anecdotal function. "After the question has been asked, the one thing to do is to sustain the asking. The last thing is to answer it," writes J.T. Dillon in *Questioning and Teaching* (Teachers College Press, New York, 1988). (Dillon's account, however, errs on the side of unchecked idealism, as certain questions must necessarily be answered, and often the state of the student's knowledge does not allow for adequate reformulation.)

20 The method I am advocating here is by no means an unprecedented one. It is the traditional mode of teaching divulged in the Hebrew Talmud as *Haggadah*, extensive anecdotal commentary on the doctrines of the Law or Halakah, and in the time-honoured usage of the parable. It finds its supreme fruition in the standard technique of Hasidic pedagogy in which, as Gershom Scholem says, "Nothing at all has remained theory, everything has become a story." The Hasidic tale systematically replaces theoretical disquisition. Scholem quotes a celebrated Hasidic story about the primacy of narrative, which I reproduce in full (cf. *Major Trends in Jewish Mysticism*, Schoken Books, Jerusalem, 1941):
   When the Baal Schem had a difficult task before him, he would go to a certain place in the woods, light a fire and meditate in prayer – and what he had set out to perform was done. When a generation later the "Maggid" of Meseritz was faced with the same task, he would go to the same place in the woods and say: We can no longer light the fire, but we can still speak the prayers – and what he wanted done became reality. Again a generation later Rabbi Moshe

Leib of Sassov had to perform this task. And he too went into the
woods and said: We can no longer light a fire, nor do we know the
secret meditations belonging to the prayer, but we do know the
place in the woods to which it all belongs – and that must be sufficient; and sufficient it was. But when another generation had
passed and Rabbi Israel of Rishin was called upon to perform the
task, he sat down on his golden chair in his castle and said: We cannot light the fire, we cannot speak the prayers, we do not know the
place, but we can tell the story of how it was done. And, the storyteller adds, the story which he told had the same effect as the actions of the other three.

It is interesting to note as well that for Jean-François Lyotard the distinction between theoretical and narrative discourse is by no means absolute: "Theory is a form of narration without the transitivity." In these
terms narrative is simply theory that takes an object, which is to say, a
subject (*The Lyotard Reader*, Basil Blackwell, Oxford, 1989).

Finally, it may be appropriate to mention that some educational
scholars regard narrative with a certain amount of suspicion and mistrust. François Tochon, for example, wonders, in the best postmodern
fashion, whether narrative does not operate as a means of promoting
ideological conformity, that is, whether the "language of freedom" that
narrative mobilizes to explore the self is not used instead "for building
obedience networks." Moreover, Tochon problematizes, in the best deconstructive fashion, the alleged Presence beyond the narrative construct: "What is then beyond the narrative? Illusion or Presence? Self or
doctrine?" In other words, narrative may not only explore the secret coherencies of the (initially) non-reflective self but in effect generate a
false or delusory model according to a recipe provided by a controlling
authority (teacher) or dictated by personal need. This essentially Freud-
ian dialectic (cf. Freud's notion of paramnesis, past events that are
chiefly *reconstructed* rather than recollected, requiring analysis to work
with metaleptic narratives) has been carefully investigated by many recent thinkers, in particular Paul Jay (*Being in the Text*, Cornell University Press, Ithaca, 1984), who in his analysis of writers like Wordsworth,
Proust, and Joyce points out how "truth becomes a function not of remembering but of fictionalizing" and flashlights the obscure mecha-
nisms by which the psychological subject (author) is transmuted into the
literary subject (protagonist). For Jay, narrative may be a technique for
avoiding or modifying or inventing, not revealing, the past. Tochon
takes the argument a step further perhaps in underlining the dangers of
"narrative fundamentalism" and suggesting the importance not of narrativizing but rather of "destorying events" – (in)auspiciously misprinted
in the text as "destroying events." (See François V. Tochon, "Presence

Beyond the Narrative: Semiotic Tools for Deconstructing the Personal Story," *Curriculum Studies*, vol. 2, no. 2, 1994.)

For my part I propose here, in the best de Manxian fashion, only to indicate the inherently problematic and perilous character of *all* "rhetorical" artifacts, be they psychological case studies, ostensibly objective reports, statistical summaries, anecdotal functions, biographical constructs, or even forms of destorying events through semiotic analysis. None of these can escape the human predicament of self-division and of the compulsive desire to embody that very "presence" that may exist somewhere *behind* narrative, come into existence *through* narrative genesis, or recede eternally, in the best Derridean fashion, *beyond* the narrative quest for origins. My point is that since all our devices of self-discovery/construction are, in the words of the poet Derek Walcott, "halved by a darkness / from which they cannot shift," the best we can do is to exercise restraint and to practise certain scruples of attention in the attempt to become "persons" with a modicum of depth, coherence, and resonance of being. Narrative, for all its pitfalls, remains one of the most effective ways of accomplishing this project, if only because it enables us both to structure the inchoate plasma of drives and impulses of which we presumably consist and to innervate the impersonal and subjectless world of theoretical discourse. And therefore, as it goes almost without saying, it remains one of the best ways of helping us to perform as teachers engaged in the act of firming up the wavering, discontinuous, and amorphous shapes of those minds we are called upon to educate – including our own. "That, anyway, is what I have learned," to cite the refrain from Mario Vargas Llosa's *The Storyteller* (Penguin, New York, 1989).

CHAPTER FIVE

1 It should perhaps be admitted that *Education Lost* (OISE Press, Toronto, 1989) was not conceived as an excursion into the murky field of education theory but as a species of cultural analysis adopting the form of a pedagogical critique as a stalking horse, straw dog, or red herring – a theriomorphic mantelet. It should be compared with books like *The Culture of Narcissim* by Christopher Lasch, *The Image* by Daniel Boorstin, and *Leisure* by Joseph Pieper. (But, as should also be noted, *Education Lost* is in some respects a barbarous book: a trifle windy, heedlessly abrasive, and somewhat opsimathic. As this one is.)

2 I have no intention or desire to take issue with all of Wilson's cavils, objections, or dismissals. For all I know, he may from time to time be right. For example, I am taken to task for the "dabs of pop social psychology that he regularly dishes out" – with one instance of this appar-

ent misdemeanour. I thought the passage in question was reasonably insightful, or I would not have included it. Curiously, Wilson compares this apparently lamentable tendency of mine, "jazzing up an argument by using pop psychology to mystify," with the practice of George Grant, a writer I have always admired and even revere. So Wilson is critically astute in detecting affinities. (Even more curiously, Wesley Cragg in his article in the same issue of *Interchange* links my book with Grant's *Lament for a Nation*.) All this is fascinating stuff. But my own threnody, if I may put it so boldly, is not the lament for a nation or a "system" or a set of circumstances as it is "the lament for the dried-up vision which enfolds us," to quote the poet Nikos Orphanides. (See his extraordinary book of poems, *Anatoliki Thalassa*, if you can find it.)

I should also anticipate an objection to the kind of vocabulary I tend to mobilize from time to time, but the discerning reader will have recognized by this time the theoretical purpose behind such tsunamic excesses. And as for the tendency to belligerence for which I have been spanked from time to time, I can only say that it suits me to practise what Michel de Certeau in *The Practice of Everyday Life* (University of California Press, Berkeley, 1984, 1988) so aptly called the "polemological analysis of culture."

3 Cf. *Martin Heidegger*, George Steiner, University of Chicago Press, Chicago, 1978; *Dog Years*, Gunter Grass, Fawcett Crest, New York, 1965; and Victor Farias, *Heidegger and Nazism*, Temple University Press, Philadelphia, 1989. Agnes Heller argues in *A Philosophy of History in Fragments* (Blackwell Publishers, Oxford, 1993) that authenticity may be a constituent of speculative thinking without being decisive for personal character. "Heidegger certainly is an unauthentic person," she writes. "But I simply do not think that the philosophical greatness or the speculative weight of authors necessarily depends on their personal authenticity." This, it seems to me, may also serve as the unintended or subliminal conclusion of Paul Johnson's unsparing analysis of the despicable streak to be found in so many authoritative philosophers and writers (Paul Johnson, *Intellectuals*, Weidenfield and Nicholson, London, 1989). Jacques Derrida accounts for the current dismissal of Heidegger, whether intellectual or social, by citing "a self-perpetuating deviance, a kind of spellbound projection, which is taking a more and more defamatory turn" (Jacques Derrida, *Positions*, University of Chicago Press, Chicago, 1981). And even Jean-François Lyotard ironically concedes that "one must admit the importance of Heidegger's thought ... without this recognition, the 'fault' (Lacoue-Labarthe) would unfortunately be ordinary" (Jean-François Lyotard, *Heidegger and "the Jews,"* University of Minnesota Press, Minneapolis, 1990).

4 For Prof. Wilson's benefit, I wish to stress that I do mean "ostensive" – deictic – and not "ostensible."

5 A notion that may have influenced Jacques Barzun in his choice of the title *The House of Intellect*
6 Claude Levi-Strauss's useful notion of *bricolage* or "tinkering" in *Structural Anthropology* (Basic Books, New York, 1963) has been aptly modified to "thinkering" by Michael Ondaatje in *The English Patient* (Vintage, Toronto, 1993). It is perhaps here, in t(h)inkering with the concept of "unhousedness," that one might launch a *legitimate* argument against Heideggerian predispositions. One could mobilize, for example, Andrei Codrescu's powerful insight that "life consists, it seems, in a variety of ways of *not being at home*. Consciousness itself is in exile from biology. History is an exile from paradise ... We are all exiles if only because, by virtue of His never having left the womb, God is the only native." The condition of unhousedness may constitute a heroic opportunity for self-making, not an impoverishment of being (cf. *The Disappearance of the Outside*, Addison-Wesley, New York, 1990).
7 Peter Sloterdijk, *Critique of Cynical Reason*, University of Minnesota, Minneapolis, 1987. This book is essential reading for contemporary educators. It is among other things a miscellany of colourful stylemes and caustic examples, devices meant to cleanse and deodorize, deposited in the porcelain declivities of the modern soul like pink urinal pucks.
8 Educators have become increasingly prone to firing the word "elitist" at their theoretical adversaries without pausing to consider the implications of what they are doing. The utopian temperament cannot tolerate the striving for excellence in a real-world context and all the hard and painful choices this necessarily entails. The devastation we confront in the present educational scene is the direct result of the utopian fiction we have so resolutely domesticated and of the sebaceous garrulity of two generations of education theorists. The dilemma is acute and persistent. What is happening today is that we are gradually and inexorably being shorn of our language by the connotative loading of important words which makes their use increasingly problematic or counter-productive. The adjective "gay" is a contemporary example, and so is the word "elitist." (As John Ralston Saul writes in *Voltaire's Bastards* (Penguin, New York, 1992), "Contemporary language doesn't equip us to distinguish between meritocracy and expertise." Worse, it scarcely permits us to use the word "meritocracy.") The aberration we are facing here is diagnosed by Conor Cruise O'Brien as deriving from the "late development of Orwellian Newspeak known as 'politically correct'" in which "no term is more comprehensively damning than 'elitist.'" According to this writer, it is nothing less than the survival of the Enlightenment tradition, "demonstrably an affair of elites," that is now being threatened. (See Conor Cruise O'Brien, *On the Eve of the Millennium*, Anansi, Concord, 1994.)
9 See Richard Rorty, *Contingency, Irony and Solidarity*, Cambridge University Press, Cambridge, 1989. Shaun Gallagher makes a similar clever

move in *Hermeneutics and Education* (SUNY Press, Albany, 1992), where the teacher is almost always "she" and the student "he." Malcolm Bradbury comments wryly on such pronominal transvestism in proposing the locution "hismeneutics" (*Mensonge*, Penguin, New York, 1987).

10 "And," she continues, "I find made-up pronouns, 'te' and 'heshe' and so on, dreary and annoying" (Ursula K. Le Guin, "Winter's King," prologue, in *The Wind's Twelve Quarters*, Harper and Row, New York, 1975). Emphasis added.

11 Agnes Heller, *A Philosophy of History in Fragments*. Also to the point here is Article 108 from the Discussion Paper on Curriculum Organization and Classroom Practice prepared for the British government by Robin Alexander *et al.* (cited in Andrew Nikiforuk, *School's Out*, Macfarlane Walter and Ross, Toronto, 1993): "The problem is partly ideological. In some schools and local education authorities the legitimate drive to create equal opportunities for all pupils has resulted in an obsessive fear of anything which, in the jargon, might be deemed 'elitist.' As a consequence, the needs of some of our most able children have quite simply not been met." Charles J. Sykes modifies the terms of the debate somewhat and lays the blame for the anti-elitist prejudice at the Gucci-shod feet of our contemporary professoriate trampling the curriculum to pulp. Teachers, he argues, strive to justify "their abject neglect and the resulting ignorance of their students" by euphemizing their customary practice as enshrining the values of pluralism and diversity. "If curricular gibberish was now 'diversity,' then the traditional standards must be elitism, and anyone who advocated even a modicum of rationality in the curriculum must not only be anti-democratic, but potentially even fascistic" (Charles J. Sykes, *Profscam*, St. Martin's Press, New York, 1990).

12 John W. Gardner, *Excellence*, W.W. Norton, New York, 1987. Jacques Barzun is even more direct: "Our real attitude toward 'excellence' – we won't have it" (*Begin Here*, University of Chicago Press, Chicago, 1992). As Simeon Potter warns, "it is essential to create and secure for present-day society a "climate of 'literacy' in which alone national democracy is able to function" (*Language in the Modern World*, Penguin, Baltimore, 1960).

13 For many of us white males today, especially in the teaching profession, I sometimes suspect that a Swedish operation is no longer necessary. Aristophanes in *Thermasphoriazusae* has caught us for all time in the character of Blepyros, a blenny-mouthed pram-pusher if there ever was one, limply surrendering to Praxagoran initiatives.

14 Verses 22 and 23 of the General Epistle of Jude may, *mutatis mutandis*, be appropriate here:

And some have compassion, making a difference;
And others save with fear, pulling them out of the fire.

But real compassion, the kind that makes a difference, also contains an element of severity, a willingness to suffer and if necessary to inflict suffering, a capacity to draw distinctions. Otherwise it is too much like Calvin's cafeteria tapioca, the "hideous blob of gelatinous muck" that threatens to engulf the spaceman Spiff (*Calvin and Hobbes: Something under the Bed Is Drooling*, Bill Watterson, Andrews and McMeel, Kansas City, 1988). Perhaps the matter is most succinctly put by T.S. Eliot, who clearly approves

> The sharp compassion of the healer's art
> Resolving the enigma of the fever chart.
> (*Four Quartets*, "East Coker")

15 I don't have the faintest clue what Wilson is getting at here, especially as I can't pretend to be anything more than a technopeasant myself. Perhaps he would need to reformulate his thesis or to reconsider mine. Apart from the curious assessment of my argument in *Education Lost*, of which the quoted statement may serve as a typical Wilsonian exhibit, the writer might at least have shown sufficient respect for my analytic candour (if not my moral rectitude) to assume that I might have rejected Rushton's claims on purely methodological grounds. Rushton, at any rate until more recently, appears to some to have practised what the Concordia University psychologist Bill Bukowski calls "penny psychology," a form of pseudo-empirical research that accounts for approximately *one per cent* of the variants in outcome measurements (personal communication). Rushton may perhaps be indictable for technical or formal reasons even before we come to a consideration of his ideas. (The problem, too, is that the shadow of Arthur de Gobineau's pernicious *Essai sur l'inegalité des races humaines* hangs over the entire debate.) Nevertheless, while recognizing the value and necessity of effort, the laudable desire to avoid drawing invidious distinctions should not blind us to the datum of individual merit. As the character called Picture Singh argues in Salman Rushdie's great novel *Midnight's Children* (Jonathan Cape Ltd., London, 1981), "You see, captain, here is the truth of the business: some persons are better, others are less. But it may be nice for you to think otherwise." In a similar vein, Nicholson Baker in *The Mezzanine* (Vintage, New York, 1986) notes with respect to supermarket cashiers that "the differential in checkout speeds between a fast, smart ringer-upper and a slow, dumb one was three transactions to one, such was the variation in human abilities and native intelligence."

16 David H. Hargreaves, *The Challenge for the Comprehensive School*, Routledge & Kegan Paul, London, 1982. He distinguishes two other categories: the instrumentalists, preoccupied with the empirical self, career, and status; and the committed, a shrinking minority.

17 The embarrassment of media exposure may persuade the authorities to

revise their decision in individual cases – as I suspect will happen here – but such ad-hocism does not touch the general structure of response, the entrenched sentimentality or underdog psychology that usually gets the real underdog wrong. Our civilization is now in the process of enacting globally what Dante called the "great refusal": that is, the refusal to see clearly, to isolate root causes, to take personal responsibility, and to make difficult choices. It is so much easier to remain content with pharisaic pieties while keeping the current distributions of power intact. The real problem, to put it bluntly, is that we have forgotten how to think. Or how to think honestly and holistically. (It is important to note that the misnamed "critical thinking" movement does not address the problem but merely reinforces the reigning platitude that thinking is something that happens in a vacuum, outside of history, devoid of context, and always innocent of the ruthless deflations of self-inquiry.)

And here lies the root of our dilemma: the inability to contextualize. We divide, enucleate, fragment the issues we confront, and then try to deal with them in isolation, throwing a switch, as it were, and presumably disconnecting what forms an integral and undetachable part of a larger field or system. We cannot hope to solve our educational difficulties if we fail to take into account the vast and intricate cultural circuit in which they flicker symptomatically. As Michael Talbot writes in his explication of David Bohm's holographic approach to social problems, "Bohm believes that our almost universal tendency to fragment the world and ignore the dynamic interconnectedness of all things is responsible for many of our problems ... for instance ... we believe we can deal with various problems in our society, such as crime, poverty, and drug addiction, without addressing the problems in our society as a whole." I submit that the state of education today is as grave a "problem" as crime, poverty, and drug addiction, and that it cannot be adjusted or rectified if we do not adopt the panoramic and catechetical view. (Cf. Michael Talbot, *The Holographic Universe*, HarperCollins, New York, 1991.) In Bohm's own terms, we need to consult an "implication parameter" to help us determine those aspects of an "implicate order that can be explicated together," that is, to avoid "fragmentary perception" (David Bohm, *Wholeness and the Implicate Order*, Routledge, London, 1983). Such ideas, of course, are enfolded in the implicate order of the philosophical tradition, for example, Maurice Merleau-Ponty's work on the perception of objects as integrating what is not immediately evident and Ortega y Gasset's provocative notion of perspectivalism – important considerations for current educational thinking.)

18 The presumed correlation between academic success and social class stressed by "reproduction" theorists like Pierre Bourdieu and Jean-Claude Passeron (*Reproduction in Education, Society and Culture*,

Sage, London, 1977) and many others too numerous to mention here
seems to be to some extent the result of a prior commitment-to-thesis or
parti pris, or an effect of local conditions and specific time periods. I
teach in a junior college that serves one of the wealthiest communities
in Canada, yet the academic performance of the students to whom we
cater is cause for depression, burn-out, and hesperine thoughts of early
retirement. The best students, i.e., the most dedicated and highly motivated, often come from the lower end of the social spectrum: poorer
families who recognize the necessity of effort, and immigrant families in
the process of integrating into their adopted society but still rooted in
old-world traditions of scholarship and discipline. In any case, in today's milieu, as it seems to me, one does not need to be poor to be culturally disadvantaged. One simply needs to be a member of the culture.
We may also wonder whether economic privilege has not become an especially pernicious form of deprivation.

19 Hilda Neatby, *So Little for the Mind*, Clarke Irwin, Toronto, 1953.

20 Jacques Barzun, *The House of Intellect*, Harper & Brothers, New York,
1959. His text makes it painfully clear that he is referring to *both*
teachers and students. Harsh words from a thinker whom anyone wishing to close "the gap between words and experience in the dream world
of professional educators" should take to heart.

As a case in point, I refer the reader to an editorial in the *Montreal
Gazette* of 26 March 1995 written by Norman Henchey, a retired McGill
University education professor, under the title "Chalking up big gains in
education." Professor Henchey seems convinced that the situation is by
no means as desperate as catastrophists like myself have claimed. Many
hopeful trends are apparently emerging: "a climate of greater collaboration," "more sensitive ways of assessing learning achievement," "innovative efforts to decentralize," "enriching methods," "imaginative programs," and so on. We must be living in different universes. I see little
"collaboration" on the educational scene: the new reforms, like the Year
2000 Proposal in British Columbia and the *réforme pédagogique* in
Quebec, are imposed by administrative fiat. Continuous assessment is
more likely intrusive and threatening than "sensitive." Methods are not
"enriching"; rather, as the educational scholar François Tochon once
confided, "methods are dead research." Most of the "imaginative programs" I have encountered are at best complex ways of avoiding hard
work. And as for decentralization, the competency-based Alverno model
coming to the fore requires, under the rubric of accountability, that
teachers follow a pedagogical recipe and take full responsibility for an
outcome over which they have only limited control. Decentralization
must be "innovative" indeed if it results in nothing so much as intensi-
fied centralized authority.

Perhaps the problem is one of cultural parallax. The view from the
rarefied heights of education departments and the camera squint necessarily adopted by the educational tourist on flying visits to schools and
conference sites must differ radically from the perspective taken up by
real teachers slogging through the murk and turmoil of daily practice.
The place looks very different when you live there. (The relation between the theorist, especially when retired, and the practitioner, still actively engaged in a hopeless task, bears an uncanny resemblance to that
between Serebryakov and Uncle Vanya in the Chekhov play.) In fact,
the actual situation is deteriorating so rapidly that it is frankly doubtful
whether anything meaningful can still be done to rectify it despite our
best efforts. And one of the symptoms of the disaster, of what Connor
Cruise O'Brien has called "cognitive degeneration," is precisely this
tendency to magic ourselves out of reality or to construct from selective
glimpses and impressions "the dream world of professional educators."

21 See Jacques Derrida, *The Post Card*, University of Chicago Press, Chicago, 1987, for a prolonged meditation on priority and corruption in the
Socratic-Platonic relationship. It is entirely possible that it is Socrates
who has corrupted Plato, speech that has infiltrated and destabilized
writing, and not vice versa – if the term "corruption" applies. Moreover,
in the context of Derrida's work in general, and of *Glas* (University of
Nebraska Press, Lincoln, 1987) in particular, the project of anamnesis
now seems remarkably naive. Derrida proposes a new pedagogy based
on *hypomnesic* principles, with reference to anasemes and paragrams,
homophones and calembours, i.e., the festival of aleatory dissemination
that may nevertheless be intrinsically motivated and requires that we
pay close attention to *linguistic productivity* – a desideratum of good
teaching. Hypomnesia entails not simply the reliance upon memory but
the *discovery of memory* in the structured effusion of a language that
"remembers" what we need to know. Genuine writers have always understood this apparent paradox. One embarks on what the poet Gaston
Miron in *L'Homme Rapaillé* calls "le voyage abracadabrant," to create
that "memory [which] believes before knowing remembers," as Faulkner
puts it. (Miron again: "*Je ne suis pas revenu pour revenir/je suis arrivé
a ce qui commence*") But this spendthrift aliquanticity is not random or
arbitrary or merely self-indulgent: "The meaning-fulness of language by
no means consists in a mere accumulation of meanings cropping up
haphazardly. It is based on a play which, the more richly it unfolds, the
more strictly it is bound by a hidden rule" (Jacques Derrida,
Dissemination, University of Chicago Press, Chicago, 1981). This "hidden rule" is to be found concealed in the paronymic stratifications of
language and the repetition of the signifier. But at the same time it also
functions in the disciplined, informed, and playful *esprit* of the teacher

who does not wish to plumb the mnemological depths the student presumably contains somewhere within the obscure recesses of the psyche,
so much as seek *to bring the student* out into the resonating structures
of language itself. These structures have been variously denominated in
the literature on the subject. For example, Ferdinand de Saussure's
study of the ubiquity of the onomastic anagram in Latin poetry and
Jacques Lacan's articulation of the principle of *lalangue*, the punda-
ment or paranomasic stratum on which each specific language is raised,
stress the element of necessity or inevitability in linguistic auto-
production. (See Gregory Ulmer, *Applied Grammatology*, Johns Hopkins University Press, Baltimore, 1985, especially chapter 7, for a detailed account of *lalangue*, or might we say *lacalangue*?) The point remains: it is in language that knowledge continues to echo, could we only
learn to hear, to pay a certain cochlear attention, and, as it were, to pal-
pate its intellectual sonorities. But then, as the poet George Walton
writes, "No noise annoys an oyster."

For those with a more psychological orientation to the subject, I
might point out that the capacity of language to generate new connections and unexpected meanings serendipitously may be subsumed under
Edward de Bono's fourth principle of lateral thinking, "the use of
chance," with respect to our linguistic behaviour. This emerges as a
maxim, preferentially governing our intellectual habits, from the cumulative thrust of the preceding three principles: recognition of polarizing
ideas, the search for different perspectives and forms of reconsideration,
and relaxation of the rigid control of vertical thinking (performing what
Maxwell Maltz calls "disinhibition"). (Cf. Edward de Bono, *The Use of
Lateral Thinking*, Jonathan Cape, London, 1967; and Maxwell Maltz,
Psycho-Cybernetics, Simon & Schuster, New York, 1960.) I would not,
however, recommend either of these two books seriously except to the
most costive and rigid of scholars, to whom I should like to say: lighten
up, folks.

22 Cf. The *Montreal Gazette*, 23 Jan. 1994, "Get Smart," by Kathy Seal,
who also quotes from Jim Stigler (*The Learning Gap*, Summit Books,
1992), Sanford Graham of UCLA's Graduate School of Education, and
Carol Dweck of Columbia University, all of whom decry the supposed
American reverence for innate intelligence and valorize the Asian emphasis on hard work. I will only comment here that hard work or stick-
to-it-tiveness is an old Puritan and American virtue as well, and although it no doubt needs to be revived, one could just as well look to
the American nineteenth century as to the Asian twenty-first for working paradigms. I should also note that I remain highly sceptical about
the validity of the hypothesis regarding the current reverence for innate
intelligence. I have not often met this assumption in my own experience

as a teacher, and in fact the contrary postulate that innate intelligence is an aristocratic prejudice seems far more preponderant. Moreover, what has gradually been devalued in our society is not innate intelligence but intelligence *per se*, in whatever way it happens to manifest. As for the born smart/get smart controversy, I think it is plausible to assume that so long as one is not born unsmart, there is a lot to be said for will power, effort, and good working habits. "We need an effort-centred model," writes David Perkins (*Smart Schools*, Free Press, New York, 1992), who also quotes Carol Dweck to good effect, and his argument is well taken. But the higher creative functions, although these clearly need to be nourished and exercised, will always remain a mystery – something that is brought into the world – which should be honoured and socially valued and lodged in the Prytaneum.

As for hard work or effort-centredness, this remains a staple desideratum. Why it should ever have been called in question and should now attract so much theoretical attention – as if the value of hard work were a revolutionary discovery – is little more than a sign of a declining, self-indulgent, and alarmingly *infantile* culture plunged in deep, radiolarian slumber. Even so astute a pedagogical thinker as Perkins bypasses the essential issue, locating the source of our educational dilemma in two naive theories of instruction – the Trivial Pursuit doctrine that advocates the stockpiling of facts, and the abilities-count-more-than-effort hypothesis – when our students arrive in the classroom, at almost any level, *already* disabled and demoralized by the attitudes and practices prevailing in the home and the culture.

23 Agnes Heller, *A Philosophy of History in Fragments*.
24 See Richard J. Herrnstein and Charles Murray (*The Bell Curve: Intelligence and Class Structure in American Life*, Free Press, New York, 1994), who present compelling statistical evidence for "a downward trend of the educational skills of America's academically most promising youngsters toward those of the average student." The authors point out that, of the $8.6 billion educational budget for 1993, 92.2 per cent was allocated for programs for the disadvantaged. Programs for the gifted received 0.1 per cent of the share. It is clear that American (and Canadian) education "has neglected the gifted minority who will greatly affect how well America [and Canada] does in the Twenty-first Century."

Curiously, even as I write, a pedagogical debate has erupted between a local school board which is proposing to dismantle one of the rare programs for gifted students and parents who are resisting the move. As usual, the board cites cost as the decisive factor. The cost of programs for the disadvantaged does not arise as an issue nor does the cost to the future welfare of the larger community.

Of course, in a truly enlightened and well-administered educational system, special programs for the gifted would be reduced to a minimum precisely because *the system itself* would constitute such a program, at least as a core presupposition about the nature of the educational commitment embodied in both practice and expectation. As Herrnstein and Murray regret, "Too few educators are comfortable with the idea of the educated person. A century ago ... people were at ease with intellectual standards, with rigor, with a recognition that people differ in their capacities. The criterion for being an educated person did not have to be compromised to include the supposition that everyone could meet it." This state of affairs is expressed even at the level of idiomatic currency. Only a generation ago, public-school teachers were fond of saying "smarten up." Today, as the critical lingo has it, pedagogical practice is geared to "dumbing down." We should do well to recall the stark apothegm the poet Hopkins confided to his journals: "From much, much more; from little, not much; and from nothing, nothing."

25 As Francis Fukuyama argues in *The End of History and the Last Man* (Avon Books, New York, 1992), "democracy's long-run health and stability can be seen to rest on the quality and number of outlets for *megalothymia* that are available to its citizens." By megalothymia he means the profound need to be recognized as *superior* in value to a variable standard or level of performance, accomplishment, or intrinsic worth. He gives three examples of such megalothymotic outlets: entrepreneurship, electoral politics, and formal or contentless activities like sports. But this list is manifestly incomplete and should include the arts and sciences, education and scholarship, and the mysterious faculty of disciplined introspection, the source of what we call "wisdom."

Nor should we doubt that the spectre of competitive foreclosure haunts our imminent future. As John Gardner writes, "In an organization or society characterized by extreme equalitarianism the greatest threat may lie in external competition, i.e., from aggressive organizations or societies that have not fettered their most talented and energetic people." Gardner's conclusion is well taken, difficult to implement as it may be: "We must learn to honour excellence in every socially accepted human activity, however humble the activity, and to scorn shoddiness, however exalted the activity. An excellent plumber is infinitely more admirable than an incompetent philosopher."

26 I mean the renovation of the student *as student* in all the dimensions this social and intellectual category entails, and not the remedialism or Ketchup pedagogy we habitually practise. This desideratum involves the re-education of parents and teachers, a massive cultural project without which school reform and curriculum juggling remain little more than cosmetic ornamentation or sops to the pedagogical conscience. Treating

education as a form of rehabilitation, as we now do, is not a feasible project for many reasons, not the least of which involves the questionable status of the "re." It is quite impossible to rehabilitate those who may not have been properly habilitated in the first place.

27 See Andrew Nikiforuk's article in the *Toronto Globe and Mail*, 3 January 1992 (Fifth Column/Education), in which the writer, commenting on a study of the Manitoba science curriculum made by Josef Macek, a Winnipeg geologist, deplores the dilution and anarchy afflicting the science programs in the province, "a microcosm of Canada's educational system." Mr Macek determined that Grade 7 students in Czechoslovakia knew more basic science than Grade 10 students in Manitoba, owing to the use of properly designed textbooks rather than incoherent curricula guides, a more rigorous classroom structure, a strict, cumulative approach to the material, and the absence of the ad hoc, impressionistic methods that characterize the activities of poorly equipped teachers. Macek concludes that "every child in the province is being intellectually retarded relative to Europe," students being in point of fact victims of a certain "intellectual abuse." Nikiforuk in partial summation of Macek's argument recuses the incompetence and self-indulgence of those responsible for what I should like to call our curriculumber, the "well-intentioned gangs of educrats who often care more about pedagogical fads and feel-good politics than content." He might have added: than method and attitude as well. Scholars such as Fred Wilson and Wesley Cragg are certainly well intentioned – all, all honourable men – but their policies and convictions in the field of education amount to nothing less than the kiss of death. (For an analysis of "educracy," see *Education Lost*, chapter 7.) Teachers are partly responsible for the disasters over which they preside, but the principal blame *within the institution itself* rests with education scholars, administrators, and government ministers. Teachers are generally as much a victim of current paradigms and policies as their students. A line of cubicle graffito says it all: Humpty Dumpty Was Pushed.

28 Peter Sloterdijk, *Critique of Cynical Reason*.

29 Prof. Wilson would no doubt regard this remark as an example of pop psychology.

30 This is the same question posed in the middle of the nineteenth century by Matthew Arnold in *Mixed Essays*: "Our society is probably destined to become much more democratic; who or what will give a high tone to the nation then?" If democracy has become an endangered political genus, the danger comes less, as Christopher Lasch argues in *The True and Only Heaven* (W.W. Norton, New York, 1991.), "from totalitarian or collectivist movements abroad than from the erosion of its psychological, cultural and spiritual foundations from within."

31 The citations in these two paragraphs are from the following: Aldous
   Huxley, *Brave New World Revisited*, Chatto & Windus, London, 1959;
   Alfred North Whitehead, *The Aims of Education*, Macmillan, New
   York, 1929, 1967; Northrop Frye, *The Educated Imagination*, CBC, Toronto, 1985; C.S. Lewis, *The Abolition of Man*, Macmillan, New York,
   1947; William A. Henry III, *In Defense of Elitism*, Anchor Books, New
   York, 1994; and Richard J. Herrnstein and Charles Murray, *The Bell
   Curve*. (This latter has been powerfully challenged by many reviewers,
   perhaps most notably Alan Ryan – see note 40 of "Grammatical Fictions" for details – in a review that must be appreciated for its intellectual virility even if one cannot endorse it wholly or help wondering
   whether a certain animus or prejudice complementary to the one as-
   cribed to *The Bell Curve* does not also compromise the review itself. It
   is hard to remain scrupulously disinterested and *clear* when dealing with
   such incendiary issues.) I should also remark that I feel somewhat uncomfortable with Huxley's "genetic" argument (as if education
   amounted to a kind of sexing the chick), but his contentions must nevertheless be met and debated – soberly. The argument is perhaps most
   tactfully and yet forcefully stated by John Gardner in *Excellence*: "The
   idea for which this nation stands will not survive if the highest goal free
   citizens can set for themselves is an amiable mediocrity ... A free society
   that is passive, inert, and preoccupied with its own diversions will not
   last long."

32 See Mark Kingwell, *Dreams of Millennium*, Viking, New York, 1996.
   Kingwell's sources make for indispensable reading as well. He cites Paul
   Fussell's concept of "revenge egalitarianism" (*Class: A Guide through
   the American Status System*, Summit Books, New York, 1983), elaborates Roger Price's notion that "Democracy demands that all of its citizens begin the race even. Egalitarianism insists that they all *finish* even"
   (*The Great Roob Revolution*, Random House, New York, 1970), and
   approves strongly of William Henry III's suggestion in *In Defense of
   Elitism* that we must create a "cognitive elite" of brains and ability before we sink into the quagmire of sameness and collective ineptitude that
   Kingwell characterizes as the "relentless celebration of the ordinary and
   the average." As Henry insists, "The fretting ... about what happens to
   average and subpar students ... is a humane concern but a misplaced
   one." Why should this be so? Because, he replies, the "very essence of
   school is elitism. Schools exist to teach, to test, to rank hierarchically, to
   promote the idea that knowing and understanding more is better than
   knowing and understanding less. Education is elitist. Civilization is
   elitist."

   I should point out, however, that Kingwell, like many other intellectual dissenters, is no fan of Herrnstein and Murray, whom he accuses of

slipshod thinking (they do not distinguish between correlation and
cause) and racial nastiness (they abandon the coloured underclass to the
discriminatory agenda of a conscienceless society). As I indicated earlier, there is much about *The Bell Curve* that is problematic and disquieting. It is certainly an uneven book. But there is much that bears
further consideration and the nearly hysterical outcry it has provoked
suggests that the response of its critics is at least as imbalanced as the
work itself. Part of the problem, I think, revolves around the tendency,
shared by both the authors and their detractors, to equate the word
"elite" with the word "class" (as in "upper class"), implying a group of
socioeconomic patricians – lawyers, engineers, athletes, entrepreneurs,
technologists, politicians, financiers, executives – a sort of *lumpenelite*
flourishing at the expense of the powerless and disenfranchised. This
conflation is unfortunate and shows how easily the word may be abused.
I do not consider a gang of mercenary cutthroats, political reactionaries, and fiscal narcissists as an "elite" any more than the officer corps of
a tribe of ruthless barbarians constitutes a genuine nobility. I reserve the
term to pertain to all who, regardless of class or stratum, combine a
small but crucial number of defining characteristics: intelligence, or the
willingness to honour it; application, or the willingness to work; reflectiveness, or the willingness to think about – among other things – thinking itself and the ambiguous nature of intelligence that resists the dictionary and the test; and moral breadth, or the willingness to engage in
the collective social project along any of the dimensions in which it
manifests, political, economic, educational, or cultural. Those who meet
or at least attempt to meet these criteria are precisely those who make
up an authentic elite.

In conclusion, we might note that Kingwell's argument chimes in several respects with Herrnstein and Murray's. For example, the latter
write: "To the extent that the government has a role to play, it is to ensure equality of opportunity, not of outcome." (Kingwell's phrasing is
almost identical.) Nor can Kingwell object to the "fear" expressed in
The Bell Curve that "a new kind of conservatism is becoming the dominant ideology of the affluent – not in the social tradition of Edmund
Burke ... but ... along Latin American lines, where to be conservative
has often meant doing whatever is necessary to preserve the mansions in
the hills from the menace of the slums below." (Yet Kingwell compares
our authors unfavourably to Edmund Burke. And his censure of the
"gated community" phenomenon in the US and Canada clearly finds its
echoes in the above.) And *The Bell Curve*, for all its statistical infatuations and unpalatable assertions and caveats, does exhibit a real concern with the question of human dignity, which it defines as people
"putting more into the world than they take out." Here we focus on the
ethical core of a book that deserves to be engaged on its merits.

33 I mean the kind of thinking guaranteed to bring its practitioners into public opprobrium, which we might call "Mandevillean thinking." As the noted eighteenth-century scholar Phillip Harth writes of Bernard Mandeville, author of the universally misunderstood and widely condemned satire *The Fable of the Bees* (which in 1723 was presented as a public nuisance by the Grand Jury of Middlesex): "He insisted that societies, like individuals, must make hard choices between clearly understood alternatives, and he noticed with amusement that most men have neither the intelligence to recognize their options nor the courage to sacrifice some of them in the course of adopting others" (Introduction to Bernard Mandeville, *The Fable of the Bees*, Penguin, 1989). The *Fable* should be obligatory reading for educators, since Mandevillean thinking requires us to be honest about our dishonesty.

The notion of choice is crucial here. We are to some extent the victims of utopian thinking which holds that solutions to fundamental problems of conduct and education can form a harmonious and symmetrical whole. But, as Isaiah Berlin argues in *The Crooked Timber of Humanity* (Fontana Press, London, 1991), "ultimate values may be incompatible with one another," and therefore the idea of a comprehensively unified institution, like that of a perfect society, is conceptually incoherent. Moreover, a demand may always turn into its opposite: measures taken to establish social (or educational) equality may eventually "crush self-determination and stifle individual genius." We need to remain in a state of perpetual alert, continually monitoring and adjusting the policies we put in place, constantly aware that all our decisions entail the necessity of trade-offs and sacrifices. And we must also remember, as Herrnstein and Murray depose, that to conflate equality of opportunity with equality of outcome is destructive of genuine learning.

34 As Martin Walker reports in a recent issue of the *Guardian*, "Kishore Mahbubani, the top official in Singapore's foreign ministry, excited by the projection that East Asia's combined economies will within 10 years produce more than the U.S. and Europe combined," bluntly dismisses the United States as a serious world competitor. Says Mahbubani: "American society is breaking down and falling apart," displaying over the last generation "a 560% increase in violent crime, a 419% increase in illegitimate births, a 300% increase in children living in single-parent homes, and a drop of almost 80 points in Scholastic Aptitude Test scores." George Soros is also extremely worried about our prospects which, given an increasingly competitive future as East Asia pursues its economic ascendancy, he brusquely characterizes as "dismal." It is appropriate, he writes, "to criticize Americans for their unwillingness to suffer any personal inconvenience for the common good. Japan is a nation on the rise; we have become decadent." (See George Soros, *The Alchemy of Finance*, John Wiley, New York, 1994.) Similarly Jacques

Attali, former president of the European Bank for Reconstruction and Development, warns that the United States "risks finding itself transformed into a kind of hinterland for a new center located in Tokyo." Like Egypt vis à vis Rome, "America may become Japan's granary." (See Jacques Attali, *Millennium*, Times Books, New York, 1991.) As both Soros and Attali ruefully note, the Japanese with their annual surplus (around $200 billion) are energetically financing the American deficit, a policy that favours their eventual economic hegemony.

The ethical rejection of Japanese educational practices (or the Malaysian, Taiwanese, or Korean systems, for that matter) smacks perhaps as much of righteous lamentation and futile hand-wringing as of enlightened sentiment. Shogunizing the educational establishment, Ken Schooland tells us, will lead chiefly to the brutality and repression associated with autocratic societies. (See Ken Schooland writing in *The Educational Liberator*, vol. 2, no. 4, Fresno, CA, May 1996, with particular reference to his recent book, *Shogun's Ghost: The Dark Side of Japanese Education*.) But, of course, no responsible educator is lobbying for recourse to terror and repression as a pedagogical alternative to our current mediocrity. The argument, rather, is an eminently reasonable one: education is labour, not entertainment, implies demand, not concession, and offers substantial fare, not junk food. Discipline is not the same thing as domination.

35 We might call this unfortunate tendency the Creticus syndrome after the agnomen of the father of Marc Antony, who, as Plutarch tells us, though he lost most of a Roman fleet against pirates in a naval action off the island of Crete, was remembered chiefly for his "philanthropic impulses." Much to his wife's discomfiture, the elder Antony, who was "by no means rich," devised all sorts of clever ways to evade the good woman's vigilance and give away the family silverware. But perhaps our educators will be remembered as much for the action which they lost as for the patrimony they surrendered – if indeed the two are not the same thing. (See Plutarch, *Makers of Rome*, Penguin, New York, 1965.)

36 The current educational dispensation ensures that the offspring of the right among the more privileged classes (the lower-class right does not receive favoured treatment) will benefit economically and socially in the lottery of life, but the joke is that they nevertheless remain largely uneducated in the meaningful sense of the term, unwitting victims of the same diluted and/or restrictive curriculum from which their less-fortunate peers suffer. (The exceptions, of course, to this law of deprivation are those who can attend the better private schools.) Donald Barthelme was particularly astute when he wrote over a quarter of a century ago, in the words of one of his characters: "What is troubling me is the quality of life in our great country, America. It seems to me

deprived. I don't mean that the deprived people are deprived, although they are, clearly, but that even the fat are deprived. I suppose one could say that they are all humpheads and let it go at that." But, of course, that is precisely what we can't let it go at. (See Donald Barthelme, *Snow White*, Atheneum, New York, 1967.)

37 In connection with the "polysemic" interpretation of the phrase, which can imply repression as well as emancipation, Apple – like so many contemporary educators but for more understandable reasons – bristles at the spectre of a re-emergent elitism. Thus he strongly recommends "an education that is grounded not in providing human capital for the profit machine or in a romantic 'return' to elite cultural literacy, but in a vision of critical literacy." But what Apple (who is targeting "conservatives" like E.D. Hirsch and Allan Bloom) calls "critical literacy" cannot be taught in defiance or rejection of what he derogates as an "elite cultural literacy." Critical literacy can make no headway in a cultural vacuum. The productive engagement with current and local issues and concerns, if it is to yield meaningful results, needs to be set in the larger temporal context of what has traditionally been counted as an education: knowledge of political history in the widest sense of the term, some familiarity with the literary and scientific inheritance, and a practical mastery of the written language. Why mince words over so crucial an issue? People cannot be expected to participate effectively, as Apple exhorts, "in the creation and recreation of meanings and values" unless they are also capable of coherent thinking and have acquired an adequate grounding in what we might call *historical literacy*.

We should also keep in mind that the sodality of educational writers who lucidly and eloquently, or with an impressive degree of epistemic authority, deprecate the "return" to elitist literacy as romantic or misguided or sinful or ineffectual or obscurantist or as a kind of preciosity and affectation are precisely those who, as I remark elsewhere, have profited from a rigorous and thoroughgoing – and largely traditional – curriculum. It is that traditional education which has provided them with the tools to chip away at its foundations and which thus paradoxically shows how powerful and indeed necessary a part of our intellectual equipment it is. Perhaps the issue is not only how to recuperate the illiterate and disenfranchised but also how to educate the educated. It seems clear than an education in the traditional sense remains indispensable, but it seems equally clear that it can offer no guarantee of appropriate application. As Nietzsche has written, "Men and eras that serve life in this manner, by judging and destroying the past, are always dangerous and endangered." To avoid this peril we also need to come equipped with practical good sense, the habit of self-interrogation, and a certain lateral awareness to temper the hierarchical rigidity that educa-

tion tends to inflict upon us as a consequence of its epistemological
structure. We all need in some sense to be scholars but it is nowhere
given that we must become academics. Education in the traditional acceptation of the term remains a *sine qua non*, but so do flexibility and
native perspicacity.

It is precisely such "native perspicacity" that seems to have grown so
distressingly scarce in today's intellectual economy. Even so intelligent
and honourable a book as Michael Keefer's *Lunar Perspectives*, Anansi,
Concord, ON, 1996, the most recent entry (as of this writing) into the
cultural lists, betrays alarming symptoms of the tendency to oversimpli-
fication and political tarbrushing that afflicts some of the "best minds of
[our] generation." I am particularly disturbed by Keefer's ready identification of the neoconservative position in current educational polemics
with the right-wing brutality of dinosaurs like Newt Gingrich, Pat
Buchanan, and Rush Limbaugh. Keefer unflinchingly contends that the
neoconservative bloc – which I do not believe possesses unitary existence – is disingenuously bent on attacking the political correctness
stance in the university and other centres of intellectual dissemination in
order to advance its own reactionary agenda. The reader will, I hope,
pardon my considerable bewilderment, since in my experience as a
teacher and lecturer in various institutions and at various levels I have
more often than not found the defenders of political correctness (which I
regard as a form of repressive orthodoxy) comfortably ensconced in the
camp of those same right-wing ideologists whom Keefer accuses of attacking it – for example, in the macrodont society of corporate "philan-
thropists" many of whom are busy funding educational programs and
university chairs, career-oriented administrators whose political correctness provides them with continued employment and increased authority
as the latest incarnation of the guardian class, and a substantial cadre of
teachers and intellectuals who have made a deep psychological investment in mental and behavioral rigidity.

Perhaps the solution to the conundrum lies in the possibility that
there exists more than one kind of political correctness – one of the left
as well as of the right, with some overlap between the two – but Keefer's
argument, which lumps all neoconservatives into one big conspiratorial
fold of the rich and powerful, which holds that the oppressors are really
attacking political correctness and, moreover, that the PC designation
actually stands for a compendium of hidden virtues, and which, finally,
sees this putative assault as a ploy or destabilizing maneuver on the part
of a privileged minority against a plural and multicultural "other" struggling for recognition, still leaves me gasping in disbelief. One of us must
be a little daft at least some of the time, but as Keefer is a self-confessed
six foot seven with the physical presence of George Frazier, I must be
circumspect in my attributions.

CHAPTER SIX

1 J.T. Dillon proposes a quantitative solution to the eristic impasse in which the profession malingers that would permit the filtering and synthesis of competing knowledge claims in the form of a graphable residue. He calls this breakthrough *superanalysis*, or the "superanalytic metrification of knowledge." Interestingly, when the results of the entire field of the distribution of human knowledge are calculated, the total metrification conveniently sums out as 0. "This much accomplished, superanalysis would in the end leave only an administrative problem," Dillon assures us. This would make the present volume unnecessary along with everything else that has ever been written, including Dillon's brilliant deflationary exercise. The latter would surely represent a serious loss on any best-fit curve of mean-effect sizes. (Cf. "Superanalysis," *Evaluation News*, 1982, vol. 3.)

2 This would be a good time to rekindle interest in the work of Peter Ramus, especially his *Scholae in tres primas liberales artes* (Frankfurt, 1581), which deals with the fundamental grammar of thought and memory. His definition of memory needs to be reconsidered in the light (or darkness) of current problematics: "Memory is the shadow of the order (of the *dispositio*), and order is the syntax of the universe." Unfortunately, we are now witnessing the advent of the *apparent self*, for whom memory functions as a species of revery and reality is equivalent to image or simulation, neutralizing the interior domestication of temporality. We are dealing with what Arthur Kroker calls the "sampler self" (on the analogy of sampler music) which is "no longer a private subject in a public space" capable of seeing itself as an actor on the historical stage "but a public self in a private imaginary time" (Arthur Kroker, *The Possessed Individual*, Culture Texts, Montreal, 1992). In other words, memory no longer reflects the "syntax of the universe." See also Walter J. Ong's magisterial *Ramus, Method, and the Decay of Dialogue*, Harvard University Press, Cambridge, MA, 1958, 1993.

3 This has nothing to do with the minimax recommendations of the new tribe of Gramtech specialists who, for all their ruddy alacrity and magnanimous concern, strike me as nothing less than a colony of hostile aliens in our midst, pseudo-cybernauts from the past – *grammatistes* – who actually believe they represent the cutting edge of the future as they proceed to wreak their customary havoc with messianic ardour.

4 L.S. Vygotsky, *Mind in Society*, Harvard University Press, Cambridge, MA, 1978. (All subsequent references to and citations from Vygotsky pertain to this volume.) Jean Piaget similarly remarks that "the language used in the fundamental activity of the child – play – is one of gestures, movement, and mimicry as much as of words" – or babble? (Jean Piaget, *Essential Piaget*, Basic Books, New York, 1977.)

5 Oddly enough, in the technique of classical rhetoric, gestures ("action") come at the *end* of the training program, preceded by invention, arrangement, elocution, and memorization. Gestural systems of emphasis and persuasion received elaborate codification, which became an anatomical language in itself incorporating the minutest details of signification equal, for example, to the sinuosities of the finger movements of Indian dance. Such gestural systems have transcended the spontaneous mimesis of the infant play-mode and must be considered as an independent semiotic function. (See H.I. Marrou, *A History of Education in Antiquity*, Sheed and Ward, New York, 1956.)

6 This is also, of course, standard-issue rhetorical technique.

7 Obviously, the rising terminal stress is meant to indicate that one or the other (or both) of the two basic interlocutors in the query situation does not know, actually or ostensibly, how to resolve a given problematic circumstance. In the instance under consideration, what is most striking is that both interlocutors are usually *fully aware* of the circumstance marked as problematic or that the circumstance is clearly *not problematic* in the first place. The interrogative marker is largely redundant and operates instead as an expression of a kind of low-grade, generalized insecurity or as a function of anxiety. I suspect this anxiety or insecurity is profoundly associated with the condition of belated and prolonged childhood promoted by the culture and institutionalized by our educational apparatus.

8 I am not lobbying for the revival of the Orbilian* classroom, but merely suggesting that we have seriously erred in reversing the elements of the

---

*The name Orbilius is introduced disparagingly in C.S. Lewis's *The Abolition of Man* (Macmillan, New York, 1947), to represent callow rationalism. The adjectival form appears in H.I. Marrou (*A History of Education in Antiquity*). The source, so far as I can tell, is Suetonius, *De Grammaticis et Rhetoribus* (cf. the recension of Rodney Potter Robinson, Librairie de la Société de Linguistique de Paris, 1925), in which the following interesting passage may be found: "*Fuit autem naturae acerbae, non modo in antisophistas, quos per omnem occasionem lacerauit, sed etam in discipulos, ut et Horatius significat plagosum eum appelans, et Domitius Marsus scribens: Si quos Orbilius ferula scuticaque cecidit.*" In his Epistle to Augustus (II, 1), Horace recalls (fondly?) his old master, Orbilius, pounding the lines of Andronicus into his head: *Quae plagosum mihi parvo / Orbilium dictare.* Perhaps there is something to be said, after all, for being quick to use the rod (*plagosum*), for not sparing the rod and whip (*ferula scuticaque*), editing our classrooms as we do our texts in the interests of Orbilian quality rather than, not to put too fine a point on it, Morbilian quantity.

formal syllabus we have inherited from the Hellenistic period, that is, in trying (with scant success) to teach *glossimatikon* (forms, rules) after *istorikon* (content, history, whole language) when the appropriate order, as ancient grammarians like Dionysius Thrax in the first century B.C. clearly understood, requires us to start, however gently and sensitively, with glossematic material, or at the very least to introduce form and content concurrently. Three hundred years before, the rhetorician Iso-crates founded his school in Athens on the principle that proper speak-ing meant proper thinking and, further, served as the cornerstone of the good life. Proper speech was regarded as the salient feature distinguish-ing the civilized man from the barbarian (an idea still very much with us, albeit in modern garb, e.g., Basil Bernstein's celebrated contrast be-tween "elaborated" and "restricted" linguistic codes corresponding to upper and lower classes respectively, or Alan Ross's distinction between U and non-U verbal sets corresponding to upper-class and bourgeois usage). And we would probably be well advised in our search for insight and encouragement to proceed earlier still into the past and consider the advantages of inculcating even so archaic an ideal as the Homeric *areti* – the agonistic spirit, the drive to excel at all costs – instead of the virus of zombification we have become so adept at transmitting.

9 Roland Barthes, *Image Music Text*, Farrar, Straus and Giroux, New York 1977.

10 Michel Foucault, *Language, Counter-Memory, Practice*, Cornell Uni-versity Press, Ithaca, 1977.

11 Emile Benveniste, *Problems in General Linguistics*, University of Miami Press, 1971.

12 Walter J. Ong, *Orality and Literacy*, Routledge, New York, 1982. What we may be remarking here is an ironic realignment of the relation that once held between speech, the written characters of the ancient syllabar-ies, and the world of experience. As Eric Havelock explains in *The Ori-gins of Western Literacy* (OISE Press, Toronto, 1977), alphabetic script constituted a great advance in communication over syllabic script be-cause the former, relying on the properties of abstract letters rather than syllabic units, ceased to interpose itself as an opaque mental object be-tween the reader/writer and the spoken tongue. But the syllabary did not permit meaning to "resound in the consciousness without reference to the properties of the letters used." Today it is the other way round: current speech, like the pre-alphabetic syllabaries of hieroglyph or cu-neiform script, obtrudes materially between the written word and the world of experience in a kind of verbal occultation. This may account in part for the baffling sense of anachronism one feels in observing and in-teracting with a generation at home in the world of electronic and cyber-netic innovation and yet so curiously obsolescent in its world view, its

predisposition to the oracular, its communicative dependence upon the image and the prosodeme, and its failure to develop the written proficiency and literate articulation on which the modern self is predicated.

13 It is easy and tempting to blame others – the system, the administration, parents, the students themselves – for the scandal of literacy and the failure of education. We would be right to do so, of course, but we should not forget the extent of our own complicity as teachers in the entropic process we are witnessing. In a letter to the *Montreal Gazette* (16 April 1993) defending current modes of language instruction, the writer, who introduces himself "as an educator," benignly cites the findings of "psycholinguistics, sociolinguistics, cognitive and developmental psychology" and a number of other resonating disciplines to reinforce the practice of teaching whole language as a system of "phonics, syntax and semantics." He concludes by affirming that he and his colleagues "are proud of the articulate and literate students who graduate from our schools." Such professions of faith should immediately provoke a defensive response on the order of Gould's Principle: "Always be suspicious of conclusions that reinforce uncritical hope." Moreover, the plethora of disciplines recruited in support of what everyone knows is really a dismal educational track record serves as an infallible indicator of theoretical bankruptcy surpassed only by the bad faith which such proclamations betoken. We too are implicated in the great betrayal. It is curious how the words "teacher" and "cheater" constitute a perfect anagram.

14 There is only one way to teach writing, according to Northrop Frye, and that is "composition from models, feeling one's way into the idiom of cultivated prose" (*On Education,* Fitzhenry & Whiteside, Markham, 1990). Frye's recommendation has a long and impressive pedigree, harkening back to the school of Isocrates in fourth-century Athens, the fountainhead of humanist scholarship. Grammar and style were taught together through *paradigma kai mimisis*, the imitation of literary models. (See H.I. Marrou, *A History of Education in Antiquity.*)

The current practice of having students report on episodic moments in their own lives, under the assumption that they will become more highly motivated to produce corrigible material, or conversely to generate isolated grammatical sequences to acquaint them with the rules that govern literate expression, both eventuate in the familiar, indigestible mess of tepid linguinicity we continue to deplore without asking ourselves how it came about. We merely go on acting as plenipotentiaries for a society that delivers into our classrooms for continued instruction in the use of language those who have been rendered unfit to receive it. In the words of C.S. Lewis (*The Abolition of Man*, Macmillan, New York, 1947), "we castrate and bid the geldings be fruitful." And, ironically, should we actually succeed in our unlikely project, we would be merely compounding the dilemma, if Simeon Potter is right when he warns us that it "is useless to teach the alphabet and the three R's to young people and then turn them back into a society that remains un-cultured and unlettered" (See his *Language in the Modern World*, Pen-guin, Baltimore, 1960).

15 To be whole, as Jerome Bruner affirms, the individual "must create his own version of the world, using that part of his cultural heritage he has made his own through education" (*On Knowing: Essays for the Left Hand*, Harvard University Press, 1962). Unfortunately, the portion of the "cultural heritage" available to the contemporary student is signally diminishing with the inexorable death of reading, as indicated by the re-sults of my latest class poll. In a sampling of twenty-one students en-rolled in my Utopian Satire course (Winter/Spring semester, 1993, John Abbott College, Montreal):

- none had heard of Dylan Thomas
- three had read *Brave New World*
- one had read part of 1984
- none had heard of James Hilton's *Lost Horizons*
- none had heard of Thomas More's *Utopia*
- none had heard of Horace, Juvenal, Erasmus, Ben Jonson, or Sa-muel Johnson
- none had read *Gulliver's Travels*, though one knew the name of its author
- eleven had heard of *Robinson Crusoe*, but none had read it and none knew the name of its author
- none had heard of Voltaire
- none could identify the author of *The Tempest*
- none could identify the authors of *The Communist Manifesto*
- none could identify the author of *The Interpretation of Dreams*
- none could identify the composers of *The Gondoliers*
- none had heard of the Book of Job
- none had heard of Dostoevsky, Nietzsche, Kafka, Joyce, or Milan Kundera (though eight had seen the film of *The Unbearable Light-ness of Being*)
- none had heard of Walden, Henry David Thoreau, B.F. Skinner, or Behaviorism
- twenty-one were familiar with the exploits of Wayne Gretzky, Hagar the Horrible, Vanilla Ice, and the Simpsons.

Needless to say, these deficits do not represent a politics of difference, modes of contingency, redemption of the excluded, rupturing of domi-nant codes, the retrieval of identity, or the radical democratizing of epistemological controls but quite simply the paralysis of the mind. Henry Giroux suggests that students may be "indifferent to the forms of authority, knowledge, and values ... produced and legitimated within our classrooms and universities" because these latter are oppressive and ethnocentric institutional structures founded on a "politics of containment." On the contrary, the flood of "multiple narratives expressed through a variety of complex discursive forms" favoured by Giroux as a countermeasure has contributed heavily to the intellectual dispersal from which our institutions suffer – these "narratives" are seldom complex and almost always anarchic, fissiparous, disintegrative, neo-ideological, and, strangely enough, whether exotic or local, exclusionary. (See Henry Giroux, *Border Crossings*, Routledge, New York and London, 1992.)

My questionnaire would no doubt be dismissed by self-styled "postmodernist" educators as exemplifying the Eurocentric master narrative or hegemonic discourse dominating a curriculum that ostensibly deprivileges the subordinate or marginal or "popular" culture represented by our students. But is it merely fanciful and self-indulgent to pretend that the traditional canon is a white supremacist conspiracy, as many regard the grammatical conventions of Standard English. As George Santayana said of Greek mythology, the canon is the mother tongue of the imagination, and moreover provides a language we can *think* in, that is, in which we can reflect on our experience as members of a civilization founded on historical precedence and continuity rather than foundering in the viscosities of mere idiomatic clamour.* In the name of freedom and equality, radical educators tend to foster anarchy and dissolution, making up in stridency and abstract jargon what they forfeit in genuine effectiveness and thus working against the best interests of their stu-

---

*This does not mean that the canon cannot be abused or that propaganda cannot be grammatical. Anything human can be deformed, and will. But it does mean that once we reject the canonical and the grammatical as the twin foundations of the curriculum, we really have little left on which to ground our collective existence in time. These issues, swirling about in the current debate on curriculum formation and grammar technology, make it somewhat problematic for the teacher trying to negotiate among competing ideologies, between, say, the Scylla of Dianne Ravitch and the Charybdis of Henry Giroux. It is becoming more and more difficult to see clearly and to keep an even keel, which does not augur well for our educational periplus into the future. Julian Barnes helps us correct the perspective when he asks, "Whose truth do we prefer ... the victor's or the victim's? Are pride and compassion greater distorters than shame and fear?" (see *The History of the World in 10½ Chapters*, Vintage, New York, 1990).

dents. The irony remains that it is precisely the rigour and amplitude of
the traditional canon that furnishes us with the stamina and lucidity to
resist the incursions of the "New Right" which the postmodern sensibility has so justly repudiated. (It was a politically conservative, business-
oriented director of my college who wished to delete Shakespeare from
the curriculum.) But a further irony must be acknowledged, for the solution proposed by the postmodern left, the construction of new "subject
positions" and the opening up of so-called new "discursive spaces," will
lead not to emancipation but to disempowerment in a Babel of marginal
tongues which the conservative restoration will effortlessly disarm and
incorporate. It is astonishing how educational insurgence slides unwit-
tingly into political collaboration.

This disempowerment follows inescapably from what Richard J.
Herrnstein and Charles Murray call "the downhill slide" in American
education, in particular in the humanities and in general verbal performance. They very sensibly locate the process of "dumbing down" to a
considerable extent in precisely those programs that the postmodernists
tout as the preferential goal of current educational theory and practice,
namely, "multiculturalism in the curriculum, the need to minimize racial differences in performance measures, and enthusiasm for fostering
self-esteem independent of performance." To our new progressivists and
latitudinarians, "the idea that people with the most capacity to be educated should become the most educated sounds dangerously elitist."
And the agendas that have been pursued in the current educational
sense to prevent this from happening are naturally "antagonistic to traditional criteria of rigour and excellence" (See Richard J. Herrnstein
and Charles Murray, *The Bell Curve: Intelligence and Class Structure
in American Life*, Free Press, New York, 1994).

To conclude this excursus: One must recognize the "essential" disin-
genuousness of the postmodernist assault upon the canon. Sometimes it
is attacked for being closed, the private preserve of a mandarin insider-
group. When this approach falters (usually in an orgy of Bloom-
bashing),* it is then condemned as being open, an omnivorous, Stephen-
King-like spider that swallows its victims whole to maintain its appetitive hegemony. But you cannot have it both ways unless you live in the
Q-continuum. The plain fact is that the canon is neither bristlingly
closed nor mephitically open: it is neither a country club nor a

---

*Another Bloom has entered the fray, no doubt to be duly bashed in turn. There
is something almost farcical about this scenario, reminiscent of the opening sentence of Marx's *Brumaire*. (I'm tempted to write *Blumaire*.) I am referring, of
course, to Harold Bloom's feisty if Shakespeariolatric *The Western Canon: The
Books and Schools of the Ages*, Harcourt Brace, New York, 1994.

quicksand bog. It is a *language* which structures our thought and which remains *accessible* to effort, will, discipline and love. And it is a language which enshrines the twin values of clarity and exuberance, of analytical rigour and rhetorical exhilaration, of the veridical and the poetic, equally hospitable to infusions of Quinine or to bouts of reJoycing – as it eschews the gormless bafflegab of the postmodern aberration.

16 In the absence of reading in either of its two dimensions, the individual is always overtaken and undermined by the historical flux (unless one happens to belong to a resolutely oral culture which has evolved its own strategies of permanence). As the poet Ciaran O'Driscoll writes in *The Myth of the South* (Dedalus Editions, Dublin, 1992):

And between the silence and the shout,
a plague of events that happens by stealth.

See also Jacques Barzun on "The Centrality of Reading" (*Begin Here*, University of Chicago Press, Chicago, 1992). "To allow the written word to be indefinite is to undo the incalculable technical advance that turned sounds into signs," writes the *eminence grise* of American education, a sentiment that accords perfectly with Vygotsky's analysis of written language. Barzun continues: "On this pedagogic ground alone, it could be said that no subject of study is more important than reading. In our civilization, at any rate, all the other intellectual powers depend on it ... *no one can write decently without reading widely and well*" (italics mine). The sober truth is: "many cannot read or understand what they do read." To address so vast a deficit in our intellectual budget, George Steiner recommends that our undergraduate colleges be turned into reading schools. He warns in his Bowker Memorial Lecture that reading is in danger of becoming "as specialized a skill and avocation as it was in the *scriptoria* and libraries of the monasteries during the so-called Dark Ages" (quoted in Neil Postman's *Conscientious Objections*, Vintage Books, New York, 1992). For a rapid and compendious summary of reading-theory in the twentieth century, see John Willinsky's *The New Literacy*, Routledge, New York and London, 1990.

17 See Sven Birkerts, *The Gutenberg Elegies*, Fawcett Columbine, New York, 1994. Birkerts believes we have encountered a "conceptual ledge ... that may mark a break in historical continuity" and that people who turn from print, "finding it too slow, too hard, irrelevant to the excitement of the present," are inhabiting a kind of mental spacetime that "has rendered a vast part of our cultural heritage utterly alien." This bravo new world, mediated through electronic circuitry, is really an oral one which, as Walter Ong in *Orality and Literacy* defines it, is chiefly participatory, communal, agonistic, homeostatic (discarding memories

regarded as irrelevant) and close to the event-filled lifeworld. (The next step, as I have argued elsewhere, is to move into the pseudoevent-filled virtual world, a process which media technology makes "virtually" inevitable and which has been underway since the irruption of television into our lives. The snarl of the pseudo and the real is now impossible to disentangle.) My student, who belongs with his congeners to an essentially non-literate world (of which the electrographic apparatus is an extension), possesses a mindset fundamentally inimical to writing and reading, one that is tuned to the outward, the adventurous, the immediate, and of course, the extraordinary (for its high mnemonic value). Now, reading a book that does not mirror raw experience heightened by cinematic fantasies of election, he is thrown back on the dwindling reserves of the solitary self. "As literary narrative moves toward the serious novel," Ong writes, "it eventually pulls the focus of action more and more to interior crises and away from purely exterior crises." Subjectivity, as Jean Baudrillard argues, is an abandoned referent.

My student also experienced great difficulty *remembering* the few passages he had actually read. Vygotsky helps us in focusing the problem. There are two types of memory, he tells us. The "natural" or eidetic is characterized by nonmediated or direct impression of materials as the basis of mnemonic traces and by the quality of immediacy. This form of memory, operating along the stimulus-response axis, dominates the behaviour of non-literate people and presumably children as well. The second type of memory is "culturally elaborated but, as it incorporates artificial or self-generated stimuli (or signs) we might more accurately designate it as semiotic (especially since all memory is in some sense culturally elaborated)." Eidetic memory may be simply diagrammed as S $\longrightarrow$ R; semiotic memory as

$$S \diagdown \diagup R \\ \diagdown \diagup \\ X$$

My student is eminently capable of eidetic recollection where the material strikes him as valid, quasi-pictorial, immediately accessible, and predictably organized; what he representatively lacks is the semiotic X provided by independent and artificial systems of discourse.

Neither does the current diluted curriculum offer much help in restoring the balance or redressing deficits, since it fails to provide our students with the obligation to stretch themselves to their limits and beyond. As Herrnstein and Murray write in *The Bell Curve*: "Plenty of students with high IQ's will happily choose to write about *The Hobbit* instead of *Pride and Prejudice* for their term paper if that option is given to them. Few of even the most brilliant youngsters tackle the *Aeneid* on their own."

18 Hockey goon Ti Domi, formerly of the New York Rangers, might serve as an eloquent spokesman for the dialogical ethos behind current lexical practice which downplays the semiotic dimension of language. Dismissing a sparring session with an opponent during a recent game as insignificant, he told reporters, "It was nothing. We just traded verbal words."

19 In a batch of forty-one student essays I recently corrected, fully seventeen exhibited at one point or another some such iconic embellishment. The word-processor, too, has become a ready Merovingian accomplice in this distracting practice, as lavishly rubricized title pages bear ample testimony. (Which suggests the formulation of a new empirical law: the quality or substance of the work varies in inverse proportion to the ornamentation of the title page.) I sometimes wonder if we are not witnessing a re-medievalization of the sensibility, though without the intense labour of application and the morality of craftsmanship we find so admirable in the techniques of manuscript illumination.

20 Sometimes the truth is found not in the bottom of a well but on the impenetrable surface of student term papers, one of my most unimpeachable sources (see previous note). In a class essay based in part on the Gospel of John, dealing with the intercession of the Holy Spirit in human affairs as a model for the work of the Imagination in literary texts, that is, an allegory for creative speech, I find the following avian phrase: "In the way we use language we must learn from the Parakeet." This is about as good a description of the current phenomenon of mimetic language as one might expect (as if in serendipitous confirmation of Walker Percy's example of totemic self-identification: "I am Parakeet") – closely rivalled by the summation of another student who, considering the subject from a different and bathetically orgiastic perspective, recommends that we "follow the example of the Paraclit."

21 The distinction between speech and script as two discrete first-order systems is evident to anyone who has enjoyed the opportunity of meeting writers whose works are appreciated for their lucidity, eloquence, and metaphorical vigour. How often in such cases do we not marvel at the disjunction between the rhetorical flow of the prose and the often casual, plain, halting, or distracted quality of the speech? The latter may surpass the norm of quotidian expectation; nevertheless, we still experience some difficulty in matching samples, almost as if we were encountering *two different people*. (I have at this moment returned from an engagement with a celebrated, prize-winning English writer whose speech was slow and pedestrian and who was deaf into the bargain.)

Both common sense and habitual experience register the validity of the distinction. We are all aware of the difficulty, the labour, and the resistance implicit in the act of formulating our thoughts in writing as opposed to the flow and spontaneity of speech. And how surprised we often are at the results of our written efforts, which reveal aspects of our thinking we were completely unaware of prior to their formulation. Why should this be the case if speech and writing are merely complementary functions of the same system of representation? Moreover, we insist on keeping these two systems separate in our customary attitudes to communication. Note how uncomfortable we become with people who "talk like a book."

22 H.J. Uldall, "Speech and Writing," in *Acta Linguistica* 4, 1944. See also Ferdinand de Saussure's *Course in General Linguistics*, chapter 6 (which antedates Uldall by more than twenty years): "The linguistic signifier ... is not ... phonic but incorporeal – constituted not by its material substance but by the differences that separate its sound-image from all others." This famous passage (or its cognates) is quoted by a host of writers on the subject (cf. *Of Grammatology*, Jacques Derrida, Johns Hopkins University Press, Baltimore, 1976; *Ferdinand de Saussure*, Jonathan Culler, Cornell University Press, 1986; *Language, Saussure and Wittgenstein*, Roy Harris, Routledge, London, 1988).

Uldall's focus on pronunciation and spacing points up the difficulty students have in moving from one independent system to another, which accounts in large measure for the infelicity of much student writing. A good example of the amphibolic practices we are trying to correct is provided by the profusion of commas students scatter randomly throughout their sentences, ubiquitous as bandaids on the bottom of YMCA pools. Similarly, the apostrophe in "it's" appears solecistically in the possessive form – the transcendent avatar of the comma. (One of my students insists on writing "Brutus" as "Brutu's" – a serious case of apostrophitis to which the commatose are especially prone.) Students know that punctuation is necessary in written language but are baffled by the rules of application since these do not pertain to spoken language in which punctuation is refracted through the medium of gesture, phasis, respiration, and tonal expressivity. In the student mind, the inoffensive and complaisant comma operates as a synecdoche for punctuation *in general*, since it is neither as teleological as the period nor as eccentric and hazardous as the colon and semi-colon. Students consequently proceed to distribute commas with generous abandon on the assumption that some are bound on probabilistic grounds to turn up in the right places while the remainder will be absorbed harmlessly into the word heap.

23 Most teachers today take up the same phonocentric position towards the

teaching of writing as the character Susan Barton in J.M. Coetzee's *Foe* (Penguin, New York, 1987) adopts toward the tongueless Friday: "How can he write if he cannot speak? Letters are the mirror of words." As Brenda Marshall comments in *Teaching the Postmodern* (Routledge, New York, 1992), for Barton "speech is primary and writing is a fallen manifestation of speech." The proper attitude is represented by Foe, who claims: "Writing is not doomed to be the shadow of speech ... We are accustomed to believe that our world was created by God speaking the Word; but I ask, may it not rather be that he wrote it ... May it not be that God continually writes the world?" Foe's God, like Jacques Derrida, combats the logocentric fallacy tooth and nail.

24 As Huck Finn says, "There orter be writing 'bout a big thing like this." What is essential – and what remains lacking in the present environment – is a respect for language that elevates it to the status of something like a miracle, which is what it is. It is not necessary to entertain or credit mystical doctrines of contemplation such as that of the great Hebrew kabbalist and teacher Abraham Abulafia, whose method encompasses distinct steps or stages, leading from articulation (*mivta*) to writing (*miktav*) to its consummation in the transcendent alphabet of thought (*mashav*), the three ascending rungs of meditation. Nevertheless, this sequence reproduces the itinerary or trajectory of all linguistic accomplishment: without articulation and writing (the latter assuming many different embodiments), the mastery of abstract thought in all its subtlety and intricacy seems unlikely. What I would like to stress in my example is that the three moments identified by Abulafia, *mivta*, *miktav*, and *mashav*, although related, remain distinct and autonomous, exhibiting a kind of domain structure, each in turn requiring independent treatment, practice, and assimilation.

In Jacques Barzun's formulation, "reading, writing, speaking, and thinking are not four distinct powers but four modes of one power." My conception of the various "functions" of articulation and expression as "related but distinct," drawing in part on psychological (Vygotskian) and mystical (Abulafian) sources, runs parallel to the robust common sense that Barzun commands. (The word "distinct" receives a slightly different inflection, modified by context, in the two formulations.)

What I have called the domain structure of these various modes or functions underlies the celebrated aphorism of Francis Bacon in "Of Studies," which the contemporary Academy might adopt as its collective watchword: "Reading maketh a full man; conference a ready man; and writing an exact man."

25 Bronowski makes a similar point with a slightly different emphasis. "You enter more fully into your own mind by entering through me into the human mind." (See J. Bronowski, *The Identity of Man*, Natural History Press, New York, 1971.)

26 Current instructional practice reminds me more and more of Stanislaw Lem's concept of "simulimbecility" or "mimecretinism," functions of a benignimized society whose children learn reading and writing, both obviously forms of mere reproductivity, from sipping orthographic sodas. Shades of Jonathan Swift's wafers imbued with a cephalic tincture. (Stanislaw Lem, *The Futurological Congress*, Avon, New York, 1974.)

27 The quotations in this paragraph and the next are from Kathy Toohy's "Language Across the Curriculum," John Abbott College, Montreal, Winter 1994.

28 Reading complex material with a "delicate sufficiency" of understanding is *always* work.

29 The reference is to Joseph Chilton Pearce, *Magical Child*, Bantam, New York, 1980.

30 Jacques Derrida, *Writing and Difference*, University of Chicago Press, Chicago, 1987.

31 Jacques Lacan, *Ecrits*, Seuil, Paris, 1966. For a rather confusing attempt (more so than mine, I think) to desediment the Lacanian notation, as well as its companion algorithm governing the operation of metonymy, which kedges along as F (S ... S1) S = S (-) s, see Jane Gallop, *Reading Lacan*, Cornell University Press, Ithaca, 1985.

32 Frank Smith, *Joining the Literacy Club*, Heinemann, Portsmouth, 1988.

33 As Andrew Nikiforuk writes, "Each family has a curriculum; each home is a child's first school." He goes on to lock horns with the whole-language movement, condemning "the myth that learning to read is ... as natural as learning to speak." We have become gullible victims of the "institutionalized confusion of speech (a biological activity) with script (a learned artefact)" (*School's Out*, Macfarlane Walter & Ross, Toronto, 1993). Jacques Barzun, while in substantial agreement with this assessment of the issue (and with the general argument I have developed in this chapter) inflects the terms of the debate somewhat. He acknowledges the "link between the bad writing now being attacked and our unexamined habits of speech" but claims that the relation holds "not because people write exactly as they talk, but because the same deep feelings accompany both forms of expression. The hidden bond is the reason why much of remedial teaching ... bring[s] about no improvement." Neither my assumption nor Barzun's can be *definitely* proven and the reader must judge which seems more persuasive. For my part, I do not see one as incompatible with the other. (See Jacques Barzun, *A Word or Two Before You Go* ... , Wesleyan University Press, Middletown, CT, 1986.)

That our students are themselves tacitly aware of this double predicament – that is, they feel obscurely that there are two distinct systems of linguistic representation but do not realize that these systems entail different rules of production – is attested in several characteristic ways. For instance, the tendency to formalize their speech, render it somehow "official," when they speak into a telephone-answering machine, generating a kind of verbal writing. (I owe this aperçu to my colleague Murray Napier.) Or the lamentable habit of "authenticating" their academic writing by lexical inflation – phrases like "The author exemplifies how history operationalizes by implementing errors into his manuscript" rather than "The author shows how history works by introducing errors into his text." In the first case, they are trying to speak writing; in the second, they are trying to *write* writing. Though sensing the difference, they do not understand that writing *as such* is neither written speech nor overwritten prose but a second first-order system of symbolic representation with its own set of rules for the codification of thought and reformulation of experience.

CHAPTER SEVEN

I "Much of our educational thinking views content either as an irrelevance or as a repressive threat to the selfhood of the learner ... Instead of seeking to restore an aggressive ideal of mastery of understanding, educational thought glorifies process and experience for their own sakes and relegates mastery to the rubbish heap of dead ideas" (Gerald Graff, *Literature against Itself*, University of Chicago Press, Chicago, 1979). This criticism of contemporary practice does not attempt to subordinate process to product but merely calls attention to the absurdity and dysfunction inherent in trying to teach performance or process *in the absence of pedagogical substance* – a caveat that I wholeheartedly endorse. But given the existence of real content, then the complementary focus on text B or the work of production itself, in the words of Genevieve Jacquinot (*Image et Pedagogie*, Besses Universitaires de France, Paris, 1977), *"fait de l'acte didactique un processus de production du sense. Dans cette perspective, le discours didactique ... se definit comme un discourse 'ouvert' ... ou questions et reponses sont generatrices d'autres questions."*

It is tempting to extrapolate from the structuralist distinction between the hermeneutic and autotelic dimensions of a work of art. With respect to fiction, for example, we may discriminate, as Ross Chambers suggests, between narratorial self-referentiality "whereby the story draws attention to its status as art" (what the Russian Formalists called "baring the device") and narrative duplicity "whereby the story pretends to be concerned only with its informational content." The relations we may detect between the narratorial and the narrative, self-reflexivity and "duplicity," the autotelic and the informational, mirror precisely the form of double textuality that prevails in the teaching protocol I am proposing in these pages. If we wish to come up with an appropriate nomenclature, we may refer to the aspect of teaching that conforms to narrative by the traditional designation of *pedagogy* and to the aspect that corresponds to the narratorial by the term *pedasophy*. The bipolar class is that which combines the pedagogical and the pedasophical in varying proportions as determined by the teacher responding to the limit-possibilities of his or her discipline. Until very recently, the pedasophical dimension in classroom practice was systematically neglected, repressed, forgotten, disguised, or otherwise deleted from the script that both teachers and students are ostensibly engaged in producing. (See Ross Chambers, *Story and Situation: Narrative Seduction and the Power of Fiction*, University of Minnesota Press, Minneapolis, 1984.)

2 The progressivist conceit or perhaps prejudice, deriving in large measure from Edward Thorndike, that skills developed from the study of specific subjects are not transferable to other subjects, is based upon a bizarrely myopic pedagogy. No serious educator would claim that the specific language or glossary or informing structure associated with one discipline automatically invades, subsumes, or edulcorates the communicative registry or inner schematism of another; such is manifestly not the issue. But the habits of good learning fostered in the proper study of any given subject, the supple and rigorous comportment of mind graced by the affective qualities of modesty, persistence, and curiosity, cannot in the nature of things be anything but transferable, binding subjects together like force-carrying particles, pedagogical bosons, virtualities of the intellect – since we are dealing with *energies of the mind* and not species-specific, isolable, encapsulated "skills." As Matthew Arnold wrote in a letter to John Henry, Cardinal Newman, "The effect you have produced on me ... consists in a general disposition of the mind rather than in a particular set of ideas."

Certainly the progressivist tendency to regard mental life as a parcel of monogrammed skills and specialized abilities neglects the psycho-cognitive foundations of all intellectual function in general: will, disposition, and interrogationality. This is why the experiments on which the progressivist thesis rests are notoriously trivial, routinely missing the essential point that intellectual function differs from instrumental function*s*, the latter comprising only one aspect of mental life.

Moreover, even if one restricts one's gaze to the horizon of pure instrumentality, I fail to see how anyone could seriously maintain Thorndike's postulate of non-transferability of specialized abilities in the light of the "conversion of function" rule, a staple of evolutionary biology. Conversion of function is a major player in the evolutionary game and provides one of the standard elements for natural selection to work with.

As William H. Calvin explains in *The Ascent of Mind* (Doubleday, New York, 1991), when natural selection acts on any serial-order skill, it works toward the improvement of a large number of serial-order behaviours "because they all utilize the same neural machinery." Consider the neural apparatus needed for accurate throwing: when not performing this primary function, nothing prevents it from being deflected toward other targets, like "speaking a sentence ... composing a melody, or playing chess."

Thus conversion of function, used to good purpose by evolutionary strategy (whether arranging the conversion of swim bladder to lung or of predatory savvy to checkmate), effectively challenges the progressivist notion that mental capabilities cannot be transferable since they are presumably dependent on the material with which they operate. It is not even necessary to recruit countervailing arguments from developmental theorists who claim, with considerable plausibility, that learning mobilizes *general structures* of adaptation which are inherently transferable, unlike specific habits or skills. Although this argument strikes me as eminently reasonable, it need not compel assent, as it is founded more on common sense than on hard, empirical evidence. On the other hand, if conversion of function is a standard technique of evolutionary processes, then extrapolation to the field of cognitive development seems warranted if not inescapable. Once we entertain the idea that *instrumental* functions are in themselves convertible, the distance to transferability shrinks to zero.

It is important that we reflect analytically on the reality of transferability, since its denial is one of the most pernicious doctrines to come out of the progressivist camp. It is comforting to be able to cite so considerable an arbiter as Jacques Barzun who condemns "the absurd dogma that there is no transfer in learning ability from one subject to another" (*Begin Here*, University of Chicago Press, 1992). But the problem with Barzun is that he tends to speak *ex cathedra*, deriving his authority from his long experience and intellectual stature and not from close and rigorous analysis. Barzun gives no *reasons* – he merely censures *de haut en bas*. The fact that he happens to be correct and that he writes with muscular candour and robust common sense does not, unfortunately, constitute evidential force. But the argument from an established fact of human development such as conversion of function does.

Nevertheless, one must be careful here. What is transferable or convertible is not an unmodified set of discipline-specific "skills" but a certain *versatility* or flexibility, a generalized decathlon-like suppleness of intellect which manifests in the ability to perform well over a range of activities.

3 Analogously, what Abraham Maslow calls the "plateau-experience," that is, the experience of a serene competence – unitive, contemplative, and appreciative – possesses a noetic and cognitive element and is far more *voluntary* than the famous so-called peak experience. For our purposes, it is important to recognize, in Maslow's words, that "Plateau-experiencing can be achieved, learned, earned by hard work," in precisely the same way that the vocational "personality" of the teacher can be richly and scrupulously perfected. (See Abraham Maslow, *Religions, Values, and Peak Experiences*, Viking, New York, 1970; Penguin, New York, 1976.)

4 Alfred North Whitehead, *The Aims of Education*, Macmillan, New York, 1929, 1967.

5 Gregory Ulmer, *Applied Grammatology: Post(e) Pedagogy from Jacques Derrida to Joseph Beuys*, Johns Hopkins University Press, Baltimore, 1985.

6 This distinction clearly derives from Frank Kermode's *The Sense of an Ending* (Oxford University Press, London, 1965) where we find good fictions (open) as opposed to bad fictions (closed, dogmatic). The former are "good" because they are not escapist, sentimental, or easily consoling. The citations from Eco circulate freely in three of the latter's works: *The Role of the Reader*, Indiana University Press, Bloomington, 1979; *The Open Work*, Harvard University Press, Cambridge, MA, 1989; and *Semiotics and the Philosophy of Language*, Indiana University Press, Bloomington, 1986.

7 As Martin Buber writes in *Paths in Utopia* (Routledge and Kegan Paul, London, 1949), "The 'real' man approximates most closely to the 'ideal' just when he is expected to fulfil tasks which he is not up to, or thinks he is not up to ... he grows to higher purposes." This is the pedagogical territory Vygotsky has named the ZPD, or Zone of Proximal Development.

8 The concept of textuality may also be regarded as a reformulation of the concept of the "dramatic paradigm" (or dramaticity) developed in my *Education Lost* (OISE Press, Toronto, 1989). There teaching was understood as a form of ritual metamorphosis in which "the teacher impersonates the initiating presence and the student impersonates his ideal or projected self." The central tenet of the book is that the teaching-learning nexus depends upon "the hierophant-postulant relationship, subliminal and at the same time a shaping or structural principle at work in the classroom," and that it is precisely here "that the real nature of 'drama' is to be found." Teachers and students were encouraged to conceive of themselves as mutually implicated in the staging of a dramatic production, its informing purpose the accomplishment of an

initiation out of confusion and dispersal into a realized and holistic, that is, a resolved and "educated" sensibility. Clearly, what I here designate as "textuality" is an adaptation of the dramatic hypothesis in the light of semiotic theory as found in the work of such thinkers as Jacques Derrida, Michel Foucault, Umberto Eco, Jacques Lacan, and Roland Barthes.

9 Ilya Prigogine and Isabel Stenger, *Order out of Chaos*, Doubleday, New York, 1984.

10 The texts cited under the rubric "narrativity" are: Richard Rorty, *Contingency, Irony and Solidarity*, Cambridge University Press, Cambridge, 1989; Fredric Jameson, *The Political Unconscious*, Cornell University Press, Ithaca, 1981; Tzvetan Todorov, *The Poetics of Prose*, Cambridge University Press, Cambridge, 1979; Gregory Ulmer, *Teletheory*, Routledge, London, 1989; and Richard Ohmann, *Politics of Letters*, Wesleyan University Press, Middletown, CT, 1987. See also chapter 4, "The Anecdotal Function."

11 The constituent factors and functions of the Jakobsonian model should be treated in some detail in the conduct and procedures of the classroom forum itself. See in particular Roman Jakobson, "Linguistics and Poetics," edited by Thomas Sebeok and published in *Style and Language* (Indiana University Press, Bloomington, 1960).

12 Mikhail Bakhtin, *The Dialogic Imagination*, University of Texas Press, Austin, 1981. I tend to think of the "superaddressee" as a kind of Emmaean interlocutor and as the conscience of the collective classroom personality (cf. the Gospel of Luke 24:13–31).

13 As Thomas Mann writes in *Freud and the Future: Essays of Three Decades* (Knopf, New York, 1971), "The happiest, most pleasurable element of what we call education (Bildung), the shaping of the human being, is just this powerful influence of admiration and love."

14 "I teach more than a body of knowledge or a set of skills. I teach a mode of relationship between the knower and the known," claims one of the most influential of the new sodality of desert teachers in the tradition of Abba Felix. Palmer's book is an important document in the anti-objectivist movement that is starting to gain ground in contemporary pedography, but it must be stated that his valuable and penetrating insights are often blunted by the somewhat naïve Christian ontotheology he professes. To accept Palmer's recommendations wholly and effectively, we would need to share both his ontotheology and his Creation premise, especially as his notion of the teaching space as a "community of truth" rests upon pure Edenic assumptions: "Truth contains the image ... of community in which we were first created." But for the majority of us as secular beings living in an evolutionary world, his premise cannot be validated. Our original home, it seems, was not the Gar-

den of Eden but Jurassic Park. (Parker J. Palmer, *To Know As We Are Known*, HarperCollins, New York, 1993.)

15 Textuality, in the larger or *general* sense, may be understood finally as embracing the dynamic schematism in its entirety. In other words, local textual production (essays and discussions on the learning protocol), narrativity, and dialogism may be regarded as aspects of the supervening class-as-text. These distinctions are essentially matters of terminology. What remains important for our purposes is the radical transformation proposed in our habitual ways of appraising and *theorizing* the classroom situation. The class viewed under the aspect of textuality, soliciting the textual collaboration of the student, necessarily entails both narrative procedure and dialogical awareness.

16 Hans-Georg Gadamer, *Truth and Method*, 1960; reprint, Crossroads Press, New York, 1989.

17 "Every communication has a content and a relationship aspect in such a way that the latter classifies the former and is therefore a metacommunication" (cf. Watslawick, P.; Beavin, J.H.; Jackson, D.D.: *Pragmatics of Human Communication*, W.W. Norton, New York, 1967). A caveat is in order here: the bipolar paradigm, as was the case with experiential learning, may be suspected of converging with the systems-communication approach toward classroom management, which treats of the problems that may arise from poor metacommunication techniques. This latter problematic takes for its field of inquiry the root causes of class *misbehaviour* (understood not so much as a function of the student but as a property of the situation which must be "punctuated" differently if it is to be rectified). (Cf. Wubbles, T.; Creton, Hans A.; Holvast, Anne, "Undesirable Classroom Situations: A Systems Communication Perspective," *Interchange*, vol. 19, no. 2, Toronto, 1988.) Bipolarity, on the contrary, does not start from misbehaviour but from the need to improve classroom dynamics.

The texts to which I refer in this section, unless otherwise indicated, are the following: Jacques Lacan, *Ecrits*, Edition du Seuil, Paris, 1966; Jacques Derrida, *Of Grammatology*, Johns Hopkins University Press, Baltimore, 1976, and *Writing and Difference*, University of Chicago Press, 1978; Michel Foucault, *The Archaeology of Knowledge*, Pantheon Books, New York, 1972; J.L. Austin, *How to Do Things with Words*, Harvard University Press, Cambridge, MA, 1962; Jürgen Habermas, *Knowledge and Human Interests*, Beacon Press, Boston, 1971; Jean-François Lyotard, *Libidinal Economy*, Indiana University Press, Bloomington, 1993; and Roland Barthes, *Image Music Text*, Farrar, Straus and Giroux, New York, 1977.

18 What I am variously calling "learning to learn," "Text B," "the meta-cognitive dimension," or "the second pole of the bipolar paradigm" ob-

viously derives in part from Gregory Bateson's fruitful distinctions between proto-learning or Learning I (solution of a problem within a context), deutero-learning or Learning II (determining the context, the rules
of the game), and Learning III (understanding the nature of the paradigm itself). But the differences are substantial.

To begin with, Bateson is studying the learning process in its largest,
overarching sense and not subjecting *pedagogical praxis* itself to latitudinal analysis. He is more preoccupied with the phenomenon of schis-
mogenesis than with the process of cognitive reception-and-production
within the educational institution *per se*. Secondly, his discriminations,
while helpful in gaining understanding of psychological functioning as a
whole, need to be tempered, modified, adapted, reformulated, and often
restructured when it comes to a question of dynamic reciprocity between teacher and student in an actual classroom situation. And thirdly,
applying the principle of Occam's razor, I would suggest that the proliferation of categories in the Batesonian model, unless handled gingerly,
may lead to confusion rather than conceptual clarity. (See *Steps to an
Ecology of Mind*, Ballantine, New York, 1972.)

19 It is important to recognize that the concept of "transparency" has nothing to do with the training of teachers to disseminate information or inculcate skills. Such training, as I have emphasized in *Education Lost*, is
more often than not unavailing, distracting, and self-defeating. Rather,
what I am advocating in these pages has to do with the induction of the student as an active co-responsible into the learning protocol.

20 Max Dublin, *Futurehype*, Penguin, New York, 1990.

21 Hilda Neatby, *So Little for the Mind*, Clarke Irwin, Toronto, 1953; and
A Temperate Dispute, Clarke Irwin, Toronto, 1954. Jacques Barzun,
Teacher in America, Little, Brown, Boston, 1945; and *The House of In-
tellect*, Harper, New York, 1959. It is only fair to concede, however, that
one must invoke the example of Jefferson with a certain diffidence, if
Conor Cruise O'Brien is right in regarding the great democrat as, in
fact, a closet slavocrat. (See *On the Eve of the Millennium*, Anansi,
Concord, 1994; by October 1996, in O'Brien's article in the *Atlantic
Monthly*, Jefferson has become an arrant racist.)

22 For Carl Rogers's take on the subject, see *On Becoming a Person*,
Houghton Mifflin, Boston, 1961. For the discussion on the relation be-
tween predicative and attributive, see G.E. Moore, *Ethics*, Oxford Uni-
versity Press, London, 1912, 1965, 1976; and Bernard Williams,
Morality, Harper, New York, 1972. Fielding's remark is from *Tom
Jones*, Penguin, New York, 1966.

23 Peter Dews, *Logics of Disintegration*, Verso, London, 1990.

24 Thus the rich ambiguity of the word "subject," which can mean both (1)
field or discipline, the "subject" to be learned or pedagogical object,

Text A; and (2) the desiring, curious self, in the process of establishing itself as a continuous learner, implicated in Text B.

25 For an extensive analysis of this phenomenon in its larger social context, see Philip Rieff, *The Triumph of the Therapeutic*, Harper, New York, 1966. Gerald Graff also comments interestingly on the diffusion of "therapeutic man" in modern society: "One's very selfhood is understood as a problem, if not as a grievance, a condition of acute vulnerability ... requiring permanent administration and 'caring.'" It is a small step from "the victimized self-conception of the therapeutic type" to the problems and grievances of the contemporary student and the concomitant tendency of teachers to therapeuticize education. (Cf. Gerald Graff, *Literature Against Itself.*) For an interesting discussion of the relation between teacher and student, see Edward T. Hall (*The Dance of Life*, Doubleday, New York, 1983, especially chapter 9): "The classroom can be an extension of the home. It is therefore necessary for the professor to discourage any impulses on the part of the students to cast him in the parental role."

26 cf. Shaun Gallagher, *Hermeneutics and Education*, SUNY, Albany, 1992. Similarly, Neil Postman, who defines education as a "becom[ing] aware of the origins and growth of knowledge and knowledge-systems," contends that "such a definition is not child-centered, not training-centered, not skill-centered, not even problem-centered. It is idea-centered and coherence-centered" (*Technopoly*, Knopf, New York, 1992).

27 Jacques Lacan, "Seminar on 'The Purloined Letter'" in *Ecrits*, in which he develops his theory of the three "epistemic" glances, which we may designate as the blind, the myopic, and the long-sighted. Interpretation, whether of a text, a situation, a dream, a therapeutic procedure, or a pedagogical encounter, is a function of which of the three positions in the hermeneutic structure we take up. The first position represents the solipsism of ignorance and self-satisfaction. The second betokens the illusion of desire and complementarity founded on the denial of precedence, generating false or imaginary relationships. The third position, because it subtends the other two, is always the position of the analyst: disinterested, stereoscopic, self-aware, and authoritative.

28 Jane Gallop, *Reading Lacan*, Cornell University Press, Ithaca, 1985.

29 Mem Fox, *Radical Reflections*, Harcourt Brace, New York, 1993. The problem with Mem Fox is not that her heart is not in the right place but that there is *no place* in which her heart is not palpitatingly visible (and thunderously audible). The book is drenched in tears and saturated in love, cloyingly shed and proclaimed at every opportunity. Despite a sparse scatter of decent insights, *Radical Reflections* (which is neither radical nor reflective) reads like a self-enamoured *curriculum vitae* extolling the accomplishments and perquisites of the Memfoxian ego: the

docile husband, the precocious daughter, the loyal friends, the grateful students, and the long list of well-received publications, all testifying to the primary self and the advantages of political correctness camouflaged beneath the rhetoric of her pseudo-revolutionary agenda. Fox remains trapped in the Lacanian imaginary, seeing her students as specular doubles of herself and at the same time blind to the distortions of her structural projections. The fairy-tale redundance of her prose gives the game away, inadvertently revealing the illusory world in which she continues to play the Mary Poppins of pedagogy.

30 Jerome Bruner, *On Knowing: Essays for the Left Hand*, Harvard University Press, Cambridge, MA, 1962.

31 Richard Mitchell, *The Gift of Fire*, Simon & Schuster, New York, 1987.

32 Israel Scheffler, *In Praise of the Cognitive Emotions*, Routledge, London, 1991.

33 Lawrence Halprin, *The RSVP Cycles*, George Braziller Inc., New York, 1969.

34 David Perkins, *Smart Schools*, Free Press, New York, 1992.

35 As I argued in *Education Lost*, the good student is one who can compensate for the bad teacher. Or the bad textbook, for that matter. But within the framework of the traditional curriculum, it is *never the subject* that is deficient. Perhaps one might put the matter this way: boredom is generally in the student, often in the teacher, and never in the subject.

36 "Reflection and 'distancing' are crucial aspects of achieving a sense of the range of possible stances – a metacognitive step of huge import" (Jerome Bruner, *Actual Minds, Possible Worlds*, Harvard University Press, Cambridge, MA, 1986). This reflective posture also invites the student to participate in the construction of metatextual meaning, to fill in what John Fiske in *Reading the Popular* (Routledge, London and New York, 1994) calls the "syntagmatic gaps" and to collaborate in the establishment of a "semiotic democracy" – which remains perfectly compatible with the first principles of intellectual constitution, namely, hard study, submission to the exigencies of the discipline, and respect for the cognitive authority of the teacher.

37 And the answer plainly does not lie in the expansion of the technological infrastructure or in the distributive processing of knowledge, as Perkins seems to believe. This solution to the pedagogical dilemma is merely another symptom of what Arthur Kroker and Michael Weinstein have called "the recline of the West," that is, "the will to be incorporated into technologically-produced environments" (*Data Trash*, St. Martin's Press, New York, 1994).

38 Lewis J. Perelman, *School's Out*, Avon, New York, 1992. Oddly, the same title, attached to a very different vision of educational felicity

though equally suggesting the reactionary nature of the educational establishment, reappears in Andrew Nikiforuk's book of the following year.

CHAPTER EIGHT

1 "No metaphor runs on all four legs," said Coleridge in the *Biographia Literaria*. My metaphor requires a return to origins while education envisions a projected destination that may correspond to the source only from a Romantic or mythological perspective.

2 Paul Virilio, *Speed and Politics*, Semiotext(e), New York, 1986.

3 Agnes Heller, *A Philosophy of History in Fragments*, Blackwell, Oxford, 1993.

4 *Bedrock*, Véhicule Press, Montreal, 1993.

5 David Carr, *Time, Narrative, and History*, Indiana University Press, Bloomington, 1991. Carr also develops an interesting discussion on the relation between Dilthey and Heidegger under the aspect of temporality and with respect to value, purpose, and meaning.

6 John Ralston Saul, *Voltaire's Bastards*, Penguin, New York, 1992. In a more recent work (*The Doubter's Companion*, Free Press, New York, 1994), Saul regards memory as "central to the idea of a Humanist equilibrium" but also as an endangered faculty, "despised by the sophisticated structures of management." And in his latest offering (*The Unconscious Civilization*, Anansi, Concord, 1995), he celebrates memory as "the first quality that differentiates us" from the inanimate and the mechanical. What I am here calling "continuous time" bears a close family likeness to the concept of "temporal integration," defined by Frank Kermode as "our way of bundling together perception of the present, memory of the past, and expectation of the future, in a common organization" (*The Sense of an Ending*, Oxford University Press, London, 1966).

7 Emmanuel Levinas, *Ethics and Infinity*, Duquesne University Press, 1985. Similarly, if memory may be considered as the interior analogue of dynamic temporality, then it does not merely reproduce the past but carries us forward into the dimension of the unexpected or unpredictable. This is precisely the way in which Michel de Certeau regards the operation of memory, which "is linked to the expectation that something alien to the present will or must occur. Far from being the reliquary or trash can of the past, it sustains itself by *believing* in the existence of possibilities and by vigilantly awaiting them ..." Levinas on time and de Certeau on memory geminate the subject. See Michel de Certeau, *The Practice of Everyday Life*, University of California Press, Berkeley, 1988.

8 As David Kolb writes, "we need a thicker identity with some historical memory ... history is not something we consult but something we are" (*Postmodern Sophistications*, University of Chicago Press, Chicago, 1990). And history is profoundly implicated in the structures of thought itself that render the individual coherent, integrating mind and sensuous experience into a unified whole. In the crisp phrasing of Pope's *Essay on Man*:

> Remembrance and reflection how allied!
> What thin partitions sense from thought divide.

9 Agnes Heller, *A Philosophy of History in Fragments*. Arnold Kroker similarly dismisses the "sampler self" as something which is "never really stable, never really localized ... with no history to inhibit its future, no encrusted identity to suppress its desire" (*The Dispossessed Individual*, Culture Texts, Montreal, 1992). Kroker is a writer I particularly admire for his defiant unintelligibility, which forces readers to slow down and take their time to avoid samplerhood.

10 At this time, as I revise my text, the suburban community in which I teach has been shocked by the brutal murder of an elderly couple at the hands of three teenage boys between the ages of thirteen and fifteen, students at a local, middle-class high school. The murder was particularly gruesome, carried out with baseball bats – eerily reminiscent of the famous episode in *A Clockwork Orange* – and prompted not by gain or resentment or any of the traditional motives but merely by the desire to experience the unique and momentary delight of killing. Reality for these "children" has become largely virtual: they are apparently unrepentant, seem devoid of a sense of responsibility, and have no awareness of consequences, that is, of temporality. Reality for them is a succession of instantaneous experiences, as if behaviour had no effect on the future or was in any way a reflection of the past.

A schoolmate reports that the boys, who boasted of their exploit, were planning to commit a second murder. Would this not suggest that they were indeed living in the stream of temporality? But one may still be able to "project" purposes into the future, as David Carr argues (see Section II), without engaging in "the development of a life." Mere repetition, brute chronicity, even if it can be previsioned, is nothing more than a function of raw, linear, segmented time in which moments succeed one another non-incrementally. Living in continuous time, which is the authentically human form of temporality, is predicated on *development*, on the dynamic of emergence into ever richer and more complex states of consciousness characterized by memory of past implications and anticipation of future consequences. What I am calling continuous time may be understood, from another perspective, as the ethical dimension of human experience.

The moral and imaginative deficiencies from which these young people suffer should not, of course, be attributed to any single, isolated cause. There are probably a concatenation of factors at work: low cognitive ability, a poor home life, TV saturation, cultural degeneracy, the growing addiction to Virtual Reality substitutes for experience, and the failure of education. But the resulting behaviour shows all the traces of the syndrome I have been analysing throughout these pages, namely, a severe temporal dystrophy which to a very real and alarming extent dehumanizes their relation to the world. As Donna Woolfolk Cross warned in *Mediaspeak* (New American Library, New York, 1983) some years before the advent of the Virtual Reality syndrome: "We are threatened by a new and peculiarly American menace ... the menace of unreality." For Arthur Kroker and Michael Weinstein, paraphrasing both Lacan and Spengler, we have now entered "the technological imaginary" which they refer to as "the recline of the West." This is a condition characterized by "the disintegration of experience into cybernetic interactivity or ... the disappearance of memory and solitary reflection." We have become "celebrants of amnesia," victims of an image-generated "recombinant history" in which not only the past but "the contemporary loses all meaning." (See *Data Trash*, St. Martin's Press, New York, 1994.)

This "condition" would also explain why it is vital to introduce young children and students to quality language experiences if they are not to be cheated of their cognitive legacy and a place in the real world. It is the symbolic transfer or disembedding process fostered by language, enabling the mind to imagine or conceive of other worlds (past, future, conditional, hypothetical, analogical, or metaphorical), that allows it to impinge upon the here-and-now to shape, modify, and improve it. Whereas those who begin with pictures, who grow up in iconic or virtual worlds that are intensively here-and-now *in themselves*, are ironically abstracted from the real, the actual here-and-now. The virtual or imaginary realm in this case, because it is so immediate and seductive and inescapable, fails to provide alternative ways for conceiving and transforming the real. *It becomes the real*. The virtual or iconic world is imagination in runaway.

Thus the paradox in which we are currently mired. Those who develop through the symbolic displacement provided by language come to live more fully in the real world of the here-and-now which enables them to imagine an equally real world of the there-and-then. But those who begin with and "develop" through the immediacy of pictorial simulation and iconic substitutes for language come to live in an empty, unreal, virtual world, a nowhere and non-time tragically mistaken for a here-and-now. No longer literants but immersants, probably the best these kids can look forward to is life in a world of Couplandian micro-serfs. The reality of the situation is mournfully summarized in John Taylor Gatto's *Dumbing Us Down* (New Society Publishers, Philadel-phia, 1992). Today's children, Gatto writes, "cannot concentrate on any-thing for very long; they have a poor sense of time past and time to come. They are mistrustful of intimacy like the children of divorce they really are (for we have divorced them from significant parental atten-tion); they hate solitude, are cruel, materialistic, dependent, passive, vio-lent, timid in the face of the unexpected, addicted to distraction."

11 Ned Lukacher, *Primal Scenes*, Cornell University Press, Ithaca, New York, 1986.

12 In defence of my bizarre terminology, I might point out that the study of tropology does tend to generate a weird, mixolydian nomenclature. Consider, for example, the work of the *Groupe Mu* in France, which, in attempting to refine the field of rhetorical figures, has distinguished four types of operations, involving both lexical units and syntactic chains, that displace the traditional codification of metaphor, metonymy, synec-doche, and irony. The new schematism comprises the metaseme, which acts upon content and is akin to metaphor; the metalogism, a figure of thought akin to irony; the metaplasm, which acts upon lexical structure (apocope, puns, etc.); and the metasyntagm, which acts upon syntactical structure (hypallage, zeugma, etc.). I am not at all sure whether such rhetorical pleaching actually clarifies the subject much.

13 Metaphor, says Umberto Eco, "is a new semantic coupling not preceded by any stipulation in the code"; that is, it restructures the semantic sys-tem by introducing linguistic circuits not previously in existence, which would account for the production of novelty (*The Role of the Reader*, Indiana University Press, Bloomington, 1984). Similarly, Paul Ricoeur defines metaphor as "semantic impertinence" (*The Rule of Metaphor*, University of Toronto Press, Toronto, 1977). In the classical discussion, the four figures of speech are understood as forms of lexical substitu-tion: irony is substitution based on negation, synecdoche is substitution based on integral association (part for whole, or vice versa), metonymy is substitution based on contiguity or functional association, and meta-phor is substitution based on the principle of resemblance in difference (and vice versa). Metaphor has come to be regarded in current literary theory as the linguistic prevention of entropy. Thoughtless, reproductive, reactive, or tautological expression ensures that information will be lost in any process of communication – the cybernetic version of the Second Law of Thermodynamics – producing a kind of semantic-temporal sta-sis. Metaphor, we might say, keeps the inner clock ticking.

This way of looking at metaphor is obviously a specification of the
Romantic theory of metaphorical transumption. Johnson in his "Life of
Pope" distinguishes "the two most engaging powers of an author. New
things are made familiar, and *familiar things are made new.*" This second, renovating function of metaphor is favoured by Coleridge in the
Biographia Literaria where he praises Wordsworth's poetry for remov-
ing the "film of familiarity" from our perception, a phrase picked up by
Shelley in the celebrated *Defence* in which we read that poetry, the natural home of metaphor, "makes familiar objects be as if they were not
familiar." That same idea reappears in the work of our near-
contemporary, the Russian formalist Victor Shklovsky, who develops the
concept of *ostranenie* or defamiliarization: art, founded on metaphorical
transformations, "exists to help us recover our sensation of life ... to
make things unfamiliar." The sense of expectation generated by the
predication of the new, the unsuspected, the unpredictable, is intimately
associated with the sense of temporal emergence generated by implication and presupposition at the heart of the metaphorical transaction
with the world.

14 The reader may recall that in the first chapter, "Grammatical Fictions,"
I located the problem of temporal dystrophy on the axis of combination
(Jakobson's "contiguity disorder"). Now I appear to be shifting my attention to the axis of selection (Jakobson's "similarity disorder"). The
discrepancy is only apparent. At the deeper levels of tropological activity, both axes of linguistic production, the syntagmatic and the paradigmatic (or the metonymical and metaphorical), form part of the original
transformational process which I have designated as metaphoronymy –
the ur-trope that generates the deep sense of temporality through the medium of implicature and presupposition and that gives us metonymical
sequences of metaphorical transformations along which we plot the
timeline of developing identity. Thus the campaign against illiteracy I
am advocating in these pages deploys its resources along two related
fronts: the metonymical, which combats the weak form of contiguity
disorder by "recapturing" historical, syntagmatic time through the revival of the humanities; and the metaphorical, which proposes to
strengthen the felt sense of continuous time. This latter operation proceeds both by recognizing the nature of metaphorical implicature in
order to *confirm* the causal relation between tropology and temporality,
rhetorical presupposition and ostensive continuity, assumption and currency (if only through developing a conscious respect for the work of
language as the source of the inner, prenoetic sense of emergence), and
by disengaging an appropriate set of temporal metaphors in which to
"place" or contextualize the educational transaction, to "frame the

pitch," building a kind of rhetorical coaming around whatever subject is being taught.

15 Having introduced my new and rather unwieldy term, I return to the handier "metaphor," not only for reasons of stylistic convenience but because I am here primarily concerned with the metaphorical process itself, that is, transformation, or what I am tempted to call *metaphormation*: the formation of metaphor as part of the metaphorical formation of the self, which is itself predicated on the metaphor of formation.

16 This would naturally require a student responsive to the demands, the exigencies, of the gradual unfolding of a subject in time, a student capable of the vestigial feat of listening to a lecture. Psychologists have discovered that certain neural and cognitive frequencies may be outside the range of normal entrainment (e.g., music that breaks certain temporal rules, abnormal light-dark cycles that desynchronize the circadian system). Is this what is happening to lectorial time? The lecture, whose periodicity does not coincide with the Sesame Street sound-bite temporal frame, is outside the range of entrainment of the student audience.

As Jerry Mander maintains in *Four Arguments for the Elimination of Television*, Quill, New York, 1978, young people who have been watching television on an average of thirty-five hours per week since infancy have been trained to expect a rapid and endless sequence of "technical events" to make what they are looking at interesting. These "technical events" consist of cuts, zooms, pans, montage, impossible camera angles, musical accompaniment, and the like, occurring every few seconds or at even greater rates of frequency in commercials and rock videos. Long exposure to this technology is probably the major cause of hyperactivity in our students and also contributes "to the decline of attention span and the inability to absorb information that comes muddling along at natural, real-life speed."

Thus, the problem for the teacher today is *lectorial disentrainment or infradian decoupling*. (Jane Healy in *Endangered Minds* [Simon & Schuster, New York, 1991] argues convincingly that the actual neurophysical structure of the brain has changed in the generation now coming of age.) Resonance has gone awry, a breaking of entrained frequencies or harmonic oscillations. There is nothing wrong with the lecture *per se*, as so many contemporary theorists contend, advising teachers who know their stuff to stop talking and begin listening to their students who know next to nothing. I am always amazed by the amount of classroom pandemonium that many teachers now regard as normal – as if quizzes, chatter, and movies were a viable substitute for learned discourse. One of my colleagues, rather more enlightened, re-establishes temporary order in his classroom by regularly blowing a whistle, the latest pedagogical proxy for eloquence. Which is certainly better than administering Ritalin, the latest pedagogical substitute for professional respect.

17 Jean Baudrillard, *Simulations*, Semiotext(e), New York, 1983; and *The Ecstasy of Communication*, Semiotext(e), New York, 1987. In an interview in the *Montreal Gazette* for 30 April 1995, the astrophysicist and programming wizard, Cliff Stoll, author of such books as *The Cuckoo's Egg* and *Silicon Snake Oil*, warns of the technological subversion of real experience. "One of the problems of technology is that people think it's a substitute for real life. I don't have to deal with my neighbour when I can log onto the Internet for two hours a night." The so-called Virtual Community is nothing more than "a weak substitute, an ersatz community." It is time now, he advises, to consult the "bogometer."

Another way of regarding this critical yet banal predicament is to see how virtuality spells the death of the imagination, that faculty, both temporal and analogical, which, in the words of Philip Sidney in the *Apology for Poetry*, enables our "recoursing to things forepast, and divining of things to come." Imagination and memory are intimately braided together: memory, writes Michel de Certeau in *The Practice of Everyday Life*, "responds more than it records." The temporal plasm of authentic human experience is an amalgam of various faculties or predispositions: memory, anticipation, imagination (or projective sympathy), and the sense of responsibility, moving between the temporal poles of guilt (the moral past) and concern (the moral future), which ground the ethical consciousness.

18 Paul Virilio, *Speed and Politics*. See also Kroker and Weinstein, *Data Trash*, who lament "the inertial gridlock of high speed" in "post-Crash society, where everything always speeds up to a standstill."

19 Paul Virilio, *The Aesthetics of Disappearance*, Semiotext(e) New York, 1991. See also Andrei Codrescu, *The Disappearance of the Outside*, Addison-Wesley, New York, 1990. Codrescu warns that "the reduction of round, biological human time to speeding-up mechanical time is almost complete."

20 Milan Kundera, *Immortality*, HarperCollins, New York, 1991.

21 *The Complete Poems of Cavafy*, tr. Rae Dalven, Harcourt, Brace & World, New York, 1948. The basic figure on which this poem is built is the alchemical notion of the *longissima via*. The *Rosarium Philosophorum* says of the educational process, the journey toward enlightenment and metamorphosis, "Know that this is a very long path." This is the same journey, the same path, though in a more "contemporary" and collective manifestation, to which the physicist Paul Davies alludes as he embarks upon an excursion into the nature of mathematics: "Though the going gets rough here and there, and the destination remains

shrouded in mystery, I hope that the journey itself will prove exhilarating" (*The Mind of God*, Simon & Schuster, New York, 1992).

It is curious to note that eighteen centuries before Cavafy, another famous Alexandrian went to the *Odyssey* for exempla touching the education of the human soul. I refer to the Christian Neoplatonist Clement, who, unlike his secular successor, recommended *undeviating* steadfastness to one's destination. The voyager must tie himself to the cross as Odysseus strapped himself to the mast in order to avoid temptation as represented by the sirens. From the standpoint we are adopting here, it is precisely the sirens, the slow meanderings of temptation, perilous as these may be, that constitute the true curriculum. See Richard Tarnas, *The Passion of the Western Mind*, Ballantine, New York, 1993, for a recent, brief, but informative discussion of Clement's Neoplatonism.

22 Ideally, the teacher may be considered – another metaphorical embodiment – as the Virgilian preceptor or Beatrice-figure for whom the student is like Dante in Purgatorio, Canto 33, drinking from the river Eunoë, which secures him against Lethean oblivion:

> Back from the waves most holy privilege
> I turned me, re-made, as the plant repairs
> Itself, renewed with its new foliage,
> Pure and disposed to mount up to the stars.

It is almost providential that the stream of temporal restoration is called Eunoë, a near homonym for "you know."

23 Cf. *Modern European Poetry*, Bantam, New York, 1966. Translation by Vernon Watkins.

24 "There is no test, textbook, syllabus, or lesson plan that any of us creates that does not reflect our preference for some metaphor of the mind, or of knowledge, or of the process of learning. Do you believe the student's mind to be a muscle that must be exercised? Or a garden that must be cultivated? Or a dark cavern that must be illuminated? Or an empty vessel that must be filled to overflowing? Whichever you favour, your metaphor will control – often without your being aware of it – how you will proceed as a teacher" (Neil Postman, *Conscientious Objections*, Vintage, New York, 1992).

25 Frank Smith, *Joining the Literacy Club*, Heinemann, Portsmouth, NH, 1988.

26 This is, of course, Heidegger's concept of *Geworfensein* or thrown-ness.

27 Terry Eagleton, *Saints and Scholars*, Verso, London, 1987. In the words of Paolo Portoghesi, "It is the loss of memory, not the cult of memory, that will make us prisoners of the past" (Paolo Portoghesi, *After Modern Architecture*, Rizzoli, New York, 1982). It is in this predisposition to atemporality, manifesting socially as indifference, brutality, a desire for mere sensation, and a crippling lack of historical curiosity, that we may

locate the irruption of a renewed barbarism. In the words of Isaiah Berlin, "Only barbarians are not curious about where they come from, how they came to be where they are, where they appear to be going, whether they wish to go there, and if so, why, and if not, why not" (Isaiah Berlin, *The Crooked Timber of Humanity*, Fontana, London, 1991).

28 In Northrop Frye's limpid sentence, "His ultimate goal is the abolition of himself, or the turning of himself into a transparent medium for his subject, so that the authority of his subject may be supreme over both teacher and students" (*On Education*, Fitzhenry & Whiteside, Toronto, 1990). This is an idea I have elaborated at considerable length, under the auspices of the Bakhtinian speculation regarding the superaddressee at the apex of the communication triangle (cf. "The Bipolar Paradigm").

CHAPTER NINE

1 Edgar Allen Poe, *Complete Tales & Poems*, Vintage, New York, 1975.
2 Jerome Bruner sets us right here. The answer to the question, "What shall be taught?" he tells us, turns out to be the answer to the question "What is non-trivial?" (*On Knowing: Essays for the Left Hand*, Harvard University Press, Cambridge, MA, 1962, 1979.)
3 See Lionel Trilling, *Matthew Arnold*, Harcourt Brace Jovanovich, New York, 1954. Arnold's use of the phrase "inferior classes" is not patronizing or invidious but intended as a form of free indirect speech, a kind of diction appropriate not to the narrator but to the character. Thus it works as an ironic critique of precisely those who are prone to use the phrase dismissively. Arnold's settled position on class distinctions is articulated in his essay of 1882, "Literature and Science," in which he castigates "our world of an aristocracy materialised and null, a middle class purblind and hideous, a lower class crude and brutal." Allowing for an adjustment of perspective and terminology corresponding to the make-up of our contemporary class structure – plutocrat, bourgeois, blue-collar – Arnold's indictment remains scrupulously accurate.

Arnold's proposal for cultural diffusion is perhaps more familiar to us as the Jeffersonian doctrine of educational leavening, that is, of bringing the "common man" into the higher world of learning. Jefferson was the first great apostle of learning up on this side of the Atlantic, a legacy we have honoured in the breach.
4 In my college at present, considerable money and effort have been squandered in institutionalizing the so-called First Semester Experience: classes composed entirely of neophytes, designated catering personnel (once called "teachers"), special calendars filled with pampering information, etc. Before the invention of the community college, freshmen at universities were left to the tender mercies of upperclassmen and frater-

nity initiations. The experience, as I can personally attest, was traumatic – but it worked. We were forced to grow up pretty fast, which seems preferable to diapering our students throughout the first year of college, coddling them through the second, and letting subsequent despair and rejection do the work of maturation for them. Meanwhile our hands remain clean and our consciences immaculate.

5 Richard Mitchell, *The Gift of Fire*, Simon & Schuster, New York, 1987.
6 See Antonin Artaud, *The Theatre and Its Double*, Gallimard, Paris, 1964.
7 See Jacques Derrida, "Freud and The Scene of Writing," *Writing and Difference*, University of Chicago Press, Chicago, 1978. The citations from Freud are in text.
8 Friedrich Nietzsche, *On the Genealogy of Morals*, Vintage Books, New York, 1969.
9 Parker J. Palmer, *To Know As We Are Known*, HarperCollins, San Francisco, 1993. I do not wish to misrepresent Palmer by shanghaiing his arguments from their context. The reader should take note that he develops his thesis from an authentically Christian perspective with the emphasis falling on truth, love, personhood, transparency, and relationship. His rejection of objectivist pedagogy is persuasive and well founded, although his passionate advocacy of the ontotheological self bypasses the entire semiotic and deconstructive thought of the postmodern era and sounds naïve indeed. His position cannot be credibly maintained without taking on and taming the revolutionary implications of the work of such thinkers as Martin Heidegger, Ferdinand de Saussure, Jacques Lacan, Louis Althusser, Gilles Deleuze, Michel Foucault, and Jacques Derrida, who pretty well define the contemporary climate of epistemological inquiry. Palmer would have to *show*, in the light of the powerful Derridean argument that origin and presence are mediated by language and constantly *deferred*, recessive, and elusive, how logocentric knowledge is possible (see for example the reasoned arguments to this effect in Donald Davidson's *Inquiries into Truth and Interpretation* (Oxford University Press, London, 1984), where referential truth is understood as a kind of logical primitive.) And at the same time he would have to explain just how the Lacanian imaginary/symbolic self and the Althusserian ideological self, both *constructed* objects, yield to the idea of the self as incarnation. (For example, Palmer claims that "the 'Word' our knowledge seeks is not a verbal construct but a reality in history and the flesh.") He would have to justify such categorical propositions as "the transformation of teaching must begin in the transformed heart of the teacher" by courageously bearding the Lacanian hypothesis of the pre-structured "subject," the Althusserian notion that personal change

may paradoxically strengthen the ISA (Ideological State Apparatus) already in place, and the well-known Foucauldian claim that such changes of heart may affect the institution without altering the system. The abstract and sentimental piety implicit in statements such as "we must allow our hearts to be known by the love and truth in which they were first formed" emerges in an evolutionary vacuum and assumes the myth of Eden rather than the reality of Jurassic Park (i.e., the reality that grounds the fantasy). This is why his argument must remain sadly ineffective in the larger world of thought and practice that does not share his ontological premises.

Nevertheless, while regretting its conceptual inadequacies, there is much I find sympathetic in Palmer's book, and I have no quarrel with his notion that a "learning space needs to be hospitable not to make learning painless but to make the painful things possible, things without which no learning can occur."

10 I think in this regard of that fortunate generation of student-goslings in James Reaney's great poem, the pastoral fable *A Suit of Nettles* (Macmillan, Toronto, 1958). The character, Valency (who stands for Hilda Neatby in the July eclogue), affectionately recalls the practice of her former schoolteacher, Old Strictus, who taught "the most wonderful list of things," including

> The eight winds and the hundred kinds of clouds,
> All of Jesus' stem and the various ranks of angels ...
> The Nine Worthies and the Labours of Hercules,
> The sisters of Emily Brontë, the names of Milton's wives ...

The goslings, realizing the importance of the material to be absorbed and profiting from good study habits, would then construct "little huts of burdock leaves, lay down on our backs with large stones on our bellies and recite the whole thing over to ourselves forwards and backwards," emerging from the burdock hut of disciplined learning only when "they knew all that a young goose was supposed to know." The second character in the dialogue, a progressive educational theorist named Anser (Latin for "goose"), whose students are presently gorging in a field of buckwheat, replies: "Pah! If they like nothing, then teach them that. The self must be free."

When she is not doubling as Dr Neatby, Valency is, of course, the nineteenth-century Canadian mythopoeic poet, Isabella Valancy Crawford. Valency also reminds me in many ways of Camille Paglia, recalling her rigorous mentor, Milton Kessler, or dismissing educational relevance as a "quickie standard of judgment," or announcing in clarion prose that educational coddling is nothing short of disastrous: "People were not coddled in the age of the immigrants. If you flunked, you flunked! The end result is that we're graduating into college people who cannot read." (See Camille Paglia, *Sex, Art, and American Culture*, Vintage, New York, 1992.)

11 See Edward Thorndike, *The Principles of Teaching Based on Psychology*, A.G. Seiler, New York, 1906.

12 In his dictionary of non-received ideas called "Sixty-Three Words" (*The Art of the Novel*, Harper & Row, New York, 1988), Kundera remarks that this portion of *The Book of Laughter and Forgetting* (Penguin, London, 1980) presents "an oneiric image of an infantocratic future," and defines infantocracy as the ideal of childhood imposed by the technological era on all humanity.

13 In defence of that state of mind which I am here calling learning-up pedagogy, Martin Buber writes in *Paths in Utopia* (Routledge & Kegan Paul, London, 1949), "the 'real' man approximates most closely to the 'ideal' just when he is expected to fulfil tasks which he is not up to ... Thus he grows to higher purposes." Similarly, though for somewhat different reasons, one of Vygotsky's most frequent experimental techniques in testing for the development of learning skills was to introduce difficulties or set tasks that exceeded his subjects' capabilities and to monitor the consequent modifications of behaviour (*Mind in Society*, Harvard University Press, Cambridge, MA, 1978). These notions are securely rooted in the ancient soil of Greek education whose aim, as H.I. Marrou remarks, "was not to make things easy for the child but to give him the hardest things first, in the belief that once those were mastered the rest would follow of its own accord" (*A History of Education in Antiquity*, Sheed and Ward, New York, 1956). But today the major impetus is toward retoddlerization, as is perhaps most conspicuous in current adolescent fashion, that bathetic parody of Harlem style: backward baseball cap (bonnet), humungous T-shirt (bib or smock), floppy, unlaced running shoes (booties), and oversized shorts or jeans fastened loosely at the level of the lower abdomen, as if to accommodate the bulky diaper within.

14 Jacques Lacan, *Ecrits*, Editions du Seuil, Paris, 1966. Trans. Alan Sheridan, Norton, New York, 1977.

15 There is always the possibility that the letter may be misdelivered. The teacher will often find himself or herself in the position, structurally speaking, of Shakespeare's Costard in *Love's Labour's Lost* who mistakenly delivers Armado's letter to Rosaline and Berowne's to Jacquenetta, leading to much hilarity, discomfiture, and perilous absurdity in about equal measure.

16 Derrida writes: "It belongs to the structure of the letter to be capable, always, of not arriving. And without this threat ... the circuit of the letter would not even have begun" ("The Purveyor of Truth," in *The Post*

Card, University of Chicago Press, Chicago, 1987). With respect to the celebrated exchange between Derrida and Lacan on this subject, John Muller and William Richardson explain that Lacan's notion of *la lettre en souffrance* paradoxically always arriving at its destination "overlooks the structural possibility that the letter can always remain in the dead letter office, and that without this possibility of deviation and remaining – the entire postal system – there would be no delivery of letters to any address at all." (*The Purloined Poe*, Johns Hopkins University Press, Baltimore, 1988). It is precisely this taking up of the wager, this willingness to gamble, this recognition of the problematic nature of the epistolary transmission endemic to education – "the entire postal system" – that constitutes the decisive moment in genuine teaching. The possibility of the letter never arriving, and the readiness to accept the basic postal uncertainty that defines the act of communication and puts all genuine transmission at risk, is nothing less than the *condition* of education. Refusing to accept the possibility of loss and deviation, or what amounts to the same thing, demanding constant verifiability and assurance, the so-called "continuous assessment," reduces the educational transaction to the level of mere banality and redundance.

It is for this reason that the cliché-driven effort to "maximize classroom instruction," for example, nearly always fails. Good teachers do not walk into class determined to maximize instruction. They enter the "scene of teaching" determined to engage their students and their subjects, radiating knowledge, wit, sceptical irony, belief, conviction, passion, doubt, anger, and sometimes even love – though the smarmier manifestations of love are generally counter-productive (too much like Stanislavsky method acting). Nor are they obsessed with the need to monitor constantly the effects of instruction in order to avoid the inescapable threat of dereliction or failure, since they know that the circuit of genuine communication rests on the willingness to take chances and necessarily involves the possibility of misunderstanding, resentment, and at least temporary confusion. Letters get lost, go astray, are misdelivered, sometimes remain unopened, and may be misunderstood when read. The fact of postal incertitude is a condition accepted by every passionate letter-writer. It is part of the wager of education.

17 See L.S. Vygotsky, *Mind in Society*, and *Thought and Language*, MIT Press, Cambridge, MA, 1986. The notion of the Zone of Proximal Development (ZPD) was not so much discovered as developed, systematized, and established by Vygotsky. The general idea has been with us in one form or another for a long time. In Jerome Bruner's lapidary phrase, "supply creates demand" in education; "the provocation of what is available creates response" (*On Knowing*). Similarly, Article 128 of the Discussion Paper on Curriculum Organization and Classroom Prac-

tice prepared for the British government by Robin Alexander *et al.* (cited in Andrew Nikiforuk's *School's Out*, Macfarlane Walter & Ross, Toronto, 1993) reads: "Good learning does not merely keep step with pupils but challenges and stretches their thinking." John Gardner argues quite sensibly that "high performance takes place in a framework of expectations." If teachers expect a lot from their students, "they increase the likelihood of high performance ... That means standards, an explicit regard for excellence" (*Excellence*, W.W. Norton, New York, 1987). And H.I. Marrou writes with evident approval of the Hellenistic ideal of education which, while by no means barbarous, was extremely rigorous in its congenial practice. It focused not on the development of the child but on the formation of the adult, viewing education as self-transcendence. "One cannot feel confident that if the Greeks could have known the endeavours that psychology and education have been making since *Emile* was written to adapt themselves to the child and the special characteristics of his mind they would have responded with anything but amused surprise" (*A History of Education in Antiquity*).

In Vygotsky's conception of the ZPD, social and pedagogical collaboration plays a far more significant role than in many of the previous formulations of the basic idea, which tend to take the tutorial stance more or less for granted, or as in Marrou, to scant it altogether. But the fundamental notion remains: high expectations and demanding teaching produce undoubted results. And if, as Vygotsky claims, "the zone of proximal development today will be the actual developmental level tomorrow," then ZPD teaching – the implantation of a Zoom Pedagogical Device in the classroom – is essential if the student's intellectual life is to grow, complexify, and transcend the limitations we habitually accept as normal or inevitable, or mobilize the usual array of ineffective techniques and reforms to combat.

18 Odysseas Elytis, *The Little Mariner*, Copper Canyon Press, Port Townsend, 1988. As Northrop Frye comments, "'elitist' is a bogey word without content ... like 'communist' ... it expresses certain social anxieties but defines nothing, and raises only pseudo-issues." And again, deploring the influence of those people, always in the ascendancy, who "cannot stand the thought of a fully realized humanity," he comments: "Words like 'elitism' become for such people bogey words used to describe those who try to take their education seriously" (*The Educated Imagination*, CBC Enterprises, Toronto, 1985). Similarly, Milan Kundera has no patience with the anti-elitist sentiment that contaminates our epoch, a time in which "the nonthought of received ideas," inflated by the mass media, is carrying us to the brink of cultural collapse. (Conor Cruise O'Brien in his most recent work makes exactly the same point,

using the term "cognitive degeneration" to apply to those who do not understand that "the Enlightenment tradition is demonstrably an affair of elites." See *On the Eve of the Millennium*, Anansi, Concord, 1994.) Kundera remarks on the mordant irony emerging from the fact that, at the same time as the word "elitist" embarked on its invidious career in the West, "official propaganda in the Communist countries began to pummel elitism and elitists ... It used the term to designate philosophers, writers, professors, historians." But, a further irony, these campaigns against elitism by no means culminated in the disappearance of elites; without using the word, two synchronous hierarchies have established themselves as pervasive yet exclusive elitist structures: the police apparatus "over there" and the mass media apparatus "here." And the manoeuvre is almost foolproof, since "no one will ever accuse these new elites of elitism" (*The Art of the Novel*). But perhaps the fear of excellence is a transhistorical prejudice. Jacques Barzun in *Begin Here* (University of Chicago Press, Chicago, 1992) draws attention to the character Jack Cade in *Henry VI, Part II*, a representative of the popular *ressentiment* against elitism. Confronted with the "monstrous" clerk who can "write and read, and cast acompt," Cade orders: "Hang him with his pen and inkhorn around his neck."

19 Mortimer J. Adler, *The Paideia Program*, Macmillan, New York, 1984. James O'Toole, also writing in *The Paideia Program*, rounds on American education for its elitist practices, but for very different reasons from Adler. He is referring to the scandal of athletic scholarships, the vast sums given over to the maintenance of semi-professional sports dynasties, and "the emphasis on interscholastic competition, in which only a few participate. If anything is elitist, that is it." America has not cashiered its elite, it has merely replaced it with a new elite composed in equal measure of barbarism and mediocrity.

20 Aldous Huxley, *Brave New World Revisited*, Chatto & Windus, London, 1959.

21 I should also say that I suspect the entire metaphor may be hopelessly skewed, founded on the etymology of the word "instruction" – a piling on or filling up – which has more to do with training or indoctrination than with education proper. Certainly, a metaphor of this kind does not allow for individual failure or perfectibility, but if we insist on using it, perhaps the analogy of the wine cask, which imparts a hint of oak or chestnut to its contents, would be more to the point – although it would still remain within the metaphorical space of "instruction." (Since we are playing with analogies, I might also suggest the appositeness of the seed metaphor: hybridization is both possible and necessary, but hybridizers need to work with original "subjects" that carry some hope for the future – heirloom seed – in order to achieve a promising cultivar.)

22 In a different and yet related sense, Northrop Frye comments as follows on the subject of teaching written articulation. "The English teacher's ideal is the exact opposite of 'effective communication,' or learning to become audible in the marketplace. What he has to teach is the verbal expression of truth, beauty and wisdom: in short, the disinterested use of words" (*On Education*, Fitzhenry & Whiteside, Toronto, 1990). Unfortunately, many teachers of English language or literature are not given to reflect on the nature of what we are prone to calling our "mandate," but merely continue to teach on the whole impressionistically, asking the standard questions about intention or meaning and "clarifying" texts without pausing to consider the principles, habits, and tacit presuppositions governing their procedures. For example, most grammatical instruction remains impenitently prescriptive. But every now and then a soupçon of descriptive linguistics, rarely identified as such, may be detected flavouring customary practice, even though these are opposing paradigms. To be sure, there seems little danger of comparative (diachronic), generative, or categorial approaches complicating the issue, but one might wish to find these various models considered and discussed from time to time. When it comes to literature courses, many teachers do not appear to have decided whether they have adopted a reproduction theory in the tradition of Schliermacher, Dilthey, and Hirsch, a response paradigm à la Gadamer, Ricoeur, and Fish, the emancipatory hermeneutics of Marx, Freud, Adorno, and Habermas, or the corrosive radical displacement of the school of Nietzsche, Heidegger, Derrida, and de Man – or some insoluble mix of the above. Or is it just the usual comfy ad hoc *explication de texte* based on the teacher's assumption of oracular privilege? Such discursive and theoretical lassitude cannot readily lead to pedagogical vitality, regardless of how generous, good natured, spontaneous, or hard-working an individual teacher may commendably happen to be. As Paul de Man notes, "Perhaps the most difficult thing for students and teachers of literature to realize is that their appreciation is measured by the analytical rigour of their own discourse about literature ... " (Paul de Man, *Resistance to Theory*, University of Minnesota Press, Minneapolis, 1986).

23 For the classical references in this paragraph, see *The Complete Plays of Aristophanes*, ed. Moses Hadas, Bantam, New York, 1971; and *Terence: The Comedies*, tr. Betty Radice, Penguin, New York, 1978.

24 John Milton, *Prose Writings*, Dutton, New York, 1965.

25 *Poems of Matthew Arnold*, Oxford University Press, London, 1926.

26 A.N. Whitehead, *The Aims of Education*, Macmillan, New York, 1929. (Italics mine.)

27 George Steiner, *Real Presences*, University of Chicago Press, Chicago, 1989. See also Aristotle, *Metaphysics*, in *Introduction to Aristotle*, ed.

Richard McKean, Random House, New York, 1947; and *The Works of Plato*, tr. Benjamin Jowett, Random House, New York, 1956.

28 Richard Ohmann, *English in America*, Oxford University Press, London, 1976.

29 Frank Smith, *Joining the Literacy Club*, Heinemann, Portsmouth, 1988.

30 Northrop Frye, *On Education*. Naturally there is a vast difference between a "good style" and simple grammatical competence. But what Frye has to say about style applies, *mutatis mutandis*, to grammatical felicity as well. Those of my students with some prior experience of reading deal far more rapidly and easily with the exigencies of grammar and syntax than their unread peers.

We might also hazard for explanatory purposes a working homology or ratio here: articulate speech is to writing as language is to perception. As Raymond Tallis says (commenting on Norman Geschwind's etiology of agnosia), "In the absence of language, sensation cannot give rise to what we could count as fully formed perception" (Raymond Tallis, *Not Saussure*, Macmillan, London, 1988). Analogously, in the absence of approximately articulate speech, students cannot be expected to consistently produce well-formed sentences.

Ultimately, what John Fiske says of reading seems equally true of writing: "Reading is not merely a decipherment of signs, but the bringing to bear upon the text of previously existing knowledge. Reading is a cultural practice, not a set of skills" (John Fiske, *Reading the Popular*, Routledge, London and New York, 1994). And this is precisely the point: writing is a cultural practice, not an assemblage of isolable skills sutured into some sort of neutral competency function and activated on demand.

31 Jeremy Campbell, *Winston Churchill's Afternoon Nap*, Simon & Schuster, New York, 1986. The "ability to represent real experience in symbolic terms" over a given interval is a function of the metonymic or syntagmatic chain of signifiers and by definition cannot be divorced from a robust sense of temporal continuity. One must distinguish between *duration* (the persistence of a content) and *development* (the elaboration of a content). The latter entails subsidiary functions like splitting, transformation, productivity, and linkaging. The difference is that between dream time and real time.

32 That is, subjective time depends on what P.E. Strawson in *Individuals* (Routledge, London, 1990) calls the "essential grammar" of a language in contradistinction to its "variable grammar," which latter is what we typically and misguidedly attempt to pummel into our students under the assumption that we are helping them to retrieve an education.

33 Max Dublin, *Futurehype*, Penguin, New York, 1990. Dublin is by no

means discounting the importance of will, habit, and culture but is pointing out that nothing can be achieved without continuity, without a genuine hospitality to the temporal.

34 *The Paideia Program.*

35 See especially *Of Grammatology*, tr. G.C. Spivak, Johns Hopkins University Press, Baltimore and London, 1976.

36 Stephen Levinson yuppifies the definition of the term "pragmatics" as "the study of those relations between language and context that are grammaticalized or encoded in the structure of a language" (Stephen Levinson, *Pragmatics*, Cambridge University Press, Cambridge, 1983). For interesting and pertinent reflections on the subject, see Hilary Putnam, "The Meaning of Meaning," *Mind, Language and Reality*, Cambridge University Press, Cambridge, 1975, and of course E.D. Hirsch, *Cultural Literacy*, Vintage, New York, 1988. I also refer the reader to Franco Moretti (*Signs Taken for Wonders*, Verso, London and New York, 1988), who develops the idea of "the *unconscious* culture, the implicit knowledge, of every civilization." Thus we might say, somewhat paradoxically, that the cultural unconscious we have always assumed is gradually ceasing to exist. More recently, Jeff Smith has coined the term *illegeracy* to signify "a kind of reading disorder – an inability to 'read' one's cultural situation. It literally affects one's command of words." Put this way, then, one of the reasons our students cannot write is that they are illegerate, victims of an infirmity that consists in equal measure of "a missing skill, an unhappy state, and a social (in)action that follows in consequence." (See Jeff Smith, "Against 'Illegeracy': Toward a New Pedagogy of Civic Understanding," in *College Composition and Communication*, vol. 45, no. 2, May 1994.)

It should be manifest in any event that the study of grammar as a set of rules and principles that are essentially *applicable* rather than *intrinsic* to a given content inevitably leads to poor or defective practice. Shaun Gallagher argues that "A text is not simply a collection of grammatically constructed sentences arranged in a certain syntactic order. It is a totality of composition that bears within itself possibilities of meaning that overflow grammatical and syntactical arrangement" (*Hermeneutics and Education*, SUNY Press, Albany, 1992). If this is the case – and I suspect the case to be a strong one indeed – then it follows that grammatical and syntactical felicity arises mainly from a "totality," a gestalt, the embrasure of context, be that textual, cognitive, empirical, or social. This, of course, is merely another way of stating Mikhail Bakhtin's famous dialogical principle that meaning is always a function of context. (See Mikhail Bakhtin, *The Dialogic Imagination*, tr. Michal Holquist, University of Texas Press, Austin, 1981.) But this also suggests that reasoning is a function of content. As Jeremy Campbell argues, the ability to reason coherently and to generate stable meanings depends "on what we know, on the way our knowledge is organized in memory." (See Jeremy Campbell, *The Improbable Machine*, Simon & Schuster, New York, 1990.)

37 Frank Smith, *Insult to Intelligence*, Heinemann, Portsmouth, 1987.

38 Umberto Eco, *The Limits of Interpretation*, Indiana University Press, Bloomington and Indianapolis, 1990. Further citations from Eco are from this text.

39 Colin MacCabe, *Tracking the Signifier*, University of Minnesota Press, Minneapolis, 1985.

40 In detecting irony, I don't mean anything so sublime as the Kierkegaardian recognition of absolute infinite negativity but the simple ability, in I.A. Richards's famous phrase, of bringing in the opposite. The knack of sorting out the symmetric complications of cognitive dissonance in speech or writing is a good indicator of "cultural literacy." And the ability to deploy irony may in fact be the signal gesture of consciousness, if Merleau-Ponty is correct in his assertion that "consciousness implies the ability to step back from any given thing and to deny it." (The phrase occurs in his commentary on Hegel in *Sense and Non-Sense*, Northwestern University Press, 1964.)

41 Otto Jespersen, *Negation in English and Other Languages* (1917; reprint, Ejnar Munksgaard, Copenhagen, 1966).

42 Cited in Eco, *The Limits of Interpretation*, from which I take my thematic direction in this portion of the argument. (As Jackendoff later argues, negative sentences do not spring into existence in full panoply but are laboriously *acquired* through a kind of queuing procedure, a sequence of systematic mistakes and corrections. See Ray Jackendoff, *Patterns in the Mind*, Basic Books, New York, 1994.)

43 Emil Benveniste, *Problems in General Linguistics*, University of Miami Press, Coral Gables, 1971.

44 T. Givon, in *Pragmatics*, ed. Peter Cole, Academic Press, New York, 1978 (italics mine). Once more I am indebted to Eco for directions.

45 Sigmund Freud, *The Psychopathology of Everyday Life*, Hogarth Press, London, 1960.

46 What we are now in the habit of calling "background information" or "schematic associations" which enable and empower literate communication, Maud Bodkin denominates "predisposing factors" (*Archetypal Patterns in Poetry*, Vintage, New York, 1958). Elaborating on both the obvious and the work of the philosopher F.C. Bartlett, Miss Bodkin remarks that "it is not mere contact with an idea's expression that secures its assimilation," but that certain "predisposing factors" must necessarily intervene. When those are absent, "the experienced futility of attempted communication is the most convincing proof ... that ... there must

stir within us 'larger systems of feeling, of memory, of ideas, of aspira-
tion.'" (The concluding citation is from Bartlett, writing in *The Journal
of Philosophical Studies*, 3, no. 9, mentioned in text.)

47 Philip Rieff, *The Triumph of the Therapeutic*, Harper & Row, New
York, 1966. For Christopher Lasch the dilemma similarly lies in "the
shift from a work ethic to a consumption ethic." It is *the ideology of
consumerism* (its addiction-structure maintained and reinforced by the
media) which with its search for novelty and constant stimulation undermines education, eroding curiosity and sustained attention while encouraging passivity and an increased susceptibility to boredom (cf.
Christopher Lasch, *The True and Only Heaven*, W.W. Norton, New
York, 1991). It is, of course, this intense proneness to boredom on the
part of the contemporary student that constitutes one of the major
"problems" for the teacher. In this context it is at least moderately brac-
ing, if ultimately ineffective, to reconsider Barthes's definition of boredom as "bliss viewed from the shores of pleasure" (Roland Barthes, *The
Pleasure of the Text*, Hill and Wang, New York, 1975). Or Lacan's
quasi-pedagogical dictum as rephrased by a recent commentator: "If you
are not prepared to stagnate, at least a little, you will not have access to
the 'symbolic polyphony' that is your rightful world of meaning" (Malcolm Bowie, *Lacan*, Harvard University Press, Cambridge, MA, 1991).
Boredom is a crucial pedagogical experience, absolutely indispensable as
an interval in the learning process, as it is in the affective reclamation of
its anagrammatic double, "bedroom." Education, like love, cannot
flourish in an environment inhospitable to boredom.

48 Max Dublin, *Futurehype*.

49 Stanislaw Lem, *The Futurological Congress*, Avon, New York, 1974.
Lem describes a society in which "children learn their reading and writing from orthographic sodas" – shades of Swift's "thin wafer" on which
propositions were written "with ink composed of a cephalic tincture" –
and the sceptics who doubt the authenticity of their environment are
given dehallucinides, which "create the illusion that there is no illusion."
If problems persist, retrotemporex effectively reverses the flow of subjective time and a dose of obliterine or amnesol purges the mind of the
burden of memory. *De nobis fabula narratur.*

50 Alfred North Whitehead, *The Aims of Education*.

51 L.S. Vygotsky, *Mind in Society*.

52 See also Jerome Bruner's notion of the spiral curriculum (*The Process
of Education*, Harvard University Press, Cambridge, MA, 1960), the
structural features or components of any given discipline repeating in
due course at increasingly "higher" or more complex levels of attainment and absorption.

53 L.S. Vygotsky, *Mind in Society.* This distinction between leaps and
lines is in a sense common intellectual property and can be formulated
in any of a number of different ways. Consider, for example, Roland
Barthes's analysis of the photograph, which would consist of two related functional elements designated as *studium* and *punctum.* The
studium is defined as "the extension of a field, which I perceive quite fa-
miliarly as a consequence of my knowledge, my culture ... a classical
body of information." The *punctum* is the disturbing and surprising element that punctuates the field "like an arrow," that which is unique,
poignant, memorable, special, unprecedented. There can be no
punctum without the underlying and sustaining *studium* from which the
former arises (Roland Barthes, *Camera Lucida*, Fontana, London,
1984). The *studium* may equally be regarded as "background information" (Hirsch) or "the unconscious culture" (Moretti). See note 36.

    The developmental or stage-specific theory of learning is still a con-
troversial topic. Some of the tenets of its most famous proponent, Jean
Piaget, have been challenged by recent thinking. (See Jeremy Campbell,
The Improbable Machine, Simon & Schuster, New York, 1990, for a discussion of these issues, including a respectful critique of Piagetian theory in the light of Peter Wason's celebrated four-card puzzle. See as
well Howard Gardner, *The Mind's New Science*, Basic Books, New
York, 1985, for a measured assessment of Piaget's contribution to cognitive psychology, increasingly under attack.) And Vygotsky's fruitful notion of the Zone of Proximal Development has clearly demonstrated
that good learning is always in advance of development. Yet that stages
and periodicities do exist in learning obviously cannot be doubted, even
if these cannot be fixed with mathematical precision, and therefore need
to be taken into account in some reasonable way in the planning of
remedial programs if the latter are not to prove embarrassingly
ineffective.

    One should note that neither Whitehead's nor Vygotsky's thinking
can be classified as "Piagetian." Piaget's stages (sensorimotor, intuitive
or preoperational, concrete operations, formal operations), while allowing for limited differential rates of development, are far more narrowly
and rigidly fixed, are in fact related to one another as an invariant sequence. Vygotsky's "leaps" and Whitehead's "greater cycles" provide for
a much richer degree of freedom.

    Educational development may be, perhaps, best represented by a the-
ory which reconciles specificity with flexibility of the kind proposed by
Jane Healy in *Endangered Minds* (Simon & Schuster, New York, 1991),
where she quite reasonably claims that "the brain grows best when it is
challenged, so high standards for children's learning are important.

Nevertheless, curriculum needs to be considered in terms of *brain-appropriate* challenge." This is Whitehead and Vygotsky riding in tandem.

Finally, to revert to the metaphor of aging-in-cask (see note 21), the temptation to compress the educational transaction rather than allow for gradual maturing (Vygotsky's "general line of development"), resembles that practice of certain contemporary wine-makers called oak-chipping, that is, accelerating the process by dipping a bag of toasted oak chips in a vat of new wine. The process works – provided your demands or expectations are moderate. (It might also be noted that pitching a subject ahead of its recipient does not *accelerate* an educational process that has been long retarded but rather *advances* it beyond the range of normative expectations.)

54 Whitehead and Vygotsky are not theorists in the dyslogistic sense of the term. One is a major philosopher developing a persuasive *hypothesis* to account for the stages of intellectual growth, the other a child psychologist and educator of undoubted genius whose conclusions are based on sound experimental results. I would also hope that my own deposition avoids the hazards of psittacine reproduction.

55 See Roger Shattuck, *The Forbidden Experiment*, Simon & Schuster, New York, 1980.

56 See especially K.W. Spence, *Behavior Theory and Conditioning*, Yale University Press, New Haven, 1956, for an early and powerful, indeed definitive, advocacy of incentive motivation, deriving from Clark C. Hull, *Principles of Behavior*, Appleton-Century-Crofts, New York, 1943, and *Essentials of Behavior*, Yale University Press, New Haven, 1951. That the motivation concept emerges from the lab-like thinking of behavioural and experimental psychology should long ago have motivated us to reject it.

57 For Frank Smith, motivation "is one of the biggest red herrings we hear from teachers. Most of the time we learn without motivation, without ever knowing that we are learning. And motivation itself does not guarantee learning." One of the unlikely "masters of suspicion" in this connection is John Dewey himself, who claims that it is because the object of learning "is assumed to be outside the self that it has to be *made* interesting, that it has to be surrounded with artificial stimuli, and with fictitious inducements to attention." He suggests as an alternative "the principle of the recognized identity of the fact or proposed line of action with the self" (*Democracy and Education*, 1916; reprint, Free Press, New York, 1966).

This is not to say that motivation, reinforcement, and incentive do not have a place in education. They probably do – in moderation – but this place should not be conceived as the vast Skinner box which the educational institution has lamentably become. "Motivation and reinforcement are only required for nonsense-learning or for other kinds of pointless or painful activity" (Frank Smith, *Joining the Literacy Club*). And again: "It is an odd educational idea that learning is sporadic, difficult, and effortful, requiring special motivation, incentives, and rewards. It is an odd educational idea based on meaningless learning" (Frank Smith, *to think*, Teachers College Press, Columbia University, New York and London, 1990).

58 See Theodore Roszak, *The Cult of Information*, Pantheon Books, New York, 1986; and Jacques Barzun, *Begin Here*.

59 This is the central theme of Huxley's *Brave New World Revisited* (as it is of its famous predecessor), from which this citation is taken.

60 The students in this particular class ranged in age between seventeen and twenty-two, with the mean age approximately eighteen and a half.

61 Umberto Eco, *The Role of the Reader*, Indiana University Press, Bloomington, 1984.

62 Franz Kafka, *Parables and Paradoxes*, Schoken Books, New York, 1975.

63 Charles K. Ogden, and I.A. Richards, *The Meaning of Meaning*, Harper Brace Jovanovich, New York, 1923.

64 The parable of education is one of the essential, structuring themes of all literary production, whether in the *Bildungsroman* where it operates visibly and insistently or in the humble folk-tale where it does its work subliminally. As an instance of the latter, consider the story of Hansel and Gretel in which the initial stages of the children's education are governed by the orality motif, pure consumption (and its complementary, famine), a lazy, passive dependence on what is given (the gingerbread house), reproducing the motions of regression or re-infantilization relieved by the occasional ingenuity of pseudo-response (pebbles, bone for finger). Hansel and Gretel begin pedagogical life as empirical students. This condition must eventually be replaced by active, goal-directed learning based on intelligent assessment of what the situation requires of them and the development of hermeneutic initiative. The teacher may be temporarily experienced as harsh and rejecting, as witch or stepmother refusing maieutic comfort and the milk of human kindness. Necessarily, as the raison d'etre of the entire process entails the transformation of the tyro into a competent, self-reliant, post-Oedipal model student willing and able to "go over," in this case to cross to the other side of the lake that magically appears at the edge of the forest and to join the family of the truly educated. But for this to happen the student must be willing to be territorialized in the parable. See Bruno Bettelheim, *The Uses of Enchantment*, Vintage, New York, 1977, for a psychoanalytical reading of the tale. (Apparently, Bettelheim himself was

just the sort of martinet mentioned above, renamed by his students as
Brutal Bettelheim. This from the education theorist, J.T. Dillon, personal communication.)

65 Seymour Chatman, *Story and Discourse: Narrative Structure in Fiction
and Film*, Cornell University Press, Ithaca, 1978. The phrase "implied
author" derives from Wayne Booth, *The Rhetoric of Fiction*, University
of Chicago Press, 1961, and its reciprocal, "implied reader," from Wolfgang Iser, *The Implied Reader*, Johns Hopkins University Press, Baltimore, 1974. The citation from Iser reproduced in the text is from *The
Act of Reading*, Johns Hopkins University Press, 1980.

66 Cf. My *Education Lost*, OISE Press, Toronto, 1989. The teacher must
not shrink from playing the role of initiator, intercessor, or thauma-
turge, inducting the student into the privileged space of the ritual text or
stage, even if at times he tends to appear faintly absurd in the solemn
conviction he maintains in the high importance of the event – like Cor-
wyn Magus who was not, as some people claimed, a quack of a chemist
but, in point of fact, an aquatic alchemist. See Douglas W. Clark in his
passatempo novel *Alchemy Unlimited* for a loving and whimsical study
of the pedagogical relationship between the patient master and the in-
corrigible apprentice.

67 In Jacques Derrida's words, we may say that the class-as-text inscribes
"the peril of inter-rogation" which entails "the response in which two af-
firmations espouse each other." Cf. *Writing and Difference*, University
of Chicago Press, Chicago, 1978, from which my references to Derrida
in this section are taken.

68 Edwin Honig, *Dark Conceit: The Making of Allegory*, Oxford University Press, London, 1966.

69 The staple theory of teaching (associated with rabbinical parable) is developed by Milton's God in Book III of *Paradise Lost*: "for I will clear
their senses dark ... / and soften stony hearts ... / Mine ear shall not be
slow, mine eye not shut." (But the stern preceptor remains close at
hand, punishing the unworthy with Hermetic assiduity: "they who neglect and scorn ... / blind, shall be blinded more/ That they may stumble
on, and deeper fall.") (See the *Complete Poetry*, Random House, New
York, 1950.)

    The rabbinical view of the parable, which Kafka is probably bur-
lesquing, may be found in another Talmudic parable (itself pre-
eminently rabbinical), which likens the parable to an inexpensive candle
by whose light a king finds a precious pearl which he has lost. See Mark
4:22, mentioned in the text, for another parable about a candle (King
James Bible, any edition).

70 For a rewarding discussion of Augustine's doctrine of rhetorical production, see Tzvetan Todorov, *Theories of the Symbol*, Cornell University

Press, Ithaca, 1982, to which I am indebted not only for the citations from Augustine but for insight and for directions to the appropriate sources.

71 That the parable, despite its appearance of simplicity, is *inherently* complex by its very nature as a material or diffracting medium should not be cause for surprise. As Maurice Merleau-Ponty writes, "The parables of the Gospel are not a way of presenting pure ideas in images; they are the only language capable of conveying the relations of religious life, as paradoxical as those of the world of sensation." (*Sense and Non-Sense.*) Similarly, Robert Farrar Capon affirms that most parables "are complex, and a good percentage of them produce more confusion than understanding." In fact, as he points out, the word *parable* occurs only in the Synoptics. John occasionally uses *paroimia* (dark sayings), and sometimes we find the word *kekrymmena* (secret or hidden things), which may provide the closest approximation to the essence of the parable as the device which reveals at the same time as it conceals. (See Robert Farrar Capon, *The Parables of the Kingdom*, William B. Eerdmans, Michigan, 1985.) Perhaps the closest approximation in the contemporary intellectual scene to the practice of the parable may be found in the quasi-oracular structure of Lacanian writing and teaching which, as Lacan himself observes, "leave[s] the reader no other way out than the way in, which I prefer to be difficult" (*Ecrits*). For a good explication of parable pedagogy (paragogy?) see Bunyan's Apology to *The Pilgrim's Progress* where meanings, like fish, "must be groped for and be tickled, too, / or they will not be catch'd whate're you do." And again, refering to his "dark and cloudy words," Bunyan writes: "who so considers / Christ, his apostles too, shall plainly see / That truth *to this day* in such mantles be." (John Bunyan, *The Pilgrim's Progress*, New American Library, New York, 1964. Italics mine.)

72 Mario Désilets, "Constructivist Principles and Their Application to Teaching," University of Sherbrooke, Sherbrooke, 1992. Difficulty promotes learning on the plane of our normal engagement with reality because it stimulates and strengthens the ability to remember. On the level of brain chemistry one might suggest, if one were so disposed, that memory storage and learning are the product of synaptic modifications. *Effort*, as experienced on the macroscopic level, generates new connections between neurons, which fire repeatedly, thus creating synaptic patterns that form a new circuitry. From a technical perspective, what appears to happen is that raising voltage along the cells by repeated stimulation (what neuroscientists call long term potentiation, or LTP) produces more dendrite per neuron which in turn allows more area for the formation of new receptors and synapses. Whether memory is presynaptic, as Eric Kandel maintains (i.e., learning causes a change in the

amount of neurotransmitter a sender neuron releases) or postsynaptic, as Gary Lynch contends (i.e., learning causes a change in the number of receptors that form on the receiver neuron) does not affect the general neurological thesis that memory is a neural function (neither a molecular event on the one hand nor an ectoplasmic phenomenon on the other). As George Johnson puts it, "Recognition would occur when we encountered something that evoked a neural pattern similar to the one that was already in storage." (See George Johnson, *In the Palaces of Memory*, Vintage, New York, 1992. Johnson's book is favourable to Gary Lynch's ideas. For a friendlier account of Eric Kandel's hypothesis, see Steven Rose, *The Making of Memory: From Molecules to Mind*, Doubleday, New York, 1992.) Of course, from the parabolic point of view, it matters little whether memory and learning are molecular or neural (pre- or post-synaptic) or ectoplasmic in nature, or are merely the beneficial outcome of hordes of infinitesimal yellow-fanged gremlins running up and down the cells jabbing pitchforks into axon fibres, inflicting memory for our sins. The point is: difficulty and attendant effort produce results.

73 *A Midsummer Night's Dream*, IV, i. The relevant passage from Corinthians I reads:

> But as it is written, Eye hath not seen, nor ear
> heard, neither have entered into the heart of man,
> the things which God hath prepared for
> them that love him.

We find the same rhetorical pattern but in reverse in John 20:29, where Jesus says to Thomas, "Blessed are they that have not seen, and yet have believed."

74 William H. Calvin, *The Ascent of Mind*, Bantam, New York, 1991. Italics mine.

75 See Mary Hyde, *The Thrales of Streatham Park*, quoted in Robert Burchfield, *Unlocking the English Language*, Faber and Faber, London, 1989.

76 T.S. Eliot, *Collected Poems* 1909–1962, Faber and Faber, London, 1963.

77 See Richard J. Herrnstein and Charles Murray, *The Bell Curve: Intelligence and Class Structure in American Life*, Free Press, New York, 1994, for a sobering account of cognitive partitioning.

78 "Balance," says Charles Van Doren in *The Paideia Program*, "must be maintained between abandoning the slower students and boring the quicker ones." Here we have precisely the inadvertent and symptomatic expression of our present dilemma: the quest for miracle. How are we to comport ourselves pedagogically in so mysterious and unprecedented a fashion so as not to abandon the poor student while at the same time not boring the good one? What possible way is there to describe and

produce a concrete instance of such blended incompatibles except in the world of the Transcendental Sublime?

79 Paul Simpson, *Language, Ideology and Point of View*, Routledge, London and New York, 1993.

80 See Carl Sagan, *Contact*, Simon & Schuster, New York, 1985.

81 Shaun Gallagher, *Hermeneutics and Education*.

82 See *The Education of Henry Adams*, Houghton Mifflin Co., Boston, 1971; in particular the concluding chapter.

83 Theodore Roszak, *The Cult of Information*.

84 Gary Snyder, *The Practice of the Wild*, North Point Press, San Francisco, 1990.

85 Martin Heidegger, *Nietzsche*, Harper & Row, San Francisco, 1991.

86 Stephen Jay Gould, *Wonderful Life*, W.W. Norton, New York and London, 1989.

All those things for which we have no words are lost. The mind – the culture – has two little tools, grammar and lexicon.

Annie Dillard

There is an obligation to remember, not in the memory cells of computers but in the heaviness of the heart.

Peter Berger